A Companion to German Realism

Studies in German Literature, Linguistics, and Culture

Edited by James Hardin
(*South Carolina*)

Camden House Companion volumes

The Camden House Companions provide well-informed and up-to-date critical commentary on the most significant aspects of major literary works, periods, or figures. The Companions may be read profitably by the reader with a general interest in the subject. For the benefit of student and scholar, quotations are provided in the original language.

A COMPANION TO
German Realism
1848–1900

Edited by
Todd Kontje

CAMDEN HOUSE

Copyright © 2002 by the Editor and Contributors

All Rights Reserved. Except as permitted under current legislation,
no part of this work may be photocopied, stored in a retrieval system,
published, performed in public, adapted, broadcast, transmitted,
recorded, or reproduced in any form or by any means,
without the prior permission of the copyright owner.

First published 2002 by Camden House
Transferred to digital printing 2009
Reprinted in paperback 2010

Camden House is an imprint of Boydell & Brewer Inc.
668 Mt. Hope Avenue, Rochester, NY 14620, USA
www.camden-house.com
and of Boydell & Brewer Limited
PO Box 9, Woodbridge, Suffolk IP12 3DF, UK
www.boydellandbrewer.com

Paperback ISBN-13: 978-1-57113-445-5
Paperback ISBN-10: 1-57113-445-X
Hardback ISBN-13: 978-1-57113-322-9
Hardback ISBN-10: 1-57113-322-4

Library of Congress Cataloging-in-Publication Data

A companion to German realism / edited by Todd Kontje.
    p. cm. — (Studies in German literature, linguistics, and culture)
Includes bibliographical references and index.
ISBN 1-57113-322-4 (alk. paper)
  1. German literature—19th century—History and criticism. 2. Realism
in literature.   I. Kontje, Todd Curtis, 1954–   II. Studies in German
literature, linguistics, and culture (Unnumbered)

PT345 .C59 2002
830.9'12—dc21

2002022600

A catalogue record for this title is available from the British Library.

This publication is printed on acid-free paper.

Cover image: Adolf Menzel, *Selbstbildnis im Walzwerk*, 1872–75.
Courtesy of Museum der bildenden Künste, Leipzig.

Contents

Preface	vii
Introduction: Reawakening German Realism 　　*Todd Kontje*	1
Adalbert Stifter's *Brigitta,* or the Lesson of Realism 　　*Robert C. Holub*	29
Mühlbach, Ranke, and the Truth of Historical Fiction 　　*Brent O. Peterson*	53
"In the Heart of the Heart of the Country": Regional Histories as National History in Gustav Freytag's *Die Ahnen* (1872–80) 　　*Lynne Tatlock*	85
A Woman's Post: Gender and Nation in Historical Fiction by Louise von François 　　*Thomas C. Fox*	109
Friedrich Spielhagen: The Demon of Theory and the Decline of Reputation 　　*Jeffrey L. Sammons*	133
Wilhelm Raabe and the German Colonial Experience 　　*John Pizer*	159
From National Task to Individual Pursuit: The Poetics of Work in Freytag, Stifter, and Raabe 　　*Hans J. Rindisbacher*	183

Das Republikanische, das Demokratische,
das Pantheistische: Jewish Identity in
Berthold Auerbach's Novels   223
   Irene S. Di Maio

E. Marlitt: Narratives of Virtuous Desire   259
   Kirsten Belgum

The Appeal of Karl May in the Wilhelmine Empire:
Emigration, Modernization, and the Need for Heroes   283
   Nina Berman

Making Way for the Third Sex: Liberal and
Antiliberal Impulses in Mann's Portrayal of
Male-Male Desire in His Early Short Fiction   307
   Robert Tobin

Effi Briest and the End of Realism   339
   Russell A. Berman

Works Cited   365

Notes on the Contributors   397

Index   401

Preface

THIS VOLUME BRINGS together some of the leading scholars of German realism working today and testifies to the vitality of the field. It includes essays on familiar authors — Stifter, Freytag, Raabe, Fontane, Thomas Mann — and canonical texts but also considers writers frequently omitted from traditional literary histories, including Luise Mühlbach, Friedrich Spielhagen, Louise von François, Karl May, and Eugenie Marlitt. Although the book does not attempt to cover every author or aspect of the period — which would, in any case, be impossible — an effort has been made to include a representative sampling of German realist prose in the second half of the nineteenth century. While the contributors vary in their choice of topic and approach, they all situate the literary works in their historical context and also suggest reasons why these texts remain of interest today. Thus, the contributors focus on questions of national identity during the period of Germany's first political unification; examine representations of Germans abroad and foreigners at home at a time of mass emigration and colonial expansion; consider attitudes toward work in a period of rapid industrialization; and reflect on questions of sexual identity and gender roles in works by both men and women in the era of the family journal, the first organized women's movements, and the earliest advocates for homosexual rights. Each essay refers to relevant literature on the particular author or topic discussed, and the volume concludes with a complete list of works cited. The book should, therefore, be of interest primarily to students and scholars of German literature but also to those concerned with the topic of realism in literature and questions of subject-formation, national identity, and cultural memory in an era of rapid historical change.

I would like to thank the contributors for their willingness to collaborate on this project, their patience with my demands, their respect for deadlines, and, above all, the quality of their work.

Introduction: Reawakening German Realism

Todd Kontje

GERMAN REALISM OF the nineteenth century has a bad reputation. Contemporary literature about the aftermath of German Reunification captures headlines; modern classics by Kafka, Brecht, and Mann remain in print and on class syllabi; and the "Age of Goethe," whether revered or reviled, retains its prominent place in German culture. While a handful of late nineteenth-century novellas still attract critical attention, most works of the period seem minor embarrassments best left to specialists. It does not help matters that German writers of the period identified themselves as latecomers on the literary scene in the wake of Goethe's death: Heinrich Heine declared the end of the "Goethean period of art" in *Die romantische Schule* (The Romantic School, 1833); Karl Leberecht Immermann titled his 1836 novel *Die Epigonen*, "those born after" greater men; and in 1842 Georg Gottfried Gervinus concluded his epoch-making *Geschichte der poetischen National-Literatur der Deutschen* (History of the Poetic National Literature of the Germans) by declaring that his generation could not hope to improve on the works of Goethe and Schiller; the time had come for politics rather than art. In the highly charged political climate of the years prior to the revolution of 1848 known as the *Vormärz* radical critics rejected Goethe for his conservatism, but after the failed 1848 revolution Goethe's stock began to rise until he became a cultural icon of monumental proportions. German literary historians celebrated his life as an inspiring example of individual harmony in an increasingly disjointed modern world and viewed the eternally striving protagonist of his *Faust* as the embodiment of imperial Germany's reckless and ruthless struggle for power.[1] Against such standards the "mild and timid liberals" of the later nineteenth century could offer only the cozy comforts of an antimodern *Heimatliteratur*, so the charge goes,² or an elitist cult of genius that ignored questions of modern urbanization and the workers' movement.³

German realism fares no better from a comparativist perspective. Erich Auerbach's damning verdict in *Mimesis* (1946) set the tone for much postwar criticism of nineteenth-century German literature. Auerbach argues that Schiller's tragedy *Kabale und Liebe* (Intrigue and Love, 1784) seemed to promise a new kind of German drama that was contemporary, tragic, and realistic but was, in fact, only "a melodramatic hit written by a man of genius."⁴ Whatever promise Schiller's early work offered was, in any case, soon lost as both he and Goethe turned away from contemporary reality to seek inspiration in works of classical antiquity. The French dominate Auerbach's account of nineteenth-century literature, and he discusses in turn the novels of Stendhal, Flaubert, the Goncourt brothers, and Zola. In contrast to the modern metropolis of Paris, life in Germany "was much more provincial, much more old-fashioned, much less 'contemporary.'" Without an appropriately modern subject matter, Germany could produce neither writers nor literature of the first rank. Hence, Auerbach declares that "there was no important realistic talent" in Germany and concludes that "it is true that the best German works of this period had no world-wide importance" (516–17).

With such critical heavyweights weighing in against the hapless German contenders, it seems remarkable that anyone would answer the bell for a new round of punishment. And yet, German realism fuels a flourishing critical industry: there are those who explain why they think German literature of the period is — or is not — so different from that of other contemporary European nations, those who argue for the unrecognized genius of exceptional writers whose works stand out like glacial erratics on the terminal moraine of nineteenth-century German prose, and an increasing number who are impatient with evaluations of individual talents and more concerned with the place of German literature within the broader discursive field of nineteenth-century cultural history. In this introduction I will discuss what German realism is, how it fits into the history of German and other European literatures of the period, and why, despite its dubious reputation, it continues to inspire critical interest today.

Defining German Realism

Efforts to define *realism* are inherently problematic.[5] *Webster's New World Dictionary* tells us that realism in literature portrays "people and things as it is thought they really are, without idealizing." Yet, since literature, like all the arts, is a representation of reality rather than reality itself, even the most "realistic" text is something of a Potemkin village, an artificial construct that creates only "the effect of the real" in the reader's imagination.[6] Nor does the literary text necessarily create the same effect on subsequent generations of readers: a work that seemed boldly realistic when first published may seem dated and clichéd today. It thus makes little sense to offer a single binding definition of *realism*. Rather, we can speak of *realism* as a relative term, a way of defining a contrast instead of identifying an object. In the history of German literature, for example, there have been many such realisms: the medieval *Schwank* has elements of crude realism that one does not find in Arthurian romance; *Sturm und Drang* drama breaks with the rigid conventions of French neoclassicism; Hitler wanted to replace "decadent" modern art with "healthy" Aryan realism; and the German Democratic Republic established an official program of Socialist Realism to counter "subversive" tendencies in the West.

The period most clearly identified with realism in literature and other arts remains the nineteenth century.[7] As Linda Nochlin argues in her seminal study of nineteenth-century painting, realism became the dominant movement in France around 1840.[8] Realists sought to see the world afresh, to break free of convention and rely instead on observation. Yet, we cannot define realist art solely in terms of verisimilitude; as in literature, many paintings of past epochs look more or less "realistic." Specific to the nineteenth century is the increased awareness that one is living in an era of unpredictable and accelerating historical change. Gone is the comforting biblical paradigm of salvation history, with its clearly marked beginning and end and its promise of redemption for the faithful Christian. Humans wander, instead, through a world of "transcendental homelessness," seeking to establish the legitimacy of the modern age.[9] Depictions of death in nineteenth-century art tend to show only dead bodies, "the bare truth, stripped of all transcendental meanings and metaphysical implications, but rich in the circumstantiality of psychological, physical and social detail."[10] The attentiveness to contemporary detail carries over, as well, to representations of the living, where we find a new range of experience depicted: ordinary people, everyday life, the worker, the peasant, the prostitute, the modern city. The artist attempts to view the world impartially and with an almost scientific objectivity. Finally, realism in French art was often left-wing or socialist in its sympathies: if not always overtly advocating revolution, then covertly reminding the respectable bourgeoisie of the threatening presence of an endangered peasantry and the new urban masses.[11]

German cities also experienced unprecedented growth in the second half of the nineteenth century, as the industrial revolution caught hold with a rapidity that made up for its belatedness. In 1820, for example, Berlin had a population of barely 200,000; by 1870 it had almost quadrupled in size, and at the turn of the century the population was approaching two million.[12] Other German cities could boast similar population gains. German industry capitalized on natural resources of iron and coal from the Ruhr valley, while adapting technological advances and business practices from abroad. In only a few decades Germany was transformed from a predominantly agricultural economy into one of the most modern industrial societies in the world.[13] In midcentury, however, Germans perceived themselves as lagging behind their European competitors. "Wir haben kein London," lamented Otto Ludwig, "keinen Verkehr mit Kolonien in allen Weltteilen, kein so großes politisches Leben; wir haben keine Flotten, und wenn wir dem Deutschen nationales Selbstgefühl geben, so fehlt dazu der Boden, aus dem es organisch hervorwüchse und berechtigt erschiene."[14]

This sense of national belatedness inspired some to hasten Germany's advance toward modern times with a compensatory aggressiveness that culminated in the "Griff nach der Weltmacht" at the start of the First World War.[15] Others in late nineteenth-century Germany reacted against the already dizzying pace of historical change by seeking refuge in idealized images of a premodern past rooted in wholesome family values and religious faith.[16] Neither trend strengthened Germany's notoriously weak democratic traditions. Martin Luther had encouraged the Germans to revolt against the religious authority of the Roman pope; but when the peasants took up arms against their secular masters at home,

Luther condemned their actions in no uncertain terms. Three centuries later Immanuel Kant challenged the Germans to think boldly in the spirit of the Enlightenment, but he ended his appeal with a reminder that intellectual freedom should never lead to civil disobedience.[17] In 1871, finally, Bismarck brought about German unification through a series of three quick wars against Denmark, Austria, and France, thus realizing the liberal dream of a unified Germany through the power of "blood and iron" rather than constitutional reform. Modernization without liberalization characterized German culture and society throughout the rest of the nineteenth century and placed its particular stamp on German realist literature of the period.[18]

The essays in this volume focus primarily on works of German realism written between 1848 and 1900. In political terms, the date 1848 is, of course, somewhat arbitrary: German liberalism died many deaths in the course of the nineteenth century, ranging from the Congress of Vienna (1815) and the Karlsbad Decrees (1819), through the prohibition of the Young German writers in 1835, to the neutralization of liberal opposition during the constitutional crisis of 1874.[19] Yet, the revolution of 1848 was certainly one of the most dramatic events of nineteenth-century German history, and it was perceived as a decisive turning point by those who experienced it.[20] Thus, Russell Berman argues in this volume that German realism begins with the repression of pre-1848 liberalism, as well as the repression of Romanticism, while Jeffrey Sammons suggests that we view Spielhagen as an agonized liberal reacting to the sharp conservative turn in Bismarck's Germany. Of course, German realism did not arise *ex nihilo* in 1848. In literary works we can already trace a move toward greater realism in the late Romantic E. T. A. Hoffmann,[21] and certainly in such diverse authors as Georg Büchner, Annette von Droste-Hülshoff, and Berthold Auerbach during the 1830s and 1840s. In the field of German literary criticism, as well, Peter Uwe Hohendahl has noted "a considerable measure of continuity" in the years from 1820 through 1870.[22] Nevertheless, Julian Schmidt's essays of 1849–50 in the literary journal *Die Grenzboten* set the tone for a new programmatic realism that was to steer a course between Romantic fantasy and *Vormärz* tendentiousness, a balancing act that Otto Ludwig dubbed "poetic realism."[23]

Setting the *terminus ad quem* at 1900 is arguably even more arbitrary and somewhat late for traditional surveys of German realism, which tend to break off with the advent of naturalism in the early 1880s. With reference to political history, one might draw the line with Bismarck's forced resignation in 1890 or even at the beginning of the First World War. Nevertheless, 1900 serves as a convenient stopping point marked by the death of Nietzsche and the publication of Freud's *Interpretation of Dreams* and followed, just a year later, by Thomas Mann's *Buddenbrooks* (1901), a novel that, together with Theodor Fontane's *Effi Briest* (1895), marks the end of nineteenth-century German realism.[24] The essays collected here all focus on German prose, either the novel or the shorter novella that older critics frequently cited as Germany's unique contribution to European realism.[25] While it is certainly possible to speak of realism in drama or poetry,[26] the nineteenth century was first and foremost a century of prose, and it is here that we must seek its most characteristic form.

German realist prose thus stands poised between the politically engaged literature of the 1840s and naturalism, or, more broadly, between Romanticism and modernism. As such, it could be viewed as part of a dialectical progression internal to the history of the German national literature. Throughout the period, however, German writers remained open to a wide range of foreign influences. After 1848 many German liberals admired the work of Dickens and Thackeray, while Scott's historical fiction continued to inspire German practitioners of the genre. Russian writers became important to the Germans in the 1860s, primarily through the work of Turgenev.[27] The importance of Ibsen, Strindberg, and Hamsun on German naturalists of the late nineteenth century is well known, but Clifford Bernd has argued that "poetic realism" actually began in Denmark during the 1820s and that the Scandinavians exerted considerable influence on the development of German realism after 1848.[28] In histories of German literature, however, French influence, or the lack thereof, plays the most important role in establishing the specific character of German realism. Between about 1830 and 1850 the works of Balzac and Stendhal were frequently translated and widely read, while the novels of George Sand influenced such feminist writers of the German *Vormärz* as Ida Hahn-Hahn, Fanny Lewald, and Louise

Aston.[29] After 1848, however, French fiction made relatively little impact: Flaubert's novels were quickly translated "but created barely a ripple and were forthwith forgotten."[30] Only with the coming of Zola around 1880 did the French novel once again assert a dominant influence on German writers.[31]

Literary historians have frequently used the French example to bemoan the shortcomings of German literature. French realism, in this view, was everything that German realism was not but should have been: focused on the impact of urbanization and industrialization on the modern masses and committed to bettering the plight of the poor. German realism, in contrast, seems more pretty than gritty, more regional than national, and more reactionary than progressive. From a German perspective, of course, such apparent flaws could be defended as national virtues. As Thomas Mann would argue, the Germans had philosophical profundity and musical spirituality on which to base their "unpolitical" *Kultur,* whereas the superficial French had only the shallow rationalism of their *Zivilisation.*[32] In this spirit, German literary historians of the late nineteenth and early twentieth centuries seized on the Bildungsroman as the specifically German contribution to the history of the novel. In Wilhelm Dilthey's influential definition, the Bildungsroman depicts an innocent young man who encounters friendship and love as he matures to become confident of his role in the world. Dilthey discusses novels written around 1800 in the pattern of Goethe's *Wilhelm Meisters Lehrjahre* (Wilhelm Meister's Apprenticeship, 1795–96), but other critics soon claimed that later novels also expressed the "typically German" traits of spirituality and inwardness. Moreover, they appropriated an increasingly triumphalist narrative of individual growth to describe Germany's path toward political unification and military might.[33]

On closer inspection, this highly selective history of the nineteenth-century German novel can be seen to misrepresent the actual state of affairs. It begins with a simplistic and overoptimistic image of the canonical Bildungsromane around 1800, which tend either to remain fragments or to end with the hero's disillusionment or even death. *Wilhelm Meisters Lehrjahre* is more the exception than the norm, and even Goethe views what he once termed his "poor dog" of a hero with considerable irony.[34] If we stop looking for happy endings and settle merely for works that focus primarily on individual development, we do find several "brothers," or at least cousins, of *Wilhelm Meister* among the most famous German novels written between 1848 and 1900, including Keller's *Der Grüne Heinrich* (Green Henry, 1854/55; 1879/80), Freytag's *Soll und Haben* (Debit and Credit, 1855), Stifter's *Nachsommer* (Indian Summer, 1857), and Raabe's *Der Hungerpastor* (The Hunger Pastor, 1864).[35] But how typical were these novels at the time they were published? If we look at a more recent history of German literature for the years 1848–80, for example, we find articles on social novels, historical novels, village tales, early workers' literature, adventure novels, and romances, together with the obligatory chapter on the Bildungsroman.[36] Thus, Jeffrey Sammons concluded his largely futile search for the supposedly typical and peculiarly German genre by stating "that the more I try to read the books the Germans actually read, which in Germany as elsewhere normally means novels, the less strange a place it seems to be."[37] Reacting against such falsifications of German literary history, some critics have begun to focus, instead, on the broad spectrum of "what the Germans really read," rather than on a handful of canonical texts, while others study the institutional history of German literary criticism that established the canon in the first place.[38]

The alleged national characteristic of apolitical inwardness has led to the charge that nineteenth-century German fiction tended toward an "avoidance of social reality."[39] While Dickens portrayed the working class in the modern metropolis, Germans began to write tales of village life; while Flaubert strove for a cold-blooded realism in his prose, Germans heeded Friedrich Theodor Vischer's call for the novelist to seek out the "green spaces" in an increasingly drab world.[40] Yet, the charge that German writers ignored the changing social reality entirely does not hold water. Although the Germans would have to wait until 1892 for Gerhart Hauptmann's famous portrait of oppressed workers in *Die Weber* (The Weavers), a now largely forgotten workers' literature had already begun to appear in the 1860s and 1870s.[41] In bourgeois literature we also find a heightened focus on the sanctity of labor as one of the central values of the rising middle class, best captured in the Julian Schmidt quotation that Gustav Freytag used as a preface to *Soll und Haben:* "Der Roman soll das deutsche Volk da suchen, wo es in seiner Tüchtigkeit zu finden ist, nämlich bei seiner Arbeit."[42] In the present volume Hans J. Rindisbacher sheds new light on the representations of work in *Soll und Haben,* Stifter's *Nachsommer,* and Raabe's *Pfisters Mühle* (Pfister's Mill, 1884). He argues that Freytag implicitly refutes the criticisms of Marx and Engels in *The Communist Manifesto* by portraying capitalism as a stable world based on order, hierarchy, and trust, all "German" virtues that can be enlisted against unscrupulous Jews and incompetent Poles.[43] Stifter counters a growing sense of alienation in modern industrial society by creating a backward-looking utopia based on an anachronistic model of unalienated labor in *Der Nachsommer,* while Raabe exposes the ecological consequences of industrial pollution in *Pfisters Mühle.* Taken together, these examples indicate that German-speaking writers were, in fact, quite aware of the social consequences of modernization and that they discussed them, at least implicitly, within their works.

German Realism and National Identity

"Seek Germans at work" — but where exactly were the Germans working? Where was "Germany" before the unification of 1871? The question had already puzzled Goethe and Schiller in one of their *Xenien* of 1796:

> Deutschland? aber wo liegt es? Ich weiß das Land nicht zu finden.
> Wo das gelehrte beginnt, hört das politische auf.[44]

The two writers distinguish between cultural and political nationalism in a way typified by Schiller's literary journal *Die Horen* (1795–97), which united leading intellectuals of the German-speaking territories in a forum that explicitly forbade discussion of political events. In his own major contribution to the *Horen* Schiller based his concept of aesthetic education on the paradoxical claim that the best way to solve political problems was to turn your back on them in the contemplation of timeless art. In the same year Goethe began his essay "Literarischer Sansculottismus" (1795) with a list of reasons why the culturally and politically fragmented German-speaking territories could not produce "classical literature."[45] Yet he goes on to insist that the Germans do not want the sort of political revolution taking place in neighboring

France that might prepare the ground for a unified national literature, and he concludes cheerfully that under the circumstances, German writers were doing pretty well. As in the quoted *Xenia*, Goethe draws a neat distinction between the political and the intellectual spheres in an essay that combines national pride with the sort of cosmopolitan generosity that informs his concept of *Weltliteratur* in the late 1820s.

By this time, however, Goethe was swimming against the tide. Napoleon's conquest of Prussia in 1806 and his subsequent defeat in the "Wars of Liberation" gave rise to a newly militant German nationalism directed primarily against the French but also against the moribund institutions of absolutist Germany. While idealistic young men enlisted in the army, Wilhelm von Humboldt restructured the German universities, and Stein and Hardenberg modernized the Prussian bureaucracy. In the years after 1815 Germans continued to forge their "imagined community" by building national monuments, staging public festivals, and writing the history of their own national literature.[46] Goethe and Schiller's neat distinction between national culture and nationalist politics collapsed as a cultural nationalism paved the way toward political unification.

Questions about the nature of German national identity remained urgent after 1871. In this context Lynne Tatlock discusses Gustav Freytag's sprawling historical epic *Die Ahnen* (The Ancestors, 1872–80) in the present volume. She discovers that Freytag does not, as one might expect in the wake of the recent unification, produce a top-down, Prussocentric version of German history but, instead, conceives of a German national identity rooted still in the local region of Thuringia, in the private domestic sphere, and in the affective realm of sentiment. Tatlock concludes that Freytag has no a priori sense of "the German," but that he conceives of the German nation as a weaving together of diverse local identities. Such literature contrasts sharply with Goethe's cosmopolitanism; yet, nineteenth-century writers could adapt his antirevolutionary stance to defend a narrowly provincial literature that extended from the popular *Dorfgeschichten* of the 1840s and 1850s to the *Heimatliteratur* of the 1890s.[47] At its worst, such reactionary fare fed into the *Blut- und Bodenliteratur* of the Nazi regime, whose literary historians categorized writers in terms of the particular patch of German soil from which they sprang.[48] Underlying such sentiment is a romantic conception of national identity based on the *Volk* as a unifying force. In contradistinction to the Western liberal tradition, in which citizenship could be extended to anyone who accepted the progressive values of an enlightened state, *völkisch* nationalism restricted membership to ethnically related individuals from a particular place and with a common history, that is, those bound by ties of blood and soil.[49]

Such racist nationalism voices confidence in the biological purity of regional and national identities. In fact, however, many prominent German realists situate their works in border zones in an often anxious effort to create a sense of national identity based on common hostility toward an external foe. As noted earlier, Freytag set his most popular novel, *Soll und Haben,* on the German-Polish frontier, while Stifter's novella *Brigitta* takes place on the eastern fringe of the Austrian empire. Robert Holub argues in this volume that Stifter links his call for the suppression of passion in individuals to a fear of the Hungarian threat to Western civilization. Raabe, too, distrusted the Hungarians: as John Pizer shows in this volume, Raabe's advocacy of the *kleindeutsch* solution to the question of German unity derived at least in part from his fear of the corrupting influence of the non-Germanic peoples in the Austro-Hungarian empire. Louis von François sets her historical fiction on the German-French border, as Thomas C. Fox demonstrates in this volume, and contrasts Germany's "masculine" virtues with the decadence of the "effeminate" French. Gottfried Keller's Heinrich Lee, finally, moves back and forth across the Swiss-German border in *Der grüne Heinrich*. In this case, however, Germany fares poorly in comparison with the democratic traditions of Switzerland, where the liberal Keller finds compensation for the failed 1848 revolution in Germany.[50]

Efforts to define external foes coincided with hostility toward perceived internal enemies. As Hans-Ulrich Wehler has argued, Bismarck forged a sense of national identity through a policy of "negative integration" that targeted "foreign" elements within the Reich.[51] In the immediate wake of Germany's unification Bismarck launched the *Kulturkampf* against German Catholics. Social Democrats were always fair game and could not expect impartial justice from the German courts.[52] Ethnic minorities who labored in the expanding German industries were viewed with suspicion and increasing hostility, directed with particular venom toward the

Poles.[53] The most disturbing tendency, in the light of subsequent developments, was the sharp rise in anti-Semitism that began in the 1870s and continued into Hitler's Germany.[54] Although such sentiments did not go unchallenged in the nineteenth century — one thinks of Nietzsche's disdain for plans to establish a racist colony in Paraguay — some prominent works of German realism, of which Freytag's *Soll und Haben* is only the most notorious, did help to fuel hostility toward the Jews, while Wagner's operas can be viewed as monumental products of the anti-Semitic imagination.[55] In this volume Irene Di Maio examines representations of German-Jewish identity in the works of Berthold Auerbach. In the 1830s and 1840s Auerbach had written historical novels about Spinoza and Moses Mendelssohn, but after the success of his *Dorfgeschichten* in the mid-1840s he no longer placed the Jewish experience at the center of his works. As Di Maio demonstrates, however, Auerbach continued to reflect in subtler ways on "the Jewish question" in his critically neglected works of the realist period. These novels are infused with a spirit of tolerant humanism that defies growing anti-Semitic sentiments in German society.

German Realism in Global Context

The question of German national identity extended far beyond European borders in an era of mass emigration and imperial expansion. As Kirsten Belgum has shown, contributors to the popular family magazine *Die Gartenlaube* insisted that Germans in foreign countries remained part of the national community.[56] In fact, the experience of living abroad seemed to reinforce a sense of national identity among many emigrants. Authors wrote with pride about industrious Germans who carried their virtues abroad while remaining impervious to the influence of indigenous cultures. Settlers did their best to retain their own native traditions, as was captured in a poignant article about Germans in Brazil trying to keep the spirit of Christmas alive without snow or a *Tannenbaum*.[57] Contributors to *Die Gartenlaube* published a steady stream of articles on the new German colonies during the last two decades of the nineteenth century. The articles informed German readers about exotic locales, while bolstering pride in the nation's increasing international strength. Germany had at last become a major industrial and imperial power within modern European society. At the same time, however, *Die Gartenlaube* portrayed such colonies as fast-disappearing vestiges of a pristine, premodern world. Thus, nationalistic celebrations of the new German empire pointed simultaneously backward and forward, celebrating Germany's modernity even as they lamented the loss of simpler times.

Karl May's popular fiction also catered to the German thirst for news of the exotic frontier — although his readers were outraged to discover that he had never been to the American West until long after he had completed most of his novels. In this volume Nina Berman reads May's fiction as an effort to come to terms with the disruptive effects of modernization and mass emigration on German society. May rejects the revolutionary sentiments of the Forty-Eighters and portrays some characters as having left Germany to do penance for their former beliefs. He does offer vicarious adventure to his readers, but is concerned to discourage further emigration. When he portrays Germans living overseas, he creates an anachronistic image of sturdy peasants and God-fearing Christians who uphold traditional values in a rapidly changing world.

While the editors of *Die Gartenlaube* took pride in the fact that their family magazine was exported to the colonies, Germans living abroad also established their own publications. One of the most important of these was the Christian family journal *Die Abendschule*, published continuously in the United States from 1854 to 1900. Brent O. Peterson has shown how Germans living abroad sought to retain their national identity through this publication, while gradually adapting to their new environment.[58] Thus, he argues that *Die Abendschule* did not merely reflect a prefabricated identity but took an active part in reformulating that identity in a new context. Peterson's work on *Die Abendschule* is part of an effort to move German-American studies away from a politically suspect "filiopietism" and ethnic advocacy based on excessive pride in German contributions to American culture[59] and toward an approach more closely linked to "ethnic, minority, diaspora, postcolonial, and subaltern studies."[60]

Some of the same theoretical concerns underlie recent work on nineteenth-century German imperialism and colonialism. Colonial and postcolonial studies have been in vogue for some time among scholars of British and Francophone literatures, but they have only recently become the focus of German Studies. One is tempted to draw a parallel between Germany's belated rush to empire toward the end of the nineteenth century and the belated rush of German scholars to postcolonial studies at the beginning of the twenty-first. Reasons for the delay include the absence, until recently, of strong minority voices within Germany, a concentration on the Holocaust, and the sense that colonialism was a brief and relatively unimportant part of German history.[61] It was only in 1884 that Bismarck embarked on an official policy to establish an overseas empire, and the Germans lost whatever colonies they had gained through the Treaty of Versailles at the end of the First World War. There are, nevertheless, compelling reasons for the recent upsurge in the study of German imperialism and colonialism. Contemporary Germany's move toward greater integration within the European Union and participation in an increasingly global economy have inspired a renewed interest in the history of relations between Europe and the non-European world. National identities have not, however, disappeared in the new global era. Even as international commerce and communication have made German borders more porous, work continues on the reintegration of the former German Democratic Republic into the Federal Republic. While the Soviet Union, Yugoslavia, and Czechoslovakia split apart in the wake of the Cold War, Germany embarked on a paradoxical program that combines national reunification with increased globalization. The influx of foreign workers, from the Mediterranean *Gastarbeiter* of the 1960s to the Eastern Europeans and former Soviet Jews of the 1990s, have made Germany an increasingly multiethnic society, prompting both revision of its citizenship laws and periodic outbursts of antiforeign violence.[62]

Thus, the ghosts of the German past continue to haunt current efforts to redefine national identity and to preserve cultural memory.[63] As a result, many critics have begun to reinvestigate the place of nineteenth-century German colonialism within the broader context of its cultural history. One lesson to be drawn from the peculiarities of German history is that we cannot view imperialism in terms of a European monolith imposing its will on an equally homogenous "rest of the world." The history of European conquest of foreign territories is also a history of conflicts between individual nations within Europe. As Russell A. Berman has argued, "the emergence of German colonialism is, at least in part, a matter of an intra-European dynamic of imitation and competition."[64] Indeed, he contends that "German material is of particular interest, not because of the significance of German colonialism per se, but because of Germany's own liminal situation — never quite a full-fledged European nation-state, never indisputably part of the modern West."[65] Thus, to investigate German efforts to take part in the European project of imperialism is simultaneously to investigate the history of German national identity within Europe. In this volume, for instance, John Pizer demonstrates how Raabe's hostility toward pan-Germanism at home informs his rejection of German imperialist aspirations abroad.

Such an investigation need not begin with Germany's official entry into the imperialist era in 1884. Susanne Zantop, for instance, began her history of German "colonial fantasies" in the seventeenth and eighteenth centuries.[66] Although Germany did not yet have colonies of its own at this time, individual Germans did take part in the explorative and colonizing missions of other European nations, while many more "armchair conquistadors" followed events from the comfort of their homes. Until about 1870 Germans drew on their largely vicarious experience of European colonization as a source of national pride, criticizing the cruelty of Spanish and other imperial powers, while implicitly suggesting that they would eventually do things better. When Germans did begin to expand their empire, they could do so confidently and with a clear conscience: "no, Germany had not come too late — there was still territory to be had; no, Germans were not incompetent colonizers — on the contrary: their proverbial courage, industry, and organizational talent predestined them for that vocation; and no, Germans had no share in colonial guilt."[67]

While Zantop documents the complicity of many late-nineteenth-century German intellectuals in a program of aggressive colonial expansion, she also notes that at least some writers resisted the trend. Gottfried Keller's novella *Die Berlocken* (The Trinkets, 1881), for instance, evokes many familiar motifs of the conquest myth, only to subvert them into a "colonial counterfantasy."[68] Zantop thus cautions against teleological narratives of German history that lead inevitably from nineteenth-century imperialism to Hitler's Germany. Countercurrents existed, and alternatives were possible, although in the end the Holocaust "is the outcome with which we must contend."[69] Berman cautions even more strongly against a simplistic equation of the Enlightenment with empire that reduces Western rationality to an agent of control: "Knowledge is not only power."[70] Blanket condemnations of European imperialism threaten to become exercises in anti-intellectualism and to deny the possibility of rational critique. In other words, if all Europeans are equally guilty in spirit, than no European is guilty of a particular crime; the accusation of collective guilt unwittingly exonerates the implicated.[71] Berman insists that the German colonial encounter included incidents of genuine exchange and the recognition of cultural alterity, as well as Eurocentric arrogance and racism. He even makes the controversial suggestion "that there is a strain in German culture that allows for the appreciation of difference, and that this strain tempered colonial discourse, directing it more toward primitivism and the possibility of a heterophilic appreciation than, by way of contrast, the more imperiously universalist discourses characteristic of the colonialism of England and France."[72]

Gender plays a central, if varying, role in the literature of German colonialism. In one version an apologist for German colonialism described the relations between the imperial power and the colonies as that between the "motherland" and "daughter states."[73] In other cases a patriarchal model held sway as a benevolent father figure extended his protection to the colonial "child."[74] In still others Europeans writers imagined relations in terms of an interracial romance between the European man and the native woman. Both the paternalistic and the romantic models could be used to legitimate European rule, stylizing violent conquest into a benign account of a father's love for his children or a submissive native's desire for the irresistible white hero. Yet, colonial literature could portray nightmares, as well as fantasies: "virgin" territories eager for the conqueror's touch can turn into Amazons who strike back against anxious intruders.[75] Women writers in the German fatherland do not necessarily share their compatriots' male fantasies. For example, Frieda von Bülow, "arguably the founder of the genre of colonial fiction in Germany" in Berman's opinion, uses her fiction of the 1890s to criticize Wilhelmine patriarchy, thus producing an "unexpected alliance of colonialism and feminism." Rather than reinforcing gender stereotypes, Bülow calls them into question by portraying the colony as a site of "radical queerness" that promises a "perpetual transgression of gender" in a "hybridizing utopia."[76]

Taken together, these varied accounts of German colonial fiction point to ways in which multiple categories combine and interact within individual texts. Paternalistic or romantic fictions of German imperialism can serve as a form of national self-assertion against the alleged shortcomings of other European nations, as a defense of bourgeois morality against aristocratic decadence, as a demonstration of European racial superiority over non-European peoples, and as commentaries on gendered relations between the empire and the colonies, and between men and women in the German nation.[77] As Anne McClintock has shown in her study of British imperialism, the categories of "race, gender and class are not distinct realms of experience, existing in splendid isolation from each other; nor can they be simply yoked together retrospectively like armatures of Lego. Rather, they come into existence *in and through* relation to each other — if in contradictory and conflictual ways."[78]

Gender and German Realism

Two of the most important developments in recent scholarship on German realism have been an increased interest in women writers and a broader concern with questions of gender relations and sexual identity in texts by both men and women of the period. The renewed attention to texts by German women began with the second women's movement of the late 1960s and 1970s.[79] In German circles much effort has been directed toward "the discovery that women writers had a literature of their own, whose historical and thematic coherence, as well as artistic importance, had been obscured by the patriarchal values that dominate our culture."[80] Elaine Showalter's designation of such scholarship as the "second phase of feminist criticism" is somewhat misleading, in that it implies that once scholars unearth the work of a forgotten women writer they can rest assured that her works will remain in the public eye and that they will be available for at least a scholarly public in reasonably priced editions. Such confidence may be warranted in the United States, but it belies the power of the German literary institution that has excluded almost all women writers from its literary histories until fairly recently and continues to marginalize feminist scholars within the university.[81] The recovery of women's writing of the nineteenth century is likely to be a continuing task in the years to come rather than a temporary phase of German literary criticism.

The belief that a woman's place is in the home has a long tradition in German letters that extends back at least as far as Martin Luther. Calls for women to fulfill their domestic destiny escalated in the eighteenth century, which witnessed the emergence of a proto-democratic public sphere restricted to men, an increasing belief that the division of labor between men and women was rooted in nature, and the rise of the novel as an agent for disseminating new attitudes toward love and the family.[82] The men of the rising middle class took pride in their new family values as they struggled to wrest moral, as well as political, authority from what they perceived as a decadent aristocracy.[83] Women were expected to restrict their attention to hearth and home and to remain silent in public. In fact, however, some women did begin to speak out in literary texts aimed at the growing body of German readers, both male and female. Beginning with such pioneers as Luise Gottsched, Anna Karsch, and Sophie de La Roche, German women published in increasing numbers throughout the eighteenth and nineteenth centuries and became some of the most widely read authors of the period.[84]

Against a persistent tendency to categorize authors of *Frauenliteratur* as a monolithic block of inferior talents, it becomes necessary to make the seemingly banal point that not all women writers were alike. One of the continuing projects of feminist scholarship has been to differentiate among individual women writers of a given period and among groups of writers in different periods.[85] Nor should we imagine that German women writers concerned themselves exclusively with private concerns in the domestic sphere. They participated in the political debates of the nineteenth century, at times directly, by voicing their opinion about issues ranging from the industrial poor to Jewish emancipation, at other times indirectly, by using representations of family life to comment on patriarchal politics. Nor, finally, can we expect women writers to conform to a consistent pattern of feminist advocacy, given the strength of repressive sexual stereotypes in Germany and the taboos surrounding female authorship. As Ruth-Ellen Boetcher Joeres observes, German women writers often gave conflicting signals in their work: "they stepped out of line, but they also toed the line, they asserted their gender, but they also acceded to gender ideologies, they took unpopular positions, but they also seemed aware of the limitations of their spheres of activity."[86]

The failed revolution of 1848 marks a turning point for German women writers, who turned away from the open radicalism of such *Vormärz* authors as Louise Aston, Fanny Lewald, Ida Hahn-Hahn, and Louise Otto. Middle-class German women began to organize for the first time, yet they tended to work for moderate reform within the existing system.[87] The fiction of Eugenie Marlitt offers an interesting case in point.[88] As the flagship author of *Die Gartenlaube*, Marlitt appealed to what for the first time could be categorized as a modern mass audience of German readers. Marlitt shared the liberal convictions of her editor, Ernst Keil, rejecting aristocratic privilege and religious intolerance, while upholding the importance of the family for the well-being of the German nation. At first glance her heroines seem to have inherited the feminist spirit of the previous generation of women writers: they tend to be intelligent, self-reliant young women who do not hesitate to condemn injustice and stand up for their beliefs. In the end, however, each woman gladly sacrifices her independence in exchange for marriage and motherhood. As a result, some feminist critics have dismissed Marlitt's work as trivial fiction that reinforces patriarchal values. As Kirsten Belgum argues in her contribution to this volume, however, we should not overlook the emancipatory potential of Marlitt's strong female characters, who consent to marry only after having persuaded their future husbands to accept their progressive social and political beliefs. Canonical works of realism often focus on male fantasies, Belgum concludes; why should we not also include works that depict female fantasies and desires within an expanded canon of German realism?

Other women writers of the realist period turned their attention to German history. One of the most popular and prolific authors of the nineteenth century was Luise Mühlbach, whose historical novels Brent Peterson examines in this volume. Peterson contrasts Mühlbach's fiction with Ranke's histories to show how the two genres offer conflicting versions of the German past. Ranke concentrates on public events in the lives of "great men" in a way that was typical of a generation of male writers establishing the academic discipline of history at the German universities. In contrast, Mühlbach's fiction reveals a more intimate side of famous figures from the past and also shows how private concerns can have an impact on political decisions. At stake is not just the conflicting social status of historical fiction versus academic historiography but a debate about what constitutes historical truth. Louise von François also wrote historical fiction, whose conflicting messages on gender roles Thomas C. Fox explores in his contribution to this volume. Although François sets the "masculine" virtues of Germany and Prussia against the "effeminacy" of Napoleonic France, she also disrupts traditional gender roles by creating a series of independent, "masculine" women in her fiction. Her work thus simultaneously upholds a view of German patriotism rooted in patriarchal values and subverts patriarchy by granting an unusually strong role to androgynous or masculinized women.

While François was creating her transgressive female characters, the medical community was beginning to focus increased attention on questions of sexual identity in general and homosexuality in particular. Same-sex desire has, of course, been part of Western civilization at least since ancient Greece; what was new in the nineteenth century, as Michel Foucault argued, was the creation of the category of "the homosexual" to set off a group of "deviant" individuals from mainstream society.[89] In his contribution to this volume Robert Tobin examines Thomas Mann's early fiction in the context of conflicting German discourses about this new category of the homosexual. He begins with a look at Karl Heinrich Ulrichs's writings about what Ulrich termed "the third sex." Although Ulrich pursued a liberal agenda that sought to decriminalize homosexual acts between consenting adults, his association of homosexuality with Jewishness and Oriental exoticism reinforced the sense that homosexuals remained on the margins of German society. The same sense of uncertainty informs Mann's early representations of same-sex desire. Again and again, Mann portrays "lonely men with problematic sexualities" who pay for their heightened artistic sensibility with exclusion from a "healthy," heterosexual German society — the same society that ostracizes "effeminate" Jews. By the early twentieth century, however, a new generation of German sexologists led by Hans Blüher emphatically rejected the notion of the third sex. For Blüher, all men were at least potentially homosexual, and same-sex desire was the glue that bonded together German society. Ulrichs's liberal politics of inclusion for the minoritized homosexual had been inverted into a reactionary agenda that equated homoerotic desire with national strength. Although Mann endorsed Blüher's theories uncritically in his nonfiction texts of the teens and the early 1920s, his fiction of the prewar period, most notably *Der Tod in Venedig* (Death in Venice, 1912), continues to associate homosexuality with illness and abnormality. In this regard, Tobin concludes, Mann remains a writer more shaped by the medical discourses of the nineteenth than those of the twentieth century.

In sum, the essays in this volume suggest that in many ways late-nineteenth-century Germany can be viewed as a not-so-distant mirror of concerns that continue to preoccupy scholars of German literature today, including questions of national unity in an increasingly global era, of gender roles and sexual identities, and of minority rights and antiforeign violence. This is not to imply that we can only reawaken interest in German realism by a desperate effort to make it seem relevant to contemporary concerns. "Always historicize!" commands Fredric Jameson,[90] and the contributors to this volume obey by carefully situating the texts they examine in the historical context in which the works were written. That certain aspects of this historical period should be of renewed interest today hardly invalidates the research; as Nietzsche argued, history is written for the living, not the dead.[91] The following essays demonstrate that it is not only possible to reawaken slumbering classics but also to discover new life in pages once cast into the dustbin of literary history.

Notes

[1] Maximilian Nutz, "Das Beispiel Goethe: Zur Konstituierung eines nationalen Klassikers," in Jürgen Fohrmann and Wilhelm Vosskamp, eds. *Wissenschaftsgeschichte der Germanistik im 19. Jahrhundert* (Stuttgart: Metzler, 1994), 605–37. See also Hans Schwerte, *Faust und das Faustische: Ein Kapitel deutscher Ideologie* (Stuttgart: Klett, 1962); Karl Robert Mandelkow, *Goethe in Deutschland: Rezeptionsgeschichte eines Klassikers* (Munich: Beck, 1980); and Peter Uwe Hohendahl, *Building a National Literature: The Case of Germany 1830–1870*, trans. Renate Baron Franciscono (Ithaca NY: Cornell UP, 1989).

[2] Roy Pascal characterizes Stifter as "a mild and timid liberal" in his highly critical *The German Novel: Studies* (Manchester: Manchester UP, 1956), 53.

[3] Jost Hermand, "Zur Literatur der Gründerzeit," in his *Von Mainz nach Weimar (1793–1919): Studien zur Deutschen Literatur* (Stuttgart: Metzler, 1969), 211–49.

[4] Erich Auerbach, *Mimesis: The Representation of Reality in Western Literature*, trans. Willard R. Trask (Princeton: Princeton UP, 1968), 441.

[5] For a detailed overview of the term and the history of German realism see Fritz Martini, "Realismus," in Paul Merker and Wolfgang Stammler, eds., *Reallexikon der deutschen Literaturgeschichte*, 2nd ed., eds. Werner Kohlschmidt and Wolfgang Mohr, vol. 3 (Berlin: de Gruyter, 1976), 343–65.

[6] Roland Barthes, "L'Effet de Réel," *Communications* 1 (1968): 84–89. "In short . . . what we call 'real' (in the theory of the realistic text) is never more than a code of representation (of signification) . . . *the novelistic real is not operable*." Barthes, *S/Z: An Essay*, trans. Richard Miller (New York: Hill & Wang, 1974), 80.

[7] As Robert C. Holub observes, there are, in fact, two realisms: one that can occur at any time and another specifically linked to the nineteenth century. *Reflections of Realism: Paradox, Norm, and Ideology in Nineteenth-Century German Prose* (Detroit: Wayne State UP, 1991), 14. See also the opening pages of his essay in the present volume.

[8] Linda Nochlin, *Realism* (Harmondsworth: Penguin, 1971).

[9] Georg Lukács, *The Theory of the Novel: A Historico-Philosophical Essay on the Forms of Great Epic Literature*, trans. Anna Bostock (Cambridge MA: MIT P, 1971), 41. See also Hans Blumenberg, *The Legitimacy of the Modern Age*, trans. Robert M. Wallace (Cambridge MA: MIT P, 1983).

[10] Nochlin, *Realism*, 60.

[11] Nochlin, *Realism*, 45–50.

[12] Koppel S. Pinson, *Modern Germany: Its History and Civilization,* 2nd ed. (New York: Macmillan, 1966), 221.

[13] See Pinson, 219–51; also James J. Sheehan, *German History 1770–1866* (Oxford: Clarendon P, 1989), 730–92.

[14] Quoted from Fritz Martini, *Deutsche Literatur im bürgerlichen Realismus 1848–1898,* 4th rev. ed. (Stuttgart: Metzler, 1981), 398.

[15] *Griff nach der Weltmacht* is the original title of the book by Fritz Fischer translated as *Germany's Aims in the First World War* (New York: Norton, 1967). The classic text on German "belatedness" is Helmuth Plessner's *Die verspätete Nation: Über die Verführbarkeit bürgerlichen Geistes,* in his *Gesammelte Schriften,* vol. 6, eds. Günter Dux et al. (1935/1959; Frankfurt am Main: Suhrkamp, 1982), 7–223. The question of assigning blame for the start of the First World War is complex and hotly debated. See, for example, Barbara Tuchmann's popular *The Guns of August* (New York: Macmillan, 1962) for an overview of the conflicting national policies that led to the outbreak of war.

[16] On reactionary tendencies in German nationalism see George L. Mosse, *The Crisis of German Ideology: Intellectual Origins of the Third Reich,* 2nd rev. ed. (1964; New York: Schocken, 1981).

[17] Kant, "Beantwortung der Frage: Was ist Aufklärung?" in his *Werkausgabe,* ed. Wilhelm Weischedel (Frankfurt am Main: Suhrkamp, 1978), 11: 53–61.

[18] See Hans-Ulrich Wehler's critical account of the German bourgeoisie's willingness to concede power to a reactionary elite: *The German Empire 1871–1918,* trans. Kim Traynor (Oxford: Berg, 1985). David Blackbourn and Geoff Eley argue against Wehler's theory of a German *Sonderweg,* claiming that his indictment of the German bourgeoisie relies on an unwarranted idealization of the equally illiberal British middle class: *The Peculiarities of German History: Bourgeois Society and Politics in Nineteenth-Century Germany* (Oxford: Oxford UP, 1984).

[19] James J. Sheehan, *German Liberalism in the Nineteenth Century* (Chicago: U of Chicago P, 1978).

[20] Clifford Albrecht Bernd, *German Poetic Realism* (Boston: Twayne, 1981), 19.

[21] See Hans Mayer, "Die Wirklichkeit E. T. A. Hoffmans," in Richard Brinkmann, ed., *Begriffsbestimmung des Literarischen Realismus* (Darmstadt: Wissenschaftliche Buchgesellschaft, 1969), 259–300.

[22] Peter Uwe Hohendahl, "Literary Criticism in the Epoch of Liberalism, 1820–70," in Hohendahl, ed., *A History of German Literary Criticism 1730–1980,* trans. Franz Blaha et al. (Lincoln: U of Nebraska P, 1988), 181.

[23] Bernd, *German Poetic Realism,* 19–28. Although he resists the tendency to view 1848 as the "zero hour" of German realism, Hohendahl also notes a general agreement on the part of most critics after 1850 "that the intimate

relation between literature and politics must be dissolved" ("The Epoch of Realism," 214). The best collection of source material and analysis of nineteenth-century German novel theory is Hartmut Steinecke's *Romantheorie und Romankritik in Deutschland*, 2 vols. (Stuttgart: Metzler, 1975, 1976). See also Eberhard Lämmert, ed., *Romantheorie: Dokumentation ihrer Geschichte in Deutschland*, 2 vols. (Berlin: Kiepenheuer & Witsch, 1971, 1975).

[24] On realism in *Buddenbrooks* see Martin Swales, *Buddenbrooks: Family Life as the Mirror of Social Change* (Boston: Twayne, 1991), 12–16. In his contribution to this volume Russell A. Berman discusses *Effi Briest* as marking the end of German realism.

[25] See for example E. K. Bennett, *A History of the German Novelle from Goethe to Thomas Mann*, 2nd. ed., rev. H. M. Waidson (New York: Cambridge UP, 1961); Walter Silz, *Realism and Reality: Studies in the German Novelle of Poetic Realism* (Chapel Hill: U of North Carolina P, 1954).

[26] For example, Horst Albert Glaser's *Deutsche Literatur: Eine Sozialgeschichte*, vol. 7: *Vom Nachmärz zur Gründerzeit: Realismus 1848–1880* (Reinbek: Rowohlt, 1982), contains several essays and extensive bibliography on the poetry and drama of the period.

[27] Fritz Martini offers a succinct overview of foreign influence in *Deutsche Literatur*, 55–58.

[28] Bernd, *Poetic Realism in Scandinavia and Central Europe 1820–1895* (Columbia, SC: Camden House, 1995).

[29] Henry H. Remak, "The German Reception of French Realism," *PMLA* 69 (1954): 410–31. See also Ruth-Ellen Boetcher Joeres, *Respectability and Deviance: Nineteenth-Century German Women Writers and the Ambiguity of Representation* (Chicago: U of Chicago P, 1998).

[30] Remak, 418.

[31] In addition to Remak, see Lämmert, ed., 2: 1–5.

[32] Thomas Mann, *Betrachtungen eines Unpolitischen* (Frankfurt am Main: Fischer, 1988). See also Norbert Elias, "On the Sociogenesis of the Difference between *Kultur* and *Zivilisation* in German Usage," in his *The Civilizing Process*, trans. Edmund Jephcott (Oxford: Blackwell, 1994), 1–28.

[33] Todd Kontje, *The German Bildungsroman: History of a National Genre* (Columbia, SC: Camden House, 1993).

[34] Novalis derided Goethe's *Meister* as an increasingly prosaic "pilgrimage toward a patent of nobility," a critique that forms the basis of Karl Schlechta's withering analysis in his *Goethes Wilhelm Meister* (Frankfurt am Main: Klostermann, 1953).

[35] Jürgen Jacobs, *Wilhelm Meister und seine Brüder: Untersuchungen zum deutschen Bildungsroman* (Munich: Fink, 1972). Goethe's enormous prestige

explains the desire on the part of many German novelists to associate their work with his and for literary historians to invent a national genre. See Hartmut Steinecke, "*Wilhelm Meister* und die Folgen: Goethes Roman und die Entwicklung der Gattung im 19. Jahrhundert," in Wolfgang Wittkowski, ed., *Goethe im Kontext* (Tübingen: Niemeyer, 1984), 89–118.

[36] Glaser, ed., *Deutsche Literatur: Eine Sozialgeschichte*, vol. 7.

[37] Jeffrey L. Sammons, "The Mystery of the Missing *Bildungsroman*, or: What happened to Wilhelm Meister's Legacy?" *Genre* 14 (1981): 229–46.

[38] Mosse, "What the Germans Really Read," in his *Masses and Man: Nationalist and Fascist Perceptions of Reality* (New York: Fertig, 1980), 52–68; Hohendahl, *Building a National Literature*; Hohendahl, ed., *A History of German Literary Criticism*; Fohrmann and Vosskamp, eds., *Wissenschaftsgeschichte der Germanistik*; Klaus Weimar, *Geschichte der deutschen Literaturwissenschaft bis zum Ende des 19. Jahrhunderts* (Munich: Fink, 1989).

[39] Pascal, *The German Novel*, 63.

[40] Friedrich Theodor Vischer, *Aesthetik oder Wissenschaft des Schönen* (1857); cited from Steinecke, *Romantheorie und Romankritik in Deutschland*, 2: 259–60.

[41] Hartmut Vinçon, "Frühe Arbeiterliteratur," in Glaser, ed., 7: 206–15.

[42] Ernest K. Bramsted, *Aristocracy and the Middle-Classes in Germany: Social Types in German Literature 1830–1900*, 2nd rev. ed. (Chicago: U of Chicago P, 1964), 107–32.

[43] On the theme of labor in *Soll und Haben* see also Holub, *Reflections of Realism*, 174–85.

[44] Cited from Friedrich Schiller, *Sämtliche Werke*, eds. Gerhard Fricke and Herbert G. Göpfert (Munich: Hanser, 1980), 1: 267.

[45] Johann Wolfgang von Goethe, *Werke* (Hamburg: Wegner, 1953), 12: 239–44.

[46] Benedict Anderson, *Imagined Communities: Reflections on the Origin and Spread of Nationalism*, 2nd rev. ed. (London: Verso, 1991); Mosse, *The Nationalization of the Masses: Political Symbolism and Mass Movements in Germany from the Napoleonic Wars through the Third Reich* (Ithaca NY: Cornell UP, 1975).

[47] Norbert Miller, "Dorfgeschichte und Dorfroman," in Glaser, ed., *Deutsche Literatur: Eine Sozialgeschichte*, 7: 179–205; Peter Zimmermann, "Heimatkunst," in Glaser, ed., *Deutsche Literatur: Eine Sozialgeschichte*, 8: 154–68.

[48] Karl Otto Conrady, "Deutsche Literaturwissenschaft und Drittes Reich," in Conrady et al., eds., *Germanistik — eine deutsche Wissenschaft* (Frankfurt am Main: Suhrkamp, 1967), 71–109.

[49] Plessner argues that the German susceptibility to romantic or *völkisch* nationalism stems from its belatedness: while nation-formation in England and

France coincided with Enlightenment pleas for universal human rights, Germany remained a political backwater of absolutist particularism throughout the eighteenth century (*Die verspätete Nation,* 46). See also Mosse, *The Crisis of German Ideology.*

[50] Georg Lukács, "Gottfried Keller," in Rodney Livingstone, ed., *German Realists in the Nineteenth Century,* trans. Jeremy Gaines and Paul Keast (Cambridge MA: MIT P, 1993), 157–247.

[51] Wehler, 91.

[52] Wehler, 128.

[53] Saski Sassen, *Migranten, Siedler, Flüchtlinge: Von der Massenauswanderung zur Festung Europa* (Frankfurt am Main: Fischer, 1996), 75.

[54] Wehler, 105–13. See also Daniel Jonah Goldhagen, *Hitler's Willing Executioners: Ordinary Germans and the Holocaust* (New York: Vintage, 1997), 49–79.

[55] On Nietzsche's rejection of anti-Semitism, see Walter Kaufmann, *Nietzsche: Philosopher, Psychologist, Antichrist* (Cleveland: Meridian, 1956) and Holub, "Nietzsche's Colonialist Imagination: Nueva Germania, Good Europeanism, and Great Politics," in Sara Friedrichsmeyer, Sara Lennox, and Susanne Zantop, eds., *The Imperialist Imagination: German Colonialism and Its Legacy* (Ann Arbor: U of Michigan P, 1998), 33–49. On anti-Semitism in Freytag's novel, see Berman, *The Rise of the Modern German Novel: Crisis and Charisma* (Cambridge MA: Harvard UP, 1986), 79–104, and Holub, *Reflections of Realism,* 176–86. For a nuanced discussion of alleged anti-Semitism in Raabe, see Sammons, *Wilhelm Raabe: The Fiction of the Alternative Community* (Princeton: Princeton UP, 1987), 73–87. On anti-Semitism in Wagner's operas, see Marc A. Weiner, *Richard Wagner and the Anti-Semitic Imagination* (Lincoln: U of Nebraska P, 1995).

[56] Kirsten Belgum, *Popularizing the Nation: Audience, Representation, and the Production of Identity in Die Gartenlaube 1853–1900* (Lincoln: U of Nebraska P, 1998), 47.

[57] Belgum, 50.

[58] Brent O. Peterson, *Popular Narratives and Ethnic Identity: Literature and Community in* Die Abendschule (Ithaca NY: Cornell UP, 1991).

[59] Valters Nollendorfs, "The Field, the Boundaries, and the Cultivators of German-American Studies," *Monatshefte* 86 (1994): 319–30. This issue reprints contributions to "A Symposium on German-American Studies," held at the University of Wisconsin-Madison in September 1993.

[60] Peterson, "Towards a 'Cultural' German-American Studies," *Monatshefte* 86 (1994): 355.

[61] Friedrichsmeyer, Lennox, and Zantop, introduction to *The Imperialist Imagination,* 1–29.

[62] On literature and identity in the New Europe see Gisela Brinker-Gabler and Sidonie Smith, eds., *Writing New Identities: Gender, Nation, and Immigration in Contemporary Europe* (Minneapolis: U of Minnesota P, 1997), and Karen Jankowsky and Carla Love, eds., *Other Germanies: Questioning Identity in Women's Literature and Art* (Albany: State U of New York P, 1997).

[63] Brian Ladd, *The Ghosts of Berlin: Confronting German History in the Urban Landscape* (Chicago: U of Chicago P, 1997); Andreas Huyssen, *Twilight Memories: Marking Time in a Culture of Amnesia* (New York: Routledge, 1995).

[64] Berman, *Enlightenment or Empire: Colonial Discourse in German Culture* (Lincoln: U of Nebraska P, 1998), 100.

[65] Berman, *Enlightenment or Empire*, 134–35.

[66] Susanne Zantop, *Colonial Fantasies: Conquest, Family, and Nation in Precolonial Germany, 1770–1870* (Durham, NC: Duke UP, 1997).

[67] Zantop, *Colonial Fantasies*, 29.

[68] Zantop, *Colonial Fantasies*, 206.

[69] Zantop, *Colonial Fantasies*, 16.

[70] Berman, *Enlightenment or Empire*, 204.

[71] See Berman, "An Imagined Community: Germany according to Goldhagen," *German Quarterly* 71 (1998): 63–67.

[72] Berman, *Enlightenment or Empire*, 235

[73] Berman, *Enlightenment or Empire*, 141.

[74] Friedrichsmeyer, Lennox, and Zantop, introduction to *The Imperialist Imagination*, 20. See also Zantop, *Colonial Fantasies*, 46–65.

[75] Zantop, *Colonial Fantasies*, 45.

[76] Berman, *Enlightenment or Empire*, 172–74.

[77] See, for example, Zantop's reading of Kleist's *Verlobung in Santa Domingo* in *Colonial Fantasies*, 141–61; also Kontje, "Passing for German: Politics and Patriarchy in Kleist, Körner, and Fischer," *German Studies Review* 22 (1999): 67–84.

[78] Anne McClintock, *Imperial Leather: Race, Gender and Sexuality in the Colonial Contest* (New York: Routledge, 1995), 5.

[79] Pioneering studies include Renate Möhrmann, *Die andere Frau: Emanzipationsansätze deutscher Schriftstellerinnen im Vorfeld der Achtundvierziger-Revolution* (Stuttgart: Metzler, 1977) and Silvia Bovenschen, *Die imaginierte Weiblichkeit: Exemplarische Untersuchungen zu kulturgeschichtlichen und literarischen Präsentationsformen des Weiblichen* (Frankfurt am Main: Suhrkamp, 1979). Both continued the important earlier work of Christine Touaillon, *Der deutsche Frauenroman des 18. Jahrhunderts* (Vienna: Braumüller, 1919).

[80] Elaine Showalter, "Introduction: The Feminist Critical Revolution," in Showalter, ed., *The New Feminist Criticism: Essays on Women, Literature, and Theory* (New York: Pantheon, 1985), 6.

[81] Feminist scholarship in Germany has not received the same institutional support that it has in the United States. See Joeres, *Respectability and Deviance*, xix–xxx.

[82] On these topics see Joan B. Landes, *Women and the Public Sphere in the Age of the French Revolution* (Ithaca, NY: Cornell UP, 1988), Thomas Laqueur, *Making Sex: Body and Gender from the Greeks to Freud* (Cambridge MA: Harvard UP, 1990), and Nancy Armstrong, *Desire and Domestic Fiction: A Political History of the Novel* (New York: Oxford UP, 1987).

[83] Lynn Hunt, *The Family Romance of the French Revolution* (Berkeley: U of California P, 1992).

[84] For a selection of German women writers in English see Jeannine Blackwell and Susanne Zantop, eds., *Bitter Healing: German Women Writers 1700–1830: An Anthology* (Lincoln: U of Nebraska P, 1990).

[85] Kontje, *Women, the Novel, and the German Nation 1771–1871: Domestic Fiction in the Fatherland* (Cambridge: Cambridge UP, 1998).

[86] Joeres, 137.

[87] Joeres regards Louise Otto, one of the leaders of the German women's movement, as typical in this regard (86). On the relative conservatism of the German women's movement as compared with that of England or the United States, see Richard J. Evans, *The Feminist Movement in Germany 1894–1933* (London: SAGE, 1976).

[88] Kontje, *Women, the Novel, and the German Nation 1771–1871*, 183–201.

[89] Michel Foucault, *The History of Sexuality*, vol. 1: *An Introduction*, trans. Robert Hurley (New York: Vintage, 1978), 43.

[90] Fredric Jameson, *The Political Unconscious: Narrative as Socially Symbolic Act* (Ithaca, NY: Cornell UP, 1981), 9.

[91] Friedrich Nietzsche, "Vom Nutzen und Nachteil der Historie für das Leben," in his *Werke*, ed. Karl Schlechta (Frankfurt am Main: Ullstein, 1976), 1: 209–85.

Adalbert Stifter's *Brigitta,* or the Lesson of Realism

Robert C. Holub

I BEGAN TO THINK about realism over a decade ago, when I was planning a course on the nineteenth century. Most of the texts I wanted to include were regarded by knowledgeable literary scholars as "realist," and so I decided to design the course rather conveniently along the lines of literary texts reflecting social reality — in particular, the social reality of the German middle class, although there were several texts that did not really fit well in this framework. In reflecting on realism and on previous theories of realism, however, I began to feel some discomfort. It struck me that in the secondary literature there were two ways in which realism was approached. One set of theorists employs realism as I did at that time: to refer to a specific period during the nineteenth century when writers dealt with the social reality of the newly established or self-conscious middle class. Particularly important for these theorists are long novels, and the names that are usually associated with realism in this sense are almost always British or French: Dickens, Thackeray, Stendhal, Balzac, Flaubert. In the scholarship about German realism one usually finds the term *realism* accompanied by an adjective, sometimes "poetic," sometimes "bourgeois," sometimes "programmatic"; and it is usually applied to such writers as Keller, Storm, Freytag, and Fontane, occasionally also to Stifter or Meyer and others. This secondary literature usually concedes that Fontane is the only classical realist in the European sense of the word; and some would argue that even he is atypical, since his writing career began when European realism was already waning, and since he deals primarily with aristocratic demise and not with middle-class life. A chief representative for a theory of nineteenth-century realism would be someone such as René Wellek, who, in a seminal essay of 1961 titled "The Concept of Realism in Literary Scholarship," defines realism simply as "the objective representation of contemporary social reality."[1]

The other type of realism is less specific with regard to epochs and considers realism to be a general characteristic of literary texts. In this sense it can be applied to the entire tradition of Western literature from Homer to the present and includes a conceptual apparatus that extends from mimesis as a concept among the ancients to socialist realism in the twentieth century. This notion of realism relates in a general fashion to the manner in which literature captures or mirrors reality, a quality of texts that is apparently considered timeless and can happen in any epoch or in any author's works. Perhaps the most celebrated scholar who sees realism as a tendency or potential inherent in all Western literature is Erich Auerbach, whose *Mimesis* (1946; trans., 1953)[2] is still one of the most worthwhile reading experiences in all of secondary literature. But even in Auerbach we see how the two definitions of realism dovetail. Although he finds realism in Homer and the Bible, as well as in Virginia Woolf, he obviously considers Western literature to possess a telos that was attained in the nineteenth century in the writings of the great novelists whom our first group of theorists considered realists. In the penultimate chapter — Virginia Woolf represents the decline from realist heights — we have reached our destination. Here, for the first time, Auerbach defines the privileged relationship between text and reality he has called *realism:* "The serious treatment of everyday reality, the rise of more extensive and socially inferior human groups to the position of subject matter for problematic-existential representation, on the one hand; on the other, the embedding of random persons and events in the general course of contemporary history, the fluid historical background — these, we believe, are the foundations of modern realism" (491).

Despite the differences between these two approaches to realism, I began to see that both parties considered realism to be a norm from which one deviated in composing literary texts that were not realist. This notion of a normative type of text disturbed me, since it was not — and is not — apparent to me why a so-called realist text should be more normative than a Romantic text or a modernist text or a fairy tale. It was also rather troublesome that no one was really able to define *realism* in a satisfactory manner. As Richard Brinkmann pointed out in 1966,[3] definitions of realism inevitably depend on a fixed set of characteristics and invariably employ circular reasoning: realism is defined in terms of features drawn from works of a certain period, and then those features are located in the works to prove that they are realist. Furthermore, the listing of characteristics — for example, the abundance of detailed description or the concern for formerly excluded social classes — leaves one with a catalogue that is either incomplete or so general that obviously nonrealist works would have to be included, as well. Detailed description is a characteristic of many Baroque novels that are obviously not realist in the sense that realism is usually employed; and pastoral poetry of the eighteenth century deals with classes excluded from the high genres of tragedy and epic, but no one is anxious to claim these poems for realism, either.

Discontented with the implied normativity of realism and the inadequate definitions, I decided to try a different approach. Common to all definitions of realism I had encountered was a set of characteristics relating to the text and its representations. Why not, I reasoned, look at the text and its relationship to the reader, instead? In lieu of asking what quality of the text and its representation makes it realist, I initially rephrased the query as follows: What makes a text have a realist effect? I found, however, that I got no further with that question than others did with their listing of representational characteristics. So I reformulated my question as follows: What *destroys* for us the realist effect of a text — at least for certain readers at certain times? A description of a trip to the moon would have seemed fantastic for readers of the nineteenth century; but if such a work were written today, it would obviously not have exactly the same effect. In certain circles the reference to miracles might be an acceptable part of reality and, hence, nonintrusive for the effect of realism, but for most educated readers today these references would disqualify the text in which they appear from realist literature. With regard to realist effect, elements of content therefore appear relative to the beliefs, biases, and even age of the readership; I could not count on them to formulate a notion of realism. Neither could I take recourse to most formal or stylistic elements — for example, narrative perspectives; although they are not so much relative to variations in the readership, they are adaptable to many different compositional situations and produce widely variant effects. Indeed, many techniques of "antirealist" modern literature — for example, montage or stream-of-consciousness — may also be employed to produce a realist impact. There would appear to be at least one stylistic trait, however, that is rarely found in realist texts. *The foregrounding of fictionality will almost always produce a nonrealistic effect.* The reason is simple. When a given text makes no claim to mirror or refer to an external reality but, instead, insists on its nonrelationship to the world and tells the readership that it is creating a fiction, it forfeits automatically and necessarily its potential for producing an effect of the real.

Realist texts, therefore, must stop short of foregrounding fictionality if they are to have a realistic effect. Indeed, if we consider the foregrounding of fictionality to be one extreme, the works of realism would appear to be at the other end of the spectrum. In most instances they must conceal any traces of their nature as fantasy and invention: *the fiction they perpetrate is that they are not fiction at all.* Accompanying this implicit self-denial is usually an absence of reflection on the relationship between text and reality. Works of realism, by the very fact that this relationship is not thematized, imply that it is natural or, at least, that it requires no clarification. For this reason omniscient third-person narrators are found in the classical novels of realism: these narrators do not question their own voice or knowledge but write as if they are reporting everything without error or prejudice.

What I found, however, in texts traditionally considered realist was that they often did not correspond to this ban on reflecting their fictionality at all. Indeed, the most I was able to say about these so-called realist texts was that their reflections remained unforegrounded and unmarked, while in texts of Romanticism or modernism the fictional nature of the enterprise was quite often obvious. Thus, realist texts became for me ones in which fictionality was unforegrounded, hidden, or concealed but just as often furtively, unconsciously, or unintentionally revealed. Furthermore, I noted that in the German canon texts that have traditionally been considered realist are most interesting and most revealing of their historical situatedness at precisely those moments when they begin to reflect on the precarious nature of their own poetics. I found that realism was, indeed, normative, but not in the way that other theorists had suggested. Instead, I believe that realist texts are normed discourses that contain and disclose contradictions and paradoxes of their ideological universe at precisely those moments in which they are covering their fictionality. In short, the normative discourse appears to be related to certain social norms that these texts wish to convey.

The readings in my book *Reflections of Realism*[4] were meant to uncover some of these norms; in the remainder of this essay I would like to present a continuation of or supplement to the readings in that volume. My topic here is a novella, *Brigitta,* usually regarded as an early example of German realism and written by probably the most accomplished Austrian prose writer of the nineteenth century, Adalbert Stifter (1805–68). It is a work from the pre-March period, although, as we shall see, it had little to do with the growing revolutionary fervor of those years. Stifter began composition on the novella as early as 1842. It first appeared in the popular Almanac *Gedenke Mein! Taschenbuch für 1844.* The author reworked this version and included it in the fourth volume of his *Studien* in 1847.[5] *Brigitta* is usually regarded as an illustration of Stifter's didactic concern with inner beauty in contrast to outward appearances. Indeed, Stifter places so much emphasis on the eponymous heroine's outward ugliness, contrasting it with her internal worth, that the reader can hardly avoid a direct confrontation with this theme. In some respects the novella is simply an abbreviated version of Stifter's lengthy novel, *Der Nachsommer* (Indian Summer, 1857), which contains a similar constellation of characters, except that Stifter, a pedagogue by profession, is rather heavy-handed in inculcating his message in the earlier work. But the most obvious and intended interpretation is not the only lesson that this novella imparts. As I hope to demonstrate, Stifter instructs us in more than inner beauty by demonstrating for us — perhaps unwittingly — that the preferred and positive values of the civilized world are always already informed by their antinomies.

Brigitta opens with an unusual series of statements. The initial paragraph is apt to give us pause: it relates to us a pedagogical, quasi-philosophical message, a generality stated in the most abstract terms. We read of mysteries of the soul, of inner beauty in ugliness, of inexplicable attractions and repulsions. Psychology has been able to explain such enigmas, we are told, but much remains inaccessible to science: "dunkel und in großer Entfernung." The narrator continues, speaking somewhat oddly of "ein heiterer unermeßlicher Abgrund, in dem Gott und die Geister wandeln." We are used to hearing about "unfathomable abysses," but only seldom are they referred to with the almost Nietzschean adjective "heiter." And we are told that the soul occasionally crosses this abyss — what could possibly be on the other side? — and that literature ["die Dichtkunst"] in childlike unconsciousness sometimes unveils it, although the metaphor of unveiling seems to be more appropriate for secrets or something hidden, such as the hidden moral reasons referred to in a previous sentence, than for an abyss, which is not usually something unveiled. Science,[6] in any case, is powerless to give us any answers in these matters. It stands at the edge of the abyss ["an dem Rande"] with hammer and spirit level and in many cases does not even begin work. With the reference to the spirit level ["Richtscheite"] Stifter seems to refer back to the unfathomable abyss — an instrument such as a spirit level is useless if the abyss cannot be measured — and some more adventurous interpreters may want to connect the hammer with the other adjective describing the abyss and tie them all together in a Nietzschean reference to philosophizing with the hammer. (Is it a total coincidence that Nietzsche was so enthusiastic about *Der Nachsommer*, the expanded retelling of *Brigitta*?) Even those who do not want to cross into this more adventurous zone of intertextuality, however, will recognize that this opening is strange in its metaphors and slightly ominous in its tone. On the one hand, it is a valorization of the project of literature, which, like the soul, is able to comprehend, according to the narrator, things that science cannot. Literature [*Dichtkunst*] is here superior in explanatory power to science [*Wissenschaft*]; it is an abysmal path to knowledge, an exploration of knowledge of the abyss.[7] On the other hand, it suggests that precisely in the arts — and, as we shall see, in art forms that adhere to realistic conventions — one achieves knowledge that eludes the scales of consciousness. We gain knowledge here not from judicious activities or reasoned argument but from an inexact realm that nonetheless delivers with precision. In any case, the opening paragraph does not suggest that what we are going to encounter in the following pages is a realist novella but, rather, if anything, an exploration or perhaps an unveiling of the abyss (411–12).[8]

But the style turns rather abruptly in the second paragraph. From this point onward we repeatedly encounter signs that assure us of fidelity to some external reality and that tell us, therefore, that the work we have before us is demanding inclusion among the texts we usually associate with realism. The first-person narrator, whom we come to know as totally — almost annoyingly — trustworthy, informs us that he is going to relate to us an event ["eine Begebenheit"] from his youth to explain the reflections with which he prefaces his story. In contrast to Goethe's famous definition of the novella, this "Begebenheit" is not initially seen as "unerhört" [unprecedented],[9] although we may come to see it in this fashion on further reflection. At the beginning of the novella, in any case, the narrator relates the story in order to demonstrate the general point he has made in the opening paragraph. Thus, we are supposed to learn something from this story; we are going to see something demonstrated. Like Stifter's own activity in Austria, this novella is defined as pedagogical, as didactic, as educational. Just as the narrator has learned from this event, we, too, should come to a similar insight. We are thus placed in an analogous position to that of the narrator. Indeed, what we have here is a continuation of the lesson of realism, a handing down from one character to another, and then to the reader, so that pedagogy disseminates, eventually encompassing the entire human race. In reading, we are pupils in an education experiment. If we learn our lessons well, if we read correctly, if we follow the path dictated to us by the realist novella, then we will experience the same rewards that have come to the main character and to the narrator.

But, of course, this analogy between reader and narrator is far from perfect. Indeed, the very fact that the narrator is a narrator and that we are the readers situates us in a completely different position vis-à-vis the reality described for us. In the first place, the lesson that the narrator learned, although we are going to learn it, as well, appeared as the result of his experiences. For us the lesson — at least part of the lesson — is the preface or introduction to these experiences. The order of experience and lesson is thus reversed. We read at the beginning what the narrator has only learned at the conclusion of his journey. For another thing, the narrative is structured so that it is not given to us in the order in which it was experienced or learned by the narrator but is presented to us in a different order to preserve a coherence for us.[10] Thus, the third section of the novella breaks off the linear plot line — and we must assume that the narrator's experience was linear — and we are informed as follows: "Ehe ich entwickle, wie wir nach Marosheli geritten sind, wie ich Brigitta kennengelernt habe, und wie ich noch recht oft auf ihrem Gute gewesen bin, ist es nöthig, daß ich einen Theil ihres früheren Lebens erzähle, ohne dem das Folgende nicht verständlich wäre" (445).

We might want to note, first, that the entire section is a bit strange. Its very title, "Steppenvergangenheit," is a misnomer, or at least misleading. As we learn during the course of our reading, Brigitta's past is not the same as the past of the steppe region in which she now lives; in fact, she grew up in the "Hauptstadt," which is far away from the desolate *puszta* region in Hungary where she settled and raised her son.[11] Indeed, what is important about the steppe region, about this Eastern area in Europe, is that it has no proper past before the arrival of Brigitta and the Major. Even after they have introduced their beneficent civilizing effects, it is repeatedly described as desolate, as "Oede," or "öde Heide" (461). Yet, at other times it is referred to as untamed and opulent. There is no contradiction here, since the steppe region is, above all characterized throughout by its lack of civilization, its lack of cultivation. The descriptions from the very beginning testify to this quality. The narrator contrasts the civilization of Italy and the Western environment in which he had met the Major with the vast and opulent surroundings of the East:

> Dort war er im Aeußern der glatte feine Mann gewesen — hier aber war alles anders, und oft, wenn ich ganze Tage nichts sah, als das ferne röthlich blaue Dämmern der Steppe und die tausend kleinen weißen Punkte darinnen, die Rinder des Landes, wenn zu meinen Füßen die tiefschwarze Erde war, und so viel Wildheit, so viel Ueppigkeit, trotz der uralten Geschichte so viel Anfang und Ursprünglichkeit, dachte ich, wie wird er sich denn hier benehmen. (417)

And a bit further on the desolation of the region is emphasized in contrast to the cultivated vineyards of civilization: "In der That war es eine Wüste, in der wir jenseits der Weinberge geriethen, und die Ansiedelung war wie eine Fabel darinnen" (420). What characterizes Hungary in the mind of the narrator is that it is the antithesis of all those qualities we associate with civilization: it is the opposite of history and narrative, the opposite of the narrator's own activities as pupil and teacher, and opposed, as we come to see, to the activities of the Major and Brigitta. Despite the bow toward its primeval history ["uralte Geschichte"], it is the seemingly infinite absence of form and order that prevails in the narrator's description. For the narrator continues: "Eigentlich war die Wüste wieder mein altes Steinfeld, und zwar sich selber so gleich geblieben, daß ich wähnte, wir reiten denselben Weg zurück, den ich gekommen bin, wenn nicht das schmutzige Rot, das noch hinter meinem Rükken am Himmel glühte, belehrt hätte, daß wir wirklich gegen Morgen reiten" (420). Everything is the same here, and that sameness or monotony is called desert ["Wüste"], desolation, wilderness, and fields of stone. The narrator rides here away from the sun and the light into the darkness that is, perhaps, alluded to in the opening paragraph by the image of the abyss. Like the philosophical lesson, he himself is plucked out of history, paradoxically by entering into a story, a private history, the history that has been carved into this natural and ahistorical landscape by the invaders from the West.[12]

Let me return to the sentence at the beginning of the third section and point out that it, like the title of the section it starts, is strange, as well. We have already observed that story and moral have been reversed for our convenience. Here we are told that information has to be inserted for our understanding. But this notion, too, is an odd one. The narrator, after all, has also reached an accurate and pedagogically correct understanding of the state of affairs without having the information presented in the order he now deems necessary for the reader's understanding. His claim in the third section is that the rest of the narrative line would be incomprehensible without the insertion of this section; but if we reflect for even a moment, we should be able to see through such a fabulous assertion. We should also recognize by this point in his story that, prior to this passage, he has hardly done everything possible to be totally comprehensible, anyway. All along he has withheld from the reader quite a bit of potentially enlightening information. For one thing, although the observant reader may suspect that the woman the narrator met in the fields on his way to see the Major was actually Brigitta, he only informs the reader about it at the start of the fourth section: "Brigitta ist wirklich jenes reitende Weib gewesen, das mir die Pferde mitgegeben hatte" (462). If the narrator had really been so intent on giving us information that would make the narrative more comprehensible, then he should have mentioned this fact at an earlier point. What is important, of course, is not that we really ["wirklich"] know who Brigitta is but that we know who she is when the narrator wants to tell us who she is. Similarly, many readers easily guess that the Major is in reality — or at least in the reality created by the text — Stephan Murai.[13] Few will have to wait until Brigitta sighs "Stephan" toward the end of the novella (472) to know his true identity. But this information was also withheld from us — again, not in the interest of clarity, which is the narrator's feigned purpose as he begins "Steppenvergangenheit," but in the interest of storytelling. The narrative reflection at the beginning of the third section is, therefore, false, a narrative lie or a lie about narrative. The story must be understandable without it, since the narrator understood it himself at one point, and thus the inclusion or exclusion of information at any point is disclosed as an ordering, a construction, an artificial structuring, a fiction necessary to produce a particular effect, to bring home with more force a lesson for the reader.

Although the narrator of this tale does not state it directly, his implicit reflection on writing does not differ significantly from that of the narrator of Romantic texts, such as Bonaventura in *Nachtwachen* (Night Watches, 1804) or Heine in *Ideen: Das Buch Le Grand* (Ideas: The Book Le Grand, 1827), those playful and self-reflective narrators who foreground the textuality and fictionality of their narration. We will recall that in those texts the narrators foreground their attempts to cope with traditional narrative. Kreuzgang states at one point: "Was gäbe ich doch darum, so recht zusammenhängend und schlechtweg erzählen zu können, wie andre ehrliche protestantische Dichter und Zeitschriftsteller die groß und herrlich dabei werden, und für ihre goldenen Ideen goldene Realitäten eintauschen."[14] In Heine this is expressed in a slightly more humorous fashion: "In allen vorhergehenden Kapiteln," Heine tells us late in the text after serving up one digression after another, "ist keine Zeile, die nicht zur Sache gehörte, ich schreibe gedrängt, ich vermeide alles Überflüßige, ich übergehe sogar oft das Notwendige."[15] The thought is the same in both. In each case the narrator comments on his own narrative techniques, on the strategies he has not employed, although these strategies may have been preferred by the sober realist tradition. Stifter's narrator also comments on the construction of his narrative, and the difference is not only that he is neither humorous nor self-reflective but also that he is thoroughly dishonest about the matter. He plays the role of forthright, reliable narrator, but, as we have witnessed, a moment's pause on the part of his reader reveals that the underlying message is really one about the constructed nature of his text. What separates him from Kreuzgang and Heine, therefore, besides honesty, is the amount of foregrounding. Ironically, the irony in the statements of both Kreuzgang and Heine makes them honest and open, while the apparent honesty of Stifter's narrator discloses him as deceptive and disingenuous.

We learn from the analysis of this passage that realism goes about its business by placing an order on its plots, but, at the same time, that the realist text makes an endeavor to cover this very ordering. The irony and concomitant playfulness associated with the Romantic tradition are excluded, only to return at the center of the realist enterprise. Thus, realism in this text works via an exclusion of whatever threatens its reflective nature — that is, it discards irony, textual ambiguity, play, intertextuality, contradiction, and self-reflection for the true mirror, the real image, accurate portrayal, authenticity, and fidelity to nature. But ultimately and inevitably this threat erupts and reappears in the text as the enabling moment for the very realism that seeks to banish it. Realism reveals itself as false necessity, as artifice. Its constant reassurances are corrupted from within, destroyed by just the forces that it pretends to overcome.

But one can say more than this. At the very point that realism covers its textual tracks, denying its own status as fiction, it also covers other, ideological traces that it conveys without foregrounding and that are central to the realist ideological enterprise. In the case of *Brigitta* the ordering we have found to be constitutive for realism is reflected in perhaps the central dichotomy in the text, one that we have already touched on. We have seen that the steppe region is characterized by desolation and disorder. Just as the narrator supplies an ordering for the story, making it palatable for the reader, so, too, Brigitta and the Major, the Germans who have come into the Eastern territories, bring with them an ordering and, hence, a civilizing influence. The opposition between civilization and raw nature in the steppe region is repeated on the level of the text by the opposition of the formal features characteristic of realist narration and the chaos of discourse. Both are accomplished by human agency constructing something that excludes a threat to civilization and civility. It is revealing to read the narrator's account of Brigitta's intervention into the natural landscape she has encountered:

> Sie führte uns in den Park, der vor zehn Jahren ein wüster Eichenwald gewesen war; jetzt gingen Wege durch, flossen eingehegte Quellen, und wandelten Rehe. Sie hatte durch unsägliche Ausdauer um den ungeheuren Umfang desselben eine hohe Mauer gegen die Wölfe aufführen lassen. (463)

Important in this depiction are the winning back of nature from its wild state, the Faustian effort that must go into this intervention against natural forces, and the exclusion of the natural elements that would threaten the enterprise — in this case, the wolves. Special care was taken to make certain that all the wolves had been excluded, we are told; only after the threat to civilization had been eliminated were the deer introduced.

But it is, of course, this very exclusion that then threatens the entire stability of the civilizing forces. Later in the novella the wolves, excluded from their natural habitat, attack Gustav, the son of Brigitta and Stephan. But it is not only this attack that indicates that the excluded threat is still present, for the threat appears in other, perhaps more important guises inside the civilized enclave. The Major himself is likened to these animals even as they are attacking his son. We read about his actions in defense of Gustav: "der Mann war fast entsetzlich anzuschauen, ohne Rücksicht auf sich, fast selber wie ein Raubthier warf er sich ihnen entgegen" (468). Later he again shows his killer instincts when he offers a reward for every dead wolf. Indeed, even in the flashback in the third section of the novella the Major, prior to his acquaintance with Brigitta, is likened to a wolf preying on innocent women: "Mehrere behaupteten, er sei ein Genie, und wie es an Verläumdungen und Nachreden auch nicht fehlte, sagen manche, daß er etwas Wildes und Scheues an sich habe, und daß man es ihm ansehe, daß er in dem Walde auferzogen worden sei" (449–50). His origins are the woods, untamed nature, not civilization. And the combination of the wild and the shy ["Wildes und Scheues"] will be repeated by the narrator in describing the wolves against whom Stephan fights.

When the wolves are not driven by hunger, Stephan tells us, they are cowardly. Thus, they, too, are a combination of aggression and its antithesis. And this odd mixture manifests itself most strikingly in Stephan when, in his fateful meeting with Gabriele, he embraces her suddenly, presses her on his heart, and then suddenly springs onto his horse and rides off. Murai is thus the epitome of the civilized man, but he is also a wolf inside the civilized world, both civilizer and destroyer of civilization, orderer and ultimate peril to that order. His wolflike nature, like the wolves themselves, is subjected to the severe civilizing procedures practiced by Brigitta.

And Murai is not the only insider who mimics the excluded others. The wolves are likewise mirrored in the civilized world by their civilized counterparts, the dogs. After the Major and the narrator have visited a portion of the estate, the Major cautions him about the dogs he has seen: "Wenn es Euch ergötzt, diese Haidewirthschaft einmal im einzelnen genau anzuschauen, und Ihr etwa einmal allein heraus kommen wolltet, um mit diesen Leuten gleichsam zu leben, müßt Ihr auf die Hunde achten, die sie haben. Sie sind nicht immer so zahm und geduldig, wie ihr sie heute gesehen habt, sondern sie würden Euch strenge mit fahren" (434). The Major warns the narrator about precisely the situation that occurs later with Gustav, except that in the latter case the dogs are cast in the role of their canine cousins. It is not just that there is a thin line separating civilization and the wilderness; rather, the wilderness continues to exist inside civilization and is even its prerequisite for existence, as we see when the wolves are set upon by the "beast of prey" called Stephan Murai and then by the "Wolfshunde" [wolfhounds] (469), a word that combines and makes undecidable what belongs to the inside and what belongs to the outside. And it is not just the animals that partake of this dual nature, at once part of civilization but also part of the wild. Murai is himself duplicated by the faithful followers he has accrued over the years. He tells his friend the narrator: "Diese würde ich sogar zum Blutvergießen führen können, sobald ich mich nur an ihre Spitze stellte" (438). The head predator needs only to place himself, wolflike, at the head of the pack to elicit violence from the natives he has hitherto taken so much time to domesticate.

This undecidable duality of civilization and wilderness underlying both the ideological and the literary structure of the text has at least one further manifestation. As the narrator is first led through the countryside, Milosch informs him about their destination, the gallows: "Hier ist der Galgen," sagte Milosch, "dort unten, wo es glänzt, rinnt ein Bach, daneben ist ein schwarzer Haufen, auf den geht zu, es ist eine Eiche, auf der sonst die Uebeltäter aufgehängt worden sind. Jetzt darf das nicht mehr sein, weil ein Galgen ist" (421). Here again we find the ambivalence caused by the introduction of civilization/realism into the wilderness. Formerly, at a time presumably predating the advent of Brigitta and the Major, the oak tree served as the instrument of punishment for the society. After the introduction of civilized juridical and punitive practices, this function has been assumed by a human construction. Punishment, of course, is an interesting phenomenon; for, like the park created by Brigitta, its purpose is to banish those who threaten society by breaking its laws, by disobeying its strictures. In the case of the ultimate punishment, death by hanging, the threat is permanently removed. Thus, the new gallows is part of an ordering that, like realism, banishes to its outside those elements that threaten its existence. But, again, the doubling effect Wolf/*Wolfshund*, civilized humans/predators, Stephan Murai/beast of prey is evident. The "Galgeneiche" (469), a word that, like *Wolfshund*, combines the civilized with its uncivilized counterpart, is the site of the attack on Gustav; without this violation of civilization the narrative could not progress. The gallows thus replaces the natural instrument for punishment by a human, ordered construction that accomplishes precisely the same purpose, but the natural site becomes, in its name and its function in the narrative, part of the civilized realm to which it purportedly no longer belongs.[16] Inherent in nature is civilization; but inherent in civilization is the wild naturalness, the outlawed criminality and violence that are never successfully banned, because they always appear as the very prerequisite, indeed, the enabling moment, for their replacement.

There is another force, of course, related to violence — at least in Stifter's texts — that is a potential threat to the serene surface of both the order of civilization and its reflection in realism. This force goes by the name of passion. Indeed, the necessity for an absence of passion in both the civilized world and the ordered text of realism is emphasized in the fourth section of the novella. Here the

Major contrasts the passionate experiences of his life as a Don Juan with his pure and ordered relationship with Brigitta:

> Freund! ich bin oft in meinem Leben heiß begehrt worden, ob auch so geliebt, weiß ich nicht; aber die Gesellschaft und die Achtung dieser Frau ist mir ein größeres Glück auf dieser Welt geworden, als jedes andere in meinem Leben, das ich für eines gehalten habe. (465)

This implicit separation between passion in sexual interaction and the ideal quality that characterizes Stephan's relationship to Brigitta merely repeats the structure that the narrator describes in the third section. We recall that Brigitta demands from Stephan "eine höhe Liebe" (454), and although she describes it as a love "ohne Maß und Ende" (454), it obviously does not entail the usual type of passion a man feels for a woman in an intimate union; that is, it does not necessarily include the intimacy associated with sexual desire. At the time of the narrator's visit the nature of the relationship between Stephan and Brigitta is aptly judged to be a type of "highest friendship" (444); once again, passion as a human emotion is called into question as a part of a relationship between a man and a woman. The words "great" or "greater," "high" or "higher" that modify "love" and "friendship" contrast in both instances with the base or low passions and desires aroused by Gabriele, "ein wildes Geschöpf" (458), associated, like Stephan himself, with the woods and unbridled nature rather than domesticated civilization.[17] In contrast to the heights, not of passion but of pure ideal love that characterize Murai's relationship to Brigitta, we find Gabriele described by the lowest of depths: "gleichsam ein Abgrund von Unbefangenheit" (458). Gabriele, defeated by Murai in a race, becomes an object of sexual passion: "verglühend" [glowing] (459) is the way she is described leaning on the tree trunk, and Murai, who has obviously been tempted by her before on his rides through the woods, can no longer resist. Of course, there is no fulfillment either for Gabriele or for Murai in their brief encounter; he steals a short embrace and races off on his horse. He has already become a dual nature, partly civilized by his marriage to Brigitta, but still partly the beast of prey. Brigitta does not recognize the act of infidelity but, rather, the existence of illicit passion when she observes the deep reddening of their faces when Stephan and Gabriele meet, and this betrayal of the heights of love for the depths of passion is enough to destroy the absoluteness that is for her, for Stifter, and for the text of the novella, a sine qua non of relations between the sexes.

This contrast between love and passion is the point of Stephan's comparison of his relationship with other women to his relationship to Brigitta, which I have already cited. But the way in which he conveys his thoughts to the narrator is also significant and is recorded dutifully for us to consider: "Er hatte diese Worte ohne alle Leidenschaft gesagt, aber mit einer solchen Ruhe der Gewißheit, daß ich in meinem Herzen von der Wahrheit derselben vollständig überzeugt war" (466). Here the narrator associates the very qualities that bring into proximity civilization and realism. For the absence of *Leidenschaft,* of passion, subjectivity, and emotion, and the concomitant valorization of serenity, reason, and objectivity are associated with the truth and with the telling of the truth. Realism involves the maintenance of an order without passion, without desire, and the relationship between Brigitta and Stephan mimics that order. It is significant, therefore, that in our most complete and informed description of their relationship passion is eliminated. Indeed, the depiction the narrator had heard earlier from Gömör turns out to be false. We recall that Gömör thought that passion was definitely involved: "und Leidenschaft sei es ganz gewiß, das erkenne ein jeder, der hinüber komme" (444). But the narrator, who has the inside information, counters later with a more accurate assessment: "Von einer unheimlichen Leidenschaft, von einem fieberhaften Begehren, oder gar von Magnetismus, wie ich gehört hatte, war keine Spur" (467). What does the relationship between the two entail, then? The narrator confirms that it was what one would call love between the sexes, but that it did not appear this way. What characterizes this love, and what the narrator does not explicitly state but everywhere suggests, is that it is love without passion, love without sexual desire. The Major hints at this when he tells the narrator that his relationship with Brigitta is a friendship of the most beautiful kind, but nothing else. It is a morally firm altar at which they stand ["diesem sittlich festen Altare"] (467). But like all altars, it is one that demands a sacrifice, a purification, or, in more psychological terms, a repression.[18]

This theme of excluded and repressed passion, of course, returns even more forcefully in Stifter's later novel *Der Nachsommer*.

As I have noted previously, the plot line is quite similar to that of *Brigitta*. Two young people deeply in love, the Freiherr von Risach and Mathilde, break off their relationship, later live on neighboring estates, and experience thus a "Nachsommer" type of relationship — a late-blooming flower, as it is called in *Brigitta*. But the polemic is even more direct and uncompromising in the later work. Here there is not even the passionate embrace we find in the earlier novella. And in *Der Nachsommer* the Freiherr von Risach takes pains to inculcate his message into his young visitor, Heinrich Drendorf, who, like the narrator of *Brigitta*, is supposed to be educated through patience and through the elder couple's example to a higher type of love. Heinrich comes to Risach well prepared for this school of renunciation, of course. We learn that in his youth Heinrich already shunned the "mere enjoyment" that most of his schoolmates pursued (6: 18).[19] The pleasures he experienced in his home, he informs the reader, were always "of a serious kind" (6: 18). The elder Drendorf, who is a carbon copy of Risach, would undoubtedly be judged today as unnecessarily harsh and repressive. He did not allow his children to go to the theater, even to see plays of a more ennobling variety, because he feared the arousal of their emotions: "Er sagte, es würde dadurch die Einbildungskraft der Kinder überreizt und überstürzt. Sie behingen sich mit allerlei willkürlichen Gefühlen und gerieten dann in Begierden oder gar Leidenschaften" (6:206). This polemic against passion is continued and augmented by the owner of the Asperhof. An "excess of wishes and desires," Risach tells Heinrich, prevents us from perceiving the "innocence of things" (6: 235).[20] Passions should not be used as a criterion for evaluating the importance of an object. Here Risach is evidently adopting a principle from Kant's *Critique of Judgment* and extending it to apply to all of our interactions. Natural science can only be pursued without interest, that is, aesthetically. Later in the novel, in what must be read as a justification for his behavior toward Mathilde years before, he expounds on this antipassionate position. Following Socrates in the *Phaidon* — and scores of philosophers in the intervening centuries — Risach separates body and spirit; the former is the realm of the passions and contains nothing noble; the latter, if properly nurtured and trained, can be employed to attain the highest goal: passionless love.

> Wenn wir hier alle die Dinge ausschließen, die nur den Körper oder das Tierische des Menschen betreffen und befriedigen, und deren andauerndes Begehren mit Hinwegsetzung alles andern wir mit dem Namen Leidenschaft bezeichnen, weshalb es denn nichts Falscheres geben kann, als wenn man von edlen Leidenschaften spricht, und wenn wir als Gegenstände höchsten Strebens nur das Edelste des Menschen nennen: so dürfte alles Drängen nach solchen Gegenständen vielleicht nicht mit Unrecht nur mit einem Namen zu benennen sein, mit Liebe. (7: 356)

Love and passion are thus placed at opposite poles, as far from one another as possible. Like scientific observation, love is brought into the proximity of the object of art, which is also to be grasped without interest or desire. That Natalie, the woman Heinrich will marry once his realist education is completed, is compared to a marble statue and a fictional princess, namely, the renunciatory Nausikaa of the *Odyssey*, is totally appropriate, since she is to be appreciated and "possessed" like a work of art.[20] Indeed, the lifelessness and coldness of the marble, often used by previous writers (for example, Eichendorff in *Das Marmorbild* and Heine in various descriptions throughout his work) to signal a lack of passion, suggests, apparently against Stifter's intention, the sterility and frigidity of the love she and Heinrich share. Risach's aesthetic and realist education therefore conveys a twofold renunciatory message. Having been taught that love is a function of a Kantian aesthetic attitude, Heinrich must accordingly deny his nature, his body, his desires. And in emulating Risach, who has been at pains to defend his own passionless actions of an earlier vintage, he partakes in a structure of renunciation identical to that of his mentor.

It is precisely in this point that *Der Nachsommer*, despite its classicist pretensions, departs from the pedagogical thought of its predecessors during the Age of Goethe. To demonstrate this difference a brief comparison with one of the chief documents of this earlier period, Schiller's *Aesthetic Education*, is instructive. Both Schiller's essay and Stifter's novel are obviously responding to recent historical events: the former to the French Revolution, the latter to the revolutions of 1848, especially to the events in and around Vienna. Both authors were basically freedom-loving democrats who had themselves suffered under the old order but who were first disappointed and then shocked by what they perceived as excesses of the revolutionary masses. In a sense, both works are, thus, responses to these excesses, attempts to come to terms with political problems within a larger, more philosophical framework. Each arrives at an apparently similar conclusion: an aesthetic education can serve to correct revolutionary abuses, to eliminate the abhorrent outbursts of base emotions and deeds. Risach's homily against passion has its origin — in part, at least — in the reaction against revolutionary violence; on the political level it implies a program of moderation. But Schiller and Stifter part company on two essential issues. For Schiller there is no question that the principles he is espousing are universal. Like Kant, he believes that aesthetic judgment involves at least a potential *sensus communis;* an "aesthetic education" is something everyone in the human species could and should enjoy. Even his frequently quoted remark about the existence of the "state of beautiful appearance" in small, exclusive circles is prefaced by a more general claim: "Dem Bedürfniß nach existiert er [der Staat des schönen Scheins] in jeder feingestimmten Seele."[21] For Stifter the exclusivity of Risach's pedagogy is never in doubt. From various comments he makes concerning his servants (6: 143–44) and the decline of appreciation for art (6: 311–12), and from Heinrich's observations on Viennese society, it is obvious that only a select few are candidates for the enlightened path. Accordingly, the Rose House is an isolated estate that Risach buys after retiring from public service; that is, the aesthetic education is a retreat from politics rather than a preparation for political activity. And Heinrich is one of only a handful of visitors who has extended contact with Risach. He and Gustav are really the only ones who will ever be educated in the Rose House. More important for the theme of renunciation, however, is the authors' disparate treatment of the pedagogical impact of art. Schiller conceives of aesthetics as a realm of harmony or compromises between opposing forces or instincts. Although he, too, would repress "raw, lawless drives," his theory endeavors to reconcile natural, sensual inclinations with reason and understanding. Aesthetics, the play-drive [*Spieltrieb*], the beautiful appearance — these terms are mediators in Schiller's essay, not (or, perhaps, as well as) absolutes. In contrast, Stifter's aesthetic program, as we have seen, is based on a nondialectical, repressive scheme. The body, passion, and desires are evils; beauty, love, and pure science must remain uncontaminated and are thus severed from contact with this world. Indeed, although Stifter evidently felt himself to be a continuator of the educational spirit of Weimar Classicism, the Manichaean framework he employs and his implicit praise of passionless old age bring him closer to Cato in Cicero's *De senectute* than to Schiller in the *Aesthetic Education*. The instruction Heinrich receives from Risach does not prepare him for a summer of fulfilled life but for a winter of renunciation.

Although *Brigitta* stems from a slightly earlier period and should perhaps be understood as a reaction against Young German sensuality rather than revolutionary fervor, the pedagogical lesson is much the same. Indeed, as most commentators have noted, the constellation of events and characters is quite similar — in fact, almost identical. The Major and Brigitta remain apart for fifteen years, the prime years of their lives, sacrificing the passion of their adulthood for a higher type of love in old age. This love must remain perfect and innocent; it must not admit of the wolflike violence that passion stirs. Thus, the narrator describes the two mature individuals as children: "in dem Augenblicke waren sie auch unschuldig, wie die Kinder; denn die reinigendste, die allerschönste Blume der Liebe, aber nur der höchsten Liebe, ist das Verzeihen, darum wird es auch immer an Gott gefunden und an Müttern" (473). Here their love has been stripped of the passion that had formerly ruined it. It is either childlike, and thus prior to sexual passion — or at least phallic passion — or likened to the relationship between God and man or between mother and child. The narrator learns his lesson well from this pair, and we as readers, pulled into an identity with him from the start, may now also recognize the moral we should have gleaned from this tale of passionless love. Throughout the story we gain only slight glimpses of who the narrator is. We learn that at the time of his visit to the Major's estate he was a bachelor, that he, like the Major before the latter settled down, had traveled to various places in the world. But we are also informed that he has since changed his ways, that he has now emulated Stephan Murai, that he has taken Murai as a model or *Vorbild*, and that he, therefore, applies a major principle of realism — the imitation of a perceived reality — to his own life. The imitation or mimetic moment in his life consists primarily in the voiding and avoidance of passion. Reflecting on the relationship between Stephan and Brigitta, he thinks: "O wie heilig, o wie heilig, muß die Gattenliebe sein, und wie arm bist du, der du von ihr bisher nichts erkanntest, und das Herz nur höchstens von der trüben Lohe der Leidenschaft ergreifen ließest" (474). It is precisely the "dim flame of passion" that must be eliminated if imitation, the realist project, is to be completed.

We as readers accompany the narrator, dressed again in his German clothing, headed for his German Fatherland, with his German walking stick, as he leaves the now civilized and passionless idyll of the Hungarian steppes. And to make certain that we do not stray from the true path, to be sure that we are not waylaid by desire as Stephan Murai once was, we pass with him a significant reminder of where passion leads: we walk by Gabriele's grave. "Ich sah auf dem Rückwege Gabrielens Grabmal, die schon vor zwölf Jahren im Gipfel ihrer jugendlichen Schönheit gestorben war" (475). The passion and sensuality affirmed by the Young Germans in their writings are here once again negated with the mention of Gabriele's early demise. The lesson we have learned, in contrast to what we may have first thought after reading the introduction, is not how to clear up a mystery of the human soul, and not the secrets of one Stephan Murai, but, rather, how to avoid being drawn into Gabriele's abyss, into the darkness of chaos and passion, that mark the ominous boundaries of both the ideological and the literary order of German realism.

Notes

[1] René Wellek, "The Concept of Realism in Literary Scholarship," *Neophilologus* 45 (1961): 1–20; here 10.

[2] Erich Auerbach, *Mimesis: Dargestellte Wirklichkeit in der abendländischen Literatur* (Bern: Francke, 1946); trans. Willard R. Trask as *Mimesis: The Representation of Reality in Western Literature* (Princeton: Princeton UP, 1953).

[3] Richard Brinkmann, *Wirklichkeit und Illusion: Studien über Gehalt und Grenzen des Begriffs Realismus für die erzählende Dichtung des neunzehnten Jahrhunderts* (Tübingen: Niemeyer, 1966).

[4] Robert C. Holub, *Reflections of Realism: Paradox, Norm, and Ideology in Nineteenth-Century German Prose* (Detroit: Wayne State UP, 1991).

[5] See Christiane Baumann, "Angstbewältigung und 'sanftes Gesetz': Adalbert Stifter: *Brigitta* (1843)," in Winfried Freund, ed., *Deutsche Novellen: Von der*

Klassik biz zur Gegenwart (Munich: Fink, 1993), 121–29. Although there are several important differences between the original version and the revised book version, I focus my analysis on the latter, which has become the standard form of the novella. For a side-by-side comparison of the two versions, see Adalbert Stifter, *Brigitta: Urfassung/Studienfassung,* ed. Max Stefl (Augsburg: Adam Kraft Verlag, 1957).

[6] Psychology (*Seelenkunde*) for Stifter is not yet a "*Wissenschaft*" or natural science; indeed, for most of the nineteenth century it was a branch of moral philosophy and would not really become a science in the modern sense of the word until the work of Wilhelm Wundt in the last few decades of the century.

[7] With regard to this introduction, Albert Meier mentions Stifter's debt to the Wolff school in philosophy, according to which there are different means of acquiring knowledge. In this case Stifter would be making the case for "aesthetic knowledge" as opposed to scientific knowledge. See Albert Meier, "Diskretes Erzählen: Über den Zusammenhang von Dichtung, Wissenschaft und Didaktik in Adalbert Stifters Erzählung 'Brigitta,'" *Aurora* 44 (1984): 213–23.

[8] Parenthetical citations are from Stifter, *Werke und Briefe: Historisch-Kritische Ausgabe,* ed. Alfred Doppler and Wolfgang Frühwald, vol. 1, part 5 (Stuttgart: Kohlhammer, 1982), 411–75.

[9] Johann Wolfgang Goethe, *Sämtliche Werke,* Münchner Ausgabe, ed. Karl Richter, vol. 19, *Johann Peter Eckermann Gespräche mit Goethe,* ed. Heinz Schlaffer (Munich: Hanser, 1986), 203 (29 January 1827).

[10] In "'Brigitta' — seelenkundlich gelesen: Zur Vewendung 'kalobiotischer' Lebensmaximen Feuchterslebens in Stifters Erzählung," in Harmut Laufhütte and Karl Möseneder, eds., *Adalbert Stifter: Dichter und Maler, Denkmalpfleger und Schulmann: Neue Zugänge zu seinem Werk* (Tübingen: Niemeyer, 1996), 410–34, Christina von Zimmermann notices the didactic structure of repetition but fails to note the differences between narrator and reader in terms of their experiences.

[11] Rosemarie Hunter-Lougheed also notes that the chapter title has no relationship to its contents but reasons that it refers to the internal desolation of the main character: "Adalbert Stifter: Brigitta (1844/47)," in Paul Michael Lützeler, ed., *Romane und Erzählungen zwischen Romantik und Realismus: Neue Interpretationen* (Stuttgart: Reclam, 1983), 354–85; here 374.

[12] On the relationship of *Brigitta* to Stifter's views of Hungary, see Moriz Enzinger, "Stifters Erzählung 'Brigitta' und Ungarn," in his *Gesammelte Ausfsätze zu Adalbert Stifter* (Vienna: Österreichische Verlagsanstalt, 1967), 134–53.

[13] There is another level to this reality if we consider that Murai was modeled after Graf Isvan (Stefan) Szechenyi, whose biography is similar to Murai's. Brigitta's historical model is Helene Charlotte von Lestwitz, Frau von Fried-

land. Enzinger mentions historical sources for various place names and persons in his essay.

[14] Bonaventura, *Nachtwachen,* ed. Wolfgang Paulsen (Stuttgart: Reclam, 1964), 48.

[15] Heinrich Heine, *Sämtliche Schriften,* ed. Klaus Briegleb, vol. 2 (Munich: Hanser, 1976), 284.

[16] Barbara Osterkamp places a slightly different emphasis on the gallows in her *Arbeit und Identität: Studien zur Erzählkunst des bürgerlichen Realismus* (Würzburg: Königshausen & Neumann, 1983). She points out that the gallows, placed in the middle of unbridled nature, is a protection against the uncivilized and also a guarantee of Stephan's and Brigitta's hegemony among the Hungarians (141–42).

[17] Ulrich Dittmann, however, in *"Brigitta* und kein Ende: Kommentierte Randbermerkungen," *Jahrbuch des Adalbert Stifter Institutes* 3 (1996): 24–28, points out that Gabriele is not simply the temptress. He argues that there is a symbolic connection between Gabriele and her biblical namesake, the archangel Gabriel, who is charged with delivering and interpreting the word of God (24).

[18] Murai's beauty and Brigitta's masculine qualities are devices that Stifter uses to shift the emphasis from traditional sexual roles. His model in this novella appears to be an androgynous society, which combines in an odd fashion traditional values with a notion of the absolute equality of the sexes. See Jochim W. Storck, "Eros bei Stifter," in *Adalbert Stifter: Dichter und Maler, Denkmalpfleger und Schulmann: Neue Zugänge zu seinem Werk,* ed. Hartmut Laufhütte and Karl Möseneder (Tübingen: Niemeyer, 1996), 135–56; esp. 145–46.

[19] Parenthetical citations are to Stifter, *Werke,* eds. Kamill Eben and Franz Hüller, vols. 6–8 (Prague: Verlag der Gesellschaft zur Föderung deutscher Wissenschaft, Kunst und Literatur in Böhmen, 1916–21).

[21] See chapter 3 in my *Reflections of Realism.*

[22] Friedrich Schiller, *Werke: Nationalausgabe,* eds. Lieselotte Blumenthal and Benno von Wiese, vol. 20 (Weimar: Hermann Böhlaus Nachfolger, 1962), 412.

Mühlbach, Ranke, and the Truth of Historical Fiction

Brent O. Peterson

THE LINE BETWEEN fact and fancy runs straight and uninterrupted until it hits historical fiction; at least, the boundary seems clear before it bumps into this curious mixture of history and fiction that seems simultaneously true and false. Historians find their truth in archives. They ransack bits of parchment, paper, and film; assess discarded objects; and analyze the traces our ancestors left on the landscape. Then they stitch the results together in a story or an interpretation of people's actions in the past. Except for those rare instances when historians wonder about how to put their truth on the page, the reading, viewing, and listening public accepts history as a true representation of the past. Novelists, on the other hand, invent. They search for poetic truth, often in the form of generalizations about human nature, but they make no claim on the facts. While authors may research locations, crib material from their friends, family, and, most important, their own experiences, their ultimate arbiter lies elsewhere, beyond fact-checkers and footnote sleuths. Novelists' truths take shape in their heads. "Fictional truth," to use Michael Riffaterre's term, functions at the level of coherence and plausibility; it resists both verification and falsification.[1] Again, the border seems clearly demarcated until it reaches historical fiction, and it was during the nineteenth century in Germany, when and where history arose as an academic discipline and historical fiction became the most widely read genre of literature, that historians and historical novelists attempted to divide the past, that is, to draw the line between history and fiction. This essay chronicles that division of labor and territory in paradigmatic fashion by examining works by two of the most prominent participants: the historian Leopold von Ranke (1795–1886) and Luise Mühlbach (1814–73), a prolific author of historical fiction.

Treating the past as fact or fancy acquired a particular relevance in nineteenth-century Germany, because the rise of these two modes of dealing with history coincided with the arrival of nationalism as a political and cultural force throughout Europe, and national identities presumed a shared past. At least, they rested as much on the assumption of a common history as on commonalties of religion, race, language, or culture. Thus, the disparate inhabitants of Prussia, Saxony, Bavaria, and Lippe-Detmold all had to learn about the exploits of ancestors they supposedly shared; and what better means of imparting that historically grounded identity to the men and women learning what it meant to be German than to offer them historical novels, popular history, and, for the educated few, academic treatises on the past? The nation functioned as the most important subject for those who wrote about the past, while the knowledge that authors imparted in works of history, both fictional and nonfictional, served as an enabling condition for national consciousness. In political terms, it mattered little whether German identity was based on truth or falsehood; but in the rhetorical battle for primacy in the discourse of history — that is, in the struggle to decide who would impart historical knowledge to the nation's readers — truth was a weapon brandished by both sides. Deciding what was true about the past also entailed choices regarding the object of inquiry, and historians differed from novelists in their view of what could and should be represented. The two genres thereby diverged not just in the question of what could be known but also over the twin issues of what was worth knowing and what was worth transmitting to a wider audience — namely, to a public of prospective Germans. Adding nationalism to the mix raised the stakes in what might have remained a confrontation between entertainment and enlightenment; but, with the two sides jockeying, at least implicitly, for primacy as the purveyors of Germany's national narrative, who wrote what, how, and for whom came to matter immensely.

When Ranke and the corps of historians he trained founded the modern discipline of history, they deemed most people's lives uninteresting. Nineteenth-century historians constructed the field of scientific or, more properly translated, academic history [*Geschichtswissenschaft*] as the record of past politics; their focus meant that the entire existence of ordinary mortals, as well as the private lives of public figures, were not history. In fact, since scholars searched the archives only for traces of men's public lives — primarily official government documents such as laws, treaties, memoranda, and speeches — what they found provided no basis for women's or social histories, even if someone had entertained the notion of writing them. There were no sources, so there could be no footnotes, no documentable truth. Just as academic libraries collaborated in collecting and establishing the literary canon, so, too, did the archives that interested nineteenth-century historians specialize in the written remains of decision-makers; archivists appear to have overlooked documents pertaining to women, the working class, and even men below the social and intellectual level of professional historians. Recent accounts of individual men and women of the lower class by Carlo Ginzburg, Steven Ozment, and others would not have interested most nineteenth-century historians. Published documents — for example, the *Monumenta Germaniae Historica,* begun in 1819 under the aegis of Freiherr vom Stein — were mainly limited to classical authors, laws, and imperial acts.[2] Of course, the letters, wills, and tax returns now mined by social and feminist scholars were always there — in fact, in much greater quantity than they are today — but these traces of past lives were irrelevant to a history concerned almost exclusively with gaining insight into the intentions behind events.[3] The result was a doubly motivated erasure. Not only did historians show no interest in women, workers, and the poor, but, since their lives appeared to be undocumented, they were also unrepresentable in the academic discipline of history.

The absence of women, which I take to be symbolic of all other exclusions, was certainly the most egregious. Men — more specifically, "great men" — made history not only biologically but also in their discursively constructed genders and as the shapers of historical consciousness. First, men produced history physically and legally. Only males played the major roles — statesmen, generals, and kings. Salic law effectively prevented women in the German regions of Europe from occupying the male institutional space of the monarch, as Queen Victoria was able to do in England but not in Hanover. Even Maria Theresa of Austria needed a husband to become Holy Roman empress, and doubts about the legitimacy of her claim gave Frederick the Great the pretext he needed to seize

Silesia. Second, while "great men" made history culturally and metaphorically as the putative fathers of their countries, economies, institutions, and governments, at the next lower tier only men — in fact, mainly men from the upper and middle classes — gained admission to society's credentialing agencies (the academic high schools, universities, and armies) and thereafter to the exercise of power. Third, men from these classes became historians, and, despite a growing number of women authors, they also wrote most of the era's historical fiction. In short, powerful men controlled the present, and they cemented their grip on contemporary events by controlling the past.

Male hegemony resonated all the more loudly because the nineteenth century was an age of history. Educated men — and those men and women who wanted to appear cultured — had to display historical knowledge in polite company, and the culture viewed history as an important guide in the realm of public policy. Officers, bureaucrats, and members of the educated middle class [*Bildungsbürgertum*] studied, read, and talked about history. They compared themselves to Greeks, worried about repeating the mistakes of Roman generals, and searched for edifying traces of ancient civilizations at home and abroad. They also subscribed to fund-raising appeals for monuments to past glories, enriched the publishers of history and historical fiction, frequented lending libraries that brimmed with works of history, and identified with the heroes and heroines of historical novels. All this history made for conversation that sounded learned, and, given the subject matter of much of the history being written, it contributed to people's growing sense of being German. Cracks and interruptions appeared, if at all, along the seemingly solid line that divided history from historical fiction.

Unfortunately, few analysts have examined either the extra-academic discourse of history or its interplay with the profession of history. Most accounts also overlook the impact of both historical fiction and such celebrated works of popular history as Franz Kugler and Adolph Menzel's *Geschichte des Friedrichs des Grossen,* a lengthy illustrated biography that was serialized in 1840, published as a book in 1842, and reprinted throughout the nineteenth century.[4] We know, however, that more people read novels than works of academic history, and we will soon see that fiction's subject matter was considerably broader than history's. Yet, except at the level of individual consumers, who read both genres, the few history professors who wrote novels as a sideline, and such rare authors and critics as the novelist Theodor Fontane, who moved in both worlds, there seems to have been little contact between historians and the authors of historical fiction.[5] Historical novelists would often boast of the academic history they read, while historians seldom admitted to a passion for historical fiction. The division of labor between the two camps remained implicit, but it is impossible to understand academic history's orientation and impact without also looking at its usually excluded other. Neither is it possible to understand historical fiction in a vacuum. Finally, and most important, we cannot know what history meant to readers without looking at both sides of this hitherto unresolved equation. Our task here is to juxtapose these competing genres while comparing their respective claims on "truth." Nineteenth-century historical fiction is not just another object of inquiry, not just academic history's unrelated and unloved contemporary; historical fiction claimed to be an alternate mode of representation, possessed of an alternate epistemology and in touch with truths that lay beyond the narrow confines of archival scholarship. The two modes of writing about the past were locked in a kind of structural opposition, each defined by the other, each becoming what the other was not, and each making claims that still need adjudicating.

The form of historical fiction, its readability, and its focus on character rather than event paralleled developments in the rest of nineteenth-century fiction, but it also reflected a mutually rewarding bargain that the writers of imaginative history struck with academic historians. Unlike academic history, historical fiction's task was either to represent the undocumented human side of great men's lives, showing their motivations and portraying them in everyday situations, among their families and friends, or it was to integrate ordinary men and women into the larger historical picture, showing how great men and their actions affected the rest of humanity, male and female. Thus we either see Frederick the Great up close or learn what the disaster at Jena and the Wars of Liberation meant to the millions of otherwise unnamed inhabitants of the German territories. Although historical fiction left the idea of greatness unchallenged and accepted the central role of powerful males and the primacy of political events, it nevertheless constituted an enormous broadening of the field of history. Moreover, toward the end of the century novelists such as Wilhelm Raabe (1831–1910) could build on the heritage of historical fiction and begin testing the limits of representation in ways that went far beyond their predecessors and even farther beyond all but the most radical of today's historians, who are still beholden to the conventions of early realist fiction: they use omniscient narrators, regard language as transparent, and view the world as both knowable and amenable to representation on paper. Rather than learn from the novelists who stretched realism to its limits and then ventured further into literary modernism, as the cultural critic and historian Hayden White puts it, most historians still combine "*late nineteenth-century* social science and *mid-nineteenth-century* art."[6]

Realism scarcely appears in today's literary debates.[7] Although the topic has attracted the attention of such notable scholars as Martin Swales and Lillian R. Furst, works on realism remain far from the cutting edge of literary-critical practice and interest. Traditionalists still concern themselves with the high modernism of Kafka and Mann, while radicals search for liberating messages in popular literature but pay scant attention to its form. With a few notable exceptions, postmodernism remains uninterested in the past, and nowadays what passes for conventional narration owes more to the quick-cutting aesthetic of film and MTV than it does to nineteenth-century novelists. Despite their widespread, albeit secret, passion for detective fiction, most academics regard realist fiction as trivial, an outmoded form that no longer warrants serious investigation.[8] As a result, the term *realism* lacks an agreed-on definition. For some it simply refers to a period in literary history that, not coincidentally, corresponds to the rise of the nation-state in Europe. Realism was the form of literature preferred by the nineteenth century's self-conscious bourgeoisie, which is another reason for academics to scorn it. In Germany the realist era stretches from 1850, just after the unsuccessful nationalist uprising of 1848, to 1890, when Bismarck stepped down as imperial chancellor. The period has at its midpoint the founding of the Second Empire in 1871 and includes most of the high literature that bears the name *realism,* but it excludes the more popular varieties of realist writing that preceded and followed canonical realism. Using the period as a definition also fails to illuminate the congruence of historical fiction and academic history.

A second approach regards realism as belief in both the transparency of language and its ability to reflect external reality.[9] Authors shared a conviction held by the period's painters, who believed that they could capture people, places, and events on canvas without interference from the paint. Readers and viewers alike gained access to what the artist had seen; the medium did nothing to hinder representation. Accordingly, there was no need in realistic art for self-reflection. Producers and consumers shared a belief in their ability to apprehend the world and were uninterested in having the matter discussed when authors could better expend their efforts developing character and moving the plot forward.

Unfortunately, this definition works better in theory than in practice. Contrary to expectations, realistic writing is filled with discussions about the manner in which the narrator came to know something and about how difficult it is for him or her to reduce life's complexities to mere words on paper. For example, after noting that he was "a child of clear observation," Dickens's David Copperfield wonders "how much of the histories I invented . . . hangs like a mist of fancy over well-remembered fact?"[10] Similarly, the narrator of Alexis's *Ruhe ist die erste Bürgerpflicht* (1852) claims the perquisites of the poet [*Dichter*], namely, the license to invent, whenever he needs to mediate between the visible and the invisible worlds.[11] Historians usually confine such musings to the critical discussion of sources, but their struggle to understand documents and reassure readers with footnotes reflects the same concern with representation that bedeviled the authors of historical fiction.[12] As will soon become clear, the conflict between these two modes of representing the past revolved around competing ideas about what constituted realistic depiction. Realism was central to both camps' views of truth; they simply could not agree on what the term meant, either theoretically or practically. Neither side could answer Thomas Pavel's question: "In *War and Peace* is Natasha less actual than Napoleon?"[13] For Germans it was just as vexing to speculate about the reality of Frederick the Great when he appeared in history versus his similarly textual form in historical fiction.

Of course, there was more to realist literature than Frederick the Great, and Pavel elides the third definition of the genre when he compares the representation of an aristocratic woman to that of the French emperor. This final view of realism maintains that its practitioners simply chose a new subject matter. In accord with their belief in democracy as a form of government, realists in the arts decided to represent classes of people who had not seemed worthy to previous generations of artists. Lessing's advocacy of the bourgeois tragedy becomes the first step along a path that leads through realism to naturalism, and realist fiction is characterized not by formal properties but by its subject matter. As Linda Nochlin puts it with reference to painting, "ordinary situations and objects of daily life were no less worth of depiction than antique heroes and Christian saints: indeed . . . the noble and beautiful were less appropriate than the commonplace and undistinguished. The very boundary-line between the beautiful and the ugly had to be erased by the advanced artist" (33).

This definition favors historical fiction at the expense of academic history, because it is only in fiction that the middle class appears — to say nothing of women and the lower orders. Thus, no matter how well documented its representations were, to the extent that history concentrated on the lives of great men it could not offer a realistic image of society. If history did not show how men and women like its readers lived, it could not be true; whereas historical fiction could base its claims on truth in the genre's implicitly democratic focus. But novelists, too, devoted considerable attention to the lives of great men, and both sides were wont to employ definitions that undercut the other. We can only resolve the matter, or acquire a better understanding of the competing paradigms, by looking closely at what several participants in the debate said and did.

Historical fiction needs a worthy champion to do battle with someone as eminent as Ranke; that person also must represent both the genre's popularity and its high cultural aspirations. He or she needs to be theoretically sophisticated, able to write for the common reader, and concerned with German history at a time when public discourse shaped and was shaped by readers and writers of Germany's national narrative. Since no such person existed, I choose instead an obscure woman author; for although they were excluded from academic history, women were increasingly active as authors during the nineteenth century — often, like their male counterparts, as the authors of historical novels. Norbert Otto Eke credits Wilhelmine von Gersdorf with writing the first German novel to bear the title "historical"; her *Aurora Gräfin von Königsmark: Ein historischer Roman* (Aurora, Countess of Königsmark: An Historical Novel) appeared in 1817, the same year as the initial German translation of Sir Walter Scott.[14] Among other things, the coincidence means that Gersdorf and other German authors of historical fiction were not, as is often argued, simply Scott imitators. In fact, Dennis Sweet goes so far as to say that the German writer Benedikte Naubert (1756–1819) "exerted an important influence on Walter Scott."[15] And Hartmut Eggert includes more than forty women among the roughly 250 authors of historical novels that he documents for the period 1850 to 1900.[16] In other words, women played an important role both in broadening and in defining the discourse of history in the nineteenth century. Thus, while I could have used any number of male authors as examples, I focus initially on a woman writer: one of the most popular, prolific, and now forgotten historical novelists of the last century, Luise Mühlbach.

Mühlbach's life was remarkably conventional.[17] Born into the provincial middle class of Neubrandenburg as Clara Müller in 1814, she married the literary critic and liberal fellow traveler Theodor Mundt in 1839. Her first novel, *Erste und letzte Liebe* (First and Last Love), appeared in 1838, when she, too, belonged to the progressive "Young Germany" movement, but Mühlbach soon shifted gears and turned her awesome productive capacities to historical fiction.[18] By the time she died in 1873, Mühlbach had written some 290 volumes of fiction! Even if we divide that number by three or four, because the fashion in her day was to produce multivolume works for commercial lending libraries, Mühlbach was something of a publishing phenomenon.[19] Eggert reports that the publisher reprinted the three volumes of her *Friedrich der Große und sein Hof* (Frederick the Great and His Court) seven times after their initial appearance in 1853–54,[20] and Alberto Martino's research into lending libraries lists Mühlbach as the single most popular German author of the period 1849 to 1888.[21] That puts her in fifth place overall, behind Alexandre Dumas, Eugène Sue, G. P. R. James, and Paul de Kock, but ahead of Scott in the number of volumes owned by private lending libraries — and owned only because they could profit by providing them to readers. During the period 1889 to 1914 Mühlbach advanced to second place behind Dumas, and an eighteen-volume English-language edition of her works is still available in most libraries in the United States.

Mühlbach's novels contain, among other things, a complete history of Germany from the Thirty Years War (1618 to 1648) to the founding of the second German Empire in 1871. Furthermore, even though it was "fiction," hers was also one of the first full-length biographies of Frederick the Great. Mühlbach's complete Frederick cycle occupies some fifteen volumes, written over the course of as many years, but they were far from the only works she wrote between 1853 and 1868.[22] It takes a close reading to see what was at stake both in Mühlbach's version of political conflict and in her "unhistorical" representation of the maids, gardeners, and courtiers who inhabited the margins of Frederick's world but the center of these novels. Before turning to Mühlbach's fiction, however, I propose to outline the position taken by the founder of modern academic historiography, Leopold von Ranke (1795–1886). Just as I use Mühlbach to represent the historical novelist, I employ Ranke as Mühlbach's exemplary and paradigmatic, albeit implicit, adversary in the early stages of debate between historians and writers of historical fiction. Luckily, both authors produced biographies of Frederick the Great; and although Mühlbach's theoretical statements are far briefer than Ranke's, she still wrote enough on the subject to allow for an assessment of how she conceived of the profession of the historical novelist.

Ranke is mainly associated with Berlin, where he was a professor for over sixty years. His first published work, a history of the Roman and German peoples, appeared in 1825, while he was still teaching at an academic high school in the provinces, but the book's critical discussion of traditional historiography so impressed the Prussian minister of education that Ranke received a position at the University of Berlin. There, his most significant achievement was the development of the "critical method" of historical scholarship. He trained generations of historians to work from primary sources, which they could accept as true only after rigorous examination. More than anyone else, Ranke invented and propagated the new discipline of academic history, which makes him an apt and worthy opponent for the historical novel's most popular author.[23] Ranke and his contemporaries might have been stunned at the pairing, but the aspirations and claims of historical fiction demand it.

Ranke's famous formulation of the historian's task, "blos zeigen, wie es eigentlich gewesen,"[24] explicitly summarizes the claim history makes on "truth": nothing added, nothing subtracted, the facts and nothing but the facts, and the historian never gets in the way. If we can believe him, that is, if we can use part of Ranke's own archive to see how he came to that position, showing "what really happened" also differentiates the historian from the historical novelist. In a memoir of 1885, some sixty years after the previous statement, Ranke confesses that he read Scott, whose novels awakened in him an interest in history.[25] But Ranke also reports feeling disgust at what he viewed as Scott's falsifications.[26] In fact, Ranke links his decision to turn to history rather than fiction to his overwhelmingly negative reaction when he compared what he could learn about the real life of one of Scott's characters with what was represented in the novel.[27] Scott put words in his characters' mouths; his fictional figures sometimes contradict archival traces or say and do things for which no proof survived. Unburdened by the documentary record, Scott could choose pleasant presentation over narrowly defined truth — much to Ranke's dismay.

Ranke's "critical method," by contrast, insists that the historian not deviate from the literal truth contained in surviving documents. Should the paper trail prove insufficient, however, Ranke lets the professional historian add to his account "was sich daraus mit einer gewissen Sicherheit entwickeln läßt." The only caveat is that the writer avoid everything "was von der beglaubigten Ueberlieferung der Thatsachen wesentlich abweicht."[28] At first glance, Ranke seems to uphold the distinction between fact and fancy; but "some certainty" and "not significantly different" are by no means ironclad barriers. By allowing the historian to work not just with "authenticated" historical reality but with that which he feels safe in deriving, Ranke may have left enough holes in the border between history and fiction for novelists to march in. Historical fiction might even displace history as the preferred purveyor of truth, unless Ranke's case against Scott remains as strong as his advocacy of academic history.

On the one hand, if Scott got things wrong, or if his fictional versions of events are less pleasing and less interesting than the facts, then Ranke's position is unassailable. Indeed, if his argument is valid, no one would write historical fiction, because novels would revolt intelligent readers, whereas history would entertain and enlighten them. On the other hand, in life, to say nothing of the marketplace, history's advantage over fiction seems less obvious, the boundary not so clear cut. In fact, if we use Ranke's own statements as evidence, it turns out that drawing a sharp border between the two genres was frequently problematic. Moreover, even if it has to squeeze into the nebulous space of some certainty, historical fiction may be better able than history to represent certain aspects of the past: the small, personal, and frequently undocumented reality that people, including historical figures and readers, occupy. Novelists can add what history lacks especially, but not only, when documents are missing. The case for fiction is both simple and obvious. As Mühlbach's publisher put it in an advertisement for the seventh edition of *Friedrich der Große und sein Hof*, "Das Volk muß seine Helden nicht blos durch die Thaten, durch die historische Begebenheiten . . . kennenlernen, . . . es muß hinter dem Helden auch den Menschen sehen und begreifen."[29] Without knowing the person behind the role, readers will miss some of history's reality.

Of course, Ranke realized that not everything worth knowing or telling about the past had been recorded and preserved in archives. While he was not shy about extolling the thrill of primary research, Ranke also agonized over gaps in the written record. He realized with regret that he could untangle only the small portion of an individual's biography that had survived in letters, treaties, wills, and other documents. Yet, even more decisive for Ranke's work than the unavoidable incompleteness of archival records are the subjective limitations that he places on his inquiry. In the short biography of Frederick the Great that Ranke wrote for the *Allgemeine deutsche Biographie* (Universal German Biography) in 1878 the narrative voice claims that he can do no more than present the nation an overview of Frederick's political and military accomplishments.[30] Not only does Ranke seem uninterested in Frederick's personal life, but he claims elsewhere that individuals matter only when they advance or direct larger historical trends.[31] Thus, for Ranke archives were mainly deficient when they lacked significant documents — the treaties, dispatches, and minutes of cabinet meetings crucial to political history; it mattered little that reliable evidence about great men's private sentiments was also missing. In other words, the historian cannot derive with any certainty — and, more important, has little interest in learning or writing about — how great men related to their wives, children, and servants. Neither can he know much about great men's personal reactions to events. Furthermore, depicting how the rest of humanity viewed such heroic figures or how people's lives changed as a result of great men's actions falls outside the realm of history. Thus, Ranke not only wants to stick to the facts but also tries to focus solely on the big picture, drawing his portrait of Frederick with the broad strokes of larger truths on a canvas that novelists seek to make more complicated.

Of course, even the most careful historian occasionally slips into the realm of the personal and the undocumentable. For example, Ranke characterizes Frederick's reaction to the execution of his friend Katte, which the prince was forced to witness: "Die Disciplin des Schreckens stählte die Seele Friedrichs, die dadurch doch nicht unterjocht wurde," as if the historian had access to the young man's soul and knew what may have steeled it.[32] But for the most part, Ranke skips over incidents from Frederick's life that Mühlbach describes in great, if sometimes invented, detail. Ranke begins his account with Frederick's birth in 1712, but he moves him all the way to the throne, that is, to 1740, in just four pages of his forty-two-page biography. By choice but also by circumstance Ranke has room to present only what Frederick did rather than to explore who he was. Mühlbach, by contrast, begins her cycle of Frederick novels not with the king's birth but considerably later — sometime after 1734 — at the court in Rheinsberg, where Frederick spent half a dozen years as crown prince in relative isolation before ascending to the throne. For several hundred pages Mühlbach keeps Frederick in the countryside, where he writes music and philosophy, plays the flute, falls in love, and prepares himself to become king. Ranke covers the years in Rheinsberg in a single sentence.[33] To be sure, Mühlbach does not ignore the political events that were for Ranke the essence of history, but she embeds them in an overwhelmingly personal and private context. Her inclusion of both "the personal" and "the common people" gives readers an opportunity to identify with familiar, but partly fictional, characters and, thus, to gain the psychological benefits that identification entails. Mühlbach's inclusivity must have appealed to the rapidly growing body of literate but unsophisticated readers. For as well written as much of nineteenth-century history was, historical fiction catered to readers' needs and desires. It was also more accessible. As a result, fiction enjoyed a competitive advantage over academic historiography. Although Ranke's life of Frederick the Great was intended for the less demanding audience of a reference work rather than for a strictly scholarly readership, as their differing treatments of Frederick's years in Rheinsberg show, his and Mühlbach's versions of Frederick's life make different claims about what readers need to know to understand both the king and his times. The question, therefore, becomes not simply how they differ, but which of these writers presents a "truer" biography of Frederick II?

Here, too, a caveat is in order: truth might have mattered little in the larger enterprise of writing Germany's national narrative. If Frederick II functioned as an "integrative figure" in the pantheon of German heroes, he acquired that status despite his preference for speaking and writing French.[34] Although writers could easily overlook inconvenient details in a biography aimed at the general reading public, the issue of truth remained an important bone of contention in the debate between historians and the authors of historical fiction. By establishing the conventions of what could be included and what had to be excluded both from academic history and its fictional counterpart, the genre discourse wrote the roles played by historians and historical novelists in the myth-making enterprise of German nationalism. For example, if truth implied a scholarly tone, buttressed by footnotes in a physically substantial volume, historical truth became inaccessible to the growing mass of ordinary readers. That version of the truth was too boring and too expensive for the masses. If fiction could produces its own "true" version of the national saga, however, then less sophisticated readers could also access German history and acquire their share of what was becoming a common past. Their alternative was historical fiction, but fictionalized accounts of the past could only function as effective purveyors of German identity to the extent that they, like history, laid claim to a form of truth. If historical fiction had simply been another name for courtly and gothic novels, where knights clanked around meaninglessly in old castles, the genre would never have had the legitimacy necessary for it to participate in the historical and ideological discourse of nationalism. Historians would never have feared or reviled fictional accounts of past events and people, nor could novelists have made their claims on the nation's history.

In essence, I take an opposite tack from Hayden White, who points to the necessary fictionalization of history, especially of narrative history, brought on by its use of emplotment and the other tools of literature.[35] For me, it is just as interesting to explore what happens to history when it is embedded or represented in fiction. In fact, given the popularity of historical fiction, the stakes involved in determining its truth would seem to be far higher than in questioning the truth of history. Fiction seems to provide an escape from reality, but many readers, most literary critics, and, oddly enough, the growing number of historians who use literary evidence all credit imaginative writers with special insight into "the human condition." Unlike historians, novelists use empathy, intuition, or a peculiar form of understanding (Dilthey's *Verstehen*) to write what I call fictional truth.[36] Goethe's *Werther*, for example, contains something so profound regarding the nature of thwarted love, excessive emotions, and youthful rebellion against repressive social conventions that it utterly captivated his contemporaries. Moreover, the novel resonated strongly enough in East Germany in the 1970s that Edgar Wibeau, the hero of Ulrich Plenzdorf's novelistic encounter with Goethe, found meaning in his own life by reading that same 200-year-old text. Similarly, few doubt that Fontane's Berlin novels present an unparalleled portrait of that city's society at the end of the nineteenth century. But when Luise Mühlbach claims to explain Frederick the Great to her readers, she purports to be writing more than mere fictional truth. Ranke, to judge by his reaction to Scott, is disgusted, and warning bells go off through the whole profession of history. One wonders about the fuss. Why defend the boundaries with such acrimony? Is there a dirty little secret that historians are reluctant to share about their own work?

Historical fiction has always occupied a middle ground between literature and history; it necessarily and unavoidably mixes fact and fancy. Yet, except in the most egregious examples of historical romances (for example, the Harlequin romances set in Regency England), the writer's creativity is limited by historically verifiable "facts"; although recent theory has made facts into a textual and contextual category, they still possess a status — not just an aura — different from that enjoyed by products of the imagination. One can argue over the definition of a fact, which means putting the dispute between history and historical fiction at its most basic, atomic level, but there are limits. Both Mühlbach and Ranke must let Frederick die in 1786; they cannot change the outcome of battles or invent visits to his palace by aliens from outer space. Hence, in talking about "truth" in history and historical fiction, it is useful to differentiate the inclusion of dates, quotations, real people, and actual events from fiction's special truth and the insight literature might provide into historical people and events. Scott's and Mühlbach's mistakes are no more interesting than the historian's shoddy editing or botched footnotes, but their sins of interpretation lie somewhere between history's truth and literature's. Their successes, if they had any, exist in the tension between history and fiction, along the murky border between fact and fancy where historical fiction resides — one is tempted to say, where it lies — or not at all. Moreover, that hotly contested space is also filled with other meaningful material. It is there, for example, that I locate German nationalism, which is neither a hard fact — not geography, biology, language, or destiny — nor complete fantasy, and all the more problem-laden because it occupies physically and rhetorically disputed territory. Here, however, the crucial issue is whether and how fiction's claim on truth stands up to history's. Where does the historical novelist gain knowledge of the past, and how does that knowledge function within the particular constraints of historical fiction?

Although Mühlbach wrote about her own culture at a distance that ranged from over 200 to less than fifty years, the imaginative distance between author and subject matter is often greater; in novels set in the Middle Ages it amounts to centuries. It can also extend to vastly different peoples, places, and social origins. Mühlbach's novelistic insights are based on notions of universality, on the eternal verities of the human condition; they seem, at first glance, to contradict the historicity, that is, the uniqueness of both the figures and the culture she represents. What she wrote about the private lives of "great men" and both the public and private lives of minor characters presupposes an underlying similarity to her own experiences. Otherwise, claims of empathy, intuition, and understanding ring hollow, although they may ring just as hollow for the historian. Additionally, even if we bracket the epistemological issues and assume that both historians and the authors of historical fiction can "know" across time, culture, and space, the question of representation remains. For historians, several factors limit the decision about what to represent: their notion of what constitutes history, the process of selection, and the adequacy of archives. Nineteenth-century historians were content to paint a picture that they knew to be incomplete; they sketched the broad outlines of past events both to understand them within their historical contexts and to elucidate causes, effects, and meanings for the historians' own contemporaries. Historical novelists, by contrast, hoped to fill in the spaces between the historians' lines; they offered readers a denser, more detailed image. They added the private sphere and the masses to their accounts, but at what cost? By attempting to represent more than politics and more than just the documentable outline of great men's public lives, did they necessarily falsify history and earn the justifiable scorn of academic historians? And how did the historians fare, according to their own standards?

Mühlbach was keenly aware of the difficulties she faced vis-à-vis historians, and she addressed those problems explicitly in the introduction to the final series in her Frederick novels, *Der alte Fritz und die neue Zeit* (Old Fritz and the New Age).[37] She was responding to her critics, but who they were and precisely what they said remain unknown. Therefore — like the novelist, without compunction, or the historian, reluctantly — we must infer from the evidence that survives. For example, someone must have accused Mühlbach of factual errors, which provoked her to irony so bitter that the translator omitted the response from the English edition of her novel. Calling her foes "small-minded quibblers" ["Krittler"], who themselves make factual mistakes, Mühlbach refuses to defend either the historical novel in general or herself on the basis of factual accuracy. Since she wants to occupy the moral and theoretical high ground, she also distances herself from those historical novels in which the past serves only as background for a pulpy plot.[38] Her concern is rather with legitimizing the idea of historical fiction, defending the genre's goals, and championing its mode of representation.

Surprisingly, given her subsequent reception, Mühlbach seems unthreatened by questions of aesthetic quality, and she makes not the faintest attempt at distancing herself from the mass of readers to whom she appeals. In fact, in an odd juxtaposition, Mühlbach borrows the aesthetic category of the "sublime" [*das Erhabene*] from the world of high literature and links it to the chief goal of the historical novelist:

> Was ist aber dieses große, dieses erhabene Ziel des historischen Romanschriftstellers? Es ist dieses: die Geschichte zu illustrieren, sie populär zu machen; die großen Gestalten, wie die großen Thatsachen, welche in den Büchern der Geschichte dem Gelehrten, dem höher Gebildeten sich enthüllen, aus der stillen Studierzimmer hinaus zu tragen auf den Markt des Lebens, und zum Gemeingut Aller zu machen, was bis dahin nur das Gut des Gelehrten war. (viii)

Unlike the historian, who hides the past in an academic shroud accessible only to his fellow scholars, Mühlbach unashamedly sets the task of the historical novelist as making history popular. Her use of the words "market" and "property," especially in connection with the sublime, is as noteworthy as her criticism of academic history's elitism. Sublimity was supposed to depend on the work of art's intrinsic qualities, not on its marketability, but Mühlbach's issue is not beauty or literary quality. She wants to overcome the strictures that Ranke and other professional historians had placed on representations of the past. Whereas they had to be content with what was visible or external, Mühlbach claims that the novelist can penetrate to the internal truth of history. The problem with her argument is the difficulty in accomplishing its didactic goals of bringing the past to life and making history popular without simultaneously falsifying it.

Mühlbach claims to have been assiduous in her own preparations, although she seems to have meant reading secondary sources, not doing the archival work historians recognize as research. She does quote from primary material — in the Frederick cycle, mainly from the king's posthumously published works — but she also insists that the novelist must live and breathe the epoch before it can become real to his or her readers. Only an intimate knowledge of the details permits empathy with people from the past. Strangely enough, Mühlbach's argument resembles one made decades ago by the British philosopher of history, R. G. Collingwood.[39] But Collingwood directed his idealism toward penetrating the minds of temporally distant peoples; he wanted to intuit what they thought in order to explain their actions. By contrast, Mühlbach's orientation was resolutely practical — like that of Thucydides, who invented the famous orations in his *History of the Peloponnesian Wars*.[40] Empathy rather than the archive provides the material, and Mühlbach links a distinctly poetic notion of historical understanding and explanation with the difficulties — and the advantages — that historical novelists face in their representations of history. As Mühlbach explains it, the division of labor between nineteenth-century historians and historical novelists involves their differing conceptions of reality and, consequently, differing views of what they can legitimately write.

Mühlbach begins this portion of her argument with a statement that Ranke might well have supported, except for its tone. As she sees it, the historical novelist can peer into dark corners and shed light on people and events that remain mysterious to the historian, dependent as he is on the written record. Since novelists accept no professional or generic limits, they can begin with what they glean from reading academic and popular history and then explain away gaps in the archival record using "die schöpferische Phantasie des Dichters" (x). The "poet" — and here Mühlbach raises her calling from "writer" [*Schriftsteller*] to "poet/artist" [*Dichter*] — understands history creatively, in a manner that is not only unavailable but also forbidden to the lowly historian. Whereas serious historians limit themselves to external truth, the novelist has access to the heart of history, which Mühlbach locates within the individual. Here it becomes clear what the historical novelist can do and what, in her view, the historian cannot even attempt: the novelist's task is to discover the human motives behind events and, by writing about thinking and feeling individuals, to make history plausible and popular to ordinary readers. At this point Mühlbach has parted company from Ranke not only in her differing use of evidence but also in her conception of where historical truth is located. While Ranke relegated individuals, even individuals as important as Frederick II, to supporting roles in the drama he called "the universal trend," Mühlbach pushes those same individuals and a host of lesser personalities to center stage, which means, quite literally, that Frederick, and his family, friends, and servants have a great deal to say in her novels — even if they may not have actually said it.

In other sorts of novels, speaking parts are only difficult to write; the dialogue must simply ring or read right. The novelist makes the written word seem like speech, knowing that real oral discourse seldom sounds authentic to the reader. In historical novels, the words of well-known figures present a different problem, which is mainly evidentiary. Historians know what famous people said and, more important, what no one can prove they said. Thus, there can be no question about what to quote as speech in history books. For Mühlbach the problem is far more complex, and she adopts two quite different strategies in dealing with it. The first is to quote wherever possible. Her Frederick the Great novels regularly contain footnotes with references to his published works and to the memoirs of his contemporaries, often with the straightforward notation "des Königs eigene Worte." Sometimes she simply says "historisch" [historical], which seems to mean "accurate, "true," or "verifiable." Although Mühlbach's citations are an attempt to justify her undertaking according to the rules laid down by academic historians, that is, to claim the legitimacy they denied her, I take these notations as a sign of just how confusing and embedded the notion of "truth," particularly "historical truth," had become — or always was. Too many citations would clutter the text and implicitly praise the enemy, but every absence calls attention to the questionable status of what lies between the quotation marks. Mühlbach rails against the second-class citizenship that her dependency on the historical record and the work of professional historians implies, but she seems to realize that footnotes impress her readers and may give her some traction in the battle she is waging against the discipline of history.

Luckily, the developing conventions of historical fiction allow a second solution to the difficulties of dialogue. Unlike the historian, the novelist can claim "auf dem Fundament der Geschichte das Gebäude der Poesie aufzuführen, das dennoch ganz durchleuchtet ist von der Wahrheit der Geschichte" (xii). "Dennoch" [nevertheless] is the key word here, because it denotes the peculiar status of historical fiction, situated between the verifiable facts of empirical historiography and the notion that fiction is solely the product of an author's imagination. Mühlbach places historical fiction above history, but she nevertheless builds her poetic temple on history's foundation and claims that history pervades the construction that rises above mere facts. In fact, she seems to have backed off from her denial of history's truth, its merely "external" status, because she wants to use the discipline's still strong claim on truth to buttress her own position. Her problem is how to reconcile the principal advantage with the principal disadvantage of the genre.

Since historical fiction is neither pure fact nor pure fiction, it is difficult to address the consequences of its mixed status. The "truth" of historical novels may lie closer to fiction, but "facts" keep intruding. Some authors negotiate these shoals by refusing to invent speeches for "historical" characters; they thereby limit their "fiction" to the minor figures — to the spouses, maids, and gardeners who left nothing for the archives. Such choices make Scott's middling heroes attractive, because they allow the author considerable freedom; but Mühlbach will have none of such hesitancy, no doubt because it would have severely limited her options in writing a novel about Frederick II — especially one 4,000 pages long. Like many "great men," Frederick simply did not say enough publicly — specifically, not enough about his private life and motivations — to satisfy either the historian or the novelist. Having read and intuited her way into Frederick's life, however, Mühlbach takes a huge leap into the fictional past, claiming,

> daß es dabei durchaus nebensachlich ist, ob die in dem historischen Romane handelnden historischen Personen dieses oder jenes Wort wirklich gesprochen, diese oder jene nebensachliche Handlung so gethan; es kommt nur darauf an, daß diese Worte und diese Handlungen in dem Geist und Character jener historischen Personen gehalten sind, und daß man ihnen nichts andichtet, was sie nicht gesprochen oder gethan haben könnten. (xii)

While it would have been anathema for Ranke to plead for history that showed "what really *could have* happened," Mühlbach apparently needed that much leeway to penetrate to history's interior, to its heart. Once she has understood — that is, lived and breathed — an epoch, Mühlbach claims the right to invent what historical figures could have done or said. The only limit is that their actions have to be in character; she prefers to invent incidental [*nebensachliche*] events, but one suspects that they would perforce be revealing of the very spirit [*Geist*] that guarantees their essential truthfulness. Aside from the slightly defensive circularity of her argument, Mühlbach's was also a much different notion of truth from Ranke's, both from the standpoint of what was representable and what mattered in historical explanation.

Now that we understand the terms of the debate between these two leading figures and their respective genres, let us look at the results, with one caveat. Since discussions of "literary value" are nowadays even more hopelessly mired in long-standing debates than notions of truth, it behooves us to ignore quality and limit the inquiry, first, to Mühlbach's historiographical vision as realized in her novels, and, second, to Ranke's practical work as an historian rather than as a theorist of history. Otherwise, we would have to decide what constitutes "good" writing and then determine whether the criteria are both timeless and equally applicable to fiction and nonfiction.[41] In addition, we would have to assess the work of (literary) historians engaged in the project of building a national literature, supposedly using measures based on quality but often resting more on a thinly veiled nationalist agenda.[42] Although important, these issues would keep us from asking, first, whether Ranke or Mühlbach presented a more credible account of Frederick's life and, second, how and why the biographies they wrote differed.

Mühlbach regarded Frederick as lonely, a man given to brooding about his fate, without the comfort of friends and family to share his burdens. She does not depict Frederick as personally cold or unemotional, however; quite the contrary. When the newly crowned king decides to wage war against Austria for control of Silesia, Mühlbach's Frederick is clear about what is at stake both for himself and for his country, and he is happy for an opportunity that arises almost accidentally. The legally questionable inheritance of Silesia by Empress Maria Theresa awakens Frederick from the torpor that had plagued him ever since his father's death. The young — and fictional — king decides that Silesia offers him an opportunity for action, the chance to show the court and his father's advisors who he really is: "Es ist nicht genug, König zu sein durch Erbfolge und Geburt, man muß auch durch seine Thaten verdienen es zu sein."[43] The passage, which occurs in a private conversation with an aide, must have struck Mühlbach as true to Frederick's character, because there is no citation; whereas, two pages earlier she claims to quote the king when he discusses the Silesian campaign: "Alles war vorhergesehen, Alles vorbereitet, und es handelt sich nur um die Ausführung und Entwürfe, die ich seit langer Zeit in meinem Kopfe habe" (80). In other words, the first quotation is invented, while the second is verifiable — although it sounds as though Frederick said it in retrospect, which might make the historian question its validity.

In fact, no less an authority than Ranke presents an interpretation of events that differs sharply from "the king's own words." While Mühlbach quotes Frederick to the effect that the decision to invade Silesia was his alone, Ranke must have disregarded his statement — apparently in order to stress the continuity of Prussian politics — for he says: "Man darf nicht bezweifeln, daß der Entwurf dazu, der zu den geheimsten Papieren gehörte, die von Fürst zu Fürst übergingen, dem neu eintretendenden König bekannt geworden ist."[44] Ranke's rhetoric is more interesting than his conclusion, because his manner of writing shows how the historian intuits details for which he has no evidence, but which he nevertheless believes must have existed. Based on what must have been considerable familiarity with Prussian archives, Ranke assumes that Frederick would have learned of long-standing plans to wage war against Austria. In a sense, Ranke intuits evidence that either could or should have existed to confirm an event that was in character not with any one individual but with the long-range course of Prussian politics. His knowledge allows Ranke to claim that one must not doubt the transmission of such information to the new king; but one might well doubt that he would have allowed Mühlbach the same freedom to draw such a conclusion, especially when it contradicts a statement made by Frederick himself. In fact, except that Mühlbach feels free to invent quotations, mostly dealing with the king's private life rather than institutional continuity, the example shows surprisingly little difference between the two writers' tactics. If not characteristic of their intellectual habits, their interpretation of the origin of Frederick's Silesian campaign nevertheless suggests that their accounts vary mainly in their choice of subject matter rather than in the stringency of their intuition.

Mühlbach dwells on Frederick's private life, returning time and again to his apparent lack of personal feelings — perhaps to counter widespread beliefs to the contrary. Various characters talk about Frederick's inability to love anything other than his flute; his scheming chief of protocol, Baron von Pöllnitz, repeatedly fails to interest the king in the dancers and actresses he procures for him. Not without reason does Frederick compare Sanssouci with a monastery, and Mühlbach even suggests that the intellectual pleasure he supposedly enjoyed there with Voltaire was an unmitigated disaster. She dwells on Frederick the man in a rhetorically interesting fashion: by omitting "historical" successes that she deemed merely external. She therefore skips the years 1746 to 1749 and starts her account with what she deems the difficult year 1750, because she believes that historians have presented a falsely triumphal image of a man whom she, as a novelist, intuits to have been deeply troubled and supremely unhappy:

> Man verzeihe es, wenn wir von der Freiheit des Dichters Gebrauch machen, diese vier Jahre überspringen, und diesem vierten Band mit dem Jahre 1750 beginnen, mit demjenigen Jahre, welches die Geschichtsschreiber gewohnt sind, als das glücklichste und sonnenhellste Jahr in dem Leben König Friedrich des Zweiten zu bezeichnen.[45]

There is, however, more at stake in the picture of Frederick that Mühlbach draws than the suffering of a high-born individual grappling with both his public and his male identities. She offers an alternative view of historical reality from Ranke's. In her introduction to *Friedrich der Große und seine Geschwister*, the third installment of her Frederick novels, Mühlbach defines her aim:

> es ist mir um die innere Characterentwicklung dieses großen Mannes zu thun gewesen, den Viele nur als den kühnen Helden, Viele als den weisen Gesetzgeber, den selbstregierenden König, sehr Wenige aber als den edlen, zartfühlenden, weichen Menschen kennen, der er wirklich war. Ich wollte Friedrich als den Menschen zeichnen, und aus seiner Seele und seinem Herzen heraus sein Leben entwickeln.[46]

By working from the inside out, rather than concentrating on external events, Mühlbach claims she can not only define the real Frederick, but she also suggests that his character provides a truer explanation of events than the version offered by historians. Perhaps the clearest example of what she means comes in an episode in *Berlin und Sanssouci*, the second installment of her series of Frederick novels. The key scene comes after Frederick has refused to allow his sister Amelia permission to marry one of his officers, a man she loves deeply, because he needs to marry her off to some prince. Although political considerations make the fulfillment of her love impossible, Frederick would like Amelia to understand and accept the burden of being a princess — just as he has resigned himself to his own fate as king. To explain her fate Frederick tries to separate the two roles he must play, king and brother: "Der König hat Dir gezürnt, der Bruder will mit dir weinen, Komm Amelie, komm an ein treues Bruder Herz!"[47] Unfortunately, the reconciliation fails miserably, apparently because Frederick is the only member of the family who can countenance such cognitive dissonance. But the failure has at least one interesting consequence. In an effort to forget the defeat he has just suffered, Frederick returns to the official papers on his desk; his eyes soon brighten, because he decides to do for his people what he cannot allow for his sister: give them freedom. He declares himself ready to sign a new code of laws that would protect his subjects from arbitrary actions by the crown and make them equal before the law. Members of the royal family — namely, his recalcitrant sister — would remain the only exceptions, but Frederick calls the whole enterprise a monument that he will erect to Amelia in his heart. According to Mühlbach, the king knows what motivated his decision, but neither Amelia nor those who attempt to explain it from surviving documents would ever know the truth.

Historians generally describe the deliberations that led to the introduction of the Prussian Uniform Code in 1794 as the result of one of two factors. The first was Frederick's philosophical concerns with equal justice, perhaps brought on by the Miller Arnold Trial of 1773 to 1780, which supposedly convinced Frederick that he needed to end aristocratic interference in the legal system. The other factor historians cite is the necessity of uniting dissimilar Prussian provinces into a single unitary state for military reasons. Ranke comes down on the side of military considerations, but he mentions only economic, not legal reforms. Ranke also fails to mention Princess Amelia and her lover, because no one other than a novelist could claim access to what Frederick was thinking when he made his decision. Again, the "truth," if there is one here, is of little interest to the debate; what "really happened" is ultimately unknowable. Even though Mühlbach's version sounds far-fetched to readers schooled in academic history, it might be accurate; but neither she nor Ranke has any means of proving their cases. Frederick's mind remains impenetrable. This episode shows, however, that for Mühlbach the personal is not just historical in the sense that such seemingly trivial events occurred in the past; a person's personal life is also historical in a manner that academic historians could well have accepted — except for the tiny detail of evidence and the presupposition that great ideas, not emotions, motivated "great men." The historical novelist claims, first, that whatever happened between Frederick and his sister is important to understanding him as a person, and, second, that it may be just as critical in understanding him as a statesman.

Essentially, Ranke and those who followed his example make a virtue out of the necessity imposed by archival incompleteness; and for the longest time historians claimed to be content to relate what had happened at the level of political events, since that was all they could talk about with any certainty. In addition, they usually limited their explanations of why things had happened to the interests of impersonal entities — states, parties, armies — or they ascribed rational motives based on external, rather than personal, considerations to the statesmen whose decisions they chronicled. Historical novels implicitly insist that history consists of more than "great men's" public lives; their private lives and both the public and private lives of ordinary people were always part of fictional history, but only recently has the academy accorded them a place in "history." In a sense, historians who write social history and psycho-biographies or investigate the history of women, minorities, and the oppressed are merely catching up to the concerns of nineteenth-century historical novelists; they might even be using some of the same techniques.

Of course, historical novelists did more than anticipate developments in the academy; they also remained rooted in their own age and shared its concern with that other member of the triangle that linked history and historical fiction to German nationalism. Writers such as Mühlbach often wrote openly about their desire to bring history to the masses, and that aim also brought them into conflict with a profession that claimed sole access to history's truth. For example, Mühlbach justifies spending so much time, energy, and paper on Frederick in her introduction to *Der alte Fritz und die neue Zeit* by reflecting on her intentions: "Aber was ich gewollt habe, und was ich will, dessen wenigstens bin ich mir klar bewußt: dem deutschen Volke seine Geschichte in angenehmer Form populär und lieb zu machen, ihm Liebe und Freude für seine Specialgeschichte einflößen, ihn das innere Verständniß für dies Getriebe der Politik zu eröffnen, ihn Thatsachen der Geschichte zu einem wirklichen Stück Leben umzuwandeln" (viii). Note the possessive "their"; Mühlbach wants to let the German people love and enjoy "their history," in part, because making history popular flowed directly into the enterprise of giving Germans a share and a stake in what was becoming "their" common past. And it was here that historical fiction won its most decisive battle. Historians might have wanted to control the dialectical interplay from which Germans' sense of themselves emerged; but as a practical matter, people read more novels set in the past than they read works of academic history. One could still argue that all of what those readers learned was true, but novelists made a strong claim for a kind of truth that exceeded archival verification. They also challenged historians, albeit unsuccessfully, to rethink their own undertaking.

The critical moment of historical fiction is twofold: first, it insists that character is just as important in historical understanding as the event, and second, it demonstrates that "the personal" is not only political; it is also "historical." Without individual motivation, to which the novelist claimed unique access, there can be no larger truth; in fact, there can easily be falsehood. By illuminating the personal and integrating character into history, with means that historians, even contemporary social and cultural historians, have been reluctant to accept, novelists succeeded in producing accounts of the past more "complete" than their academic counterparts' histories. If Mühlbach and the other historical novelists of the period accomplished nothing else, their theoretical and commercially practical "victory" pushed the boundaries of historical knowledge, historical understanding, and historical representation far beyond the limits still adhered to by all but the most untraditional contemporary historians. And since novelists were the common people's teachers, it is just as important to understand the theoretical underpinnings of historical fiction as it is to grasp what Ranke and his followers meant when they founded academic history. In fact, one needs both the academic discipline and historical fiction to explain the larger discourse of history in the nineteenth century, particularly if the task is to untangle their combined role in writing Germany's national narrative, that is, in providing the content necessary for people to know what the label "German" meant.

In a sense, the point of this theoretical discussion has been to assess the sources of information about the German past that were available to nineteenth-century readers. Even if historians judged the genre harshly, people who read historical fiction (as well as popular and academic histories) learned from it. At the very least, they used novels to confirm and augment what they had already learned in school. First, readers learned or re-remembered actual facts — some incidental, some trivial, but some that became important to their understanding of the German past. Second, readers learned things, both large and small, that they believed true, but that may have been as far-fetched as Mühlbach's assessment of Frederick the Great's character and motivations. Third, they learned or accepted overarching viewpoints about what mattered in German history: who were its heroes, what had gone right and wrong in the past, where the nation had been, and where it was headed in the future. Moreover, this learning took place in an atmosphere utterly unlike the classroom. Nineteenth-century readers read historical fiction for pleasure. These works had not yet found their way into the schoolroom or the academy; they were simply fun to read. Historical fiction surrounded itself with an aura of moral or cultural uplift, but readers also got to see how plots turned out and what happened to these books' heroes. Being filled with "truths" from history did not prevent this literature from also containing much that readers found true about their families, their relationships, and society in general. But they found historical truth, too.

Notes

[1] Michael Riffaterre, *Fictional Truth* (Baltimore: Johns Hopkins UP, 1990). See also Burghard Damerau, *Literatur und andere Wahrheiten: Warum wir ohne Bücher nicht sein wollen* (Berlin: Aufbau, 1999).

[2] Carlo Ginzburg, *The Cheese and the Worms: The Cosmos of a Sixteenth-Century Miller*, trans. John and Addne Tedeschi (Baltimore: Johns Hopkins UP, 1980), and Steven Ozment, *The Bürgermeister's Daughter: Scandal in a Sixteenth-Century German Town* (New York: St. Martin's P, 1996). On the *Monumenta*, see G. P. Gooch, *History and Historians in the Nineteenth Century*, 3rd ed. (Boston: Beacon, 1959), 60–71.

[3] Friedrich Jaeger and Jörn Rüsen, *Geschichte des Historismus* (Munich: Beck, 1992), 1; the classic account is Georg G. Iggers, *The German Conception of History: The National Tradition of Historical Thought from Herder to the Present* (1968; Hanover NH: Wesleyan UP, 1983).

⁴ See Peter Paret, *Art as History: Episodes in the Culture and Politics of Nineteenth-Century Germany* (Princeton: Princeton UP, 1988), esp. 13–60. Publishing anecdotes about Frederick II seems to have been something of a cottage industry, and libraries bulged with military and local histories produced by amateurs. According to Susan A. Crane, *Collecting & Historical Consciousness in Early Nineteenth-Century Germany* (Ithaca NY: Cornell UP, 2000), the same sorts of passionate amateurs also founded the first historical museums at roughly the same time.

⁵ Franz Kugler, professor of history at the University of Berlin and the author, with Adolph Menzel, of a popular illustrated biography of Frederick the Great (1840), published novels under a pseudonym; Felix Dahn, who wrote one of the century's best-selling works of historical fiction, *Ein Kampf um Rom* (1876), was also a professor, as were the novelists Georg Ebers and Adolf Hausrath. Gustav Freytag's career as a novelist began when he was unable to secure a professorship, and he published many popular histories.

⁶ Hayden White, "The Burden of History," in his *Tropics of Discourse: Essays in Cultural Criticism* (Baltimore: Johns Hopkins UP, 1978), 43; emphasis in original. As a sign that things might be changing, if ever so slightly, see Simon Schama, *Dead Certainties (Unwarranted Speculations)* (New York: Knopf, 1991), a self-conscious mixture of history and historical fiction written by an eminent historian. Not only does Schama turn to fiction but he has also gone beyond realist representation. As he writes in an afterword: "In keeping with the self-disrupting nature of the narratives, I have deliberately dislocated the conventions by which histories establish coherence and persuasiveness" (321).

⁷ One exception is Lilian R. Furst, *All Is True: The Claims and Strategies of Realist Fiction* (Durham, NC: Duke UP, 1995). Much of the argument below is indebted to Martin Swales, *Epochenbuch Realismus: Romane und Erzählungen* (Munich: Schmidt, 1997). See also Klaus-Detlef Müller, ed., *Bürgerlicher Realismus: Grundlagen und Interpretationen* (Königstein: Athenäum, 1981).

⁸ I admit to the same vice, which provides an opportunity to illustrate how novelists play with the boundary between fiction and fact. Hillary Tamar, the narrator of Sarah Caudwell's novel *The Shortest Way to Hades* (New York: Dell, 1984) and a professor of history, laments the constraints her profession places on what she claims, within the world of the novel, to be factual: "Would that the historian might be permitted to have regard to Art rather than Truth and so enliven the narrative with descriptions of scenes known only by hearsay or speculation" (2).

⁹ The classic statement of this position is Erich Auerbach, *Mimesis: The Representation of Reality in Western Literature,* trans. Willard R. Trask (Princeton: Princeton UP, 1953). For an account of realism in art, see Linda Nochlin, *Realism* (New York: Penguin, 1971). Swales calls mimesis a breath-

taking swindle in which the creative process of human perception is reduced to writing; the lack of textual awareness is realism's greatest fiction (132).

[10] Charles Dickens, *David Copperfield* (1850; New York: Modern Library, n.d.), 14, 179.

[11] Willibald Alexis, *Ruhe ist die erste Bürgerpflicht* (1852; Frankfurt am Main: Ullstein, 1985).

[12] See Anthony Grafton, *The Footnote: A Curious History* (Cambridge, MA: Harvard UP, 1997). It is worth noting that Grafton first published this book in Germany, where its title was *Die tragischen Ursprünge der deutschen Fußnote*.

[13] Thomas G. Pavel, *Fictional Worlds* (Cambridge, MA: Harvard UP, 1986), 16.

[14] Norbert Otto Eke, "Eine Gesamtbibliographie des deutschen Romans 1815–1830: Anmerkungen zum Problemfeld von Bibliographie und Historiographie," *Zeitschrift für Germanistik*, n.s. 2 (1993): 301.

[15] Dennis Sweet, introduction to Benedikte Naubert's "The Cloak," in Jeannine Blackwell and Susanne Zantop, eds., *Bitter Healing: German Women Writers 1700–1830. An Anthology* (Lincoln: U of Nebraska P, 1990), 204.

[16] Eggert, 213–46.

[17] For a complete bibliography and a brief interpretation of Mühlbach's life and work see my entry on Mühlbach in James Hardin and Siegfried Mews, eds., *Dictionary of Literary Biography,* vol. 133: *Nineteenth-Century German Writers to 1840* (Detroit: Gale Research, 1993), 204–10. There is also a useful introduction to Mühlbach in "Clara Mundts Briefe an Hermann Costenoble: Zu L. Mühlbachs historischen Romanen," in William H. McClain and Lieselotte E. Kurth-Voigt, eds., *Archiv für Geschichte des Buchwesens* 22 (1981): 917–52.

[18] I think the case for Mühlbach's radicalism is somewhat overstated; the early novels all pull back from the political positions with which they start. Compare Renate Möhrmann, *Die andere Frau: Emanzipationsansätze deutscher Schriftstellerinnen im Vorfeld der Achtundvierziger-Revolution* (Stuttgart: Metzler, 1977), esp. 60–84.

[19] These so-called double-, triple-, and quadruple-deckers kept the libraries' patrons coming back for more, and they also circulated more rapidly (and more profitably) than thick one-volume editions.

[20] Eggert, 212. There were three editions in 1857 and one each in 1858, 1859, 1862–64, and 1882.

[21] Alberto Martino, "Publikumsschichten und Leihbibliotheken," in Horst Glaser, ed., *Deutsche Literatur: Eine Sozialgeschichte*, vol. 7 (Reinbek bei Hamburg: Rowohlt, 1982), 404, 410; Alberto Martino, *Die Deutsche Leihbibliothek: Geschichte einer literarischen Institution (1756–1914)* (Wiesbaden: Otto Harrassowitz, 1990); on Mühlbach's American career, see Lieselotte E. Kurth-Voigt and William H. McClain, "Louise Mühlbach's Historical Novels: The

American Reception," *Internationales Archiv für Sozialgeschichte der deutschen Literatur* 6 (1981): 52–77.

[22] The complete cycle includes *Friedrich der Große und sein Hof,* 3 vols. (Berlin: Janke, 1853); *Berlin und Sanssouci oder Friedrich der Große und seine Freunde,* 4 vols. (Berlin: Simion, 1854); *Friedrich der Große und seine Geschwister,* 3 vols. (Berlin: Janke, 1855); and *Deutschland in Sturm und Drang: Historischer Roman,* 17 vols. (Jena: Costenoble, 1867–68). The first four volumes of *Deutschland in Sturm und Drang* are titled *Der alte Fritz und seine Zeit,* but Frederick does not actually die until the fifth volume, *Fürsten und Dichter.*

[23] Although Grafton demonstrates how dependent Ranke was on earlier scholars, for all practical purposes the Berlin historian remains the father of modern academic history. See Grafton, 62–93.

[24] Leopold von Ranke, *Geschichten der romanischen und germanischen Völker von 1494 bis 1514,* in his *Sämmtliche Werke,* 2nd ed., 54 vols. in 43 (Leipzig: Duncker & Humblot, 1867–90), 33: vii.

[25] Ranke, "Aufsätze zur eigenen Lebensbeschreibung: 4. Diktat vom November 1885," in his *Sämmtliche Werke,* 54: 61.

[26] Ranke, "Am neunzigsten Geburtstag, 21. Dezember, 1885," in his *Sämmtliche Werke,* 52: 596. The offending novel was *Quentin Durward.*

[27] Ranke, "Aufsätze zur eigenen Lebensbeschreibung," 61. Ranke reports comparing Scott's novel to an account written by a contemporary, Phillipe de Commines (1445–1511), whose memoirs were so even-handed that some consider him, not Ranke, the first modern historian.

[28] Ranke, "Am neunzigsten Geburtstag," 596.

[29] The advertisement is bound inside the back cover of George Hesekiel, *Stille vor dem Sturm,* vol. 2 (Berlin: Janke, 1863).

[30] Ranke, "Friedrich II. König von Preußen," in his *Sämmtliche Werke,* 51: 359.

[31] Ranke, "Hardenberg und die Geschichte des preußischen Staates von 1793–1813," in his *Sämmtliche Werke,* 46: vi.

[32] Ranke, "Friedrich II. König von Preußen," 361. Of course, popular historians were far guiltier of psychologizing beyond the evidence; for a typical example from *Die Gartenlaube,* see Kirsten Belgum, *Popularizing the Nation: Audience, Representation, and the Production of Identity in Die Gartenlaube 1853–1900* (Lincoln: U of Nebraska P, 1998), 22.

[33] Ranke, "Friedrich II. König von Preußen," 362. The sentence is: "Dann aber zog er sich auf seinen Landsitz Rheisberg zurück, um sich mit seiner Musik und seinen Büchern zu beschäftigen; mit den Studien der früheren Jahre machte er nun Ernst; sie erhoben ihn über den geistigen Horizont seines Vaters."

[34] The term comes from Theodor Schieder, "Friedrich der Große — eine Integrationsfigur des deutschen Nationalbewußtseins im 18. Jahrhundert?" in Otto Dahn, ed., *Nationalismus in vorindustrieller Zeit* (Munich: Oldenbourg, 1986), 115–128.

[35] See Hayden White, *Metahistory: The Historical Imagination in Nineteenth-Century Europe* (Baltimore: Johns Hopkins UP, 1973).

[36] For want of a better term, I reluctantly use Michael Riffaterre's phrase. Riffaterre seems content to label as "true" those works that are internally consistent, while I make a claim for historical fiction that parallels the truth claim made by historians for their work.

[37] Mühlbach, "Vorwort," in her *Deutschland in Sturm und Drang, Teil 1: Der alte Fritz und die neue Zeit*, vi–vii.

[38] For Georg Lukács, it is the use of history as "mere costumery" that separates genuine historical novels from potboilers that happen to be set in the past. See his *The Historical Novel*, trans. Hannah and Stanley Mitchell (Lincoln: U of Nebraska P, 1983), 19. It is worth noting that practitioners seem to have found it difficult to make the distinction.

[39] R. G. Collingwood, *The Idea of History* (Oxford: Oxford UP, 1946).

[40] Auerbach comments on the common practice of fictitious speeches in antique history using Tacitus as an example (*Mimesis*, 39–42).

[41] For a convincing historical survey of the issues and the dilemmas any criteria raise, see Jochen Schulte-Sasse, *Literarische Wertung*, 2nd ed. (Stuttgart: Metzler, 1976). Ruth-Ellen Boetcher Joeres has taken a new look at the exclusion of woman from the canon in her *Respectability and Deviance: Nineteenth-Century German Women Writers and the Ambiguity of Representation* (Chicago: U of Chicago P, 1998), 35–77.

[42] See Peter Uwe Hohendahl, *Building a National Literature: The Case of Germany 1830–1870*, trans. Renate Baron Franciscono (Ithaca, NY: Cornell UP, 1989).

[43] *Friedrich der Große und sein Hof*, 3: 82.

[44] Ranke, "Friedrich II. König von Preußen," 364.

[45] Mühlbach, *Berlin und Sansouci*, 4: 7.

[46] Mühlbach, *Friedrich der Große und seine Geschwister*, 3rd series, part 2, vol. 1: ix.

[47] Mühlbach, *Berlin und Sansouci*, 2: 165.

"In the Heart of the Heart of the Country":* Regional Histories as National History in Gustav Freytag's *Die Ahnen* (1872–80)

Lynne Tatlock

IN THE FINAL DECADES of the nineteenth century Freytag's *Die Ahnen* (The Ancestors, 1872–80) graced many a middle-class German "Geschenktisch" at confirmation and at Christmas time.[1] It was recommended as reading for educators as well as for bourgeois "young girls," and it sold quite well.[2] By 1907 a thirty-fifth edition of the first volume had appeared from the original publisher, Hirzel, and the book, including an illustrated version, was listed among the titles available from several additional publishing houses.[3] For some contemporary critics, *Die Ahnen* exemplified a national literature appropriate to solidifying the new national aggregate that had come into being under Prussian leadership. Indeed, in 1888 one School Inspector Grüllich could scarcely contain his enthusiasm for this Song of Songs "das uns Mannhaftigkeit und Hochherzigkeit, Treue und Liebe ins Herz singt."[4] The Saxon bureaucrat went so far as to assert that *Die Ahnen* took up subjects that only Germans could understand. Why is it, he asked in a voice bursting with nationalist pathos as he reviewed the German virtues he believed incorporated in *Die Ahnen*, that it is precisely this ancestral language that other nations have not understood?[5]

Such ethnocentric reactions on the part of nineteenth-century contemporaries may tempt us to read this cycle of historical novels as but one more straightforward example of the invention of a common German past, an idealized and monumentalized one that was to promote in German-speaking readers — from the center of power and from the top down — universal identification with the newly formed empire. Certainly one of Freytag's central themes in his pre-unification popular history, *Bilder aus der deutschen Vergangenheit* (1859–67), supports such a reading of *Die Ahnen*. In *Bilder* Freytag had stressed that writing in and of itself — and literature in particular — had served and could serve to bind all Germans together in, to use Benedict Anderson's oft-cited coinage, an "imagined community."[6] And in 1854 Freytag himself had insisted in his well-known review of Willibald Alexis's *Isegrimm* on an aesthetic of novel writing that corresponded to such an imagined harmonious national whole; that is, he had demanded of the historical novel a unified and conclusive plot (16: 189).

But not every contemporary considered *Die Ahnen* successful national literature, and from the beginning evaluations of the cycle varied. The irritation of one reviewer suggests, in fact, that some of Freytag's contemporaries recognized immediately that the author viewed German history through a markedly provincial window, a vision in which the inhabitants of the various regions were not yet integrated into an undifferentiated national totality. "Vergebens habe ich nach einem Grunde gesucht in dem ganzen Buch," the historian and novelist Felix Dahn complained in 1882 of the final volume of the cycle, "weßhalb jene Scheußlichkeiten gerade von Deutschen begangen werden müssen: es durften (nach der Anlage der Verwicklung) nicht Franzosen sein: aber Napoleon führte Polen, Italiener, Holländer mit sich: warum also Süddeutsche in diesem nationalen Werk so brandmarken?"[7] Certainly, as Dahn implies here, the Germany of Freytag's *Ahnen,* like the Germany of his other works, is decidedly North German and Protestant in outlook; but since 1882, when Dahn lodged his complaint, some have perceived the novel as offering a still narrower view.

In the late twentieth and early twenty-first centuries what was once touted as national literature is being marketed as regional literature. In 1992 a small publishing house, G. & M. Donhof, located in Arnstadt in Thuringia and specializing in local history, began issuing the first new edition of *Die Ahnen* since 1966. The four volumes that have appeared boast scenic covers ostensibly depicting local landscapes with a vaguely nostalgic appeal. In the summer of 1998 at least two bookstores in Arnstadt prominently displayed the three then extant volumes of the work, along with other historical and literary materials potentially of interest to locals or to tourists. The circumscribed setting of *Die Ahnen,* in fact, suggests such local appeal. In a review of the third volume of the cycle, for example, Fontane highlights precisely this narrow focus when he meticulously maps out the confined space of the setting of the first three volumes for the purpose, as he claims, of orienting the average reader, who, he thereby implies, is unlikely to recognize the area without some prompting.[8]

Together, Dahn's remarks, Donhof's new edition, and Fontane's review not only identify a regional bias but also forcefully raise the possibility that the account Freytag offers in *Die Ahnen* is less firmly identified with a new Prussian-centered culture of empire than might appear at first glance and than one would expect of a text generated by a self-declared Prussian patriot, an author whose longing for national unification had made him a Prussian sympathizer in the 1860s.[9] As I shall demonstrate, *Die Ahnen* does not present a harmonious national whole as a finished product of history but, instead, offers a collection of invented historical artifacts with tenuous connections to one another. Such an approach projects an integrated whole but, in the end, does not actually portray it; either the author cannot or will not do so. While such nineteenth-century reviewers as Karl Landmann praised *Die Ahnen* as depicting German life, German thinking, and German sensibility,[10] it remains unclear what this idea of German life, thought, and sensibility actually has to do with the politics of the new Prussian-led state. In fact, Freytag's cycle of novels projects a different kind of national community.

The View from the Margin

Prussia's rise to political power, of course, constitutes the extratextual historical surround to Freytag's cycle of novels, and the average reader — even girls — could be expected to know full well the telos of this history (the new German empire), even if they did not know the historical details. But Brandenburg, the territory that Freytag in an obituary for Willibald Alexis (1871) called "das Mutterland des neuen Reiches," the "Heimat" of the "Stammvolk des deutschen Kaisergeschlechts" (16: 197), is virtually absent from the cycle. Moreover, Freytag's novel creates a picture of national belonging that on the whole relies not on the bombastic, grandly militaristic, and spectacular centralizing images of nation for which Imperial Germany is known, and which would especially predominate in Germany under William II, but rather foregrounds the sentimental, regional, domestic, and intimate — this, I argue, despite the text's obvious interest in military matters and despite Freytag's claim that his witnessing the pan-German army of 1870–71 inspired the cycle (1: 222). In choosing the provinces as his settings in *Die Ahnen,* Freytag offered his contemporaries an alternative *affective* means of national identification and integration, one to some extent at odds with Germany as it was being constituted under Prussian hegemony but, nevertheless, one that obviously held enormous appeal for the German middle-class reading public in the Second Empire.[11]

The narrator concludes the first part of the last volume of *Die Ahnen,* the story of the defeat of Napoleon, with a programmatic statement that characterizes the tendency of the entire work, a statement that articulates his refocusing of national history:

> Die beste Kraft der Nation ist in diesen Jahren der Niederlage und Erhebung bei euch, den kleinen Leuten, nicht bei den Regierenden, deren Stolz und Wille als allzuschwach erfunden ist und nicht bei den Hoch- und Feingebildeten, deren Leuchte unsicher umherflackert und die auch nach dem Frieden noch nicht wissen, wo das Vaterland anfängt und aufhört. . . . Und wenn die späteren Geschlechter einst auf eure Zeit zurückschauen, werden sie, was gesund und groß war, am reichlichsten in den engen Stadthäusern und in den Dorfhütten finden, in denen ihr gelebt habt. (13: 244)

In this retelling of the national story, those in power are sometimes only a pale reflection of the nation, even at odds with it. Freytag seeks the pith of the nation rather in insignificant individuals living their lives in relative obscurity in the provinces, removed from the new capital city — the very title of this final volume, *Aus einer kleinen Stadt,* flags the provincial bias of the cycle. And just as School Inspector Grüllich recognized, Freytag's provincial protagonists do embody precisely those middle-class virtues that Freytag had long touted as typical of Germans in general: loyalty, sense of duty, sentimentality, warmth, enthusiasm, industry, democratic sensibilities, even temper, deliberateness, honesty, genuineness, domesticity, and sexual moderation.

Thomas Nipperdey rightly maintains that *Die Ahnen* in fact focuses not on the rise of the German national state per se but on the development of the German people; it represents an attempt to write "ein Epos des Volkes als des eigentlichen Subjekts der nationalen Geschichte."[12] The decision to foreground the German people most certainly frees Freytag from the obligation to trace the rise of Prussia per se, but it does not entirely explain his deliberate recentering of the nationalist vision on the local histories of politically insignificant territories. Let us consider this choice of setting.

The "Green Heart" of Germany as National Museum

Although eastern sites — Silesia, the place of Freytag's birth, and Torun on the Vistula in Polish territory that was later annexed by Prussia — gain in importance as the cycle advances toward the present, Thuringia, Freytag's second home, remains the key site of the enactment of the selective history presented in *Die Ahnen*. Local geography helps to cement the link between these nine discrete and only tenuously related stories that span 1400 years. Despite the shifting of scene over the course of the six volumes, the novel begins and ends on the same spot, in what was in the 1870s a part of Thuringia, that is, in Coburg — in the fourth century, atop the mountain on which the imposing fortress of Coburg would later stand, and in the nineteenth century in the museum within the fortress itself, a museum sponsored in Freytag's day by Duke Ernest II of Saxe-Coburg-Gotha (1818–93). Moreover, several generations in between return to this site. In the second part of the first volume we see Ingraban in the eighth century atop the same mountain with St. Boniface; at the conclusion of the fourth volume in 1530, the members of the König family turn up once again in the fortress of Coburg, asking Martin Luther for spiritual guidance.

Freytag's Thuringia is by no means the Thuringia of Weimar classicism, nor even the home of the "Klassikerstraße Thüringen" promoted by today's post-Cold War German tourism.[13] Weimar plays no role in any of the volumes,[14] and Goethe and Schiller are absent from the saga — as they nearly are from Freytag's *Bilder*, as well. Furthermore, during the years of the blossoming of German Romanticism in Jena, Freytag's focus in the cycle lies elsewhere — not in Thuringia but to the East, in Silesia. And, as I shall detail below, even the important high culture of medieval Thuringia, richly and repeatedly celebrated for a receptive German public in Richard Wagner's *Tannhäuser und der Sängerkrieg auf Wartburg* (premiere 1845), receives only a passing glance.¹⁵ Indeed, in *Die Ahnen* Freytag does not seek to re-create the cultural nation, the land of poets and philosophers, in which high culture — German literary and philosophical heritage — compensates for the absent unified state.¹⁶ If not on account of Weimar, the galvanizing center of German classicism, nor on account of Thuringia's literary and artistic production in general, why, then, did this sparsely populated and, in political and economical terms, relatively insignificant province present a suitable locale for Freytag's vision of a German nation?

Freytag, of course, knew Thuringia well, for he had spent his summers in Siebleben, near Gotha, since 1852; furthermore, he had found refuge in Gotha in 1854 when Prussia issued a secret warrant for his arrest. From 1867 to 1870 he had served as the representative of Erfurt in the North German Parliament. Through his friend Duke Ernest II, Freytag had come to know in Thuringia a local political culture that was both liberal and nationalist, the political and social direction that, as is well known, Freytag advocated for *his* Germany. Crown Prince Frederick William and Crown Princess Victoria, the hope of German liberals for the future united Germany, frequented the ducal palaces at Coburg and Gotha, and the duke maintained close ties to the British royal family, Europe's model constitutional monarchs — ties that had been established earlier in the century when his brother Albert had become the British prince consort. In the 1860s Coburg itself, with the support of Duke Ernest II, generally became a site of national foment: the first *Turn- und Jugendfest* took place in 1860, along with the first plenary meeting of the *Deutsche Nationalverein*. In 1862 a German *Sängerbund* was founded there. Furthermore, like Coburg, nearby Eisenach bore the weight of a rich history, one associated with Luther and German Protestantism and one that Freytag saw as liberating the common man. Eisenach had been frequently reaffirmed as a key site for the celebration of the German national idea since the famous Wartburgfest of 1817.¹⁷ At some level, then, we might see the regional setting of *Die Ahnen* simply as a tribute to the duke and to the national-liberal culture he fostered; certainly Freytag dedicates the book to Crown Princess Victoria. But, in fact, Freytag had more compelling reasons — both aesthetic and political — for locating his saga in Thuringia.

The Thuringia of the nineteenth century surfaces in *Die Ahnen* only in the form of the museum in the fortress at Coburg, but in precisely this museum lies the key to Freytag's choice of locales. Despite Thuringia's long and varied history, nineteenth-century contemporaries saw this province not as a center of power politics but as a different kind of center, as "das grüne Herz Deutschlands."[18] August Klippenberg wrote of the Thuringian Forest in his *Deutsches Lesebuch,* a reader for German girls' schools: "Man hat ihn einem frischen, grünen Blatte verglichen, das sich Deutschland zu Schmuck und Zierde an die Brust gesteckt hat."[19] Moreover, a French commentator observed, it was Germany's park.[20] Thuringia, with its spas and healthful climate, thus represented a benignly pastoral spot, a more or less empty geographical center of the German-speaking world and the new German empire, a space available to the play of the imagination and, in particular, of the historical imagination; and precisely this historical imagination had been hard at work in Thuringia throughout the century.

As a result of nationalist sentiment in Thuringia, the Wartburg and the fortress at Coburg had been transformed in the nineteenth century into expansive museums — indeed, especially in the case of the Wartburg, into temples to the nationalist historicism of the day.[21] In some sense they were emblematic for all of Thuringia: perhaps even more than the banks of the Rhine, Thuringia was acquiring the image of a vast museum, a sort of historical theme park filled with the ruins of the past: "Die meisten der hohen und starken Burgen die einst kühn und stolz sich auf den Bergspitzen erhoben, sind längst verfallen; nur Trümmerhaufen und geborstene Türme, welche der Efeu umrankt, sind noch von ihnen vorhanden," instructed Klippenberg. "Die Tore sind mit Schutt und Gesträuch verdeckt, in den öden Fensterhöhlen nisten die Eulen. Manche sind auch ganz von der Erde verschwunden, und die Tannen wurzeln auf ihrem Grunde. Mit Wehmut gedenken wir der Zeit, wo in diesen festen Schlössern mächtige Ritter lebten."[22] What better screen on which to project a historical fiction centered on private persons? Freytag exploits this green museum to present nine generations of a family, each with its attendant love story, while binding together *his* Germany. Thus, in some sense Freytag produced in this novel what Alon Confino has characterized as the past displayed in the *Heimat* museums that came into existence in the late nineteenth and early twentieth centuries: "popular, not elitist; local, not centralist; a simple past, easy to grasp, whether one was a historian or not."[23]

Situating the Universal German within Local Diversity

To understand Freytag's approach to imagining national community in *Die Ahnen* it is instructive to consider his best-selling *Soll und Haben* (Debit and Credit, 1855), a novel that at midcentury had sought to promote a sense of both national and class belonging. Here he had evoked the provincial setting of Breslau to stand in for the universal German. The phenomenal sales of this novel with a broad German-speaking public suggest that, at some level, he had succeeded.[24] In *Soll und Haben* the characters explicitly discuss the German national character, enabling Freytag to finesse the tension between local and national allegiances. He invokes the individual German's bond to the intimate and local, what he calls "Heimat," and claims that precisely this nostalgic bond to one's place of origin — *but not its particular content* — constitutes the universal German.[25] In universalizing such a capacity, he posits a German unity that transcends the particular and, at the same time, preserves it. His allegiance to this idea shapes his representation of the past, both in his *Bilder* and his *Ahnen,* and informs his strategy by which local histories represent the German nation. Indeed, in 1896 a school principal from Erfurt attempted to describe this double vision when he characterized Freytag in a commemorative speech as a "Mann von Heimatsgefühl und Vaterlandsliebe."[26]

A second key to Freytag's strategy for representing national community in *Die Ahnen* can be found in his popular history, *Bilder aus der deutschen Vergangenheit.* In this work Freytag occasionally displays an acute awareness — especially in his treatment of the borderland territory of Silesia — that varied groups comprise greater Germany, and, furthermore, that individuals are multiply determined by the circumstances into which they are born.[27] Such awareness also informs his later narrative of himself. "Daß es für mich leicht wurde," Freytag writes in the opening pages of his autobiography of 1887, "in den Kämpfen meiner Zeit auf der Seite zu stehen, welcher die größten Erfolge zufielen, das verdanke ich nicht mir selbst, sondern der Fügung, daß ich als Preuße, als Protestant und als Schlesier unweit der polnischen Grenze geboren bin" (1: 4). Given the now infamous caricatures of Jews and of Poles in *Soll und Haben,* one may well be inclined to overlook Freytag's sometimes complex understanding of German nationality: yet, here in his memoirs, even as he positions himself on the side of the triumphant forces of the age, he also proposes a hybrid identity for himself, one that incorporates both the Prussian at the center and the Silesian at the margin. Sympathy with the new Germany has come easily for him personally, he declares, not because he possesses a priori a universal German identity but, rather, because of a fortunate and fortuitous intersection of identities, one that matches perfectly with the dominant and, in his opinion, best strains of the new state. To some extent *Die Ahnen* is about the weaving together of such diverse identities, a process that creates citizens appropriate to a projected German national state.

In *Die Ahnen* Freytag picks up and expands precisely the theme of ethnic mix and diverse identities that he had developed in *Bilder,* where he had contended that the Germans were a blended people. Even as Freytag depicts the struggles of regional Germans against the Poles and Sorbs in black-and-white terms, he attempts in this cycle of novels to make certain that the various German-speaking groups are not foreign to one another. He begins weaving the nation together as his characters migrate back and forth along an east-west axis, intermarrying not only with the locals but also across class lines.

In the first volume Freytag's protagonist Ingo is a Vandal king who has fled from the east to Thuringia. As I shall discuss below in greater detail, in the third volume the knight Ivo and his family travel eastward with the Teutonic Knights and aid in the founding of Torun on the Vistula. In the fourth volume the son of a prominent citizen of Torun marries a scholar's daughter from the Electorate of Saxony and migrates back westward to serve Luther in Thuringia and eventually to establish himself in Frankfurt. In part one of the fifth volume the soldier Bernhard König has traveled with his regiment to Thuringia, where he meets Judith, who was driven from Silesia and wishes to return there. Bernard and Judith are murdered at the very moment when they catch sight of Judith's childhood home in Silesia. Their descendants turn up in Saxony in part two of volume 5, and one of them travels to Torun to rescue his beloved, whose family has strong ties there. In volume 6 Dr. König settles in a small town in Silesia, but during the wars of liberation he finds himself guarding the main road to Erfurt. König's son Viktor eventually moves westward in pursuit of his studies and a career, finally to appear as a visitor in the museum in the fortress of Coburg on the spot where the cycle began. In the process, the König family has ramified in many directions and absorbed different peoples; in fact, in the last volume Freytag surprises us with the existence of a French branch of the family.

Die Brüder vom deutschen Hause: National Brotherhood and Middle Class

A closer look at volume 3 of *Die Ahnen, Die Brüder vom deutschen Hause* (The Brothers of the German House, 1874), positioned roughly in the middle of the cycle and teetering on the brink of the modern world, can clarify the drift and substance of Freytag's project. Here, in a novel that combines elements of medieval romance and modern stories of male coming of age, we see how the local history of Thuringia provides the opportunity for the author to knit together his two central themes: the formation of the middle class and the mixture of German peoples across various territories. Conceived as a pivotal moment in German history, this fiction of thirteenth-century Thuringia at the time of the sixth Crusade brings home Freytag's alternative vision of national belonging.

Die Brüder vom deutschen Hause — the title alludes to the Teutonic Knights, who, as we shall see, play a significant role in the novel — opens "auf dem Wege von den roten Bergen nach Erfurt" (10: 3) in the year 1226. This is not the Thuringia of Landgrave Hermann (1190–1217), the patron of Heinrich von Veldeke, Wolfram von Eschenbach, Herbort von Fritzlar, and Walter von der Vogelweide; indeed, the narrator summarily dismisses Hermann as a weak man, without mentioning his patronage of the arts (10: 32). Rather, Thuringia constitutes a site of struggle between clergy and layman, between landgrave and free knight, between rival branches of noble families, between free peasants and petty nobility — struggles that, the novel hints, are taking place throughout the empire even as the Holy Roman Emperor, Frederick II, pursues other ambitions in Italy and Palestine.

An early episode in which we view the free peasants of Friemar in the midst of their May festivities sets the tone for the class instability and class conflict that constitute a central theme in this volume. Local petty nobility attempt to join in festivities where they do not belong, and Berthold, the son of the village judge, prances about in fancy clothes that testify to his social aspirations — eventually, Berthold will abandon his father and, to the latter's chagrin, will give up his status as free peasant to serve a master as a knight, a choice diametrically opposed to the central message of the novel: that it is better to be the master of oneself than a vassal, no matter how powerful a vassal (10: 308). To evoke thirteenth-century Thuringia, Freytag relies on two literary works from the period (N.B.: neither of them from Thuringia): the poetry of Neidhardt von Reuenthal, written between 1210 and Neidhardt's death in 1250, and *Meier Helmbrecht* (1250/80); Freytag's female protagonist Friderun owes her name to the peasant girl who figures in Neidhardt's bawdy satiric poetry. Seven years earlier, in *Bilder,* Freytag had called on both of these thirteenth-century works as historical documents to testify to his assessment of the age, that is, to precisely his sense of the age as riven with social conflict: "Groß war in den Jahren des reisigen Minnegesangs die Abneigung zwischen Hof und Dorf, zwischen höfisch und bäurisch . . ." (18: 50).

Although relying on literature from the period for historical background, the novel on the whole takes a dim view of the poetry of high court culture, the cult of *Minne* — the love of a high-born lady — and jousting for the sake of a lady's favor or for personal glory. Freytag unsurprisingly positions himself squarely on the side of those who oppose courtly practices — unsurprisingly, given his modern-day views of aristocracy and his own stubborn refusal of an aristocratic title offered him by Ernest II.[28] Although our hero, the petty aristocrat Ivo, pursues these courtly activities for the sake of his love for the exotic Hedwig, the niece of the Holy Roman Emperor, he ultimately proves to be immature and misguided, neglectful of his obligations to his dependents, and unable to settle down and start a family until he abandons these pursuits.[29]

Literacy of a kind other than the composing of love songs at which Ivo is so adroit proves far more important in this novel in establishing the dignity of a projected German middle class: as a kind of foreshadowing of the Bible translations that will one day take place in Thuringia, Bernhard, the elderly judge of the free village of Friemar, tries to learn to read; he aims to read the translation of pieces of the New Testament that came into his possession when, at Ivo's request, he aided a battered vagrant. Near the conclusion of volume three Bernhard finds the courage to resist the power of the papacy, for he knows that the demands of the pope contradict Holy Scripture: "An der Aufforderung des Papstes aber, welchen Ihr den Heiligen Vater nennt, erkennen wir, daß sie hohem Zeugnis der Schrift widerstrebt" (10: 311).

Freytag leans heavily on Thuringia's geographical location at the putative center of the kingdom of Germany and the German empire — his conception of the dimensions of thirteenth-century Germany seems to be influenced by the dimensions of the Germany of the 1870s; in the thirteenth century Franconia, not Thuringia, lay at the geographical center of the kingdom of Germany — when Hermann von Salza, the Grand Master of the Teutonic Order, himself a Thuringian,[30] calls on Ivo to join the Holy Roman Emperor in a crusade to the Holy Land:

> Vor anderen aber sind es Edle und Ritter des Thüringer Landes, auf die er [der Kaiser] hofft. Denn wie ein Herzland liegt es in der Mitte und die größte Kraft ist hier gesammelt, ich darf das zum Lobe meiner Heimat wohl sagen. Wenn wir jetzt in edler Schar über das Meer ziehen, so tun wir dies auch, um den Namen der Deutschen zu Ehren zu bringen und eine Herrschaft unseres Blutes über die Länder am Südmeere zu begründen. (10: 137)

Like the author himself,[31] Hermann has come to a German identity of sorts by comparing his own people with the foreign peoples he has met in his travels to Jerusalem: "Da lernte ich unsere heimische Art mit der fremden vergleichen, und ich fand, daß wir nicht schlechter waren als jene" (10: 137). At the very moment at which Hermann addresses Ivo as a fellow German, Ivo feels a personal bond to his people as never before: "Aber während er den Grund eines tiefen Quells erschauen wollte, gewahrte er darin plötzlich sein eigenes Bild. Ihm stieg das Blut ins Gesicht als er fühlte, daß eine Kränkung seines Volkes auch Kränkung seiner eigenen Ehre war . . ." (10: 138).

In allowing Ivo to confront his own image at the very moment he becomes conscious of his membership in a nation, the author has briefly made his hero privy to his own liberal sense of history, one in which the individual carries within himself, in miniature, the spirit of the entire people. "Jeder Mensch trägt und bildet in seiner Seele die geistige Habe des Volkes," Freytag writes in *Bilder* of the relationship between the individual and the whole, "jeder besitzt die Sprache, ein Wissen, eine Empfindung für Recht und Sitte, in jedem aber erscheint dies allgemeine Volksgut gefärbt, eingeengt, beschränkt durch seine persönliche Eigenart" (17: 23). Like Hermann, Ivo in turn comes truly to know himself, to test his mettle in encounters with foreign peoples. As parts of a whole, the diverse German localities function similarly: they both contribute to and reflect the whole, albeit in various individual garbs.

Ivo does far more in the Holy Land than test his prowess in the art of war. Although born to bear arms, he dons a work apron to aid the Teutonic Knights in the building of a fortress (10: 178–81). Untutored in surveying and architecture, Ivo nevertheless manages to win the favor of Brother Sibold, a one-time merchant from Bremen, to whom he has been detailed. Brother Sibold hints that such a fortress might be expanded to a city if one knew the art that the North Germans and the Magdeburgers have learned in their travels in the Baltic. Prophetically, he instructs Ivo, "Solche Werke gedeihen bei uns überall, wo die Kaufleute ihre Bank unter den Ostleuten aufschlagen und die Bauern ihnen nachziehen, um auf neuer Scholle zu siedeln" (10: 182).

The title of volume three, *Die Brüder vom deutschen Hause,* refers to the Teutonic Knights, who play a central role. Given Freytag's undisguised advocacy of the bourgeois family throughout his writings, particularly in a work titled *Die Ahnen*, this celibate religious brotherhood may initially seem an unlikely choice as usher to the modern world. Yet, precisely in this choice we can observe Freytag working his central themes of local history and national unity. While the novel reveals the conquest of the Holy Land to be a dubious adventure, led by a German emperor whose sense of his own Germanness is at best uncertain,[32] the Teutonic Knights prove themselves in Freytag's rendering as in some sense a model national force, even as they retain a strange otherworldliness as the bearded Brothers of Mary (*Marienbrüder*). The brotherhood absorbs members from many parts of Germany — the members are identified by their point of origin — and various social classes,[33] merchants as well as knights; the brotherhood is even able to absorb non-Germans, as witnessed by the presence of Brother Gottfried, the Saracen.[34] Its members wield the sword not so much as a way of life but for strictly defined and limited purposes. More important, they devote themselves to constructivist activities: healing and building fortresses — indeed, cities. Freytag launches here a fantasy of equality and unanimity that bridges difference, one in which alert readers might see the faint reflection of a wished-for modern orderly state composed of male citizens from all regions of Germany, citizens who will bear arms as necessary but who pursue what he sees as civilizing activities in their daily lives. Freytag projects the brotherhood into the future when he has his protagonist, Ivo, join the order as a *"Zugewandter,"* a lay brother who is not obliged to take vows of celibacy, who will produce offspring. In the end the knight and lay brother Ivo marries his childhood friend Friderun, the daughter of a freeman, thus providing the foundation of a middle class that will turn up 300 years later in the following volume, *Marcus König,* as the patricians of Torun.

The eastward migration, led by the Teutonic Order, provides a stirring conclusion to *Die Brüder vom deutschen Hause* and constitutes a defining moment of the entire cycle, for it reverses the westward movement of the first volume. In these final pages Freytag employs a vocabulary that recalls that of Manifest Destiny in the American context: "tausend Jahre nach der Auswanderung jener alten Germanen begannen die Thüringe und Sachsen an der Stromgrenze auf neue den Kampf gegen die Fremden, mit stärkeren Waffen und festerer Kraft" (10: 324). The train of colonists leaves behind the red hills of Thuringia, singing the song of the crusade and seeking land where they can live in freedom and where they will found the city of Torun.

Given his well-known colonialist views toward the Poles and Poland, as evidenced in both *Soll und Haben* and *Bilder,* the allure of Thuringia's local history for Freytag as he wrote this volume of *Die Ahnen* once again becomes clear: the Grand Master Hermann von Salza sent the Teutonic Order from the heartland to the east to convert the heathen Prussians, a Slavic people; to this day Erfurt commemorates with a plaque the one-time presence of the Teutonic Order. But more important for our understanding of Freytag's vision of German nation than the particular prejudices he harbored against the Poles is his representation here of the Germans in general as a people of colonizers, a view he had expressed in *Bilder*.

Even in 1874, when Freytag was writing *Brüder*, Germany had not yet entered the European colonialist game in Africa and Asia in a significant way; but as Susanne Zantop argues, abundant colonial fantasies preceded the fact of German colonialism in the third world. In particular, the Germans saw themselves as good colonizers who did not necessarily employ force as they civilized and absorbed foreign peoples.[35] Freytag's work shares in such fantasies. In Freytag's vision the German penetration of Eastern territories constitutes a productive civilizing process; it leads to the building of towns and the cultivation of farms. Ivo fights against the heathens as a warrior, but as the final line of the novel brings home, the role of warrior is superseded by another role when he makes his new home in Torun: "aus einem thüringischen Edlen der Ivo, den sie den König nannten, [wurde] ein Burgmann von Thorn" (10: 329).

From a nationalist point of view this final chapter arguably constitutes a high point of the novel, one scarcely reached again in the cycle — except, perhaps, in volume 6 in the reading of the king's call to arms against Napoleon in the village church (13: 207–8). In briefly summarizing the Germans' frontier encounter with the Slavs in the final chapter of *Brüder,* Freytag comes close to offering a broad and unified vision of the German people, a wide-angle focus that in this cycle of novels he generally shuns in favor of the detail of private lives — or, rather, he demonstrates here how private lives are interwoven with a national sweep of history. This brief picture of unity and national destiny will, of course, be quickly shattered in the following volume, *Marcus König,* where, 300 years later, Torun has lost its independence and owes allegiance to the Polish crown.

One final aspect of *Brüder* may serve to bring home Freytag's strategy in representing regional histories as national history: his construction of the female protagonist of the story, Friderun, the daughter of a free peasant. At the emperor's court in Otranto, Friderun, identified as the girl from Thuringia (10: 277), appears in the gray cloak of the Teutonic Order, "daß sie aussah wie ein Geist der heimatlichen Berge" (10: 277). Even as she here incorporates the particular spirit of the Thuringian heartland, her physiognomy elsewhere recalls nineteenth-century nationalist renditions of a vigilant blonde Germania, both martial and motherly. All eyes are on Friderun when she first appears in the novel:

> [W]ie eine Herrin empfing sie Gruß und Huldigung, eine hochgewachsene kräftige Gestalt von vollen Formen, in dem runden Gesicht strahlten zwei tiefblaue Augen, ihr blondes Haar war so lang, daß sie die Zöpfe um das Haupt geschlungen trug, und doch hingen sie ihr bis tief über den Gürtel hinab. Die hohe Stirn, die starken Brauen gaben ihr einen ernsthaften Ausdruck, darunter aber lachten rosige Wangen, ein kleiner Mund und das Grübchen am Kinn. (10: 21)

The "masculine" determination of her brow, combined with the girlish lower half of her face, reproduces the curious combination of mother-warrior seen repeatedly in graphic and poetic representations of Germania.[36] Friderun will, of course, not only become the mother of Ivo's children and the ancestor, albeit a forgotten one, of the protagonists of later volumes; in her lifetime she has her own mission to fulfill: she must rescue Ivo. Her composite parts and roles include the "masculine" spirit of nationalism and the "feminine" intimacy and comfort of "*Heimat*."

When Friderun at another point in the novel appears at Christmastide in the role of Mary, the Queen of Heaven, enveloped in her own golden hair, the narrative once again highlights the thick blonde hair that repeatedly symbolizes the vitality of the nation in nineteenth-century representations of Germania: "die Fülle des langen blonden Haars hing gelöst über den Mantel und umgab ihr Haupt und Leib wie ein goldener Schleier" (10: 123). This syncretic representation pays homage to medieval images of Mary but also foregrounds the national type embodied by the allegorical figure of Germania in the nineteenth century.

Precisely this national type helps Ivo to free himself of the lethargy that has overtaken him while in Arab captivity. Here Ivo, who is painfully slow to come to a realization of his feelings for Friderun — indeed, of his love, his homesickness, for his Thuringian homeland in general — has a vision of Friderun's blonde braids even as he watches a scantily clad, brown-skinned Arab woman dance "und ich schob das [arabische] Mädchen zur Seite, um das Haar der Deutschen zu fassen" (10: 265). From this moment onward Ivo actively seeks his freedom and his return from the Middle East to the German world: that is, to his home in Thuringia.

Postunification Nostalgia for a Projected Liberal State

In the final volume of *Die Ahnen* the descendants of the characters who figure in the first volumes turn up in rival fraternities — notably, they are still identified regionally, indeed, tribally: they are "Thüringe" and "Vandale" and not "Germanen," "Teutonen," or "Deutsche." Freytag has dispensed with the founding nationalist idea of the "Allgemeine Deutsche Burschenschaft" of 1817 as including all German men in a single fraternity and has presented fraternities as local rival university clubs (as they, in fact, were at the time he was writing his novel). The König family member who figures in this final part of *Die Ahnen* is, unsurprisingly, a bourgeois; the descendant of König's thirteenth-century ancestor's marshal, Henner, is an aristocrat. Despite their initial clash, these characters learn to live with one another, and the aristocrat marries a bourgeoise and the bourgeois König marries an aristocratic woman.

The final glimpse of these descendants who unwittingly recall their own most ancient ancestors may not be the trivialization of the first volume for which some contemporaries took it. If the König family began as kings, as it were, then Freytag makes here the important point that in the larger scheme of history these were only kings of the tiniest of kingdoms, no more than a farm in one of present-day Germany's many tiny regions. More important than their one-time political power over others are the virtues that they embodied and embody and that they have cultivated over the centuries within tight family units, the virtues that mysteriously resurfaced in each generation of Königs and eventually formed the middle-class ethos on which a national — and, as Freytag hoped — liberal state could be founded.

Scholars have frequently remarked that Freytag had his cycle conclude in 1848, twenty-three years before German unification under Prussia and thirty-two years before the publication of the last volume of *Die Ahnen*. As Otto Brahm noted in 1881, some contemporaries were dismayed that Freytag's national saga ended, as he phrased it, in the realm of the petty bourgeois and provincial instead of portraying Prussia's glorious victory over the French in 1871.[37] And Freytag's decision to end his novel in 1848 is all the more striking given that in his memoirs he cites his experiences observing the battlefields of the Franco-Prussian War as the impetus for the cycle of novels. Freytag himself offered as an explanation for truncating the novel that he was writing fiction and that fiction would suffer if it came up too hard against the political reality that his readers knew so well (1: 254–55). At first glance this explanation may appear disingenuous; but, in fact, the national political climate of the present that his readers knew all too well *was* at odds with the liberal, provincial, and multifaceted Germany that his *Ahnen* evoked. By concluding his story of the König family before unification he did not have to confront the disparity and could, instead, project a national-liberal ideal from the standpoint of 1848.[38]

Claus Holz maintains in an insightful and highly critical study of *Die Ahnen, Flucht vor der Wirklichkeit* (Flight from Reality), that Freytag presents a decidedly unrealistic view of the new nation, one that fails to take account of the central political, economic, and social changes of the second half of the nineteenth century.[39] Holz's criticism is well taken if we evaluate the realism or truth-value of works of the imagination by their fidelity to historical fact. As Holz claims, Freytag does not present an accurate historical-political account of the nineteenth century. Nevertheless, in positing mere escapism, Holz misses the opportunity to assess the cultural significance of *Die Ahnen,* which, after all, never pretends to be anything but fiction and which, as a cultural artifact, does embody a kind of truth — or, we might say, realism about the culture that produced it. Indeed, the interesting point about *Die Ahnen* is not its historical inaccuracy but the fact that this historically inaccurate vision of Germany played so well with the middle-class reading public when it first appeared. In other words, the reading public seems to have willingly participated in Freytag's "unrealistic" but intimate and cozy view of the nation — at least in their leisure hours.

In sum, this tale is not the seamless narrative that one might expect of a family saga, written postunification, that begins in the fourth century and marches toward the present; rather, it is an assemblage of stories. *Die Ahnen* does not trace ancestry per se, despite the implications of the title; it is not a German *Roots*.[40] In fact, for most of the cycle only the reader bears knowledge of the generations from volume to volume, generations who in the earlier volumes are separated from one another by 200 to 300 years and who have little, distorted, or no knowledge whatsoever of one another. In the dedication of the novel Freytag stresses the lack of nostalgia of the last descendent of the König family: "Dies Werk ... beginnt mit Ahnen aus früher Zeit, und wird ... allmählich bis zu dem letzten Enkel fortgeführt werden, einem frischen Gesellen, der noch jetzt unter der deutschen Sonne dahin wandelt, ohne viel um Thaten und Leiden seiner Vorfahren zu sorgen."

Freytag's characters do not, in fact, display a longing for the past in this historical novel but, rather, tend to exhibit a buoyant amnesia that keeps the past from weighing too heavily on them. The past haunts the present of each subsequent volume in the form of legends, which, as only the reader knows, do not correspond to the historical facts; impersonal artifacts, such as the flint arrowheads found in the final volume at the ramparts of the Vandals; and even ghosts, namely, the "*Brunnenweib*" (woman of the well) of volume six, whose appearance allegedly portends misfortune — possibly a misremembering of the tragedy that concludes volume five (13: 41). In the end, Freytag depends on the reader's knowledge, perception, and imagination — indeed, on the reader's, not the characters', nostalgia for the lives that filled past volumes to hold together the histories he displays.

This cycle thus creates allegiance to a new national aggregate through a collection of the individual and local. It presents not the mythologizing heroic frescoes found in public buildings and not the larger-than-life monuments that had sprung up and would spring up throughout Germany over the course of the century but, rather, the intimacy of the *Genrebild*.[41] We see this perhaps most graphically illustrated in a tender scene in the final volume, *Aus einer kleinen Stadt* (From a Small Town), that takes place at what had once been a site of bloody conflict, the ramparts of the Vandals. Freytag writes: "Der Doktor stand wie bezaubert, der Wallring umschanzte das liebe Mädchen und ihn gegen die ganze Welt, nichts war zu sehen, als der Himmel, welcher wie eine lichtblaue Glocke über dem Ringe stand" (13: 39). This blue sky stretches over the lives of Freytag's characters and over those of his readers, uniting them in a sentimentality that is paradoxically, by means of the act of reading, both private and shared. For Freytag, Germany remained, to borrow Celia Applegate's coinage, "a nation of provincials,"[42] and in the 1870s he was not wrong to think so. His account of the König family amounts, in the end, to a sort of *Heimatmuseum* before the fact, a collection of sentimental local and private histories that both displace and project a national history. This quality may explain its healthy sales, which occurred despite the fact that the reviews by the pundits in the new empire were decidedly mixed.

Notes

[*] I borrow the phrase from my colleague William H. Gass, whose anthology *In the Heart of the Heart of the Country and Other Stories* appeared in 1977.

[1] The publication of each successive volume was, in fact, timed to take advantage of the Christmas market. Fontane remarks on this marketing strategy in the opening lines of his review of the third volume of *Die Ahnen*. Theodor Fontane, "Gustav Freytags Die Ahnen," in his *Sämtliche Werke*, ed. Kurt Schreinert (Munich: Nymphenburger Verlagshandlung, 1963), 21.1: 231. Freytag himself wrote to Duke Ernest II that he was earning a great deal of money with *Die Ahnen* and later claimed in his autobiography that of all his works his publisher had earned the greatest profit with this family saga. *Gustav Freytag und Herzog Ernest von Coburg im Briefwechsel 1853 bis 1893*, ed. Eduard Tempeltey (Leipzig: S. Hirzel, 1904), 256, 291; Gustav Freytag, "Erinnerungen aus meinem Leben," in his *Gesammelte Werke*, 22 vols. (Leipzig: S. Hirzel, 1896–98), 1: 238. Further references to this edition of Freytag's works will appear parenthetically in the text with volume and page number.

[2] See, e.g., Caroline S. J. Milde, *Der deutschen Jungfrau Wesen und Wirken: Winke für das geistige und praktische Leben*, 4th ed. (Leipzig: C. F. Amelang, 1878), 157. As Gisela Wilkending points out, *Die Ahnen* inspired Brigitte Augusti's (1839–1930) series of historical novels "für das reifere Mädchenalter" [for more mature girlhood] titled *Am deutschen Herd* [On the German Hearth] that appeared in the 1880s. Gisela Wilkending, *Kinder und Jugendliteratur: Mädchenliteratur vom 18. Jahrhundert bis zum Zweiten Weltkrieg, Eine Textsammlung* (Reclam: Stuttgart, 1994), 496.

[3] Gustav Freytag, *Die Ahnen: Roman*, 35th ed. (Leipzig: S. Hirzel, 1906–07). The individual volumes are listed as various editions: vol. 1, *Ingo und Ingraban*, 35th ed. (1907); vol. 2, *Das Nest der Zaunkönige*, 30th ed. (1906); vol. 3, *Die Brüder vom deutschen Hause*, 24th ed. (1906); vol. 4, *Marcus König*, 21st ed. (1906); vol. 5, *Die Geschwister*, 20th ed. (1906); vol. 6, *Aus einer kleinen Stadt*, 17th ed. (1906). The editions appearing simultaneously from other publishers that I have been able to confirm include *Die Ahnen, bebilderte ungekürzte Ausgabe* (Berlin: Kurt Wolff, n.d.), *Die Ahnen: Roman*,

vollständige Ausgabe (Berlin: Th. Knaur, 1900), *Die Ahnen, vollständige Ausgabe* (Berlin: Schreiter, 1900); *Ingo und Ingraban* (Berlin: Wegweiser-Verlag, 1910), *Die Ahnen*, pt. I, *Ingo,* authorized ed., ed. Otto Siepmann (London & New York: Macmillan, 1906), and *Die Ahnen: Roman, vollständige Ausgabe* (Berlin: M. Maschler, 1900).

[4] Schulrath Grüllich, *Was können wir aus Freytags "Ahnen" lernen. Vortrag, gehalten im Bezirks-Lehrerverein Dresden-Land* (Meißen: H. W. Schlimpert, 1888), 28.

[5] Grüllich, 21.

[6] Benedict Anderson, *Imagined Communities: Reflections on the Origin and Spread of Nationalism* (London: Verso, 1983).

[7] Dahn (1834–1912) was born in Hamburg but had spent his adult life in Bavaria, studying in Munich and teaching at the University of Würzburg.

[8] Fontane, 231–32.

[9] See, e.g., Freytag's letter of 30 January 1860, in *Gustav Freytag und Herzog Ernest von Coburg im Briefwechsel,* 130–32. In this exchange the duke is considerably more skeptical of Prussia than is Freytag, who believes that Prussia is Germany's only hope for unification. Freytag, however, shows himself not to be uncritical of Prussia.

[10] Karl Landmann, "Deutsche Liebe und deutsche Treue in Gustav Freytags 'Ahnen,'" *Zeitschrift für den deutschen Unterricht* 6 (1892): 81.

[11] For a discussion of similar strategies in his *Bilder aus der deutschen Vergangenheit* in the period before the founding of Imperial Germany, see Lynne Tatlock, "Regional Histories as National History: Gustav Freytag's Bilder aus der deutschen Vergangenheit (1859–67)," in Nicholas Vazsonyi, ed., *Searching for Common Ground: Diskurse zur deutschen Identität* (Cologne: Böhlau, 2000), 161–78.

[12] Nipperdey, qtd. by Peter Sprengel, "Der Liberalismus auf dem Weg ins 'neue Reich': Gustav Freytag und die Seinen 1866–1871," in Klaus Amann and Karl Wagner, eds., *Literatur und Nation: Die Gründung des deutschen Reiches* (Vienna: Böhlau, 1996), 154.

[13] See, e.g., Erich Taubert, *Classical Road Thuringia,* 2nd ed. (Weimar: Weimardruck GmbH, 1994): "The name 'Klassikerstraße Thüringen' has been used since 1992 for a 300 km route along the paths of the German classicists.... The term 'classicism' ... should be understood in a general sense and includes all the historic achievements of literature and fine arts" (3).

[14] In the final volume one of the leaders of the national rebellion alludes disparagingly to Weimar intellectuals' admiration of Napoleon (13: 162).

[15] Ivo alludes briefly in volume 3 (10: 265) to the Thuringian legend of the *Venusberg* [Mountain of Venus] that figures so largely in Wagner's opera.

[16] This is, of course, not to say that Freytag's Thuringia owes nothing to German literature. On the contrary. Medievalists and early modernists will readily recognize literary influences, especially in the third, fourth, and fifth volumes.

[17] In setting much of the cycle in Thuringia, Freytag might have leaned heavily on the myth of Barbarossa — Kyffhäuser, after all, lies in Thuringia — but even this centralist national legend, which just happens to have its home in Thuringia, receives little attention. Instead, in volume 3 the narrator merely alludes in passing to the court of Barbarossa (10: 40) and the legend of Kyffhausen (10: 273).

[18] While Duke Ernest's ultimate support of Prussia had important symbolic force, the principal economic and social developments of the nineteenth century — urbanization and industrialization — were taking place elsewhere: along the Rhine, in the Ruhr, in Berlin, etc. Thuringia, on the other hand, was devoid of important rivers and lacking in population.

[19] August Klippenberg, *Deutsches Lesebuch für höhere Mädchenschulen*, Edition A, pt. 3, 22nd ed. (Hannover: Norddeutsche Verlagsanstalt O. Goedel, 1903), 191.

[20] Édouard Humbert, *Dans la forêt de Thuringe (1862)*, qtd. in *Deutsches Lesebuch für höhere Lehranstalten: Bearbeitung des Döbelner Lesebuchs für Mittel- und Norddeutschland in engem Anschluß an die neuesten preußischen Lehrpläne von Direktor M. Evers und Professor H. Walz*, Edition A, pt. 5: *Für evangelische Anstaltungen* (Leipzig: Teubner, 1903), 217.

[21] In 1853 the duke had offered to make the *Ausschuß für die Errichtung eines Germanischen Nationalmuseums* [Committee for the Establishment of a Germanic National Museum] a present of the Veste Coburg and its art treasures, only to have the offer turned down. Norbert Klüglein, *Coburg Stadt und Land*, 3rd ed. (Coburg: Verkehrsverein Coburg e.V., 1995), 83.

[22] Klippenberg, 193.

[23] Alon Confino, *The Nation as a Local Metaphor. Württemberg, Imperial Germany, and National Memory, 1871–1918* (Chapel Hill: U of North Carolina P), 153.

[24] Hartmut Steinecke, "Gustav Freytag: *Soll und Haben* (1855). Weltbild und Wirkung eines deutschen Bestellers," in Horst Denkler, ed., *Romane und Erzählungen des Bürgerlichen Realismus: Neue Interpretationen* (Stuttgart: Reclam, 1980), 138–52.

[25] See Tatlock, "Regional Histories and National History," esp. 172–73.

[26] H. Neubauer, Schuldirektor a.D. *Zur Erinnerung an Gustav Freytag: Vortrag, gehalten in der ordentlichen Sitzung der Königlichen Akademie gemeinnütziger Wissenschaften zu Erfurt am 29. Mai 1895*. Sonderdruck aus den Jahrbüchern der Königl. Akademie gemeinnütziger Wissenschaften zu Erfurt, n.s. 22 (Erfurt: Carl Villaret, 1896), 5.

[27] See Tatlock, "Regional Histories as National History," esp. 176–78.

[28] Friedrich Seiler, *Gustav Freytag, mit 28 Abbildungen* (Leipzig: Voigtländer, 1898), 217–18.

[29] Similarly, in *Soll und Haben* Freytag presents the protagonist's love for an aristocratic woman as derailing a promising middle-class career. Of course, the interludes in which the protagonists of these two novels pursue these foolish adventures may have provided the contemporary reading public with the more pleasurable reading.

[30] Hermann von Salza was thought to come from Langensalza in Thuringia.

[31] In his memoirs he writes of the formative experience of growing up on the border between Germany and Poland: "Als Kind der Grenze lernte ich früh mein deutsches Wesen im Gegensatz zu fremden Volksthum lieben. . . ." [As a child of the borderland I learned early on to cherish my German nature in contrast to foreign nations. . . .] (1: 2).

[32] When Frederick II asks about his own identity as a German, Hermann answers him with a parable. Hermann once had a silver plate from Goslar that he had refashioned by an Arabian goldsmith into a chalice. The goldsmith covered the silver with gold plate from Roman coins and colored it in the artful manner known only to the "infidels." After many years the gold plate has rubbed off in places, and the German silver is shining through again. Hermann suggests that in the emperor's case, the weight of the years has enabled his Germanness to shine through again (10: 153–54).

[33] In the following volume, set 300 years later, we learn that the order, which has fallen on evil days, no longer accepts those who are not of noble descent (11: 26).

[34] Freytag touts the Germans' alleged ability to absorb and learn from non-German peoples in *Bilder*. See Tatlock, "Regional Histories as National History," esp. 176, 178–79. This motif is repeated in the final volume of *Die Ahnen*, in which a French officer turns out also to be a *König* and the Polish officer Witkowski effectively serves the Silesian corps.

[35] Susanne Zantop, *Colonial Fantasies: Conquest, Family, and Nation in Precolonial Germany, 1770–1870* (Durham NC: Duke University Press, 1997).

[36] See, e.g., Ferdinand Freiligrath's poem of 1870, "Hurra Germania," in which a Germania who is peacefully harvesting her fields is transformed into a warrior by the aggression of the French: "Wie kühn mit vorgebeugtem Leib / Am Rheine stehst du da! / Im vollem Brand der Juliglut, / Wie ziehst du [f]risch dein Schwert! / Wie trittst du zornig frohgemut/ Zum Schutz vor deinen Herd! / Hurra, hurra, hurra! / Hurra, Germania!" [How boldly with body bent forward / You stand there at the Rhine! / In the full flame of the July heat, / How you briskly draw your sword! / How, filled with anger, you step before your hearth, exultant, in its defense]. Ferdinand Freiligrath, *Freiligraths Werke in 6 Teilen*, ed. Julius Schwering (Berlin: Bong, n.d.), pt. 3: 47. See also, e.g., Marie-Louise von Plessen, *"Germania aus dem Fundus," Marianne und*

Germania 1789–1889: Frankreich und Deutschland: zwei Welten — eine Revue (Berlin: Argon, 1996), 31–36.

[37] Otto Brahm, "Der Schlußband von Freytag's 'Ahnen,'" Deutsche Rundschau 26 (1881): 315.

[38] In fact, as Daniel Fulda argues, Freytag displays in *Die Ahnen* much less confidence in an emergent national totality than he had some fourteen years earlier, when he completed *Bilder* shortly after the Austrian defeat in the Austro-Prussian War. Daniel Fulda, "Telling German History: Forms and Functions of the Historical Narrative against the Background of the National Unifications," in Walter Pape, ed., *1870/71–1989/90: German Unifications and the Change of Literary Discourse* (Berlin: de Gruyter, 1993), 195–230.

[39] Claus Holz, *Flucht aus der Wirklichkeit. "Die Ahnen" von Gustav Freytag: Untersuchungen zum realistischen historischen Roman der Gründerzeit 1872–1880*, Europäische Hochschulschriften, ser. no. 1, Deutsche Sprache und Literatur 624 (Frankfurt am Main: Peter Lang, 1983).

[40] I refer here to Alex Haley's best-selling novel (Garden City NY: Doubleday, 1976) and the ABC Novel for Television made from it and broadcast January 23–30, 1977. Freytag does note in his memoirs that he is interested in the effect of inheritance, but points out that in *Die Ahnen* the generations are too far apart for this theme to dominate (1: 240–41).

[41] It should be pointed out, however, that the first story in *Die Ahnen*, "Ingo," seems to have been interpreted by some contemporaries as belonging to a heroic tradition, like that invoked in Wagner's *Ring* cycle. An example of this interpretation may be seen in the illustration contributed to the magazine *Deutsche Dichtung* by Alexander Liezen-Mayer. It depicts the final scene of "Ingo," in which Ingo lies dying in Irmgard's arms as their farmhouse goes up in smoke. In Liezen-Mayer's rendition we see a couple of heroic dimension in the foreground — a half-clad blonde woman in robes somewhat reminiscent of classical antiquity, and a bearded warrior in a helmet and armband. In the upper right corner a horned warrior is visible — perhaps this is meant to be Wotan. While the conflagration at the end of "Ingo" is somewhat reminiscent of that in the Icelandic *Njal's Saga,* and while Freytag's characters speak an odd poetic language reminiscent of this heroic literature — one, as Freytag explains, he felt appropriate to the age (1: 247) — the next story, which takes place nearly 400 years later, makes quite clear that the story involves tiny, geographically limited settlements (9: 212–13). Curiously enough, Liezen-Mayer's illustration is bound between pages three and four of Theodor Storm's "Ein Doppelgänger," a story about domestic violence in Schleswig that has no apparent connection to Freytag (*Deutsche Dichtung,* October 1886).

[42] Celia Applegate, *A Nation of Provincials: The German Idea of Heimat* (Berkeley: U of California P, 1990).

A Woman's Post: Gender and Nation in Historical Fiction by Louise von François

Thomas C. Fox

THIS ESSAY EXAMINES the intersection of gender and nation in four pieces of historical fiction by Louise von François: the story "Der Posten der Frau" (The Woman's Post), published anonymously in 1857 and one of François's first works; the story "Fräulein Muthchen und ihr Hausmeier" (Miss Muthchen and Her Chief Steward, 1859); the novel *Die letzte Reckenburgerin* (1870; translated as *The Last von Reckenburg*, 1887, rpt. 1995); and the succeeding novel *Frau Erdmuthens Zwillingssöhne* (Mrs. Erdmuth's Twin Sons, 1872). Judging from the holdings of private, for-profit lending libraries, historical fiction constituted the most popular literary genre in Germany for most of the nineteenth century, including that period we call realism.[1] To take one example, between 1858 and 1861 historical novels represented almost fifty percent of German novels published.[2] As Brent O. Peterson points out, however, the wide field of historical novels remains largely unexplored. The past thirty years have produced only four full-length studies of German historical fiction, none of which deals with aspects of gender as they pertain to the narration of nation. And yet, writes Peterson, "to understand 'Germany' as a discursive formation, i.e., as a set of ideas rather than merely a place or a political entity, one needs to examine how gender was encoded in the emerging nationalist narrative. Historical fiction ... provides unparalleled access to the gendered construction of the German nation."[3]

Whereas Peterson's work primarily investigates novels by men (with a brief glance at François), we need to remember Todd Kontje's dictum that "often-marginalized or -trivialized novels by German women played a central role in shaping attitudes toward class, gender, and the nation."[4] Francois's "Der Posten der Frau" deals with the Seven Years' War (1756–63), *Frau Erdmuthens Zwillingssöhne* with the period from 1770 to 1813, "Fräulein Muthchen und ihr Hausmeier" with the year 1813, and *Die letzte Reckenburgerin* with the time between 1780 and 1836. The works emphasize Prussian military triumphs over the French, especially what Anthony D. Smith terms "the myth of a heroic age" (Frederick "the Great"), and the "myths of decline" (1806–12) and "regeneration" (1813–15). Smith sees these elements as constituent in the project of constructing what Benedict Anderson terms an "imagined community" in the form of a nation.[5] As Peterson notes, it remains unclear to what extent a popular German nationalism in fact developed during the struggles against the French (who, of course, had many German-speaking allies); certainly, after the conclusion of the Napoleonic wars no common Germany developed, nor did many want it to.[6] Nonetheless, the story of a monolithic resistance to the French proved a convenient vehicle with which to develop the history of German nationalist consciousness. My examination of François's work is guided by the axiom, formulated in 1858 by Wilhelm Heinrich von Riehl, that the subject of historical fiction is, in fact, the present. At the same time, historical fiction, with its attendant structuring devices of dates, historical personages, and familiar, verifiable facts, is well suited to further the realist fiction that it is not fiction. It is useful at this point to remember Robert C. Holub's view that "realist" writing often serves as a cover for ideological programs, and that realism can be viewed as a series of exclusions of otherness.[7] I will be looking at what a nineteenth-century Prussian-Saxon woman writer, one who enjoyed a modicum of success both with the public and with literary critics, includes and excludes from the imagined Germany of her historical fiction, and why.

Together with Annette von Droste-Hülshoff and Marie von Ebner-Eschenbach, Louise von François is one of the few nineteenth-century women writers of German to have maintained a continuous, though often minimal, presence in literary histories. The author of three novels and twenty-eight stories, François remains best known for *Die letzte Reckenburgerin*, a hybrid historical novel and female Bildungsroman. Scholars of the historical novel have always acknowledged François, and in recent years practitioners of feminist or gender studies have also demonstrated increasing interest in her work.⁸ A new edition of *Die letzte Reckenburgerin* appeared in 1988, and an English translation, out of print since the nineteenth century, was reissued in 1995.⁹ Perhaps to signal François's inclusion in the new, improved canon of German literature, Wulf Koepke groups her with Storm, Keller, Fontane, and Raabe in the fifth edition of his college textbook on German culture, *Die Deutschen* (The Germans, 2000).¹⁰

François was born in 1817 in Herzberg on the Black Elster River and grew up in Weissenfels on the Saale River. Both of these Saxon towns had become Prussian in 1816. Her aristocratic father died in 1818, and in 1819 François's mother married the civil servant August Hohl. François enjoyed a financially comfortable childhood and in 1834 became engaged to an aristocrat. At twenty, however, she ended the engagement when it became clear that her guardian had squandered her inheritance. As an unmarried woman burdened with the care of increasingly ailing parents, François began to publish her writing in 1855, in part to earn money to support herself and her family. Hence, like many nineteenth-century German women writers, François's public career commenced later in life. Although she was the same age as Theodor Storm and Georg Herwegh, and nearly contemporary with such writers of the *Junges Deutschland* or *Vormärz* as Ferdinand Freiligrath (born in 1810) or Karl Gutzkow (born in 1811), her work belongs to the *Nachmärz* or to realism.

As Sandra M. Gilbert and Susan Gubar point out, however, a literary history that valorizes male writers will find women writers to be odd or eccentric,¹¹ and within traditional German literary history François has never seemed to fit the available categories (with the exception of those histories that included sections on *Schreibende Frauen*).¹² As a reclusive nineteenth-century German woman — in other words, as an autodidact cut off from participation in most aspects of the public sphere — François was long considered by literary scholars a naive writer uninfluenced by contemporary society, one who drew, often in an epigonal fashion, on German literature of the eighteenth century. Recently Uta Schuch has revised this widespread assumption, arguing that the fashion in which François placed her stories for publication demonstrated a keen awareness of the marketplace, and that the market, in turn, shaped the composition of her stories. She sees the influence of such realist writers as Riehl, Berthold Auerbach, and Gustav Freytag in François's early stories. In François's later work, however, especially the novels, Schuch maps the development of a style in conscious opposition to prevailing trends. François's novels unfold against the grain of realist theories as advanced by Friedrich Spielhagen or by such French realist authors as Stendhal and Flaubert. To combat what she viewed as the pessimism of her times, François consciously turned to the ideals of the German Enlightenment and German idealism in order to include often didactic and uplifting denouements. Schuch rightly identifies irony and humor as two essential narrative elements in François's writing, for with these techniques François attempted to make her world less oppressive for readers.[13] Schuch does not, however, show to what extent François's "Christian" perspective is also a gendered one.

First published in 1857 in *Der Morgenblatt für gebildete Leser*, "Der Posten der Frau" takes place in a small Saxon town during the Seven Years' War. The protagonist, Eleonore, is a Prussian countess who has been married for seven years to the gallant Saxon count Moritz von Fink. Moritz sympathizes with the French troops who have occupied the town, and he serves as host to his friend Duke von Crillon. After Moritz discovers the French officer passionately kissing Eleonore's hand, he forbids his wife to attend a ball organized for the benefit of the French officers. Eleonore refuses to obey, and her husband locks her in a small room. Humiliated and enraged, Eleonore removes her skirt and crinoline and escapes through a narrow window. As one critic points out, this is a symbolic act of transgression,[14] and the narrator describes the crinoline as "das eiserne Gerüste gleich einem Haus, das erste Hindernis auf neuer Bahn, ein Symbol des Herkommens, mit dem sie bricht."[15] During Eleonore's flight she encounters a unit of the Prussian army that intends to attack the city. An officer, whom Eleonore later discovers to be King Frederick II, lectures her (as has, previously, a Saxon pastor) about a woman's duty to her child and husband. A woman's post, she hears, is always with her child, under her husband's roof. Eleonore returns to her husband. Thus, the story, which is told by an omniscient narrator, reestablishes the patriarchal order represented by husband, pastor, and king.

We are not, however, simply confronted with the status quo ante, for Eleonore has changed. One critic has called attention to the motif of dreaming in the story and demonstrates that Eleonore discards her youthful, immature dreams of heroes, knights, and fairy tales in order to adopt a mature, realistic stance of duty.[16] (Of course, this occurs after her encounter with a "real" hero, King Frederick, and one could argue that the entire story emplots a dream fantasy of François or her narrator). Eleonore does, indeed, break with the heritage represented by the crinoline, for she will no longer indulge in the decadent diversions of high society; instead, she will manage her husband's many properties, a "male" task. When, in the middle of the narrative, she realizes that a ferryman beats his wife, she regrets that she had not done more to prevent such abuses. It is clear that at the end of the text she will set out to reform people, as well as estates, and she begins by preventing her husband from striking a servant. She reorders her relationship with her husband more or less along the lines of a business partnership, one in which she considers herself at least an equal partner; indeed, she dictates the terms. Her husband appears to accept this arrangement, as well, for his last words to their servants, uttered as he flees the Prussian army, establish Eleonore as his "alter ego" (262). Among other things, this means that she will replace him as father to their son. One wonders, however, whether it is King Frederick, not Moritz, who, in fact, functions as Eleonore's alter ego. (It is worth recalling that as a young man Frederick II also undertook an abortive attempt to flee his "post"). The conclusion of François's text confronts us with an absent Saxon father and an absent Saxon king; the Prussians Eleonore and Frederick, both of whom are gendered male and are rulers, fill the void. The narrator has already asserted that Eleonore is as decisive as a man; now Frederick confides to her in admiring fashion that wearing the pants suits her. Earlier in the story we learn that Frederick's pants symbolize great power; the metaphor underscores the connection between him and the heroine.[17]

Eleonore's husband is a feminine man.[18] Moritz is gallant, beautiful, and elegant but no hero and not, as Eleonore regrets, a real "man." "Oh, daß er ein Mann wäre," she exclaims (199).[19] A lisping courtier who is vacillating, vain, superficial, and petty, Moritz symbolizes the weak subject of a weak king. He admires and imitates things French, though he also possesses an inferiority complex regarding them. Aligned with French foreignness, he also stands metaphorically associated with blackness, being mentioned in parallel terms with Shakespeare's Othello[20] and later, in a dream of Eleonore's, being raised up by the hands of demonic slaves. At the conclusion of the story the narrator presents Moritz as a ridiculous figure. Linda Kraus Worley argues against this interpretation (181), but it seems clear that the embarrassed wife tries to justify Moritz's actions in order to save his honor in front of her servants, herself, and the Prussian king, who openly displays his ridicule. Moritz vanishes from the story, symbolically by hiding behind a door, then by fleeing into exile — an action that is not inconvenient for François and her heroine.

The French Duke Crillon belongs to a long and honorable line of aristocrats, and Eleonore's Prussian servant pays him the highest compliment by noting grudgingly that the man appears as handsome and gentlemanly as a Prussian. Crillon demonstrates his nobility by sparing Frederick's life in battle, a favor Frederick returns at the conclusion of the story. But in crucial ways he is not Prussian. Crillon drinks, gambles, and dances, all markers for François of the decadent aristocracy. More important, he embodies a particularly dangerous "French" characteristic: lust. Early in the story Eleonore's loyal Prussian servant comments on the licentiousness of the French soldiers, characterizing it as a plague, and his train of thought leads him then to Crillon and Eleonore. Indeed, Crillon's passion for Eleonore does not go unremarked by the servant, the Protestant pastor, or Moritz, and Eleonore finds herself attracted to this man who is "der fremde Gast ihres Hauses, der Gegner ihres Königs, ihres Gatten Freund" (200). Just as the Saxon ruler invites French troops into his country, Moritz invites them into his house, irresponsibly putting German virtue at risk. It is a sign of Eleonore's development when, after her meeting with Frederick, she encounters Crillon on the battlefield and, despite his entreaties, tells him firmly that she cannot see him again. And just as Eleonore bans the French from her intimate domestic sphere, Frederick bans them from Saxony. The Saxon Moritz, associated with the female, blackness, decadence, and Frenchness, leaves for Poland, which signifies an additional set of negative connotations.

The exclusions delineated above leave the imagined Germany of this story a cold one, bereft of passion, suspicious of foreigners, with marriages that resemble business arrangements. Celebrating military virtues and language, the female author clearly sees Germany as male. This Germany assigns women a place and a military post; intriguingly, that post considerably expands and reorders traditional nineteenth-century women's roles. As Worley notes, François accords women a kind of moral and ethical parity with men (185). It is easy today to see the limitations and contradictions of François's views concerning a woman's post, which can be regarded in many respects as reinforcing patriarchal structures. But Ruth-Ellen Boetcher Joeres is also correct when she notes that

> the ambiguities and innovations are intriguing enough to make us wonder what it was that Louise von François had in mind. Irony is never far away in her novella, and despite François's avowed conservative political stance, the reader is left with a sense of uncertainty about the stability of established gender roles and the sphere in which they are to be practiced. (285)

In other words, this text that attempts so intently to exclude various kinds of difference ultimately reinscribes it through the creation and valorization of a more manly or androgynous woman. We will trace that pattern in the other texts we examine.

Two years after "Der Posten der Frau" François wrote "Fräulein Muthchen und ihr Hausmeier," which, like the previous story, is a historical fiction that concerns itself with the intertwined themes of national unity and a woman's post. In 1813 three "disunited"[21] Germans — one a French sympathizer, one a fervent proponent of German national unity, and one an adherent of Saxon neutrality — share a coach as they leave Leipzig. The coach loses a wheel near the estate of Fräulein Erdmuthe Kettenloss,[22] whom they then visit. Erdmuthe's father, a Saxon officer who had resigned from the military after Saxony became a French ally in 1806, perceived in his generation "Verweichlichung, Entartung und Zerfall" (501), a diagnosis that the French Revolution, the disastrous Prussian intervention, and the defeats of 1806 all confirmed for him. He had seven children, but the first six, all boys, died. He subjected his girl to a "male" education but declared that Erdmuthe will be both son and daughter, hence signaling that she will also have "female" traits. The androgynous Erdmuthe inherits and firmly manages her father's estate at a young age; she wears clothes that, unlike Eleonore's in "Der Posten der Frau," are not à la mode but practical and unrestrictive of her movements; and observers refer to her — not pejoratively — as an Amazon.

Erdmuthe's father insists that "die Frau in ihrem Gebiet braucht dieselben Kräfte und Tugenden wie der Mann, ja sie braucht sie doppelt, denn sie hat mehr zu leiden und das nämliche zu tun" (502). As in "Der Posten der Frau," the narrative attempts to upgrade the "female" sphere without ultimately calling it into question; but also like the earlier story, this text challenges the neatness of the spheres. The omniscient narrator, which refers to him- or herself as "we," accomplishes this through the symbolism of the sword, with all its connotations of manliness. Almost at the outset of the story the narrator mentions that, uncharacteristically for students of the time, the pro-unification Hermann Wille wears a sword. At Erdmuthe's estate the *Hausmeier* taunts the student, challenging him to use it. Before the three Germans arrive at Erdmuthe's house they witness a brief meeting between Erdmuthe, standing on a hill, and Napoleon, who is reconnoitering the battlefield for the battle of Gross-Görschen. On account of Erdmuthe's beauty Napoleon refers to her as Kriemhild, the heroine of the *Nibelungenlied;* but the German reader will also associate Kriemhild with the motif of revenge (for example, the wars of "liberation" as revenge for the defeats of 1792–93 and 1806) and, more specifically, with her killing, using Siegfried's sword, of Hagen. The three Germans suggest, only half in jest, that had Erdmuthe possessed a sword she would have murdered Napoleon, thus joining the ranks of Judith and Charlotte Corday (and Kriemhild).

The sword motif climaxes in the attack on Erdmuthe's passionately pro-unification *Hausmeier* by two Cossacks who strip him of his shoes and attempt to take his clothes, a violation that may be read as a symbolic rape. Erdmuthe seizes the *Hausmeier's* sword and, wielding it, sends the two Cossacks into retreat. The disrobing of the German by the Russians turns the former, one observer notes in jest, into a kind of German sansculotte (and we have already read in this story that the French Revolution led to a "feminization"); thus, the masculinized German Amazon saves the fatherland. The symbolism of the sword concludes when the German student marries Erdmuthe and exchanges his weapon for plowshares, suggesting both the biblical invocation and fertility; by plowing Mother Earth (Erdmuthe = "earth" plus "courage") he produces six sons, one of whom later has a daughter, thus regenerating patriarchal order and offsetting the "feminization" that caused Erdmuthe's father to lose six sons and produce only a daughter. The *Hausmeier*, referring to his loss of shoes and symbolic violation, declares that no shoe length of German earth should be lost to the *Fremdling* (foreigner or other) in East or West (514). Here he is referring not only to the Russians[23] but also to Napoleon, who in this story is described as not only as French-Italian[24] but, more importantly, as a leader with figurative *Mamelucken*, which can be translated as the Turkish slaves or mercenaries of an Islamic despot (505). "Napoleon" thus signifies threats from the west, south, and orient, threats that the masculine Germany constructed in this text must exclude.

Like "Der Posten der Frau," this narrative challenges the patriarchal order only to reconstitute it in a different form. Yet this story, like its predecessor, cannot entirely reconcile its transgression, for Hermann has lost an arm, a metaphorical castration,[25] to a German fighting for the French (the Russians who violate the *Hausmeier* are also mercenaries or *Mamelucken*). Like Jane Eyre, Erdmuthe marries a cripple. As a manly woman who has reached for the sword (and who also, in contrast to her student husband, possesses land and money), she maintains the power in her marriage, and this serves to problematize the *Ermannung* (etymologically, the making masculine) of the German *Volk* that this story valorizes (512).

François's first and best-known novel, *Die letzte Reckenburgerin,* appeared in Otto Janke's *Novellenzeitung* in 1870 (during the Franco-Prussian War) and a year later (during German unification) in book form, although François had completed the manuscript around 1865. In a review that made François famous, Gustav Freytag praised the novel as "ächte Dichterarbeit" and François as a "Dichterin von Gottes Gnaden." He noted approvingly that only small details reminded the reader that a woman held the pen.[26]

The novel takes place from approximately 1780 to 1836 and details the life of Hardine von Reckenburg, daughter of an impoverished noble Saxon family. Hardine ultimately inherits a vast estate from her aunt, who is called the Black Reckenburg. Like Countess von Fink in "Der Posten der Frau," Hardine reforms her holdings into a model ("Prussian" or "manly") estate.

Die letzte Reckenburgerin investigates many of the concerns we have traced in François's previous historical fiction. It describes

Prince Christian, who, like Moritz von Fink, is a decadent Saxon aristocrat. He belongs to a court characterized by "Eastern" corruption, sensuality, and decadence; the narrator speaks of a sultan's whims and of slaves.[27] We recall that in "Fräulein Muthchen und ihr Hausmeier" Napoleon is associated with oriental despotism, and, not surprisingly, the narrator of the Reckenburg novel connects Christian with things French. He is "ein durchlauchtiger Libertin nach dem Schlage des Maréchal de Saxe," August the Strong's illegitimate son who ultimately commanded France's armies (116). Hardine, the narrator of this part of the story, can only find a French word to characterize him: *coqueluche* [heartthrob] (116). Prince Christian's son August is connected to his father's wantonness symbolically, by his Turkish pipe. An admirer of the decadent French aristocracy, Prince August desires ardently to invade France in order to restore the monarchy, an action that leads to his death. Although handsome like his father, he appears effeminate: he has a "schlanke, geschmeidige Gestalt," a "rosige Farbe von fast mädchenhafter Transparenz," and "Züge, welche vielleicht zu weich und fein erschienen" (166). To underscore his homoerotic appeal, the text three times compares him with Antinous, the beautiful young lover of Hadrian (154, 157, 167).

The narrator figures the Black Reckenburg as male. Even as a young girl at Brühl's court, she is able to guard and increase her fortune "mit der nüchternen Berechnung eines Mannes" (115). Later she rebuilds her fortune with exertions that are clearly Faustian. Hardine shares her aunt's gender. As a child she demonstrates a (male) thirst for learning, and her aunt thinks her niece not destined for love or passion; accordingly, Hardine receives what amounts to a business apprenticeship during her stay at Reckenburg. As the heroine ages and her work matures, the attribute "manly" occurs with increasing regularity. In the "Introduction" to the novel the omniscient narrator notes that the Reckenburg populace spoke of Hardine with the deepest respect, as one would speak not about a woman but about the most intelligent and resolute man whose agricultural innovations served far and wide as paradigmatic. Later, the narrator himself speaks of Hardine's manly strength and endurance. Hardine also views herself in that fashion, noting that her relationships with men were conducted not as between a man and a woman but, rather, as between two men.[28]

Hardine's childhood friend Dorl functions as her binary opposite, for the two are radically different in appearance, temperament, and class. Within the conventions of the book Dorl represents female attributes, while Hardine signifies masculinity. Throughout the text the narrators figure Dorl in terms of the traditionally female, and exaggeratedly so. She is diminutive, graceful, and breathtakingly beautiful. Associated with music, dance, and animal nature, she is also often described as childlike. Like Prince August, with whom she has much in common, Dorl possesses unbridled passion; the two conceive an illegitimate child that Dorl abandons. Unlike Eleonore von Fink, Dorl, the narrator twice notes, abandons her post (318, 331). Within the universe of this novel, Dorl's desertion of her post presents an insult to nature, which avenges itself on her through insanity. Dorl's "nature" not only disrupts the order of nature, but disrupts the order of society, for Dorl represents the French Revolution.

The novel expresses ambivalence regarding that revolution. When the decadent Prince August sets out with German troops to restore the French monarchy, he discovers, the narrator notes in a telling aside, that the French do not welcome the "liberators" as enthusiastically as the Germans had expected (197). Hardine narrates with a bifocal lens, writing late in life about her youthful feelings. As a young woman she considered the campaign in France without doubt to be a justified, indeed "holy," war to restore the monarchy. But the same sentence demonstrates that later in life she finds it ironic, indeed scandalous, that the Germans are sacrificing themselves for a foreign king, when Germany itself lies in disarray (186–87; see also 219–20).

All of this informs the important chapter "Der Kehraus," set in 1792. (The German title is ambiguous, with connotations of sweeping out or cleaning). At a reception for Prince August organized by the elite of Hardine's city the bored prince espies the bourgeois Dorl, who is at the event to help her father serve refreshments. Drinking quantities of French champagne, the prince flirts with Dorl, who, in Parisian fashion, is not wearing powder or a toupee.[29] She is dressed in a white dress with blue trim, a blue hair band, and red roses: the French *tricolore*.

At the conclusion of the evening the prince demands a last dance. After the dancers have lined up, the prince pulls Dorl into their ranks, causing a "revolution" (174). The aristocrats break ranks, leaving the dance floor in indignation. Hardine, however remains, constituting, as the text notes, the "Übergang" from the aristocracy to the bourgeoisie. The latter, following Hardine, remains, and the dance begins. It grows ever wilder, ending with a passionate kiss between the blueblood and Dorl, the *Schenkdirne*. "Er küßt ihren Mund, umschlingt sie, preßt sie an seine Brust und jagt mit ihr durch den Saal. . . . Die Ordnung ist zerstört" (176). Dorl's licentiousness causes revolution, destroying the aristocracy and, indeed, all order.

Hardine will later use an additional word to describe the Revolution after the murder of the royal family: cannibalistic (215). In her utilization of raging passion and cannibalism to describe the Revolution, she reaches back to tropes that Susanne Zantop has traced in contemporary accounts of the French Revolution by German writers. "As Germany received the news that masses of 'unbridled' women were marching to Versailles to demand bread from the king . . . depictions of revolutionary scenes abounded with references to 'amazons' and 'cannibals,' who, transgressing gender and moral taboos, declared war on the established order and patriarchal authority."[30] Zantop asserts that "women become the emblem of chaos and licentiousness" (224); Schiller's "Lied von der Glocke" compares revolutionary women with hyenas.

Dorl is no hyena, however, and "Fräulein Muthchen und ihr Hausmeier" demonstrates that the word "Amazon" is not, for François, negatively charged. As I have noted, Hardine's text expresses ambivalence regarding the Revolution, and her own feelings about the German intervention range from the word "holy" (186) to "indifference" (220). The chapter "Der Kehraus," in which Hardine describes how Dorl's sexuality sparks a revolution, is narrated by the mature Hardine with ironic distance and humor. Hardine often comments on her fascination with and attraction to Dorl — even if she ultimately rejects Dorl's actions — and François reserves her finest language for descriptions of Dorl.[31]

The novel demonstrates a certain ambivalence regarding the Revolution, because Hardine is cognizant of the need for change. She condemns the excesses of the aristocracy and the injustices and absurdities of a system built on a hollow and mechanical definition of class; but she cannot accept the eruption of sexual passion, leading to cannibalism, that the Revolution entails. The explicit coupling of the last dance with the French Revolution, of the personal with the historical, is a technique François uses often in her book. Prince August dies on August 2, 1792, at Valmy, the same day on which Hardine, years later, also dies. Hardine's mother and father and her aunt, the Black Reckenburg, all die in 1806; as representatives of the old Germany, they must die during the year in which Napoleon nearly destroys Prussia. After 1806 Dorl's fatal illness is explicitly tied to the "Qualen und Enttäuschungen des Vaterlandes"; she must pay the penalty for her actions against the natural and social order (332). As the cipher for passion, revolution, and femininity, Dorl embodies the lurking disease (described as *Elend* and *Siechtum,* 273) in the German body politic. She threatens the nascent Germany of this text, and for this reason she must be excluded.

Hardine's program is one of reform, not revolution. After 1806 she assumes authority over the Reckenburg estate and institutes a new regime (the chapter heading is "Die neue Herrschaft") that parallels the Hardenberg/Stein reforms undertaken in Prussia.[32] She twice refers to her "Fritzian" activity (304, 310), and characterizes the rejuvenated Prussia as a land of "Recht und Ehren," the Reckenburg family motto. She views the defeat of 1806 as a catalyst for the growth of this strongly rooted people. The organic metaphor connects Hardine, a planter, to the Prussian *Volk,* whose rejuvenation Hardine can prophesy.

Hardine's reforms of the Reckenburg land and people are successful, though limited. She notes that the community she has created is upright and honest but joyless and loveless, and she views that fact in gendered terms, as resulting from her masculinity. Only late in life, when she begins to love and foster Dorl's grandchild (to whom she leaves her estate), does Hardine become "eine beglückte Mutter und erst ein Weib" (374). She does not regret her masculinity, however, noting that she entered a male sphere of activity and worked productively in it for many years.

Hardine's education at the conclusion of the novel occasions a break in style; the protagonist explicitly compares her life to a fairy tale. Until that point the novel had contained a strong element of anti-Romanticism, and its realist conventions include many attempts to "document" the story with "evidence" that includes memoirs, a birth certificate, letters, and an epistolary confession. In this fashion, as Peter Demetz has demonstrated, fiction attempts to hide its fictionality by assuming the guise of a report.[33]

If the major part of *Die letzte Reckenburgerin* serves as fiction masquerading as a realist narrative, at the conclusion François, by explicitly equating Hardine's life with a fairy tale, removes the mask. The title of the final chapter is "The Fountain of Youth"; thus, the story calls attention to its own fictionality and assumes the self-conscious posture of allegory. The allegory features the Reckenburg, with its rejuvenated androgynous ruler, as a metaphor for a unified Germany. This Germany recognizes the necessity of peaceful, organic change and the concomitant resolution of class conflict. In Hardine's vision the aristocracy gracefully abdicates to the younger, more vigorous bourgeoisie.[34] In the personal sphere, Hardine manages to avoid what she perceives to be the shackles of marriage, while attaining a position that combines the rewards of productive work outside the home and motherhood. In the real Germany, as François well knew, a different constellation existed. The 1860s brought expanding industrialization and growing class antagonisms such as those portrayed by Spielhagen; the decade also brought military tensions and war. François, writing in her attic apartment in Weissenfels, could only dream of managing an estate as large as a province, and Hardine's androgynous solution must have appeared utopian when compared with the real situation and possibilities of nineteenth-century women in an emerging Germany of blood and iron. Like Willibald Alexis, François measures her vision of a potential Prussia against the real one; the self-conscious artifice of her conclusion underscores the fragility of her alternative. Reading through the lens of prescriptive realism, Freytag found the conclusion lacking. Among other criticisms, he remonstrated that a trace of bitterness remained.[35] In precisely that bitterness, however, we may discover the most stubbornly "realistic" aspect of François's novel.

Published in 1872, just after the Franco-Prussian War, during which it was written, *Frau Erdmuthens Zwillingssöhne* presents François's most radical examples of inclusion and exclusion. Based in part on the earlier story, "Fräulein Muthchen und ihr Hausmeier," the novel shares with its predecessor many features and themes. Hence, Erdmuthe von Fels in the novel receives, like Erdmuthe in the story, a man's education from her father, who underscores the constructed nature of gender by referring to his daughter in quotation marks, as "her" and "she."[36] The girl learns about finance and agriculture and serves apprenticeships with foresters, game wardens, and lumberjacks. The narrator, Erdmuthe's childhood friend who becomes a pastor and spends his life serving her, assures us, however, that this education did not turn her into a huntress, an Amazon, or even into a learned woman ("gelehrte Frau," 44) but, rather, turned her into a mother. One of the first exclusions in the novel is his passion for Erdmuthe, for the narrator notes that while one might covet another man's wife, one could never desire the mother of another man's children. With this act of "German" self-control he exiles his own desire, which, apparently, never resurfaces, even after Erdmuthe is widowed young.

Erdmuthe marries Raul von Roc, a Saxon officer of modest means whose family had left France after the annulment of the Edict of Nantes. He feels himself a Saxon and after four generations has acquired such "German" characteristics as trust and loyalty, while maintaining "French" characteristics that include a fiery, romantic temperament, gallantry, a beautiful voice, and attractive features. Their twin sons exude national stereotypes.[37] Hermann is tall, blond, honest, somewhat lethargic, and develops into a fanatically ardent supporter of German national unity; he loves his homeland as one loves a father. Born a Saxon, he serves the Prussian cause. Raul is smaller, dark, attractive, lively but superficial, vain, a *cocqueluche,* and a passionate supporter of Napoleon and France. He remains a Saxon only because his homeland maintains an alliance with France. France is female, a country Raul woos like a bride; according to the narrator, Raul chooses a homeland as he would choose a beautiful woman. Paradoxically, as in much of François's other historical fiction, this Francophile suitor is also feminized; a respected family friend notes that Raul, in contradistinction to Hermann, would never be able to become a real "man" (151). The story, which begins around 1770, builds to the battle of Leipzig in 1813, when Saxons and Prussians, and Raul and Hermann, face each other on the battlefield.

The two Rauls bring an element of foreignness into the Germany conjured in this text, but the ultimate Other is Liska, a young woman born in Italy of a French father and Polish mother. We meet the Polish mother on her deathbed; still young and beautiful but dissolute, she wears "ein türkisch bunter Schal als Turban," thus magnifying her orientalism (240). The narrator informs us that the

Polish *Volk* is talented but lacks a practical sense of order; this leads to its downfall. After the death of her mother, Liska receives refuge at Erdmuthe's estate. But this act of kindness comes back to haunt the family, which will learn that it is not wise to accept foreigners. Liska shares several characteristics with Dorl from *Die letzte Reckenburgerin*. She flits about like a butterfly and is diminutive and melodious as a bird. She possesses a seductive attractiveness and magical charm and is impulsive, childlike, and passionate. Dorl neglects her duty to her son, Liska hers to her mother. Dorl becomes infected with the French disease that has entered the German body politic; Liska carries that disease into Germany. This French/Italian/Polish woman represents the countries to the west, south, and east of "Germany," and the narrative contains repeated references to the barbarism of the East and the West (for example, 195, 201, 221, 278, 323). François furthermore connects Napoleon, as we recall from "Fräulein Muthchen und ihr Hausmeier," with Italy, and the novel refers to Liska, who was born in Italy, as "Mignon." Finally, the narrative brings Liska, who has brown skin, into association with Jewishness (238) and, on repeated occasions, with blackness (for example, 216, 217, 220, 221, 222, 272, 334). She embodies overdetermined difference and threatens German unity.

Just as the French invade and conquer Germany (and Zantop is surely correct in surmising that in order to avoid a humiliating feminization of the fatherland, which was being violated by the French, the Germans needed to feminize the French [221]), Liska invades the family sphere. Hermann, who, like his mother, is attracted to difference, falls in love with Liska and becomes engaged to her. As does Dorl's fiancée in *Die letzte Reckenburgerin*, Hermann leaves Liska alone for long periods, and into those interstices steps Raul, who seduces his brother's bride. Soon thereafter, Raul dies fighting for the losing cause of the French during the battle of Leipzig; Erdmuthe returns Liska to France, where a kind of imprisonment in a cloister will presumably contain her destructive passion. Thus, the text purges Germany. "Die Fremde muß fort" (229), demands a German innkeeper soon after Liska enters the narrative, and her expulsion provides one of the novel's final elements.

The question as to whether people of opposing or similar natures are best suited for marriage functions as a leitmotif in this novel. The masculine, Ur-Saxon Erdmuthe marries a man quite different from her; her somewhat feminized husband continues to possess "French" blood and characteristics, although his family has been in Saxony for four generations. The narrator describes the marriage as happy, though François removes the husband, who dies a soldier's death, rather early in the narrative. When Erdmuthe's friends discuss a suitable partner for Erdmuthe's son, Hermann, they again return to the question of difference. They mention Othello and Desdemona; keeping with the image of miscegenation, they then speak of a milk-white English nobleman who becomes passionately enamored of a Moorish queen. Liska becomes for Hermann the Moorish queen; she represents his opposite, though he believes she resembles his brother Raul "like a sister" (233), thus also associating Raul with blackness. Early in the story the narrator has asserted that *only* the relationship between man and woman can contain and reconcile different natures; he specifically notes that such differences within a state would destroy harmony. But even if Erdmuthe and her Raul are happy, their marriage produces offspring whose difference(s) lead(s) to disaster, thus undercutting the narrator's one obeisance to otherness. One can only speculate on the psychology involved for François, herself of Huguenot descent, in creating a feminized Saxon man of Huguenot origin, whose feminized Saxon son feels himself French and triggers a familial catastrophe that is also national — the German word for civil war is *Brüderkrieg,* or war between brothers.

In this novel, as in all of François's historical fiction, an element of ambiguity remains. In *Die letzte Reckenburgerin,* for example, one can read Dorl as a victim of class and patriarchal structures,[38] and in *Frau Erdmuthens Zwillingssöhne* Liska's story is told by a first-person narrator with his own agenda. To his credit, the narrator twice wonders whether he has figured her "correctly" (312, 339), and the text includes diary entries from Liska that allow her to speak in her own voice and suggest a different story. The narrator, who, after all, is a pastor and a man of peace, also expresses a certain ambivalence toward the German nationalist project he in general supports. He recoils in horror from the slaughter at the battle of Leipzig, a slaughter he describes in graphic detail. On the final page of the text he prays that the day will come "wo es nur noch Brüder gibt: Blutesbrüder, Volkesbrüder, Menschen-, Christenbrüder" (503).[39]

Published between 1857 and 1872, the four narratives I have discussed here ostensibly treat the Seven Years' War or the Wars of Liberation, but they are clearly at least as concerned with the German situation of the 1850s and 1860s. These texts all call for a strong and united fatherland not, as Hermann notes in "Fräulein Muthchen und ihr Hausmeier," for the sake of Prussia but in order to prevent the civil wars and internecine horrors outlined in that text and in *Frau Erdmuthens Zwillingssöhne*. All of these stories demonstrate at some point a prostrate, feminized Saxony continually occupied, demeaned, and ravaged by foreign armies. Eleonore von Fink, Erdmuthe von Kettenloss, Hardine von Reckenburg, and Erdmuthe von Fels are women in charge of large estates during those most difficult times. As Hardine notes, a landowner who has worked hard to increase her holdings looks to a strong fatherland to protect them. Despite the "conservative" political views often attributed to François, most recently by Joeres (285), François's last novel, *Stufenjahre eines Glücklichen,* demonstrates a certain sympathy for the revolution of 1848, and her calls for a united Germany under a strong Prussia do not necessarily contradict the goals of 1848. Schuch, for example, understands François's demands for national unity, together with her criticism of the aristocracy, as signals of German liberalism (91).

Regardless of François's politics, she clearly imagines her Germany — at least sometimes — as a manly one that rises up, as it were, to purge itself of foreign elements. Adopting military virtues, including, foremost, a rather abstract sense of duty, this fetishized fatherland steels its body and masculinizes its women into Amazons and Kriemhilds. This Germany excludes, often in radical fashion, much that is gendered female: licentiousness, blackness, orientalism, and the "barbarism" of South, East, and West. François's characters see a strong state as the guarantor of peace and prosperity but also as a bulwark against difference and French disease. François could not have foreseen that her recipe against one German catastrophe would lead to another, but certainly the ingredients are there. Five editions of *Die letzte Reckenburgerin* appeared during the Third Reich; in 1935 Hermann Harder published an article in the Nazi periodical *Die Sonne* celebrating *Frau Erdmuthens Zwillingssöhne* as a prophetic novel about race;[40] and various titles by François appeared as *Bayreuther Feldpostaus-*

gaben, designed for soldiers in the field.⁴¹ As Nazi soldiers set out to rid the world of otherness in our time, some carried in their rucksacks texts by Louise von François.

Nonetheless, those gender-bending texts remain riven with ambiguities, for as they attempt to narrate the nation, they simultaneously essay to reorder relationships between women and men. Military virtues for women did constitute an upgrading of a woman's post, and François's strong, transgressive, androgynous women carry a revolutionary, utopian potential. Peterson's assertion that German historical fiction marginalized women, especially those who proved "too strong, too intelligent, or too independent," needs to be qualified.⁴² While François's fiction, on the one hand, does tend to valorize patriarchal structures — leading to the not infrequent praise in literary histories that François could write "like a man" — on the other hand, it undermines those very structures. Like Marlitt, but in a more sophisticated fashion, François has things both ways. Hardine von Reckenburg does not marry but has a child; Erdmuthe von Fels marries, but the text kills her husband young; Eleonore von Fink remains married but lives apart from her husband; Erdmuthe von Kettenloss marries a cripple. If François's texts masculinize the women, one should not forget that Hardine von Reckenburg, after her narrative abandons realist conventions and enters the utopian realm of the fairy tale, also calls for a more feminized state. Her estate, like those of François's other heroines, exemplifies what that larger imagined state could or should be. Our four historical texts from Louise von François feature aporias that cannot be resolved by the author or her narrators. Precisely those tensions and clashes make her realist narratives of interest to us today.

Notes

¹ Brent O. Peterson, "The Fatherland's Kiss of Death: Gender and Germany in Nineteenth-Century Historical Fiction," in Patricia Herminghouse and Magda Mueller, eds., *Gender and Germanness: Cultural Productions of Nation* (Providence RI: Berghahn, 1997), 83.

² Hartmut Eggert, "Der historische Roman des 19. Jahrhunderts," in Helmut Koopmann, ed., *Handbuch des deutschen Romans* (Düsseldorf: Bagel, 1983), 342–43.

³ Peterson, "The Fatherland's," 82.

⁴ Todd Kontje, *Women, the Novel, and the German Nation 1771–1871: Domestic Fiction in the Fatherland* (New York: Cambridge UP, 1998), 1.

⁵ Cited in Peterson, "German Nationalism after Napoleon: Caste and Regional Identities in Historical Fiction, 1815–1830," *German Quarterly* 68, no. 3 (1995): 289.

⁶ Peterson, "The Fatherland's," 84–85.

⁷ Robert C. Holub, *Reflections of Realism: Paradox, Norm, and Ideology in Nineteenth-Century German Prose* (Detroit: Wayne State UP, 1991), 17–18.

⁸ Werner Kohlschmidt, for example, writes in his *Geschichte der deutschen Literatur vom Jungen Deutschland bis zum Naturalismus*, vol. 4 (Stuttgart: Reclam, 1975), 673, that *Die letzte Reckenburgerin* belongs to the classics of the historical novel form. François scholarship from the past twenty years that deals in some way with issues of gender includes Ruth-Ellen Boetcher Joeres, *Respectability and Deviance: Nineteenth-Century German Women Writers and the Ambiguity of Representation* (Chicago: U of Chicago P, 1998), 280–86; Thomas C. Fox, "Louise von François: Between *Frauenzimmer* and *A Room of One's Own*" (Diss. Yale U., 1983); Fox, "Louise von François: A Feminist Reintroduction," in Marianne Burkhard and Jeanette Clausen, eds., *Women in German Yearbook* 3 (1985): 123–38; Fox, "Sexist Literary History? The Case of Louise von François," in Ginette Adamson and Eunice Myers, eds., *Continental, Latin-American, and Francophone Women Writers* (Lanham MD: UP of America, 1987), 129–38; Fox, *Louise von François and Die letzte Reckenburgerin: A Feminist Reading* (New York: Lang, 1989); Fox, "Louise von François Rediscovered," in Gerhard P. Knapp, ed., *Autoren Damals und Heute: Literaturgeschichtliche Beispiele veränderter Wirkungshorizonte* (Atlanta: Rodopi, 1991), 303–19; Martin Gregor-Dellin, "Louise von François," in his *Was ist Größe? Sieben Deutsche und ein deutsches Problem* (Munich: Piper, 1985), 175–96; Tiiu V. Laane, "Louise von François's Critical Perspectives of Society," *European Studies Journal* 8, no. 2 (1991): 13–41; Laane, "The Incest Motif in Louise von François's *Der Katzenjunker*: A Veiled Yet Scathing Indictment of Patriarchal Abuse," *Orbis Litterarum* 47 (1992): 11–30; Laane, "Louise von François and the Education of Women," in Ginette Adamson and Eunice Myers, eds., *Continental, Latin-American, and Francophone Women Writers*, vol. 3 (Lanham, MD: UP of America, 1997), 1–16; Laane, "Comic Mirrors and Sociological Implications in Louise von François's Narratives," in Adamson and Myers, eds., *Continental, Latin-American, and Francophone Women Writers*, vol. 4 (Lanham, MD: UP of America, 1998), 95–107; Uta Scheidemann, *Louise von François: Leben und Werk einer deutschen Erzählerin des neunzehnten Jahrhunderts* (Bern: Lang, 1988); Uta Schuch, *"Die im Schatten stand." Studien zum Werk einer vergessenen Schriftstellerin: Louise von François* (Stockholm: Almqvist & Wiksell International, 1994); Eleonore Sent, ed., *Louise von François: Zum 100. Todestag am*

25.9.1993 (Weissenfels: Druckhaus Naumburg, 1993); Linda Kraus Worley, "Louise von François: A Reinterpretation of Her Life and Her 'Odd-Women' Fiction" (Diss. U of Cincinnati, 1985); Worley, "The 'Odd' Woman as Heroine in the Fiction of Louise von François," in Marianne Burkhard and Jeanette Clausen, eds., *Women in German Yearbook* 4 (Lanham, MD: UP of America, 1988), 155–65; Worley, "Louise von François (1817–1893): Scripting a Life," in Ruth-Ellen Boetcher Joeres and Marianne Burkhard, eds., *Out of Line/Ausgefallen: The Paradox of Marginality in the Writings of Nineteenth-Century German Women* (Atlanta: Rodopi, 1989), 161–86. François has also been regularly included in the newer literary histories and encyclopedias.

[9] François, *Die letzte Reckenburgerin* (Bonn: Latka, 1988); François, *The Last von Reckenburg*, introduction by Tiiu V. Laane (Columbia, SC: Camden House, 1995).

[10] Wulf Koepke, *Die Deutschen: Vergangenheit und Gegenwart*, 5th ed. (Fort Worth: Holt, Rinehart & Winston, 2000), 122.

[11] Sandra M. Gilbert and Susan Gubar, *The Madwoman in the Attic: The Woman Writer and the Nineteenth-Century Literary Imagination* (New Haven: Yale UP, 1979), 72–73.

[12] For an overview of the reception of nineteenth-century German women writers by literary historians, see Herminghouse, "The Ladies' Auxiliary of German Literature: Nineteenth-Century Women Writers and the Quest for a National Literary History," in her and Mueller's *Gender and Germanness*, 145–58.

[13] See Schuch, note 1.

[14] Joeres, *Respectability*, 283. Other citations are in the text.

[15] François, "Der Posten der Frau," in her *Gesammelte Werke in fünf Bänden*, vol. 4 (Leipzig: Insel, [1918]), 216. Subsequent citations will be in the text.

[16] Worley, "Louise von François: A Reinterpretation," 169. Other citations from this dissertation are in the text.

[17] Frederick dutifully watches over Eleonore, just as Eleonore will now watch over her son. Also, the battle described in this story is part of the battle of Rossbach, during which Frederick defeated an army far greater than his in size. The story celebrates this victory as a triumph of the weak, and this phrase, in a sense, describes Eleonore's victory, as well. Although she is a stronger personality than Moritz, she is a member of the "weaker sex." See Worley, "Louise von François: A Reinterpretation," 182–83.

[18] My use of such terms as "feminine man" or "masculine woman" in this essay corresponds to the norms established by the texts themselves.

[19] Eleonore later tells her son that he, as opposed to his father, must learn to love a fatherland in order to be a real "man": "Du aber, mein Sohn, daß du ein Mann werdest, kenne, liebe ein Vaterland" (262).

[20] The reference also, of course, reinforces the jealousy motif.

[21] François, "Fräulein Muthchen und ihr Hausmeier," in her *Gesammelte Werke,* vol. 1 (Leipzig: Lippold [1930]), 493. Subsequent citations are in the text.

[22] As is often the case in François's writing, the characters' names have symbolic connotations. "Erdmuthe" is a combination of "earth" and "courage," while "Kettenloss" translates as "without chains." She marries Hermann Wille. "Wille" connotes "resolution" or "will," while "Hermann" ("Heer" = army, "Mann" = man) is the name of the Germanic prince credited by Tacitus with preventing the Romans from occupying the right side of the Rhine.

[23] As allies of the Prussians during the battle of Leipzig, the Russians are figured more positively in this text than the French. But as the anecdote about the Cossacks demonstrates, they constitute a threat nonetheless.

[24] France obtained Corsica in 1768, the year before Napoleon's birth.

[25] The Amazon imagery attending to Erdmuthe can also be associated with mutilation; but in her case it signifies a loss of femininity, whereas Hermann's loss of a member makes him less a "man."

[26] Gustav Freytag, "Ein Roman von Louise von François," in his *Vermischte Aufsätze* (Leipzig: Hirzel, 1901), 139–47.

[27] François, *Die letzte Reckenburgerin* (Leipzig: Insel, [1918]), 218. Subsequent citations are in the text.

[28] Hence, when a neighboring count proposes marriage to the fifty-year-old Hardine, he makes no claim to passion but proposes a business deal. Inasmuch as he is often absent, she should manage his estates, making them bloom as does Reckenburg, and oversee the education of his sons (similar tasks to those assumed by Eleonore Fink at the conclusion of "Der Posten der Frau"). In a further reference to Hardine's "masculinity" the count notes that she is a woman who can complement and even (like Eleonore Fink) replace a father (319). During this scene the narrator suggests Hardine's equality by noting that she is as tall as the count. She wears a medal she has received for her services in the Wars of Liberation. Like the heroines in "Der Posten der Frau" and "Fräulein Muthchen und ihr Hausmeier," Hardine has achieved a moral-ethical equality with men.

[29] Hardine's aristocratic mother remarks that if it is, indeed, a (revolutionary) Parisian fashion not to wear powder, that is all the more reason for Hardine and her to wear it (162).

[30] Susanne Zantop, "Crossing the Border: The French Revolution in the German Literary Imagination" in James A. W. Heffernan, ed., *Representing the French Revolution: Literature, Historiography, and Art* (Hanover NH: UP of New England, 1992), 214. Further citations are in the text.

[31] The complicated relationship between Hardine and Dorl does appear to be erotically charged. Late in her life Hardine admits: "Denn ich hatte auch

darin einen männlichen Geschmack, daß nur die frauenhaftesten Eigenschaften der Frauen mir zu Herzen gingen. . . . Das Kind Dorothee hatte selbst als Sünderin den Reiz für mich nicht eingebüßt" (316).

[32] Peterson sees this as a parallel to Frederick II's rebuilding of Prussia after the Seven Years' War, but within the context of François's novel the post-1806 reforms in Prussia are at least as important ("The Fatherland's," 95).

[33] Peter Demetz, "Über die Fiktionen des Realismus," *Neue Rundschau* (Dec. 1977): 554–67.

[34] To be sure, Dorl's grandchild, though raised to be bourgeois, does have some royal blood.

[35] "Aber wenn man nach eifrigem Lesen das Buch aus der Hand legt und als ehrlicher Kritiker die eigene stille Erregung prüft, in welche der Roman versetzt hat, so fehlt der großen und edlen Wirkung doch eines: die freudige und gehobene Stimmung, welche bei schönem Kunstwerk auch nach Darstellung düstrer Ereignisse zurückbleiben soll. Ein Ton von Trauer und Entsagung, derselbe herbe Ernst, welcher durch das Leben der Heldin geht, bleibt auch in dem Leser zurück." Freytag, 146.

[36] François, *Frau Erdmuthens Zwillingssöhne* (Zurich: Manesse, [1954]), 42. Subsequent citations are in the text.

[37] I find it difficult to understand Schuch's assertion that Hermann and Raul embody "die typischen nationalen Züge des Deutschen bzw. des Romanen" (59) or that the narrator "hat weder Vorurteile anderen Völkern gegenüber noch ein Feindbild. . . . Aus diesem Grund gelingt es ihm auch, die französische Art so vorurteilsfrei und einfühlend zu erfassen" (228).

[38] For more on this topic, see Fox, *Louise von François and Die letzte Reckenburgerin;* also Leonie Marx, "Der deutsche Frauenroman im 19. Jahrhundert" in Helmut Koopmann, ed., *Handbuch des deutschen Romans* (Düsseldorf: Bagel, 1983), 439–59.

[39] The formulation is ambiguous and may well be creating new exclusions — for example, of non-Christians.

[40] Hermann Harder, "Ein Rassenroman der Louise v. François," *Die Sonne: Monatsschrift für Rasse, Glauben, und Volkstum. Im Sinne Nordischer Weltanschauung und Lebensgestaltung* 12 (1935): 265–68. Harder takes issue with the final sermon by the narrator, in which he prays for harmony among nations.

[41] For example, *Die letzte Reckenburgerin: Geschichte einer deutschen Frau*, Bayreuther Feldpostausgaben, ([Bayreuth]: Gauverlag, 1943) and *Frau Erdmuthens Zwillingssöhne: Roman aus dem Zeitalter der Befreiungskriege*, Bayreuther Feldpostausgaben ([Bayreuth]: Gauverlag, 1944).

[42] Peterson, "The Fatherland's," 96.

Friedrich Spielhagen: The Demon of Theory and the Decline of Reputation

Jeffrey L. Sammons

IN 1899 A PORTION of the German literary community organized a seventieth-birthday celebration for Friedrich Spielhagen. Such occasions had become customary in German cultural life, although sometimes they seem to have been more gratifying for the celebrants than the celebrated. Ten years earlier Gottfried Keller had simply boycotted his. Two years after Spielhagen's, Wilhelm Raabe approached his with considerable trepidation. Although the event came off all right, some of the antecedent anxiety is evident in his posthumous, fragmentary novel *Altershausen* (1911). Spielhagen, too, was uneasy, as he reports in a reminiscence titled "*Post Festum*"; he felt that he had been forced into the affair by his friends and wanted to escape.[1] But his distress must have been even greater than he reports, for it had by then become unavoidably evident that his once-gleaming career was in ruins. Spielhagen belongs to that pitiable category of writers who become decanonized in their own lifetimes. Some of the effect can be seen from the ninety-nine page celebratory album.[2] First of all, no responsible editor is named, although a good guess would be Gustav Karpeles, who had published an intensely idealizing little book on Spielhagen in the year of his sixtieth birthday[3] and who signed the introduction to the album. The contributions tend to light verse and bread-and-butter notes, many of them quite terse — doubtless telegrams. A toast by the eminent literary historian Erich Schmidt lectured Spielhagen on Goethe;[4] Victor Klemperer, who knew Spielhagen personally, says that it made him feel like a schoolboy.[5] Some colleagues are conspicuous by their absence — notably Raabe, whose own event was much more productive of honors.[6] On other such occasions Raabe tried to work up some politeness, but not for this one, although he was well aware of it.[7] Spielhagen grumbled in a letter of November

17, 1896, that he had been thrown onto the scrap iron,[8] which may be an allusion to Raabe's title *Im alten Eisen* (On the Scrap Iron, 1887), although I have not been able to find a single explicit mention of him in any of Spielhagen's writings.

His fall from literary eminence was dramatic. His first novel, *Problematische Naturen* (Problematic Characters, 1861), with its sequel, *Durch Nacht zum Licht* (Through Night to Light, 1862), were successes of a magnitude of which many authors can only dream. It has been said that girls born at that time all through Germany were named after the alluring, elegant heroine, Melitta von Berkow.[9] These and several following novels went into many editions, and Spielhagen, whose life up to then had been unsettled and penurious, made a great deal of money. Indeed, he may be the only major author among the German realists to have become prosperous from his writing. He was published in relatively large editions and serialized in every important German-language newspaper; *Sturmflut* (Storm Flood, 1877) was serialized in five newspapers simultaneously.[10] The ambitious late Bildungsroman *Was will das werden?* (What Meaneth This? 1887) was serialized in the venerable *Gartenlaube* in 1885 in, as has been pointed out, respectable company: the preceding year the periodical had brought out Theodor Fontane's *Unterm Birnbaum* (Under the Pear Tree, 1885), Raabe's *Unruhige Gäste* (Restless Guests, 1886), and Heinrich Heine's recently discovered memoirs.[11]

The early novels were translated into all the major languages. In Russia a committee celebrating Gogol's 100th birthday in 1909 elected Spielhagen as an honorary member.[12] The French Swiss literary historian Eduard de Morsier in 1890 opened a 120-page chapter on Spielhagen with the somewhat anachronistic declaration that for twenty years he had been the most celebrated of contemporary German writers.[13] American periodicals kept track of him down to notices of his death one day after his eighty-second birthday on February 25, 1911.[14] The reception was not always positive. In Henry James's story "Pandora" (1884) "a very intelligent girl, who came from Boston," engages Count von Vogelstein, a pleasantly dim young diplomat, in a conversation on the novels of Spielhagen, "a voluminous writer," without eliciting much response; the count is glad when the subject is changed.[15] In 1913 the most comic of his works, *Das Skelet im Hause* (The Skeleton in the House, 1878), was edited for American classroom use, although the pedagogues had decided after extensive discussion that, in general, he was too democratic and socialistic to be put before schoolchildren.[16] In the following year it could be asserted that he was one of the best-loved German writers in America and France and was popular in Russia.[17] As for Germany, a former student friend, the Heine biographer Adolf Strodtmann, declared flatly in 1879 that Spielhagen was the most brilliant novelist of the present.[18] Such statements are occasionally encountered even after they ceased to be strictly true. Peter Rosegger's son declared on Spielhagen's death that he was incontestably the greatest German novelist of the time.[19] His books are found in the library of Empress Elisabeth[20] and, for that matter, in Raabe's.[21]

Today there is barely a trace of all this glory. There is no modern edition. Only a couple of his works are currently in print, and those in little-known publishing houses.[22] There is no edition of his correspondence; small batches of his letters are scattered in various places, mostly in periodicals that have become difficult of access. There is no modern biography; to be sure, his life was not especially eventful after he settled permanently in Berlin in 1862 as a writer and periodical editor. We are largely dependent on an informal memoir by a friend of the family.[23] Indeed, the most substantial current biographical account may be the thirteen-page entry in the *Dictionary of Literary Biography*.[24] The decanonization has been thorough. Literary critics and historians regularly assure us that Spielhagen's fiction is of no value, and there is no need to become acquainted with it. Franz Mehring remarked that one seemed like a boor when one spoke of him at all.[25] An observation nearly forty years ago that it was "unlikely that Spielhagen will ever be widely read as a novelist again . . . a renascence seems improbable"[26] has been borne out. The process, especially as applied to nineteenth-century German realism, leads inexorably into the catacombs of literary history.[27]

Spielhagen was not immediately abandoned by his public, however. The evidence indicates that he continued to be read into the 1930s, especially by the working class.[28] A statistical survey of popular reading habits in 1900 put Spielhagen in sixth place, before his good friend Berthold Auerbach and after Heine.[29] Consequently, there has been a tendency for left-wing critics to defend him, although sometimes in a qualified way.[30] His last illness was followed in the press, there were many notices and condolences on his death, and his funeral was a public event; there were many articles on his hundredth birthday in 1929, but by that time it was acknowledged that he was no longer much read.[31] Some of the literary historians remained respectful of him[32] or at least acknowledged his preeminence as a critic of his times and an "agitator."[33] The fatal blows to his reputation, the impulses to today's oblivion, came, rather, out of the literary community.

Raabe's hostility is not surprising, considering that Spielhagen's theory of objective narration was directly opposed to his authorial manner;[34] furthermore, Raabe's literary fate embittered him into spitefulness toward his successful contemporaries. In fact, much like Raabe, Spielhagen despaired of maintaining a popular readership, as literature can survive only for the dwindling "*happy few*" of exquisite culture.[35] A curious case is that of Thomas Mann. Bertolt Brecht, with a perfect instinct for what would cause Mann pain, had declared him a successor to Spielhagen. In a testy and haughty retort, Mann declared that though Spielhagen might not have been so bad, he, Mann, was unable to read him and, in fact, never had read a line because he knew in advance that all German prose from that period was unreadable.[36] In 1939 he declared to an audience of American students that Spielhagen's works were so insipid that one could not consider them a contribution to the European novel.[37] Had Mann, then, read him in the meantime? It seems unlikely. Here is a striking example of the way in which his worthlessness had become a received opinion, relieving readers of any direct experience with him. Such assurance is often reiterated. Only occasionally does one encounter a suggestion that he has been too lightly dismissed.[38]

The usual account is that the rebellion against Spielhagen came from the Naturalists. Sometimes mentioned in this connection is Carl Bleibtreu, who dashed off an attack on a defensive open letter Spielhagen had published in 1887.[39] One of his objections is to what he regards as erotic excess. It is true that a certain erotic excitement and fascination is detectable in Spielhagen's writing; in this respect he may be close to a boundary of the conventional in the Victorian age. He once commented that all poets must be sensual like Goethe, Heine, even Schiller, not chaste like Lessing, who was, therefore, not a poet,[40] and in another place he remarked quaintly that the writer must be scientifically informed about the physiology of love (*NB*, 231). In fact, in a rather comic episode in 1881, the newspaper serializing his novel *Angela* was confiscated for what were taken to be lesbian insinuations in one episode; this, in turn, led to a brisk, fictionalized satire of the courtroom scene by Eduard Engel, directed against the censorship but even more against Spielhagen himself as a long-winded bore who could not possibly titillate anyone.[41] The suspicious ease with which his protagonists, such as Oswald Stein in *Problematische Naturen,* attract the devotion and passion of women of all stations drew censorious comment[42] and was one of the objects of parody in 1878.[43] Julian Schmidt, whom one might have expected to find on this line, while remarking that Spielhagen's representations of female characters were not as pure as one might wish, nevertheless acknowledged his warm sensuality and defended Oswald.[44] But to claim, as Bleibtreu did, that the erotic is the kernel of the oeuvre[45] is absurd.

The pivotal event was a seventy-four-page philippic delivered against Spielhagen by Heinrich Hart in 1884.[46] The very length and intensity of this screed suggests something about Spielhagen's continued standing; one does not usually beat a dead horse so vigorously. The rambling, repetitious polemic turns on a few main points. The novel itself is an inferior genre that will never reach the ideal of poesy (*H*, 9, 73). The generic touchstone is the Homeric epic, embodying a totality to which a modern literature cannot aspire; the only "modern" works Hart acknowledges as approaching the ideal are the *Nibelungenlied,* Cervantes's *Don Quixote,* Grimmelshausen's *Simplicissimus,* and, somewhat oddly, Fielding's *Tom Jones* (12). The ideal is objective narration, free of any partisan purpose, creating the world in imitation of God; authorial intrusion undermines illusion and makes us aware of fictionality (20, 22, 57, 38). Spielhagen's tendentiousness depresses the aesthetic and inhibits totality, defined as comprehending the whole people and universal human feeling; Hart links him in this connection with Zola, 15–16, 52,). Spielhagen is a wordy phrasemaker like Auerbach (16–17). Such symbolism as he employs is forced on the reader, as in *Sturmflut* (33). He was a poor prophet in his skepticism about Bismarck, for it is now evident that the chancellor realized the dreams of the masses, even if against their will; the democratic idea that actuates Spielhagen's writing is false (46, 28). He is monotonous, writes the same novel over again; one could melt his oeuvre down to one novel; his setting is always the same, his imagination limited to a space from Stralsund across the Baltic to the island of Rügen; his plotting is melodramatic, sensationalistic, and improbable (50–51, 52, 58, 63). Like Bleibtreu, Hart complains that every novel exhibits sensual and passionate women (51). Spielhagen lacks the idealistic humor that looks on the apparent contradictions of the world from a sublime height of equanimity (63). His style is complex, too difficult, too elevated, lacking in vividness (64–65). His Goethean model is not *Wilhelm Meisters Lehrjahre* (Wilhelm Meister's Apprenticeship, 1795–96), which is a novel, but *Die Wahlverwandtschaften* (Elective Affinities, 1809), which is actually a novella (70). Thus, he lacks a basic grasp of genre.

This portrayal is a caricature for polemical purposes, but it is not wholly impertinent. Any reader will discover a similarity in situation and characterization in many of the novels; there is a problem about style, though, as I shall note further along, I locate its origin in a different place; complaint about melodrama and sensationalism persists to the present day.[47] Whether the regional specificity characteristic of many, though certainly not all, of his texts is a weakness or a strength might be debated; I do not believe that it should be tarred with the brush of the suspect genre of *Heimatkunst*.[48] But there are several peculiarities of Hart's critique that have not always been clearly registered. Conventionally it has been seen as a manifesto of the younger generation of Naturalists against a mode of literature still rooted in idealism and moralism, the sort of displacement of the fathers by the sons that is routine in literary history. But, apart from the reproach of stylistic artificiality, there is little of Naturalism in Hart's attack. The principles are, in fact, deeply conservative. The allegiance to objectivity and totality, the rejection of tendentiousness, the nostalgia for the epic, and the skepticism about the genre of the novel are all grounded in the aesthetics of the age of Goethe. To this has been added a substantial dose of Wilhelminian nationalism, evident in the defense of Bismarck against Spielhagen's skepticism, in the dismissal of democratic ideas as antiquated,[49] and in the quite correct implication that Spielhagen had been unable to get with the program of the German Reich.[50] Far from contrasting Spielhagen unfavorably to the Naturalists, Hart yokes him to the arch-Naturalist, Zola, the chief example for all those resistant to the modern of how not to write, with the additional taint of being *French*, that is, heartless, materialistic, reproducing the vulgar, the ugly, and the salacious.

One might dismiss this performance as an eccentricity if it had not been so influential — as late as 1928 the premier American Germanist, Kuno Francke, declared that, while Hart was not Spielhagen's equal in cosmopolitanism, the critique of his technique was fully justified[51] — and if it were not so illustrative of the bitter ironies that beset his reputation and must have dismayed him almost beyond bearing. For the most diabolical aspect of the critique is that it turns his own values against him in a way that anticipates large areas of the case against him from his own time to the present. He placed an extremely high value on poesy and aspired to the sublime status of *Dichter;* yet, he found himself charged with pursuing a debased and popular mode of subliterature. While he rejected tendentiousness in literature, he was once said by Raabe to have pronounced himself a "Dichter-Journalist."[52] No one has been able to document such an utterance, and it seems most unlikely; Spielhagen wrote that one should not confuse *Dichter* with journalists (*BT,* 98) and, made uneasy even by agreeing to contribute drama criticism to a magazine, insisted forcefully that he was not and never had been a journalist (*NB,* vii). Nevertheless, Engel also charged him with descending with a work like *Angela* to the level of journalistic reading matter for boarding-school girls; *Susi* (1895) has also been declared a newspaper novel.[53] Spielhagen was strongly opposed to Naturalism, especially in the drama, imported as it was, via Ibsen, from abroad. He asserted hyperbolically that the whole world found *A Doll's House* (1879) distressing to any healthy spirit (*BT,* 299; his attitudes toward Ibsen are quite similar to Raabe's). On the matter of foreign literature he was often in substantial agreement with Hart, writing near the beginning of his career that the Germans were falling victim to the sensationalism and coquetry in the French novel[54] and near the end that, despite the achievements of foreign nations in the novel, the Germans were still superior (*NB,* 88); even Thackeray and Dickens are shallow compared to Auerbach and Freytag, not to speak of the French (*BT,* 262). He persistently combated Zola, though with the further irony, as I shall suggest, that Zola came, nevertheless, to infect his later writing; still, Hart's linking of him to Zola strikes one as a particularly perfidious maneuver. Spielhagen's allegiance to the aesthetics of the age of Goethe, most particularly of Wilhelm von Humboldt, was copiously on the record;[55] the commitment grew stronger as his situation worsened[56] until, just before the end of his career, he began at last to doubt that there were eternal laws of art (*NB*, 11). This initial commitment compelled the elevation of Homer as the unreachable model of the epic genre, along with the goal of totality, the dubious admissibility of the genre of the novel to poesy, and the demand for objective narration. Hart does not attack Spielhagen's theoretical convictions from a modernist and Naturalist position; from a conservative and at least implicitly antimodern position he associates himself with them and charges Spielhagen with gross failures to adhere to them. Particularly in the matter of objective narration Hart is able to mark up, with the greatest of ease, any number of violations in Spielhagen's narrative practice.[57] Thus, he is caught in a pincer: while for modern literary historians he was too much oriented on the past and old verities,[58] for Hart he was insufficiently oriented on the past or faithful to old verities.

The impeachment of Spielhagen as a novelist has led to claims that his real significance is to be found in his theoretical work. It is hard to think of any other nineteenth-century German writer, except, perhaps, Otto Ludwig, who wrote as much and as insistently about literary theory. These writings are wide-ranging, dealing with, among other things, genre definition, the relationship of authorial experience and imagination, and character models and typology, along with a large body of practical criticism. They are best known, however, for a reiterated and, one might fairly say, fanatical insistence on the doctrine of objective narration. Since few in our time seriously believe in objective narration, it turns out that the theoretical work, though declared to be his most important achievement, is a historical curiosity of no intrinsic value. With this move, he is catapulted into the black hole of decanonized oblivion from which no known force has been able to recuperate him.

His fixation on objective narration began at a fairly young age with what he initially thought of as a doctoral dissertation. In it he meant to apply an allegiance to Humboldt's aesthetics to the refutation of Schiller's distinction of naive and sentimentive poetry.[59] This need to combat a sixty-five-year-old essay with the aid of a doctrine from the same era is, in itself, an indication of the burden of immobility that the achievements of the age of Goethe imposed on Spielhagen's generation. The corollary to the principle, argued against Schiller's dualities, that there is and can be only one poetic substance (*BT*, 112) came to be the precept of objective narration, which Spielhagen continued to affirm, though with sometimes confusing variations, practically to the end of his life. The principle is of suspect simplicity: the writer of prose fiction may not intrude into the text in his own authorial voice. The author must be silent and invisible; the poet has nothing to do with the reader and nothing to say to him (*BT*, 91). Authorial utterance speaks directly from the author's to the reader's understanding [*Verstand*], disillusions the imagination, and is therefore unpoetic (*VS*, 209). No exceptions or variations are permissible. To Spielhagen this was law; he could not understand why it was not universally acknowledged. He grieved that he lacked the ability to convince others of what was absolutely certain to him (*FE*, 2: 222). Late in life he wrote that it was as clear to him as two plus two equals four; why would it not go into the heads of the teachers of literature and aesthetics?[60]

Today, after a century of narratology, it is difficult to regard these propositions with any seriousness at all.[61] One of the pioneers of narrative theory in Germany, Käte Friedemann, began her programmatic study with an attack on Spielhagen's position.[62] Even earlier, however, the distinguished literary scholar Wilhelm Scherer had defended Goethe's flexible narrative practice and explicitly contradicted Spielhagen.[63] Almost all modern commentaries are exercises in displaying the theory's untenability.[64] Spielhagen seems to have had little or no idea of the author's voice as a created one, part of the fiction, and he only intermittently recognized that the author's organization, setting of values, and moral system are forms of voice. For Bakhtin, Spielhagen's principles could result only in "unnovelistic novels. . . . As a theoretician Spielhagen was deaf to heteroglot language and to that which it specifically generates: double-voiced discourse."[65] At times, to be sure, he admitted that the "Homeric" objectivity is no longer achievable in the more disparate, class-riven modern world (*NB* 53) — a lesson he might have learned from Schiller — but he was unable to sever the genre of the novel from the model of the ancient epic. He exempts first-person narration from his strictures altogether, for in that mode he can recognize the fictionality of the narrator (*BT* 131–32, 208). There is a trace of Raabe's instinctual awareness of the porous boundary between first- and third-person narration in the fleeting comment that, compared to Homer, every modern novel is subjective and first-person (*BT* 132; cf. 203) and in his recognition that *Problematische Naturen* had the external form of a third-person novel but was first-person in its essence (*FE* 2: 394, 443). But he cannot integrate these insights and can only conclude from them the inferiority of the novel genre (*BT,* 133–34).

As pointless as his theory may seem to us today, it was not eccentric in his own time, even if some contemporaries were inclined to evade his nonnegotiable stance in propagating it. Everyone after 1848 agreed on the exclusion of tendentiousness.[66] Fontane acknowledged the objective principle while, characteristically, trying to be less rigid about it. He wrote to Spielhagen on February 15, 1896, that authorial intrusion is always a failing, but it is not always easy to tell when it is occurring, for the author has to *do* things; on the following November 24 he sent a copy of *Die Poggenpuhls* (1896) with a puckish apology for having violated Spielhagen's principles but adding that rules are there to be broken.[67] Still, one observer has concluded that Fontane reduced his level of authorial intrusion under Spielhagen's influence.[68] There were many who regarded the standard of narrative objectivity as axiomatic.[69] Its survival seems to be a conservative marker. In the revision of Tony Kellen's novel theory by the anti-Semitic Heinrich Keiter, Friedemann's critical position on objectivity is said to be an obvious error.[70] As late as 1959 Heimito von Doderer — oddly, a notably intrusive and digressive narrator — acknowledged Spielhagen's insistence on objectivity as one of the fundamental propositions of novel writing.[71] A version of it may be thought to survive in the modern critical doctrine that the narrator must show, not tell.[72] But Percy Lubbock's elaboration of this doctrine, exemplified in Flaubert's impersonality (occasionally mentioned in our connection) is incomparably subtle, flexible, and sensitive compared to Spielhagen's obstinacy. As we have seen, Hart did not oppose the principle but marked up Spielhagen's own violations of it. This is childishly easy to do. Anyone could see that Spielhagen, the enemy of the authorial voice and of tendentiousness in literature, was a crowdingly insistent evangelist, urging his worldview on the reader, and a liberal-democratic partisan evolving from a bourgeois class allegiance to an independent affinity for social democracy. The modern orthodox view that these attitudes cannot be charged to a nonexistent, empirical narrator, only to the created fictional consciousness,[73] I regard as pettifogging and unrealistic in regard to reception. In fact, he was often regarded as a successor to the generation of activist Young German writers and particularly to Karl Gutzkow, in whose periodical Spielhagen's first publication appeared.[74] Thus, it was evident to the naked eye that the prohibition was purely formal,[75] directed against an explicit narrative "I" or visible, self-conscious management of the text, and had nothing to do with a severe objectivity of tone.

Spielhagen as a theoretician might have had fewer difficulties with his younger contemporaries and become less notorious today if he had not been so fiercely insistent on his position and so extreme in his critical application of it. Given his allegiance to the age of Goethe and his profound veneration of Goethe himself, one might suppose that he would relax a bit when he finds Goethe at odds with the principle — for example, in the famous opening of *Die Wahlverwandtschaften*: "Eduard — so nennen wir einen reichen Baron im besten Mannesalter."[76] No, no, no; one may not do such a thing (*BT*, 92). This opening seems to have soured him on what he regards as an overgrown, disordered novella, starting with the title; thus, it is bitterly ironic that Hart declared it to be Spielhagen's model (*H*, 70). His recommendation would have been to get rid of the chemical symbolism, tighten the text, title it *Ottilie*, and excise Ottilie's diaries (*NB*, 96; *VS*, 215). Goethe should have avoided the editor's intrusion at the end of *Werther*, as well (*NB*, 70). Spielhagen's literary criticism often sounds like this. He read widely, not only in German but also in English, American, French, Scandinavian, and Russian literature. But he seems to have liked little of what he saw; no one knows how to do it. An example is a lengthy reckoning with George Eliot's *Middlemarch* as a botched novel, an almost unbelievable display of narrative barbarism patched together from novella pieces (*BT*, 67–99). One may be inclined to think that a reader who cannot appreciate *Middlemarch* is disqualified as a literary critic; Otto Ludwig praised Eliot "for her skill of interposing reflections in her story."[77] Erich Schmidt took the occasion of the birthday celebration to preface a brief lecture on *Die Wahlverwandtschaften* with the remark that Spielhagen had not upset *his* partiality for *Middlemarch*.[78]

Spielhagen was not a stupid man; such fervor on such a recondite topic invites explanation. Several considerations, which he regarded as imperatives, converged in the particular historical moment of his consciousness. The one usually highlighted is his allegiance to the German "classicism," sometimes regarded as a symptom of the stunted maturation and resistance to modernization of the German bourgeoisie. To this it might be said, as a corrective to today's attitudes in this matter, that it was the great age of Goethe, with values reinforced by the Revolution of 1848, that certified for the cultured bourgeoisie the status of the inchoate German nation, a status that was widely acknowledged throughout the civilized world and of which, in Spielhagen's view, the Reich was a far from adequate successor and conserver, a status, finally, that he was obviously not wrong in conjecturing that the Reich might at length ruin in the world at large. If the Germans were to disappear, he wrote, they could be recreated from Goethe, who was more truly German than Luther, Frederick the Great, or Bismarck (*AW*, 90). It is perhaps optimistic to equate German idealism and humanism with a tradition of civil rights,[79] but he did assert that the real strength of the German nation lay in humaneness; Germany will never start a war (*AW*, 91, 197–98).

But this tradition created difficulties for the novelist. Subsumed under the category of the "epic," the modern novel could never hope to equal "Homeric" totality or unity of creation and reception. It *had* to be an inferior genre, a symptom of cultural decadence. Spielhagen made this matter as difficult as possible for himself by taking the most normative possible position in genre theory: literary genres are fixed once and for all; there never could be, he once wrote, a new genre (*BT*, 108). The anxiety came to be focused on a perhaps more casual than systematic remark of Schiller that the novelist was the "half-brother" of the poet.[80] Spielhagen declared that he was ashamed of the novel-reading of his youth, of his attachment to the half-brother (*FE*, 1: 327). This half-brother turns up constantly in Spielhagen's writings; he even jokes about him wryly in his fictional texts — for example, in *Sturmflut* and *Die schönen Amerikanerinnen* (The Beautiful American Girls, 1868).[81] Since his only conceivable ambition was to be a poet, a *Dichter*, a permanent dissonance came to be installed in his conception of himself, which goes some way to explain the comic pedantry[82] and nonnegotiable character of his theoretical writings. Even though at one point he hoped that Schiller may not have been entirely serious and was not referring to the master writers (*NB*, 54–55), Spielhagen never overcame the scruple that the novel was, in fact, poetologically inferior. Preoccupied as always with the anxiety of influence, he quotes at length the letter to Goethe of October 20, 1797, where Schiller, with his customary irritating forthrightness, declares that the form of *Wilhelm Meister*, like that of any novel, is utterly unpoetic (*BT*, 198–200).[83] This view was widely shared in Spielhagen's time (e.g., *H*, xlvi, 9). One index of this is the custom of depreciating what are perceived as sensational or melodramatic elements as "novelistic" [*romanhaft*], a locution that occurs in critiques of Spielhagen up to the present day.[84] In Germany, at any rate, the novel may not be novelistic; it must strive to be something other than it is, an effort in which it can, of course, never succeed except in eccentric cases, which then come to be canonized and create the impression that the German novel tradition is essentially different from that of other nations. For his part, Spielhagen intended to free the novel from the novelistic, only to be perpetually charged with this very fault.[85]

Other problematic elements of Spielhagen's theoretical efforts are related to the aporia of realism he shared with his literary generation: how to achieve mimetic fidelity without violating aesthetic canons of beauty and propriety. One is his extensive rumination on the relationship of experience and imagination, of finding and inventing, a dialectic that provided the title of an autobiography (*FE;* see also *AW*, 93). Experience is the principle of realism, and it must be one's own (*BT*, 180); invention is the principle of poiesis; the real cannot be unmediatedly represented but must be given shape, perhaps idealized, in the imagination. So much is clear, but beyond this I cannot provide any help. I still do not understand how the relationship actually works; it seems to oscillate opportunistically between contrary commitments without ever providing a formula of realistic poiesis. Something similar is the case with another element, his insistence that characters must be derived from real-life models, persons one knows or has seen. But, of course, the characters cannot be the same as the models but must be different;

in wrestling with this topic he approaches without actually developing the concept of typology we know in the tradition from Friedrich Engels to Georg Lukács (*BT,* 180).

Finally, there is the contradiction between "objective" narration and the pronounced political and socially critical commitment of Spielhagen's fiction. The only explanation for this is an assumption that the liberal view is the true and real one; as reality narrates itself,[86] objective representation will permit the liberal truth to emerge unencumbered by mere personal opinion or subjective intention. The "idea" is supposed to speak for itself.[87] Tendentious writers, on the other hand (with a tag from *Faust*), do not allow "den Geist der Zeiten" to speak, only "ihren eigenen Geist,"[88] the assumption being that the spirit of the times is objectively knowable (*BT,* 59). Strodtmann agreed that the illusion of reality conjured by the objective narrator, despite his *engagement,* is never tendentious.[89] Spielhagen's social novels, Karpeles noted on the occasion of the birthday celebration, pursued the goals of the progress of freedom, becoming increasingly objective and nonpartisan.[90] Early in his career, in a letter of 1862, Spielhagen allowed that the hermaphroditic nature of the novel must be borne, for it was the art of the present whose content was the emancipation of the poor and the simple from the curse of the common and the obsolete.[91] When the representation of the value-laden world is identified with reality itself, "objectivity" is duplicity, though quite unaware of itself, for Spielhagen in his conscious being was the most honest of men. Nothing else, I believe, calls the quality of his intellect and perspicuity more cruelly into question than this consideration.

Even if his self-imposed regimen of "objectivity" was illusory and, fortunately, infeasible, his theoretical preoccupations did exercise qualitative constraints. Peter Demetz has observed acutely that "objectivity" compels a scenic narration that tends to the dramatic, the melodramatic, and the theatrical, thus subverting probability and, one might add, Spielhagen's rigid genre distinctions.[92] The demand for transparency is also inhospitable to creativity at the level of style, for the writing is not supposed to get in the way of the representation of reality; the word is not an end in itself, he wrote, but a means to an end (*AW,* 136). The elegance of French literary style he regarded as a defect (*VS,* 302). Opinions on Spielhagen's own style range widely from piquant and effervescent and, while unremarkable, pleasant and cultivated, to gleaming but empty, garrulous and trivial, bloated and theatrical, or banal.[93] There has been a good deal of complaint about its bookishness regardless of the speaker's cultural level or dialect. My own opinion is that, since Spielhagen was a high-strung, to some degree neurotic, personality,[94] his style has a certain edge and vivacity; but in general it is undistinguished, even programmatically so. I think, incidentally, that this is a problem with German realism generally and may partly account for its modest standing in general literary history. Similarly, the insistence on transparency is unfriendly to symbol and metaphor, for to do anything artistic with the surface of narration is a form of intrusion, of the author calling attention to himself and his fiction-making. Spielhagen was generally impatient with symbolic devices, as appears in his ambivalence toward Goethe.[95] His most overt effort at employing a symbol as an objective correlative, the flood in *Sturmflut,* seems to have made him uncomfortable; he confesses apologetically that, in reality, the events linked by the symbol, the inflationary flood of French gold reparations after the Franco-Prussian War and the inundation of Germany's north shore, had nothing to do with one another chronologically (*NB,* 220). Others shared the suspicion of symbol; Julian Schmidt wrote that Spielhagen should have left the hammer and anvil out of *Hammer und Amboß* (1869).[96] But Swales, who sees the relative absence of symbol as a marker of Spielhagen's inferiority to Balzac and Dickens, singles out the scene of the flooding storm as a uniquely successful passage.[97]

For all of the weight of the case that can be maintained against Spielhagen and the agreement to keep him in the decanonized outer darkness, from time to time there have been voices suggesting a reconsideration. Usually such arguments are made on political and ideological grounds, giving him credit for maintaining a discourse on social problems in inhospitable times.[98] He was, after all, one of the most democratic writers in German literature of the nineteenth century, especially recognized as such in foreign countries. Löwenthal from his left-wing position asserted that Spielhagen had been silenced by the dominant order and that this was to his credit.[99] That judgment may be excessive, but more recently he has been described as "one of the most important literary representatives of a liberal Germany which would be ruled through political participation and democracy."[100] In conclusion, I should like to venture briefly three suggestions as to how one might try to recover for Spielhagen some measure of reputation.

My first proposal would be to sever his theoretical work entirely from the fiction; to forget about it as far as possible. This might seem bizarre, both from the general consideration that the parts of a creative person's oeuvre must have some internal coherence and from the specific one that the theoretical enterprise mattered so much to him. But because it is so misguided and damaging to his modern reputation, and because modern scholars constantly recur to its incongruity with his fictional practice,[101] one might try experimentally to do without it altogether. Second, one might redirect attention to a different body of texts. Within the decanonized reception there is a kind of minicanon of remembered works, especially five novels from the first third of his career, which were among his most popular: *Problematische Naturen, Die von Hohenstein* (The von Hohensteins, 1864), *In Reih' und Glied* (In Rank and File, 1867), *Hammer und Amboß,* and *Sturmflut.* Of these, *Problematische Naturen* and *In Reih' und Glied* were of more interest in the past as enacting the concerns and frustrations of the post-1848 generation of liberals — particularly its class concerns in opposition to and envy of the aristocracy.[102] *In Reih' und Glied* was also of interest because of its portrayal of a figure resembling Ferdinand Lassalle, whom Spielhagen admired, but skeptically.[103] *Die von Hohenstein*, which had been the least liked of the five because it was felt it had carried the hostility to the aristocracy to caricatured extremes,[104] has more recently been the object of a study of its own.[105] Of greater interest in recent years have been *Hammer und Amboß,* the first important German novel to attempt a representation of modern industry, and *Sturmflut,* the major fictional treatment of the financial crash of the 1870s as a harbinger of the predatory but erratic capitalism that was to become characteristic of the Reich. These texts have come to be reasonably well understood; therefore, my second suggestion is to move beyond them to later ones that were less popular but perhaps can arouse a retrospective interest that they were not able to achieve in their own time.

My third proposal is to employ as a principle in this inquiry the agonized disappointment, frustration, and ultimate pessimism of a national liberal as he contemplates his dream of achieved unity and greatness evolving under Bismarck away from the moral and ideal energies that had impelled it in his generation as he "grows more and more pessimistic and at the same time radical."[106] As examples, let me propose four works that have been slighted by majority opinion but have had occasional defenders. The first is a strange novel so contorted over the problem that readers at the time seem not to have been able to understand it: *Allzeit voran* (Ever Forward, 1872).[107] A central figure, Hedwig, is an uncommonly beautiful woman of servant-class origins, who, in her morganatic and unconsummated marriage to an elderly, soon to be mediatized North German prince, applies herself to relieving poverty and oppression. The loving prince longs for sexual fulfillment, but he is in physical and political decline, hopelessly committed to the preservation of his particularist sovereignty and destroyed in a trap set by conniving French agents. Hedwig is impetuously wooed by a violently nationalist Prussian count and Franco-Prussian war hero and quietly loved by a competent and kindly bourgeois physician. None of these men succeeds in life or love; Hedwig evades them all. She is, it seems to me, an allegory (for all that Spielhagen professed to despise allegory as unpoetic, *NB*, 81) of the inability of the aesthetic and humanistic principle to find a partner in the formation of the nation.

Occasionally noticed in the critical literature is *Was will das werden?* (the title refers to the puzzlement of the Apostles in Acts 2:12), one of the longest of Spielhagen's novels; as a Bildungsroman it may seem in 1887 to be an example of his adherence to vanishing forms and concerns, but, in fact, it antedates by a couple of years the definitive version of Keller's *Der grüne Heinrich* (Green Henry, 1889–90), with which it shares several structural features: first-person narration, a severe retrospective on youthful naïveté and self-absorption, the successive failures of projects of self-realization, and a resolution in a minor key with questionable prospects for the future. It also breaks with the prohibition on the depiction of the ugly and vulgar in scenes in which the protagonist finds himself down and out in the Hamburg underworld. This is a sign of one of the most interesting developments in Spielhagen's late career, determined by the deterioration, in his eyes, of the German environment: after years of repetitive repudiation of the spirit of contemporary French literature and particularly of the Germans' *bête noire*, Zola, he comes under their influence, surely willy-nilly. There is no end to his attacks on Zola in his theoretical and critical writings; yet, the historian of Zola's German reception has remarked perceptively that Spielhagen was potentially approaching him.[108] In retrospect he was obliged to admit that Zola's ugliness was drawn from reality, if not the whole of it (*FE*, 1: 186–87), and eventually that he was powerful, surprising, and humane, even if he was only an inventor without an imaginative heart (*NB*, 45–46, 81).

One symptom of this evolution across the grain, so to speak, is the very late *Susi*, which has been condemned by almost all conventional opinion and therefore might be of interest to us today:[109] a novel of high-society intrigue in which the good and kind Baron Astolf comes to a sad end, while the pert and pretty vixen Susi, who cheerfully maneuvers herself into the position of the duke's mistress, and her amoral confidant von Brenken are, on the whole, quite successful. Some of this tone, in which satire has edged into cynicism, infects the oddest creation of Spielhagen's late career: *Zum Zeitvertreib* (To Kill Time, 1897), a novel based on the same scandal in the Ardenne family that impelled Fontane's *Effi Briest*. Naturally a fair amount has been written about this coincidence and its place in the uneasy relationship of the two writers, but always on the assumption that Spielhagen's work is hopelessly inferior.[110] No one will want to put it into competition with Fontane's finesse, but in its sad and ultimately lethal comedy of the vain and delusory class-bound desire of a thwarted petty-bourgeois quasi-intellectual, it has less of Fontane's imposed conciliation and forgiveness and might be looked on as a bitter valedictory to the foundered aspirations of the poetic realism.

Notes

[1] Friedrich Spielhagen, *Am Wege: Vermischte Schriften* (Leipzig: Staackmann, 1903), 34–35. Henceforth cited as *AW*.

[2] Festausschuss der Spielhagen-Feier, ed., *Friedrich Spielhagen: Dem Meister des deutschen Romans zu seinem 70. Geburtstag von Freunden und Jüngern gewidmet* (Leipzig: Staackmann, 1899).

[3] Gustav Karpeles, *Friedrich Spielhagen: Ein literarischer Essay* (Leipzig: Staackmann, 1889).

[4] Festausschuss der Spielhagen-Feier, ed., 6–7.

[5] Victor Klemperer, *Curriculum vitae: Jugend um 1900* (Berlin: Siedler, 1989), 1: 475.

[6] See Werner Fuld, *Wilhelm Raabe: Eine Biographie* (Munich: Hanser, 1993), 349; Walter Hettche, "Nach alter Melodie: Die Gedichte von Julius Rodenberg, Wilhelm Jensen und Paul Heyse zum 70. Geburtstag Wilhelm Raabes," *Jahrbuch der Raabe-Gesellschaft* (1999): 144–45.

[7] Gabriele Henkel, *Studien zur Privatbibliothek Wilhelm Raabes: Vom "wirklichen Autor," von Zeitgenossen und "ächten Dichtern"* (Braunschweig: Stadtbibliothek, 1997), 122.

[8] Ella Mensch, "Erinnerungen an Friedrich Spielhagen," *Westermanns Monatshefte* 110 (1911): 358.

[9] Hans Henning, *Friedrich Spielhagen* (Leipzig: Staackmann, 1910), 110.

[10] Rosa-Maria Zinken, *Der Roman als Zeitdokument: Bürgerlicher Liberalismus in Friedrich Spielhagens "Die von Hohenstein" (1863/64)* (Frankfurt am Main, Bern, New York & Paris: Peter Lang, 1991), 16.

[11] Volker Neuhaus, "Der Unterhaltungsroman im 19. Jahrhundert," *Handbuch des deutschen Romans,* ed. Helmut Koopmann (Düsseldorf: Bagel, 1983), 410–11.

[12] Henning, *Friedrich Spielhagen,* 117.

[13] Edouard de Morsier, *Romanciers allemands contemporains* (Paris: Perrin, 1890), 4.

[14] For a particularly encomiastic example, see Harold Berman, "Friedrich Spielhagen: The Novelist of Democracy," *Twentieth Century Magazine* 4 (1911): 347–49.

[15] Henry James, *The Complete Tales,* ed. Leon Edel (Philadelphia & New York: Lippincott, 1963), 5: 38. On James's insuperable dislike of things German, see Evelyn A. Hovanec, *Henry James and Germany* (Amsterdam: Rodopi, 1979). She concludes that Spielhagen is an "imaginary writer" whose name James made up (100), a particularly striking instance of his disappearance from the cultural memory.

[16] John Hargrove Tatum, *The Reception of German Literature in U.S. German Texts, 1864–1914* (New York, Bern, Frankfurt am Main & Paris: Peter Lang, 1988), 130–33.

[17] Hermann Schieding, *Untersuchungen über die Romantechnik Friedrich Spielhagens* (Borna-Leipzig: Noske, 1914), 138.

[18] Adolf Strodtmann, *Dichterprofile: Literaturbilder aus dem neunzehnten Jahrhundert* (Stuttgart: Abenheim, 1879), 195.

[19] [Hans Ludwig Rosegger, ed.], "Briefe von Friedrich Spielhagen an den alten Heimgärtner," *Roseggers Heimgarten* 35 (1911): 608.

[20] Neuhaus, "Der Unterhaltungsroman," 410.

[21] Henkel, *Studien zur Privatbibliothek Wilhelm Raabes,* 121.

[22] The only titles I can find in print at this writing are *Platt Land* (Recklinghausen: Manuscripte, 1996), and *Sturmflut* (Rostock: Hinstorff, 1996). In 1973 a paperback edition of *Hammer und Amboß* was published in a "nostalgia" series by Heyne in Munich, but it appears to be out of print.

[23] Henning, *Friedrich Spielhagen.*

[24] Katherine Roper, "Friedrich Spielhagen," in James Hardin and Siegfried Mews, eds., *Dictionary of Literary Biography,* vol. 129: *Nineteenth-Century German Writers, 1841–1900* (Detroit & London: Gale Research, 1993), 348–60.

[25] Franz Mehring, *Beiträge zur Literaturgeschichte,* ed. Walter Heist (Berlin: Weiss, 1948), 216.

[26] Alexander Robinson Anderson, "Spielhagen's Problematic Heroes" (Diss. Brown U, 1962), 6.

[27] Mehring, *Beiträge zur Literaturgeschichte,* 216.

[28] Ernst Alker, *Die deutsche Literatur im 19. Jahrhundert (1832–1914),* 3rd ed. (Stuttgart: Kröner, 1969), 124.

[29] Ulrich Ott, ed., *Literatur im Industriezeitalter: Eine Austellung des Deutschen Literaturarchivs im Schiller-Nationalmuseum* (Marbach am Neckar: Deutsche Schillergesellschaft, 1987), 1: 215–17; table, 1: 226.

[30] Mehring, *Beiträge zur Literaturgeschichte,* 216–17; Leo Löwenthal, *Erzählkunst und Gesellschaft: Die Gesellschaftsproblematik in der deutschen Literatur des 19. Jahrhunderts* (Neuwied & Berlin: Luchterhand, 1971), 137–75; Jürgen Kuczynski, *Gestalten und Werke: Soziologische Studien zur deutschen Literatur,* vol. 1 (Berlin & Weimar: Aufbau, 1969), 194–203.

[31] Henrike Lamers, *Held oder Welt? Zum Romanwerk Friedrich Spielhagens* (Bonn: Bouvier, 1991), 12–14.

[32] E.g., Hellmuth Mielke, *Der Deutsche Roman des 19. Jahrhunderts,* 3rd ed. (Berlin: Schwetschke, 1898), 289–302.

[33] Richard M. Meyer, *Die deutsche Literatur des Neunzehnten Jahrhunderts,* Volksausgabe (Berlin: Bondi, 1912), 424.

[34] Hans-Jürgen Schrader, "Gedichtete Dichtungstheorie im Werk Raabes. Exemplifiziert an 'Alte Nester,'" *Jahrbuch der Raabe-Gesellschaft* (1989): 23–27.

[35] Spielhagen, *Neue Beiträge zur Theorie und Technik der Epik und Dramatik* (Leipzig: Staackmann, 1898), 5. Henceforth cited as *NB.* English in the original.

[36] Thomas Mann, *Gesammelte Werke in zwölf Bänden* ([Frankfurt am Main]: S. Fischer, 1960), 11: 753–54.

[37] Hans Mayer, *Von Lessing bis Thomas Mann: Wandlungen der bürgerlichen Literatur in Deutschland* (Pfullingen: Neske, 1959), 301.

[38] E.g., Franz Rhöse, *Konflikt und Versöhnung: Untersuchungen zur Theorie des Romans von Hegel bis zum Naturalismus* (Stuttgart: Metzler, 1978), 177.

[39] Carl Bleibtreu, *Revolution der Literatur*, ed. Johannes J. Braakenburg (Tübingen: Niemeyer, 1973).

[40] Spielhagen, *Finder und Erfinder: Erinnerungen aus meinem Leben* (Leipzig: Staackmann, 1890), 2: 407. Henceforth cited as *FE*.

[41] Eduard Engel, "Stereographischer Bericht über die Gerichtsverhandlungen im Prozesse: 'Angela.' Roman von Friedrich Spielhagen," *Magazin für die Literatur des In- und Auslandes* 50 (1881): 399–404, 413–17. On this episode, see Hellmuth Mojem, "Literaturbetrieb und literarisches Selbstverständnis: Der Briefwechsel Wilhelm Raabes mit Eduard Engel," *Jahrbuch der Raabe-Gesellschaft* (1995): 63–64; Henkel, *Studien zur Privatbibliothek Wilhelm Raabes*, 117; cf. Spielhagen's own wry commentaries, *AW*, 192, and *Beiträge zur Theorie und Technik des Dramas* (Leipzig: Staackmann, 1883), 292–93 n., Henceforth cited as *BT*.

[42] See, for example, Victor Klemperer, *Die Zeitromane Friedrich Spielhagens und ihre Wurzeln* (Weimar: Duncker, 1913), 72, 83, 134.

[43] Fritz Mauthner, *Nach berühmten Mustern: Parodistische Studien* (Stuttgart: Spemann, [1878]).

[44] Julian Schmidt, "Friedrich Spielhagen," *Westermann's Jahrbuch der Illustrirten Deutschen Monatshefte* 29 (1870–71): 424, 428, 430.

[45] Bleibtreu, *Revolution der Literatur*, 28.

[46] Heinrich and Julius Hart, *Kritische Waffengänge*, ed. Mark Boulby (New York & London: Johnson Reprint, 1969); henceforth cited as *H*. The Hart brothers are usually treated as coauthors of the *Kritische Waffengänge*, but Boulby assigns the Spielhagen essay to Heinrich on good grounds (*H*, viii), and I shall follow his expert opinion. The segments are paged separately in Boulby's reprint; references are to the sixth one, entitled "Friedrich Spielhagen und der deutsche Roman der Gegenwart." Interestingly, Julius Hart published a eulogy on Spielhagen's death (Ott, ed., *Literatur im Industriezeitalter*, 1: 110–13).

[47] See, for example, Lamers, *Held oder Welt*, 120; Eda Sagarra, *Tradition and Revolution: German Literature and Society 1830–1890* (London: Weidenfeld & Nicolson, 1971), 216; Martin Swales, *Epochenbuch Realismus: Romane und Erzählungen* (Berlin: Erich Schmidt, 1997), 102–3. Swales makes a comparison with soap operas.

[48] On this point I disagree with Martha Geller, *Friedrich Spielhagens Theorie und Praxis des Romans* (Berlin: Grote, 1917), 96.

[49] This view was taken also by Schmidt, "Friedrich Spielhagen," 448.

[50] On the Harts' nationalism, see Boulby's introduction (*H,* iv–v, x, xvii) and, with particular stress, Rolf Sälter, *Entwicklungslinien der deutschen Zola-Rezeption von den Anfängen bis zum Tode des Autors* (Bern, Frankfurt am Main, New York & Paris: Peter Lang, 1989), 79–80.

[51] Kuno Francke, *Weltbürgertum in der deutschen Literatur von Herder bis Nietzsche* (Berlin: Weidmann, 1928), 116.

[52] To Paul Heyse, March 2, 1875, in Wilhelm Raabe, *Sämtliche Werke,* ed. Karl Hoppe et al. (Göttingen: Vandenhoeck & Ruprecht, 1960–94), Ergänzungsband (supplementary volume) 2: 183.

[53] Engel, "Stereographischer Bericht," 401, 414; Alfred F. Goessl, "Die Darstellung des Adels in Prosaschriften Friedrich Spielhagens" (Diss. Tulane U, 1966), 199.

[54] Spielhagen, *Vermischte Schriften: Sämtliche Werke,* vol. 7 (Berlin: Jancke, [1870]) 302, 305. Henceforth cited as *VS.*

[55] See Arthur H. Hughes, "Wilhelm von Humboldt's Influence on Spielhagen's Esthetics," *Germanic Review* 5 (1930): 211–24.

[56] Lamers, *Held oder Welt?* 158.

[57] See John R. Frey, "Author-Intrusion in the Narrative: German Theory and Some Modern Examples," *Germanic Review* 23 (1948): 277.

[58] See, for example, Geller, *Friedrich Spielhagens Theorie und Praxis des Romans,* 10; Hugo Bieber, *Der Kampf um die Tradition: Die deutsche Dichtung im europäischen Geistesleben 1830–1880* (Stuttgart: Metzler, 1928), 472; Fritz Martini, *Deutsche Literatur im bürgerlichen Realismus 1848–1898* (Stuttgart: Metzler, 1964), 431; Günter Rebing, *Der Halbbruder des Dichters: Friedrich Spielhagens Theorie des Romans* (Frankfurt am Main: Athenäum, 1972), 30, 99; Joachim Worthmann, *Probleme des Zeitromans: Studien zur Geschichte des deutschen Romans im 19. Jahrhundert* (Heidelberg: Winter, 1974), 100.

[59] Henning, *Friedrich Spielhagen,* 73–74; see *FE,* 2: 202–12, 222.

[60] Mensch, "Erinnerungen an Friedrich Spielhagen," 359.

[61] An exception is the eccentric effort of Andrea Fischbacher-Bosshardt, *Anfänge der modernen Erzählkunst: Untersuchungen zu Friedrich Spielhagens theoretischem und literarischem Werk* (Bern, Frankfurt am Main, New York & Paris: Peter Lang, 1988), to see him as anticipating modern theory in the abolition of the empirical author/narrator, sometimes exhibiting, in her critique of Spielhagen's imperfect practice, judgments no less dogmatically inflexible than his own.

[62] Käte Friedemann, *Die Rolle des Erzählers in der Epik* (Berlin: Haessel, 1910; rpt. Darmstadt: Wissenschaftliche Buchgesellschaft, 1965), 3–6.

[63] Wilhelm Scherer, *Geschichte der deutschen Litteratur* (Berlin: Weidmann, 1883), 682; *Poetik* (Berlin: Weidmann, 1888), 249–50.

[64] E.g., Winfried Hellmann, "Objektivität, Subjektivität und Erzählkunst: Zur Romantheorie Friedrich Spielhagens," in Reinhold Grimm, ed., *Deutsche Romantheorien* (Frankfurt am Main: Athenäum, 1968), 165–217; Rebing, *Der Halbbruder des Dichters*; with greater tolerance, Rhöse, *Konflikt und Versöhnung*, 176–204, and Worthmann, *Probleme des Zeitromans*, 104, 112.

[65] M. M. Bakhtin, *The Dialogic Imagination: Four Essays*, ed. Michael Holquist (Austin: U of Texas P, 1981), 327.

[66] Rhöse, *Konflikt und Versöhnung*, 176.

[67] Theodor Fontane, *Briefe*, 5 vols., ed. Walter Keitel and Helmuth Nürnberger (Munich: Hanser, 1976–94), 4: 533, 615.

[68] David Turner, "Marginalien und Handschriften zum Thema: Fontane und Spielhagens Theorie der 'Objektivität,'" *Fontane-Blätter* 1 (1968–69): 265.

[69] E.g., *H*, 20; on the generally positive response, see Rhöse, *Konflikt und Versöhnung*, 193.

[70] Heinrich Keiter and Tony Kellen, *Der Roman: Theorie und Technik des Romans und der erzählenden Dichtung, nebst einer geschichtliche Einleitung*, 4th ed. (Essen: Fredebeul & Koenen, 1912), 288.

[71] Heimito von Doderer, *Grundlagen und Funktion des Romans* (Nuremberg: Glock & Lutz, 1959), 17–18.

[72] Percy Lubbock, *The Craft of Fiction* (New York: Viking, 1957), 62, 67.

[73] Fischbacher-Bosshardt, *Anfänge der modernen Erzählkunst*, 43 and passim.

[74] Karpeles, *Friedrich Spielhagen*, 29–30; Henning, *Friedrich Spielhagen*, 65; see Rudolf von Gottschall in Festausschuss der Spielhagenfeier, ed., 24; Heinrich Spiero, *Geschichte des deutschen Romans* (Berlin: de Gruyter, 1950), 319; Alker, *Die deutsche Literatur*, 124; Bernd Neumann, "Friedrich Spielhagen: Sturmflut 1877. Die Gründerjahre als die 'Signatur des Jahrhunderts,'" in Horst Denkler, ed., *Romane und Erzählungen des Bürgerlichen Realismus: Neue Interpretationen* (Stuttgart: Reclam, 1980), 261; cf. Spielhagen's denial of discipleship to Gutzkow, *FE*, 2: 338–39.

[75] Friedemann, *Die Rolle des Erzählers*, 6.

[76] Johann Wolfgang von Goethe, *Werke*, vol. 6, eds. Benno von Wiese and Erich Trunz (Hamburg: Wegner, 1958), 242.

[77] Frey, "Author-Intrusion in the Narrative," 277. With another of the many ironies, an American reviewer ascribed the "clumsy form" of *Sturmflut* to the influence of *Middlemarch* and *Daniel Deronda*: Anonymous, [review of *Sturmflut*], *Atlantic Monthly* 40 (1877): 383.

[78] Festausschuss der Spielhagen-Feier, ed., 6.

[79] Volker Neuhaus, "Friedrich Spielhagen — Critic of Bismarck's Empire," in *1870/71–1898/90: German Unifications and the Change of Literary Discourse*, ed. Walter Pape (Berlin & New York: de Gruyter, 1993), 138–39.

[80] Friedrich Schiller, *Werke: Nationalausgabe*, vol. 20, ed. Benno von Wiese and Helmut Koopmann (Weimar: Böhlau, 1962), 462.

[81] Spielhagen, *Ausgewählte Romane* (Leipzig: Staackmann, 1889–93), 1st series, 8: 324; 2nd series, 4: 150.

[82] Klemperer, *Die Zeitromane Friedrich Spielhagens*, 151.

[83] Schiller, *Werke: Nationalausgabe*, vol. 29, eds. N. Oellers and F. Stock (Weimar: Böhlau, 1977), 148–50.

[84] E. g., Anderson, "Spielhagen's Problematic Heroes," 142, n. 4; Martini, *Deutsche Literatur im bürgerlichen Realismus*, 405; Goessl, "Die Darstellung des Adels," 147; Paul Jackson, *Bürgerliche Arbeit und Romanwirklichkeit: Studien zur Berufsproblematik in Romanen des deutschen Realismus* (Frankfurt am Main: Rita G. Fischer, 1981), 240.

[85] Rebing, *Der Halbbruder des Dichters*, 92.

[86] Hellmann, "Objektivität, Subjektivität und Erzählkunst," 184.

[87] Rhöse, *Konflikt und Versöhnung*, 185.

[88] Cf. Goethe, *Werke*, vol. 3, ed. Erich Trunz (Hamburg: Wegner, 1957), 26.

[89] Strodtmann, *Dichterprofile*, 208.

[90] Festausschuss der Spielhagen-Feier, ed., 3; see also Karpeles, *Friedrich Spielhagen*, 17–18, 72, 84.

[91] Adolf Stahr, *Aus Adolf Stahrs Nachlaß: Briefe von Stahr nebst Briefe an ihn*, ed. Ludwig Geiger (Oldenburg: Schulze, 1903), 258.

[92] Peter Demetz, *Formen des Realismus: Theodor Fontane. Kritische Untersuchungen* (Munich: Hanser, 1964), 24.

[93] Gottschall in Festausschuss der Spielhagen-Feier, ed., 24; Schmidt, "Friedrich Spielhagen," 423; Bleibtreu, *Revolution der Literatur*, 26–27; Engel, "Stereographischer Bericht," 401–2; Goessl, "Die Darstellung des Adels," 65; Kuczynski, *Gestalten und Werke*, 194–95.

[94] As he confessed in a letter to Peter Rosegger, in Rosegger, ed., "Briefe von Friedrich Spielhagen," 609.

[95] On the relationship of "objectivity" to the loss of Goethean symbolism, see Jürgen Kolbe, *Goethes "Wahlverwandtschaften" und der Roman des 19. Jahrhunderts* (Stuttgart, Berlin, Cologne & Mainz: Kohlhammer, 1968), 146.

[96] Schmidt, "Friedrich Spielhagen," 441.

[97] Swales, *Epochenbuch Realismus*, 103–7.

[98] Rhöse, *Konflikt und Versöhnung*, 191.

[99] Löwenthal, *Erzählkunst und Gesellschaft*, 175.

[100] Neuhaus, "Friedrich Spielhagen — Critic of Bismarck's Empire," 135.

[101] Rebing, *Der Halbbruder des Dichters*, 214; Rhöse, *Konflikt und Versöhnung*, 177; Worthmann, *Probleme des Zeitromans*, 112; again, Fischbacher-Bosshardt, *Anfänge der modernen Erzählkunst*, is the eccentric exception.

[102] On the much-discussed topic of the conflicted representation of the nobility, see Patricia Herminghouse, "Schloß oder Fabrik? Zur Problematik der Adelsdarstellung im Roman des Nachmärz," in Peter Uwe Hohendahl and Paul Michael Lützeler, eds., *Legitimationskrisen des deutschen Adels 1200–1900* (Stuttgart: Metzler, 1979), 245–61, and Goessl, "Die Darstellung des Adels."

[103] See *FE*, 1: 276–77, and Adolf Schumacher, "Ferdinand Lassalle as a Novelistic Subject of Friedrich Spielhagen" (Diss. U of Pennsylvania, 1910).

[104] E.g., Schmidt, "Friedrich Spielhagen," 438; Klemperer, *Die Zeitromane Friedrich Spielhagens*, 81; for a revision of this view, see Rhöse, *Konflikt und Versöhnung*, 194.

[105] Zinken, *Der Roman als Zeitdokument*.

[106] Neuhaus, "Friedrich Spielhagen — Critic of Bismarck's Empire," 141.

[107] For a negative judgment, see Klemperer, *Die Zeitromane Friedrich Spielhagens*, 112–14; more positively, Mehring, *Beiträge zur Literaturgeschichte*, 216–17.

[108] Sälter, *Entwicklungslinien der deutschen Zola-Rezeption*, 68–69; see also Geller, *Friedrich Spielhagens Theorie und Praxis des Romans*, 49, 110.

[109] For an unusual positive judgment, see Mielke, *Der Deutsche Roman*, 426.

[110] Schieding, *Untersuchungen über die Romantechnik Friedrich Spielhagens*, 84–87; Christa Müller-Donges, *Das Novellenwerk Friedrich Spielhagens in seiner Entwicklung zwischen 1851 und 1899* (Marburg: Elwert, 1970), 99; Kolbe, *Goethes "Wahlverwandtschaften,"* 149, n. 71; Hans Werner Seiffert with Christel Laufer, "Zeugnisse und Materialien zu Fontanes 'Effi Briest' und Spielhagens 'Zum Zeitvertrieb,'" in Seiffert, ed., *Studien zur neueren deutschen Literatur* (Berlin: Akademie, 1964), 258; for a critique of Seiffert's dismissal, see Dieter Kafitz, *Figurenkonstellation als Mittel der Wirklichkeitserfassung: Dargestellt an Romanen der zweiten Hälfte des 19. Jahrhunderts (Freytag — Spielhagen — Fontane — Raabe)* (Kronberg: Athenäum, 1978), 121.

Wilhelm Raabe and the German Colonial Experience

John Pizer

THE FLOURISHING OF postcolonial studies in recent decades inspired Germanists to focus critical attention in the 1980s and 1990s on a previously neglected field: Germany's literary engagement with its colonial past and with colonialism in other nations. The two most prominent English-language treatments of this subject, Russell A. Berman's *Enlightenment or Empire: Colonial Discourse in German Culture* (1998) and the late Susanne Zantop's *Colonial Fantasies: Conquest, Family, and Nation in Precolonial Germany, 1770–1870* (1997), are paradigmatic instances of the highly disparate points of view to which these analyses have led. Berman never loses sight of the often brutal treatment to which German settlers subjected native populations during Germany's brief but intense colonial activities at the end of the nineteenth and beginning of the twentieth centuries or of the texts supportive of this treatment. Nevertheless, he articulates a unique strain of Enlightenment-grounded German discourse, stretching from Georg Forster in the eighteenth century to Emile Nolde in the twentieth, that was drawn to and respected the Southern Hemisphere's cultural alterity, while writers reared in Europe's great imperial motherlands sought to efface this otherness by intellectually imposing their traditions on the geographic space of their colonies.[1] Zantop, on the other hand, highlights the Germans' own *self*-perception from the eighteenth century onward as, at least in potential, uniquely ideal colonists who would enlighten and educate rather than exploit indigenous peoples. She believes that this was a fantasy engendered (in both senses of that term) by Germany's exclusion from empire building prior to the late nineteenth century. This precolonial "moral impulse"[2] was supplanted, according to Zantop, by more outspokenly racist and sexist discourse when Germany actually began its imperial adventures, though a belief in Germany's special civilizing potential is never completely abandoned in the texts belonging to this later period.

Neither Berman nor Zantop mention Wilhelm Raabe (1831–1910) in their books. This omission is understandable, since Raabe only wrote one work that directly thematized colonialism outside Europe, the novella *Sankt Thomas* (Saint Thomas, 1866).[3] Nevertheless, the subtlety and breadth of Raabe's engagement with Germany's experience of colonial lands and subjects as it joined Europe's great powers in empire building is such that both Berman and Zantop could have drawn upon him to sustain their arguments. Raabe's similarly ambiguous treatments of noncolonial minorities, such as Jews and Wends, in Germany has led some scholars to accuse him of a strong bias against such groups, while others argue that he treated them sympathetically and at least tacitly refuted his country's anti-Semitism[4] and xenophobia with respect to other peoples regarded as nonethnic Germans.[5] Though, as far as I am aware, no sustained analysis of Raabe's attitude toward Germany's colonial experience in the broad thematic and chronological range of his works has heretofore been published, some National Socialists proclaimed him a strong supporter of territorial aggrandizement and imperial ambition who would have enthusiastically embraced the Third Reich's endeavors in this regard,[6] while others have argued that Raabe's oeuvre, particularly *Sankt Thomas,* offers a strong (albeit historically veiled) warning against Germany's colonial aspirations.[7]

This essay will attempt to show how such antithetical views are possible by examining what one controversial work on Raabe, in a different context, has termed his "doppelte Buchführung" (double system of bookkeeping). While Irmgard Roebling used this term to indicate how Raabe's texts reflect a contemporary crisis — indeed, a cleavage (*Spaltung*) — in the psyche of the bourgeois individual,[8] I am borrowing it here to suggest that Raabe imaginatively constellated Germany's presence in colonial space or, more often, the presence of colonial space in Germany in the figures of settlers, explorers, and persons of color in order to pursue a twofold, often conflicted, agenda. On the one hand, Raabe was extremely uncomfortable with the idea, debated in Germany until 1866, that German unification should take place in the context of a larger unification with Austria and its ethnically diverse crownlands. In 1866 Otto von Bismarck led the Prussians and their allies to a military victory against the Austrians in the second of his wars of unification, dispelling further talk of Germany's fusion with the Hapsburg empire. While the debate still raged, Raabe was an ardent proponent of a lesser-Germany (*kleindeutsch*) approach to an undivided Germany. His novel *Gutmanns Reisen* (Gutmann's Travels, 1892) takes place in Coburg in 1860, when the German National Association met to discuss the country's consolidation and considered whether they should embrace a lesser- or greater-Germany (*großdeutsch*) model. Though many of Raabe's works contain unreliable narrators, no critics dispute that *Gutmanns Reisen* articulates his lesser-Germany stance. A principal reason presented in the novel for Raabe's opposition to a merger with Austria was a recoil against weaving the crownlands' dominant Hungarian and Slavic populations into the German social and political fabric. The hero of the novel, Wilhelm Gutmann, an ardent lesser-Germany proponent, calls himself and his allies "wirkliche, reine Deutsche," while labeling his Austrian rival in love and politics, Alois Pärnreuther, "ein halber Ungar."[9] He is unquestionably speaking for Raabe when he explains to Klotilde Blume, the Bavarian maiden for whose affections he competes with Pärnreuther (the political implications of this contested courtship are obvious) that all the peoples surrounding Germany are like closed fists, while the German fatherland is like a defenseless, "offene Hand" (18: 338). Historical novels such as *Das Odfeld* (The Odin Field, 1888) and *Hastenbeck* (1899), both of which take place during the Seven Years' War (1756–63), reveal Raabe's deeply rooted anguish at Germany's long standing status as an "open hand," which rendered it vulnerable to the ruthless depredations of foreign troops treated in these novels. Raabe wanted to close Germany's fist to the foreign "Other," European and non-European alike, and this is one of two central aspects of his engagement with German colonial experience.

Raabe's profound fear of unfettered cosmopolitanism in a Germany that would have been geographically and politically "greater" through union with Austria and the establishment of a large overseas empire (a fear probably also linked to his rather introverted personality and the generalized fear of the world he imparted to many of his characters)[10] is counterpoised by his dissatisfaction, even contempt, for many facets of nineteenth-century German provincialism. He invested considerable creative energy into exposing the pettiness, hypocrisy, and narrow-mindedness he associated with the small-town mentality of his fellow citizens, even those who inhabited larger urban centers. To do so, he drew subtle parallels between the German mindset and that of the putatively primitive denizens of colonialized spaces. This is particularly true in the novel *Abu Telfan* (1867), but the tendency is evident in several other works, as well. This second primary facet of Raabe's treatment of colonial subjects must inevitably conflict with the first, creating antithetical constellations of non-European lands and peoples, a circumstance reflected in the diverse scholarly opinions in regard to Raabe's visions of the Southern Hemisphere and of the non-German "Other" in general. Indeed, Raabe's complex characterizations can imbue a single person of color with attributes supportive of both Berman's belief in German colonial discourse's unique "heterophilic appreciation"[11] and Zantop's view that such discourse was tinged with a particularly virulent racist strain in the second half of the nineteenth century. Such bifurcation is evident not only in *Abu Telfan* but also in several other works focused on Raabe's contemporary Germany: *Meister Autor* (Master Author, 1873), *Fabian und Sebastian* (1881–82), and *Stopfkuchen* (Stuffcake, 1891).

Nevertheless, we begin with *Sankt Thomas* — not only because it preceded these other works but also because it represents, in spite of its much earlier historical setting and non-German combatants, Raabe's most direct assumption of a stance in opposition to Germany's impending colonialism. It takes place in 1599 on the island off the coast of Africa that gives the story its title and is based on an account, published by Karl Curth in 1823 in his addition to Friedrich Schiller's *Geschichte des Abfalls der vereinigten Niederlande von der Spanischen Regierung* (History of the Revolt of the Netherlands, 1788), of the battle between Dutch naval forces and St. Thomas's Spanish and Portuguese settlers for possession of the island. Under the leadership of Spanish governor Don Franzisko Meneses the settlers valiantly attempt to defend their colony, but Raabe makes it clear from the outset that this endeavor will be futile. Not only does Meneses indicate to his citizens early in the struggle that they are outmanned and outgunned, but his appearance is likened to that of Don Quixote (9/2: 10), modern literature's most paradigmatic instance of a man who strives in vain. Although they finally overcome the Spanish/Portuguese resistance after an enormous loss of life on both sides, the Dutch are stricken and die from a heat-induced kind of plague. Only the island's native black inhabitants, whose free mountain-dwelling segment had formed a provisional alliance with the Dutch during the battle, emerge fully triumphant, overjoyed to be rid of all the Europeans after the small band of Dutch survivors sails away from the island.

The unique ability of St. Thomas's indigenous population to survive battle, pestilence, and oppressive heat, and their ecstasy at being left alone as the novella closes, sends two powerful anticolonial messages: colonialism with its attendant intra-European conflicts and difficulties in adapting to a tropical climate is ultimately self-destructive, and the natives who inhabit colonial spaces have no desire to share them with European settlers. Frequent flashbacks to a life in the Dutch countryside enjoyed by the Dutch sailor Georg van der Does and Camilla Drago, the Spanish commander's daughter who had been a well-treated — indeed, pampered — hostage in the Netherlands but is a clearly doomed ward of Meneses during the present narrative time, allow Raabe to evoke a stillborn love affair through the isolated reveries of the two young protagonists. By highlighting the contrary climates of the Netherlands and St. Thomas through these flashbacks Raabe anticipates, in reverse, a technique he constantly employs in his contemporary narratives where colonized domains are thematized: in the later works the temperate European settings of present narrative time are contrasted with the oppressive heat and humidity of Southern lands. Though Raabe presents such antitheses with greater subtlety and less dramatically in works subsequent to *Sankt Thomas,* one simple tacit message is evident in all of them: Europeans are neither mentally nor physically suited to live in the tropics.

African detestation of the European occupiers of their land and African jubilation at their (albeit temporary) extirpation were never presented as directly and explicitly in nineteenth-century German literature as in *Sankt Thomas*. The rapture is particularly evident in the monologue of a young island girl, the king's daughter, at the tale's close. She expresses relief and happiness at no longer seeing the settlers' "Zauberschiffe," at her people's having been saved by their gods, and at the prospect of huts being rebuilt on the ashes of the Spanish fortress (9/2: 58). Raabe was not inherently bold when it came to forcefully expressing controversial political views, but he did not shy away from indirectly expressing such opinions. Certainly, employing a historical episode from the distant past in an imaginative novella was a reasonably safe way to present an anticolonial stance at a time and in a country where such a stance would have been extremely unpopular. Raabe composed *Sankt Thomas* in Stuttgart, a strongly pro-Austrian and "greater-Germany" city in the 1850s and 1860s, and being a lesser-Germany advocate there instilled him with a certain paranoia; he even felt on the verge of being banished as a "sehr gefährliches Individuum."[12] Thus, experience taught him to be circumspect in expressing his sociopolitical sentiments.

Nevertheless, the anticolonial message *Sankt Thomas* intended to send to Raabe's contemporaries has not been lost on his critics. Even in 1939, at a time when right-wing readers of Raabe were engaging him as an authorizing voice in the service of Nazi expansionist propaganda, Friedrich Bamler recognized that the novella's true purport was to give expression to the "Dämonie und Widernatürlichkeit" of efforts at colonization overseas. He calls Raabe a true German "Eckehart" who attempted to sound a warning to his people twenty years before the empire began its colonial endeavors. Bamler recognizes that the abnormality (for Europeans) of this site and the relationships it engenders is made to seem responsible for the isolated lovers' tragic fate.[13] More recently, Jeffrey L. Sammons has cited *Sankt Thomas* as evidence of Raabe's anti-imperialist stance, his belief in the ultimate "futility of colonialism."[14] Julia Bertschik has tied Raabe's feeling of homelessness, his self-perception as a foreigner in Stuttgart because of his lesser-Germany politics, to his anticolonial stance in *Sankt Thomas* and *Abu Telfan* and finds in his characterization of the island's native population in *Sankt Thomas* a reworking in a colonial-black context of the primal qualities he perceived in Germany's earliest inhabitants.[15] Hans Otto Horch goes so far as to assume that the Dutch-Spanish conflict in the tale is intended to mirror the Prussian-Austrian and German-Danish clashes in Raabe's age, and that the inhabitants of Schleswig-Holstein, the focal point of Bismarck's first two wars of unification (against the Danes in 1864 and the Austrians in 1866) are to be equated with the indigenous blacks of *Sankt Thomas*.¹⁶ Though distilled and perhaps a bit distorted through a historical filter, Raabe's warning against future German expansionism sounds clear, indeed, to his post-nineteenth-century interpreters. It is a prophecy that the German colonial experience would be disastrous if it took the form of actual overseas empire building. Whether or not Raabe intended *Sankt Thomas* to be read as a parable of contemporary imperial politics in Schleswig-Holstein or simply as an imaginative statement against the follies of colonialism, its brevity and lack of ambiguity with respect to authorial purport make its anticolonial message relatively easy to discern. Subsequent texts that constellated imperial domains outside Europe make this purport more difficult to tease out, both because their present-time narrative setting is usually Germany and because Raabe's opposition to Germany's budding empire-building beyond Central Europe becomes imbricated with subtextual invective against his nation's sociopolitical milieu. This is particularly true of *Abu Telfan,* the tale of a maladjusted young man, Leonhard Hagebucher, who returns to his home village of Bumsdorf, near the capital city of Nippenburg (probably fictive denominations for Wolfenbüttel and Braunschweig, Raabe's respective domiciles before and after he lived in Stuttgart) after being freed from many years of cruel captivity at the hands of Madame Kulla Gulla in the fabricated African habitation to which the book owes its title. First setting foot on European soil in Trieste at the novel's outset after having been liberated by a man who will eventually play a prominent role in the novel's present time frame, Hagebucher shocks the customs officials in this port city of the Dual Monarchy by his half-African appearance. The narrator claims that Hagebucher could have credibly described himself in his hotel's guest registry as "particolarissimo," "most peculiar" (7: 7). He is subjected to much bureaucratic scrutiny during his subsequent journey home, which also passes through Hapsburg territory. Immediately, then, Raabe has introduced the novel's two primary but conflicted messages. On the one hand, nineteenth-century Europe, particularly Austria and Germany, are narrow-minded and petty and thus loath to welcome those it perceives as outsiders and misfits. On the other hand, one is in danger of acquiring such a status, or at least of enhancing a reputation for eccentricity like Hagebucher's, if one succumbs to the sort of thirst for colonial adventures that helped lead Hagebucher to become involved first in the Suez Canal project and then to fall in with a group of notorious ivory traders, a decision that brings about his capture and enslavement by indigenous tribespeople in Abu Telfan.

Bumsdorf's citizenry regards its prodigal son as an exotic curiosity on his return home; but even when he loses this initial aura after a brief time, he continues to be called an "African" — thus intensifying the outsider reputation the putative ne'er-do-well had attained even before departing for the "Dark Continent." Of course, the failure of family and friends to make him accept a regular occupation and become an integrated, productive part of the community guarantees that his marginalized status will solidify, but Hagebucher's long forced stay in Abu Telfan is made to seem responsible for the insurmountable gap now separating the "African" from the rest of the Bumsdorf community (7: 137). Indeed, his many years under the hot African sun dash (or so he believes) his prospects for a successful union with the professor's daughter he comes to love in Nippenburg (7: 315). Again, authorial intentions are tangled here: Raabe undoubtedly wants to expose the stultifying quotidian quality and conformist pettiness of small-town nineteenth-century Germany, but he also makes it clear that the suffering this can cause a somewhat rebellious individual is greatly intensified when that individual is subjected over many years to a colonial experience, to years spent apart from the fatherland. Raabe himself never ventured outside Central Europe; his only foray outside exclusively German-speaking lands was to the Hapsburg empire in 1859, an experience that decisively influenced his embrace of lesser-Germany politics. Despite his adulation for Goethe, Raabe never embraced the ideal of a journey of acculturation (*Bildungsreise*) promulgated by the sage of Weimar as integral to the character formation of a well-rounded individual. Indeed, the impact of significant time spent in a foreign, especially a tropical/colonial, milieu is usually quite baleful for Raabe's Germans; years of life in Brazil, for example, turn Agostin Agonista into a ruthless destroyer of a gentle, innocent pharmacist in *Zum wilden Mann* (At the Sign of the Wild Man, 1874).[17] Hagebucher does not lose his humanity through enslavement in Africa, but he does lose whatever chance he had to become a respectable German — a loss that forces him to suffer much anguish, even as it makes him an interesting, appealing character for Raabe's readers.

Another technique employed by Raabe to counter imaginatively Germany's appetite for imperial expansion in Africa is the disenchantment, or de-exotization, of the African milieu. While Berman feels that some German colonial discourse is marked by a unique "appreciation of difference,"[18] and Zantop feels that this putatively discrete appreciation was a thin veneer for the impulse to conquer and to sexually, militarily, and economically dominate what nineteenth-century Germans came to see as an alluring feminized space — indeed, a "virgin territory" (at least in Latin America)[19] — they agree that the urge for empire building was greatly fueled at the time by images in popular literature of the Southern Hemisphere's alterity, its lush, torrid exoticism. The narrator of *Abu Telfan* explains at the outset that the most manifold, colorful, dangerous, esoteric adventures in Hagebucher's life took place not in Africa but where "der mythische Name Deutschland auf der Landkarte geschrieben steht" (7: 12). Hagebucher's descriptions of Abu Telfan in response to the initially fascinated interest of his family and Bumsdorf's denizens make the African environment appear almost hideously tedious (7: 28–29; see also 84–87). As Horst Denkler has noted, *Abu Telfan* inverts the structural model of the "exotic novel" by beginning with Hagebucher's return trip,[20] and we can add that this inversion is enhanced by the extremely bleak portrait of the African milieu that emerges from Hagebucher's narrative descriptions.

The process of stripping Africa of the allure of alterity is also strengthened by the narration's consistent drawing of parallels between social, political, and cultural domains in Africa and those in Germany.[21] Hagebucher scandalizes an audience gathered to hear a lecture he delivers in Nippenburg, an audience undoubtedly hoping for tales of spellbinding adventure in a faraway land, precisely by allowing himself to describe German and African customs coextensively (7: 187). Hagebucher's equation of the sociopolitical domains of Africa and Germany in a lecture that shakes his audience's philistine self-assurance (7: 189), a parallelism underscored later in the novel when the narrator equates courtship, marriage, and birth in the two regions in a pithy passage bereft of the slightest trace of romantic sentimentality (7: 295), causes Nippendorf's royal police director, Johann von Betzendorff, to forbid any further presentations by the region's prodigal son. Nevertheless, Betzendorff is unable to discern a brewing scandal that ultimately blows up in his own home during the course of a ball he gives. A Lieutenant Kind crashes the ball and reveals that one of the town's leading citizens, Baron von Glimmern (who is bound in a loveless marriage to Nikola von Einstein, a woman linked to Hagebucher through a mutual sense of alienation from the dominant society), has been embezzling money from the royal coffers. Kind's disclosure is motivated by a desire for revenge: the baron had seduced Kind's daughter, had caused her fiancé to be expelled from his service through disobedience, and had sent the fiancé to Kind's penal company, where the unsuspecting Kind had to shoot his erstwhile future son-in-law when the enraged young man attempted to assassinate his former commander. The sordid complexity of this affair, juxtaposed through the novel's frequent flashbacks to Hagebucher's African captivity, makes the straightforward brutality of Madame Kulla Gulla and her compatriots against a group of men themselves involved in an illicit, corrupt, and violent ivory trade seem tame and almost innocuous by comparison. The juxtaposition allows the most subtextual but most powerful anticolonial argument of *Abu Telfan* to emerge: what right does a society so deeply infected by corruption and mendacity at the highest levels, and by smug pettiness and philistinism in its middle class, have to presume to impose its "civilization" on a relatively straightforward people living in a distant land?

Corrupt behavior and influence are also major narrative ingredients in Raabe's next work to deal, at least tangentially, with the problematic of colonialism: *Meister Autor*. The eponymous protagonist is another of Raabe's misunderstood outsiders, a man who lives in bucolic isolation but nevertheless helps his friend, the forester Arend Tofote, raise the latter's daughter, Gertrud. The author Kunemund's younger brother, described early in the narrative as "den reichen Onkel aus Surinam" (11: 28), bequeaths his estate to Gertrud. Kunemund suspects his brother's motives are malevolent rather than fraternal, since the brother's complete self-centeredness had always been his most defining personal trait. The misery into which Gertrud is plunged as a result of her being swept into high-society decadence on taking possession of the uncle's estate confirms the surmise of the "master author." Unlike Agonista, whose evil seems to have been engendered, or at least brought to life, through his years in Brazil, there is no suggestion that the colonial experience in Surinam is responsible for the younger brother's calculating wickedness. Nonetheless, in both cases, Raabe suggests, the money and duplicitous knowledge gained in Latin America as a result of this experience makes both expatriates perfect conduits for the enactment of malice and corruption in their German homeland. Precisely this configuration will be reenacted in *Prinzessin Fisch* (Princess Fish, 1882–83) when the evil Alexander Rodburg returns to his native Ilmenthal from Mexico and perpetrates a massive swindle. Such corruption is given literally concretized, crystallized, albeit metaphoric shape in a peculiar object discovered by the sailor Karl Schaake, one of Gertrud's childhood playmates, on her estate. It is a bad-luck charm of the sort Karl believes he had seen in Malaysia and that the "uncle from Surinam" had undoubtedly obtained in his dealings with the Dutch empire. Indeed, the property itself reminds Karl of old Batavian garden houses doomed to sink into the swamp (hence the novel's subtitle, "Die Geschichten vom versunkenen Garten." The omen augurs not only Gertrud's misery and Karl's (eventually fatal) injuries in a train wreck but also the transformation of the entire charming domain in and around Gertrud's estate into a soulless, barren cityscape. Of course, Raabe cannot blame colonialism for what he considered the unfortunate effects and side effects of modern progress, the destructive march of civilization he so often thematized in his work. The concatenation of the colonial world and its objects with modernism's desultory advances, however, demonstrates Raabe's belief that they belonged to the same matrix of contemporary moral, spiritual, social, and even physical putrefaction.

The most remarkable character in *Meister Autor* is Ceretto Wichselmeyer, the black servant Gertrud virtually inherits along with the Surinam uncle's estate. To paraphrase the title of an essay by Gayatri Chakravorty Spivak considered seminal in the development of postcolonial studies, "Can the Subaltern Speak?"[22] the "subaltern" Wichselmeyer not only *can* "speak" the most eloquent German imaginable but also expresses wisdom and insights rarely matched by Raabe's ethnic Germans. This is not, however, to deny the veracity of Spivak's answer to her own question: "For the 'true' subaltern group, whose identity is its difference, there is no unrepresentable subaltern subject that can know and speak itself; the intellectual's solution is not to abstain from representation."[23] The complexity of Wichselmeyer as a fictive representation of the intellectual Raabe's genuine feelings about such "subaltern" individuals stems from his presentation to the reader through the distorting prism of one of Raabe's highly unreliable first-person narrators, the self-described aesthete and dilettantish writer of novellas, Emil von Schmidt. To be sure, we can safely judge the objectivity of Schmidt's observations on how third parties respond, initially, to Wichselmeyer; Gertrud is afraid that he might be a cannibal (11: 28), and Tofote's servant woman evinces abject terror followed by a somewhat erotically tinged fascination at their first encounter (11: 30–31). Wichselmeyer describes his profession as "der wilde Meß- und Jahrmarktsindianer" (11: 29), thereby conflating his own ethnically African heritage with that of the New World's colonized natives to underscore accurately how deeply his "identity" resides in his "difference" for and from Europeans. Though Schmidt is worldly enough quickly to grasp and admire the "Moor's" powers of erudition and discernment, his "heterophilic appreciation" (Berman) for this colonial subject (an appreciation based on the perceived contrast between Wichselmeyer's race and his discourse, rather than on the love of sensuous primitive exoticism a creative individual such as Nolde found in non-European art)[24] often gives way to the powerful racist invective Zantop regards as endemic to nineteenth-century colonial discourse. Schmidt compares Wichselmeyer, for example, to the devil at his blackest (11: 96).

Given Schmidt's questionable reliability as an arbiter of the events and characters of *Meister Autor,* it would be an error to equate his judgments of Wichselmeyer with Raabe's views on Europeanized colonial subalterns. Nevertheless, Siegfried Hajek's characterization of Gertrud's servant as "weltklug und ungerührt, illusionslos und lieblos" and as "der frivole Spötter" like his biblical ancestor, Noah's son Ham (11: 97, 98),[25] is accurate in capturing how not only Schmidt but also Raabe intends us to regard this figure. After all, these attributes are on display in all of his responses to the narration's incidents, including its tragedies. Julia Bertschik is certainly correct in noting that Wichselmeyer's self-conscious mimicry of the cliché of the uncanny exotic is intended by Raabe as a skewering of colonialist attitudes, and that his presence allows Raabe to turn the motif of cannibalism situated in precivilization on its head by causing us to equate this practice with the German empire's own cannibalistic modernization; Karl's long-drawn-out death from his injuries in the train wreck and the cold-hearted tearing down of historical buildings in the increasingly urbanized milieu around Gertrud's estate are intended to be seen as the "menschenverschlingend-kannibalischen" affects of contemporary technologizing.[26] The coldness Wichselmeyer displays at Karl's demise and at Gertrud's even slower downfall, however, must also strike the reader as somewhat monstrous, irrespective of Schmidt's commentary on this matter.

This same emotional coldness is displayed by another colonial subject displaced in Germany in the later novel *Prinzessin Fisch*. The apparently beautiful Mexican woman Romana Tieffenbacher has followed her husband to Ilmenthal after he was forced out of her native land because of his service as an army paymaster under the defeated imperialist regime of Emperor Maximilian. She becomes the object of Theodor Rodburg's pubescent fantasies, a flesh-and-blood personification of the lovely damsel in distress in Goethe's poem "Der neue Amadis" (The New Amadis, 1771) who inspired the novel's title. Raabe disenchants her, much as he did the African milieu and its inhabitants in *Abu Telfan*, by revealing her to be lazy, dreary, passionless, and cruel. She is "die gelbe Hexe" (15: 373), in the words of Theodor's worldly-wise surrogate mother. Romana, Alexander Rodburg's mistress, ultimately plans to flee with him to Mexico when his scandalous intrigues are on the point of coming to light, abandoning her gentle, distraught husband and helping Alexander to steal some of his goods. Theodor, Alexander's innocent brother, comes to see her in her true guise as he matures, even before the scandal erupts, and Raabe undoubtedly hoped that it would dawn on his readers that this colonial person of color, like Wichselmeyer, was out of place in Germany.[27] It is fair to extend Jeffrey L. Sammons's comments (in the conclusion of his essay on *Der Hungerpastor*) on Raabe's attitudes toward the anti-Semites among his admirers to cover his feeling toward minority ethnic groups themselves: "We do not know what Raabe, in his innermost heart, thought of any of these people."[28] Given the impression we carry away from *Meister Autor* of a colonial subaltern who, like the later Romana Tieffenbacher, is fundamentally lacking in human warmth, however, it is reasonable to believe that part of Raabe's anticolonial message lay in convincing his readers that real-life Wichselmeyers had no place in the fatherland.

The same cannot be said of the Sumatra-born heroine of *Fabian und Sebastian,* Konstantia Pelzmann, the blond orphan of a German father and a Dutch-Creole mother. This young woman embodies attributes utterly antithetical to those of the subaltern of *Meister Autor* and the femme fatale of *Prinzessin Fisch:* warmth, love, innocence, and naiveté. She is the niece of the brothers named in the title, who are polar opposites with respect to personality, their roles as confectioners in a family firm, and in the attitudes they assume toward Konstantia. She comes to live with them on the death of her father in Sumatra. The third-person narrator describes her as "ein Blondinchen aus dem Mohrenlande" who could just as easily have been born in one of the streets in the German city of her uncles (15: 56). Though this narrator is faceless and, thus, not overtly inscribed with the quirks and prejudices of a first-person chronicler such as Emil von Schmidt, we cannot assume that his perspective is to be equated with Raabe's. Raabe was worldly wise enough to distinguish between the ethnicity of Africans and Asians, though he may well have been comfortable with the circumstance that his fellow Germans, like the narrator of *Fabian und Sebastian,* saw them as undifferentiated colonial Others, marked by an unbridgeable alterity and not assimilable into the German social fabric. This attitude would accord with the images of Wichselmeyer presented in *Meister Autor* and of Romana Tieffenbacher in *Prinzessin Fisch* and with Raabe's wish to keep the "German fist" as closed as possible to the outside world.

Of course, Konstantia's racial purity[29] and half-German ancestry allow her quick, unqualified acceptance into society; her only impediments (again, antithetically to Wichselmeyer but similar to Romana) are linguistic. This successful assimilation is symbolized by her name change; "Konstantia" becomes Germanized into "Konstanze." She immediately becomes the joy of Fabian Pelzmann's life, and the cold rejection she suffers at the hands of Sebastian is due to her patrilineal rather than her matrilineal ancestry. Sebastian was a rival of both brothers for the affections of a girl he seduced, impregnated, and abandoned to her fate after she committed infanticide. Through the machinations of Sebastian and this girl, Marianne Erdener, Konstantia's father Lorenz was shipped off to Dutch India and became a destitute soldier. Thus, Sebastian's guilt over his brother's fate causes his antipathy toward his niece; but her presence at his deathbed allows him to die with the pleasant illusion that she is his daughter, who, thus, was never really drowned. Indeed, Konstantia becomes an angel of mercy to several protagonists whose lives are ruined or at least touched by the scandal through the sheer warmth and purity of her character. At the novel's conclusion, for example, she breaks through the powerful emotional barrier Marianne's father has built up through the years of Marianne's incarceration, a deed that begins to relieve his suffering. In a twist that reverses the personality configurations enmeshed in the web of intrigue woven in *Zum wilden Mann, Meister Autor,* and *Prinzessin Fisch,* this young lady from a strange/foreign ("fremd") colonial territory is an innocent who finds herself in, and must puzzle out, a guilt-ridden house. This circumstance is explicitly underscored in the novel (for example, 15: 117 and 120). The narrator notes: "Sie war aus der Fremde in eine fremde Welt hineingekommen" (15: 146); but Konstantia feels that her childhood in the Dutch colonial world helps her face challenges such as dealing with the mortally ill and half-mad Sebastian (15: 148).

This brief consideration of *Fabian und Sebastian* allows us to glimpse some balance in Raabe's perspective on the German colonial experience. Clearly, he did not believe a lifetime or a long sojourn in Latin America, Africa, or Asia inevitably creates or enhances evil tendencies of the sort evidenced by Agonista in *Zum wilden Mann,* the Surinam uncle in *Meister Autor,* and Alexander Rodburg in *Prinzessin Fisch.* Such a life does not have to result in the emotional coldness displayed by Wichselmeyer in *Meister Autor* and Romana Tieffenbacher in *Prinzessin Fisch. Fabian und Sebastian* also paints an inhospitable picture of life in Sumatra, however; Konstantia's descriptions of its dangerous wildlife and forbidding climate, and the untimely deaths of her parents, contribute to Raabe's overall portrait of the colonial world as a realm his countrymen would best avoid. What, then, are we to make of the narrator of *Stopfkuchen,* a gentleman named Eduard who, in the present-day time frame of the novel, is returning by ship (where he composes his narrative) to his comfortable life in South Africa after a brief but remarkable visit to his German hometown? Certainly, Raabe was not one-sidedly negative in representing colonial life; such one-sidedness would have called his authorial credibility into question.

Nevertheless, recent critics have plausibly seen in *Stopfkuchen* not only a skewering of colonialism but a parody of the German colonial novel, which was in the process of becoming a highly popular genre at the time of the composition of *Stopfkuchen*.[30] For while Eduard's life is prosperous, he perceives it as anything but exotic, adventurous, or morally, spiritually, and educationally beneficial to himself and Africa's indigenous peoples, the putative aspects of life in Europe's outlying empires imaginatively lauded in colonial novels in the late nineteenth century. On the contrary, he speaks of his return trip in almost despairing terms as a journey back to "das ödeste, langgedehnteste, wenn auch nahrhafteste Fremdenleben" (18: 81). What is more, his brief German sojourn reveals that the man he idolized in childhood, the postal delivery man Friedrich Störzer, who inspired Eduard's move to South Africa by singing the praises of his favorite book, the German translation of François Le Vaillant's account of his adventures in Africa, was, in fact, a murderer. Störzer's decision to keep his slaying of the bully Kienbaum a secret brings in its train many years of persecution for the peevish farmer Andreas Quakatz, believed by the townspeople to be the murderer, and a miserable childhood for the latter's daughter, Valentine. This is revealed to Eduard in the course of the framed past-time narration by his childhood friend and now husband of Valentine, Heinrich Schaumann, the rotund "Stuffcake" whose nickname gives the novel its title. The disclosure constitutes the climax of the framed retrospection, and the shock it produces in Eduard causes him to be transported in reverie to his youth, when he sat with Störzer and heard tales of Africa's beauty, adventurous possibilities, but also peaceableness from the exquisite book of "Herrn Levalljang" (18: 184).

Though tacit, the message produced through Eduard's rumination on his misplaced adulation of Störzer is clear: his own life's most momentous decision was grounded in fraud. The intense guilt-ridden agony burdening Störzer — a guilt revealed in his confession to Schaumann — undoubtedly led to his fixation on Le Vaillant and Le Vaillant's book. His reading has cathected Africa into the locus of escapist flight, a site where he can imaginatively forget his misery-inducing culpability because it signifies absolute alterity, a space of pure, uncontaminated origin. In other words, to cite Zantop once again, his configuration of Africa allows Störzer to forget his cares by indulging in a "colonial fantasy," but a fantasy that determines the real-life choice of the narrator of *Stopfkuchen*.[31]

After taking the Quakatz family under his considerable wing and marrying Valentine, Schaumann rarely ventures forth from their family estate, the "Rote Schanze"; thus, when he accompanies Eduard into town, his appearance creates genuine astonishment among its inhabitants (18: 155). As Schaumann observes, however, one does not have to leave one's little nook in the world to attain a panoramic worldview, a perspective to which Eduard sighingly assents from the bottom of his soul and "vom untern Ende Afrikas her" (18: 66–67), already hinting at the doubt at his choice of a colonial abode that will strike him more profoundly at the novel's conclusion. Schaumann most assuredly speaks here for Raabe, a German never deeply smitten with the wanderlust associated even to this day with his countrymen. Eduard comes to see himself as Raabe would have seen such roamers, as a commonplace character who wanted to run to Africa to experience his "trivialen Abenteuerrhistorien" (18: 109), the kind of racist, imperialist tales cropping up at that time in colonial novels. Thus, it is left to Schaumann to make astute allusions to present-day Africa. He praises and tacitly identifies himself with the Zulu King Ketschwayo (18: 114 and 142–43). Noting that this warrior became a paradigmatic figure for the brave but futile struggle of indigenous South Africans against the European colonizers, and that Raabe was aware of his notorious reputation in Europe, Philip J. Brewster has shown that this configuration of Ketschwayo as Schaumann's "geistiger 'Onkel'" underscores the anticolonial message implicit in *Stopfkuchen,* as does the problematizing of colonialism's foundations through the calling into question of Eduard's motives for moving to South Africa.[32]

Raabe directly alludes in *Stopfkuchen* to *Abu Telfan* by naming the ship on which Eduard returns to South Africa the *Leonhard Hagebucher*. Reflecting on this circumstance, Hubert Ohl sees in the later novel a radicalizing of positions expressed in the earlier one. While Hagebucher cannot accommodate himself to his society's philistine hypocritical norms but sustains his own identity through resignation, both the homecomer Eduard and his stay-at-home friend Schaumann are ensnared by these same petty, quotidian values. Schaumann is, however, able to disclose and, thus, personally delimit the blindness of his bourgeois milieu. His insights force Eduard to confront a painful revelation never faced by Hagebucher: that he has been a conformist who always accommodated himself to middle-class conventions in spite of his life in a new world. This realization makes his own life's path questionable to him, a torment Hagebucher avoided by opting for an outsider's lifestyle.[33] Schaumann's ability to make Eduard recognize his fundamental myopia also allows us to perceive a radicalization in Raabe's position on colonialism in the transition from *Abu Telfan* to *Stopfkuchen*. For while Hagebucher embarked on his African adventures because his nonconformity made life impossible for him as a young man in the fatherland, Eduard settles in Africa, in spite of his early self-image, because he, *as* a conformist, can be blinded by another man's guilt-engendered colonial fantasy. This is the reason Valentine Quakatz's praise of her husband forces Eduard to count himself among the ordinary, even "coarse" ("den ganz Gewöhnlichen, den ganz Gemeinen") individuals one finds everywhere in having sought to live out his trivial adventures overseas (18: 109). If Raabe creates a certain justification for the embrace of a colonialist lifestyle in *Abu Telfan* (devastating though that choice turns out to be for the man who made it), he causes it to appear to be the product of self-delusional philistinism in his later novel.

To be sure, Raabe was quite cautious about expressing his anticolonialism in a nonfictional guise because of Germany's enthusiastic embrace of overseas imperialist ventures late in the nineteenth century. In a letter to Gustav Frenssen dated May 25, 1900, he responds to his fellow novelist's claim that the German people's romantic spirit ("Gemüth") was detrimental to the nation's colonizing endeavors by noting that his own writing had never impeded the current German *Volk* from taking possession of Samoa and conquering China, and by pointing out his own son-in-law's engagement in colonialist activities (*Ergänzungsband*, 2: 413). Since Frenssen does not appear to have impugned Raabe's personal views on colonizing, his response probably indicates the sort of nervousness Raabe began to feel as a lesser-Germany advocate in greater-Germany-oriented Stuttgart, a fear that his fictively cloaked anticolonial sentiments might be correctly interpreted, thus exposing him to majority opinion's displeasure.[34] Even more telling is a letter of January 4, 1900, to Paul Gerber, in which he expresses pride in having introduced the Boers, Oom Paul Kruger, and his city of Praetoria into German literature. This remark is undoubtedly a reference to *Stopfkuchen,* since Eduard, apparently married to an Afrikaaner woman, refers at the conclusion of this novel to his "deutsch-holländische Brut" (18: 207) and speaks at its outset of "unser Präsident, mein guter Freund daheim im Burenlande" (18: 8); as Sammons points out, this is quite likely a reference to Kruger.[35] Immediately after he claims to have brought the Boers into German literature, however, Raabe qualifies his enthusiasm about this accomplishment by noting that he has been a "Realpolitiker" since the time of Bismarck's early battles (*Ergänzungsband,* 2: 411).

The allusion to Bismarck is quite revealing. Raabe was an admirer of the "iron chancellor" and once referred to *Gutmanns Reisen* as his "Bismarckias" (*Ergänzungsband,* 3: 461). Though twentieth-century historians recognized that Bismarck was quite an active player in Germany's pursuit of colonies, the perception was widespread in Bismarck's — and Raabe's — day that the architect of German unification was extremely reluctant about permitting his nation's overseas land grabs to take place. Bismarck encouraged this view by proclaiming in a speech delivered to the Reichstag on January 26, 1889 (almost exactly a year before Raabe wrote his letter to Gerber), that he had "never been a colonial man" and only pursued colonial initiatives because of "the pressure of public opinion."[36] Some contemporary European diplomats, such as Lord Sanderson of the British Foreign Office, also believed that Bismarck was personally opposed to Germany's overseas imperialism and "was driven into a policy of colonial expansion against his will."[37] Even though Zantop opens *Colonial Fantasies* by remarking that Bismarck's extension of "'imperial protection'" to land possessed by a Bremen trader in South-West Africa is believed by historians to be "the first official act in the history of German imperialism,"[38] she also notes that "imperialist propaganda became even more unabashed" after Bismarck was forced to resign in 1890.[39] When one considers that Emperor Wilhelm II coerced Bismarck's removal from office in large part because he believed Bismarck was too tepid in his foreign-policy initiatives, it is easy to see that Raabe's embrace in the letter to Gerber of Bismarck's realpolitik was an adroit, cautious way of proclaiming his own anticolonialist perspective.

Though German realism has been defined and delimited in many ways, it has consistently been critically configured in its oppositional stance to Romantic fantasy, even if this fantasy is not inherently the product of the German Romantic movement itself. Seen in this light, Raabe's treatment of colonialism was an important and unique element in German realism. Sometimes exhibiting the "heterophilic appreciation" underscored by Berman in his analysis of German imperialism but at times exploiting the racist perceptions Zantop sees as more typical of the nation's colonialist crusades, Raabe painted the overseas territories still controlled by Europe in the nineteenth century, their climate and indigenous peoples, in exaggeratedly bleak, unattractive hues. When we consider this circumstance in connection with his tacit imaginative calling into question of the motives behind Germany's colonialist adventures and his highlighting of their potential dangers, Raabe's anticolonialism becomes evident. Though his use of colonial subjects and domains to criticize refractively domestic hypocrisy, philistinism, and corruption — the other facet of his "double system" of colonial "bookkeeping" — sometimes blurred his attitude toward the colonial experience, Raabe generally articulated a subtle but powerful minority discourse against the backdrop of German imperialist propaganda during the age of realism.

Notes

[1] In Berman's words, the writings of Forster, Nolde, and others indicate "that there is a strain in German culture that allows for the appreciation of difference, and that this strain tempered colonial discourse, directing it more toward primitivism and the possibility of a heterophilic appreciation than, by way of contrast, the more imperiously universalist discourses characteristic of the colonialisms of England and France." Russell A. Berman, *Enlightenment or Empire: Colonial Discourse in German Culture* (Lincoln: U of Nebraska P, 1998), 235.

[2] Susanne Zantop, *Colonial Fantasies: Conquest, Family, and Nation in Precolonial Germany, 1770–1870* (Durham, NC: Duke UP, 1997), 39. Zantop was coeditor, along with Sara Friedrichsmeyer and Sara Lennox, of another important book on the intersection between German culture and colonialism: *The Imperialist Imagination: German Colonialism and Its Legacy* (Ann Arbor: U of Michigan P, 1998).

[3] The translations of the titles of Raabe's works are borrowed from Jeffrey L. Sammons's *Wilhelm Raabe: The Fiction of the Alternative Community* (Princeton: Princeton UP, 1987).

⁴ The controversy concerning Raabe's treatment of Jews is primarily concentrated in scholarship focused on his best-known work, *Der Hungerpastor* (The Hunger Pastor, 1863–64). Works arguing against the notion that Raabe was genuinely anti-Semitic include Horst Denkler, "Das 'wirckliche Juda' und der 'Renegat': Moses Freudenstein als Kronzeuge für Wilhelm Raabes Verhältnis zu Juden und Judentum," *German Quarterly* 60 (1987): 5–18, and Julia Bertschik, *Maulwurfsarchäologie: Zum Verhältnis von Geschichte und Anthropologie in Wilhelm Raabes historischen Erzähltexten* (Tübingen: Niemeyer, 1995). A different view is taken by Robert C. Holub, "Raabe's Impartiality: A Reply to Horst Denkler," *German Quarterly* 60 (1987): 617–22. Sammons's chapter on *Der Hungerpastor* in *The Fiction of the Alternative Community* (73–87) provides a moderate and nuanced position on this issue.

⁵ For example, Sammons (249–54) discerns a sympathetic treatment of the Wendish piper Kiza in the story "Die Hämelschen Kinder" (The Pied Piper of Hamelin, 1863), while another critic believes that Raabe's sympathies lie with Kiza's persecutors once this marginalized figure transgresses class and ethnic boundaries. See Elke Liebs, *Kindheit und Tod: Der Rattenfänger-Mythos als Beitrag zu einer Kulturgeschichte der Kindheit* (Munich: Fink, 1986), 98–105.

⁶ See Denkler, *Wilhelm Raabe: Legende — Leben — Literatur* (Tübingen: Niemeyer, 1989), 67, and Irene Stocksieker Di Maio, "The 'Frauenfrage' and the Reception of Wilhelm Raabe's Female Characters," in Leo A. Lensing and Hans-Werner Peter, eds., *Wilhelm Raabe: Studien zu seinem Leben und Werk* (Braunschweig: pp-Verlag, 1981), 409.

⁷ Examples include Friedrich Bamler, "St. Thomas," *Mitteilungen für die Gesellschaft der Freunde Wilhelm Raabes* 29 (1939): 107–12, and Hans Otto Horch, "Historische Standortbestimmung vor Guinea: Zu Wilhelm Raabes Erzählung 'Sankt Thomas' (1865)," *Jahrbuch der Raabe-Gesellschaft* (1986): 114–28.

⁸ Irmgard Roebling, *Wilhelm Raabes doppelte Buchführung: Paradigma einer Spaltung* (Tübingen: Niemeyer, 1988).

⁹ Wilhelm Raabe, *Sämtliche Werke*, 26 vols., eds. Karl Hoppe et al. (Göttingen: Vandenhoeck & Ruprecht, 1960–94), 18: 312. Hereafter cited in the text by volume and page number.

¹⁰ See Denkler, *Neues über Wilhelm Raabe: Zehn Annäherungsversuche an einen verkannten Schriftsteller* (Tübingen: Niemeyer, 1988), 57–58.

¹¹ Berman, 235.

¹² See Raabe's letter to his mother, Auguste, dated September 11, 1866 (*Ergänzungsband*, 2: 116).

¹³ Bamler, 111–12.

¹⁴ Sammons, 104.

¹⁵ Bertschik, 51 and 77.

[16] Horch, 118–19.

[17] For a brief discussion of Raabe's expatriates who return home inwardly destroyed or proactively destructive, see Peter J. Brenner, "Die Einheit der Welt: Zur Entzauberung der Fremde und Verfremdung der Heimat in Raabes 'Abu Telfan,'" *Jahrbuch der Raabe-Gesellschaft* (1989): 47.

[18] Berman, 235.

[19] Zantop, *Colonial Fantasies,* 171–72.

[20] Denkler, *Wilhelm Raabe,* 194.

[21] This parallelism is a central topic of Brenner's article (45–62).

[22] Gayatri Chakravorty Spivak, "Can the Subaltern Speak?" in *Marxism and the Interpretation of Culture,* eds. Cary Nelson and Lawrence Grossberg (Urbana: U of Illinois P, 1988), 271–313.

[23] Spivak, 285.

[24] See Berman, 227–31.

[25] Siegfried Hajek, "'Meister Autor.' — Sprachschichten und Motive," *Jahrbuch der Raabe-Gesellschaft* (1981): 159.

[26] Bertschik, 211–12.

[27] Though the antiforeign sensibility of the narrative is modified when it indicates, regarding Romana, that such a "Princess Fish" could be Romanic, German, or Slavic (15: 363).

[28] Sammons, 86.

[29] As a note to *Fabian und Sebastian* in Raabe's collected works explains, "Creole" in this novel is meant to refer to white people born in the colonies (15: 589); thus, Konstantia's "Creole" mother is Caucasian.

[30] See Philip J. Brewster, "Onkel Ketschwayo in Neuteutoburg: Zeitgeschichtliche Anspielungen in Raabes 'Stopfkuchen,'" *Jahrbuch der Raabe-Gesellschaft* (1983): 96–118, and Michel Gnéba Kokora, "Die Ferne in der Nähe: Zur Funktion Afrikas in Raabes 'Abu Telfan' und 'Stopfkuchen,'" *Jahrbuch der Raabe-Gesellschaft* (1994): 54–69.

[31] Cf. Wolfgang Struck, "See- und Mordgeschichten: Zur Konstruktion exotischer Räume in realistischen Erzähltexten," *Jahrbuch der Raabe-Gesellschaft* (1999): 60–70. Struck claims that Brewster's and Kokora's reading of *Stopfkuchen* as an anticolonial novel does not explain the function of Eduard's second "flight" to Africa, nor what Africa he is trying to construct in the ship's isolated space. Through a comparative reading of *Stopfkuchen* and stories authored by Raabe's friend Wilhelm Jensen, Struck attempts to demonstrate that Eduard's metanarratological reflections set up a network of affiliations between his African and German homelands in such a manner that, as with

Jensen and other German writers, the "Kolonialroman" becomes a "Heimatroman" (70). This thesis ignores the likelihood that Eduard's flight home is caused by his painful realization that his "Africa," and thus his own most important choice in life, have their origin in guilty deceit; his is a flight from revelation, from the scene of Störzer's crime. The ship is, indeed, the "Ort des Dazwischen" (70) that enables narration, but it is the "place between" the locus of unbearable truth in the German town of Eduard's youth and the new "homeland" in Africa, stripped of any originary colonial fantasy.

[32] Brewster, 112–13, 117.

[33] Hubert Ohl, "Eduards Heimkehr oder Le Vaillant und das Riesenfaultier: Zu Wilhelm Raabes 'Stopfkuchen,'" in Hermann Helmers, ed., *Raabe in neuer Sicht* (Stuttgart: Kohlhammer, 1968), 269.

[34] Cf. Brewster (117–18), who regards the letter as highly provocative, given its perspective on the Social Democratic Party as the most enterprising in Germany and a reference to Christ's family that the conservative, nationalist, strongly Christian Frenssen could have considered blasphemous. Brewster also notes that Raabe put a clear question mark next to a passage on the putatively deserved death of the "pagan" blacks (the Hereros) in his copy of Frenssen's novel *Peter Moors Fahrt nach Südwest: Ein Feldzugbericht* (1906; translated as *Peter Moor's Journey to Southwest Africa*, 1909). For an analysis of this novel's racist, imperialist, but consciously self-deconstructive tendencies, see John K. Noyes, "National Identity, Nomadism, and Narration in Gustav Frenssen's *Peter Moor's Journey to Southwest Africa*," in Friedrichsmeyer, Lennox, and Zantop, eds., *The Imperialist Imagination*, 87–105.

[35] Sammons, 285. As Denkler (*Wilhelm Raabe*, 139) has noted, Raabe supported the Boers in their resistance against English colonial troops at the beginning of the twentieth century but felt that an English defeat would be disastrous if it meant a major loss of English influence in the world. This attitude is evident in the letter to Gerber (*Ergänzungsband*, 2: 411).

[36] I am citing here a translated excerpt of Bismarck's speech in W. N. Medlicott and Dorothy K. Coveney, eds., *Bismarck and Europe* (New York: St. Martin's P, 1972), 177.

[37] See A. J. P. Taylor, *Germany's First Bid for Colonies 1884–1885: A Move in Bismarck's European Policy* (1938; rpt. Hamden, CT: Archon, 1967), 4. Medlicott and Coveney (132) and Taylor (5) find the view of Bismarck as an anticolonialist to be highly dubious.

[38] Zantop, *Colonial Fantasies*, 1.

[39] Zantop, *Colonial Fantasies*, 199.

From National Task to Individual Pursuit: The Poetics of Work in Freytag, Stifter, and Raabe

Hans J. Rindisbacher

IN FICTION — in literature as well as in film — work is not usually the central issue. On the contrary: the main characters of most more or less plausibly realistic fictional narratives are provided at the outset with some means, however sketchy, of supporting themselves so that the story can focus on something else that is presumably more interesting: a love story, a passion, a crime, a mystery, self-realization, personal growth, psychological development, etc. The (semi-) literary depiction of work is usually relegated to "engaged writing," pamphlets, political tracts, propaganda, *Arbeiterliteratur,* documentaries, diaries, and so forth. This well-established generic division reflects a fundamental perception of work as something necessary but rarely pleasurable, a chore whose rewards — a salary — allow us to be and to do what we would rather do if we had our choice. Work, in short, is the mundane *base* onto which we build our *superstructures* of personal growth, leisure, fun, and pleasure.

The backgrounding of work even in so-called realist novels — often qualified as "bourgeois" or "poetic" in the German nineteenth-century context — provides the starting point for the present inquiry into aspects of the vast and multifaceted realm of *work*.[1] The essay poses a simple question: how is work, labor, one's professional occupation, one's ways of earning a livelihood depicted in three representative nineteenth-century German novels? This is not the same, of course, as asking what role work plays in nineteenth-century German society and economy or what role it plays for specific groups of people — the declining nobility, the rising bourgeoisie, peasants moving into cities as workers, the industrialists and entrepreneurs, the emerging management class, or the political and social theorists — although the views of all of these groups would no doubt warrant their own inquiries.

In this study work is framed primarily in the context of a literary inquiry, with reference to extraliterary aspects when necessary. Discourse boundaries are blurry at best. The genre of the realist novel in particular, with its implied theoretical claim to providing plausible extensions of reality into the literary realm, is programmatically linked to extraliterary social, political, and other issues. This analysis of three German realist novels, therefore, aims at two things: to pull work-related issues from the background into the center and to discuss the role work plays for the narrative structure, plot, character development, aesthetics, mood, or ideology. The three novels are Gustav Freytag's *Soll und Haben* (Debit and Credit, 1855);[2] Adalbert Stifter's *Der Nachsommer* (Indian Summer, 1857);[3] and Wilhelm Raabe's *Pfisters Mühle* (Pfister's Mill, 1884).[4] There is, moreover, a fourth text — highly literary in its diction and imagery, even if not outright "literature" — that permeates the present discussion: Karl Marx and Friedrich Engels's *The Communist Manifesto* (1848). In the chorus of nineteenth-century public discourse, where labor issues are addressed with increasing disciplinary specificity, realist literature appears as the voice perhaps best suited to providing a coherent — albeit fictional — "big picture" overview of work.[5]

Two aspects of work are at the center: work as it affects the individual and comes down on the body in the "daily grind," the fatigue and exhaustion of (physical) labor, but also in a sense of pleasure and achievement; and work as conceived in Marxist terms, as a collective force that can be organized, bought, sold, refused, and so forth. Beyond these categories, each novel places work in its own contemporary discursive context. For *Soll und Haben* this is, on the one hand, the context of nationalism, the issue of national work, the German intra-European colonial task, the *Drang nach Osten,* and the mission to spread German work and German work ethics eastward; on the other hand, it is the presentation of bourgeois values as the rock of both national and individual moral stability in an age of change. The story of Anton Wohlfahrt contains, as do the other two novels, elements of a Bildungsroman: the induction of a young man into the adult world of work and responsibility; but it is evident from the rather thin psychology, limited introspection, and the general outside perspective on Anton that Freytag's focus aims far beyond the account of an individual.

Der Nachsommer, published in 1857, just two years after *Soll und Haben,* by an Austrian author, is virtually free from nationalist-imperialist pathos. The novel forms part of a different debate about work, the incipient discussion of unalienated work that will culminate around the turn of the century in the attempted fusion of craft and industrial production (John Ruskin and William Morris in the British context; the *Werkbund* movement and the later Bauhaus in the German are landmarks along this path). But for the most part, *Der Nachsommer* outlines a more comprehensive debate about the social and moral function of work and is thus more generally about work ethics and its implication for society at large than about any specific profession. Stifter's proposed models amount to a backward-looking utopia, craft-based work, and always appropriate use of materials. Such highly site- and circumstance-specific work is, at the time of the novel's publication, already being relegated to the decidedly elite niche of amateur pursuits.

Raabe, finally, in *Pfisters Mühle* prefigures a third discourse: the environmental one. The environment is understood comprehensively in its natural and social dimensions, as a creek in a landscape as well as a mode of work, a type of technology, and a way of life. While Raabe's tone is nostalgic, as is Stifter's, it is more personally, less culturally so. The novel ultimately looks forward but betrays a sense of the inevitability of (technological) progress, environmental degradation, and changing human interaction as unavoidable consequences of progress. In the ambivalence about weighing the effects of change, *Pfisters Mühle* fits also into another contemporary discourse, that on *Heimat.* Spatial and social displacement, as well as a sense of accelerating time, are key features of this debate, as well as of Raabe's novel.

For all three novels this study also addresses aspects of personal relationships among characters in terms of generation, social rank, and class. In all three novels change — in the types of work, the work environment, and the meaning of work for individuals, as well as for larger groups — is a central issue. The attitudes to these changes and the fixed points from which they are observed or at which they ought to be stopped, together with the posited values and suggested paths of action tie each text into its respective wider contemporary discourse. Additionally, their juxtaposition in this study, together with the resonance of the *Communist Manifesto*, adds further depth to the inquiry.

1. *Soll und Haben:* The Poetics of Business

Soll und Haben is a much-discussed and well-analyzed text. Its nationalist dimension; its emphasis on work; its quintessential bourgeois worldview and set of values; its representational accuracy, as well as its biases; and, finally, its strict adherence to realist theories have all been noted and commented on by Freytag's contemporaries and later scholars alike. This essay focuses on trade, the kind of work that dominates the novel as a *relational field*. Work, conceptualized as a field of relations — a network of personal, financial, commercial, geographical, material, and informational ties — appears as the connective tissue of the narrative. It anchors not only the German bourgeoisie, so central to the text, but also the bourgeoisie as a universal, cosmopolitan class in the sense in which Marx and Engels had described it only a few years earlier. For Freytag, work-as-trade ties together several social classes in what Marx would no doubt label false consciousness.

Soll und Haben was generally positively, even enthusiastically, received and went on to become one of the most successful German novels of all time.[6] Theodor Fontane, for instance, praises the novel as "die erste Blüthe des modernen Realismus."[7] But there was criticism, too, not infrequently triggered by the very issue of work that Freytag, by placing Julian Schmidt's motto at the head of his text, had declared his central concern: "Der Roman soll das deutsche Volk da suchen, wo es in seiner Tüchtigkeit zu finden ist, nämlich bei seiner Arbeit."[8] Karl Gutzkow points critically to the issue of work. He admits that there is — and lists it in some detail — a lot of activity in the novel; there are many strands of narrative and many characters doing all sorts of things, but one nevertheless ends up asking, "Wo ist hier die Arbeit? Individuelle, der Poesie und nicht der Statistik angehörende Arbeit?"[9] Hermann Marggraff makes a similar point. After Schmidt's motto, he claims, the reader hopes to be transported into a realm of real work, "ein Klopfen und Hämmern, ein Pochen und Sägen, in ein Messen und Wägen, in ein Richten und Bauen, in die laute Werkstätte der

Handarbeit wie in die stille Arbeitsstube des Forschers und Denkers."[10] Marggraff is not denying the poetics inherent in business but misses "real work" and resents as forced the relational aspects of business as presented by Freytag, the artificial and unrealistic "verzwickten Combinationen" (342) of unrelated, faraway objects and (business-related) actions performed on them as work. Such connections are too far-fetched and socially implausible. A "Commis räsonnirt und combinirt so nicht" (341). Marggraff laments the fact that among all the types of work, only commodities trade and agriculture are deemed worthy topics by the author.

Robert Giseke raises another issue: the fundamental anachronism of Freytag's merchant world.[11] It may be objected that up-to-dateness was not Freytag's intention, as he himself describes Schröter's business as old-fashioned and solid and of a vanishing kind. Gabriele Büchler-Hauschild, in her extensive study of Freytag's novel that centers on issues of work, emphasizes this point and sums it up by saying that Freytag, rather than aiming for the depiction of cutting-edge business practices, aimed primarily at creating the impression that *any* kind of work contributes to the common wealth and provides satisfaction as long as it observes the bourgeois "rules of the game."[12]

Robert Schweichel's criticism of 1876 points up another work-related issue. Schweichel thinks that the Schmidt quote placed over the novel is "durchaus unrichtig. Das Volk ist bei der Arbeit gar nicht das Volk, es ist Handwerkszeug, Maschine, und diese sind wahrlich keine Gegenstände für die Dichtkunst."[13] Instead, Schweichel argues, poetics has to find the *Volk* where it appears as *Mensch*. But if the *Volk* at work is not the *Volk*, what is it? And where, in turn, does it appear as *Mensch*? Schweichel's remark exhibits an awareness — growing at the time — of issues of class and alienated labor that do not surface in Freytag's novel, preempted by the "natural" assumption that the bourgeoisie equals the *Volk* — or, inversely, that the *Volk*, as far as Freytag is concerned, is bourgeois. Under this assumption the businessman, the merchant, the trader, and the entrepreneur-producer are promoted as the quintessential bourgeois representatives. By means of paternalistic structures such as those in the Schröter business the bourgeoisie simply subsumes its inferiors — the workers, the packers and shippers, the movers and wagoners. They are consistently presented as individuals rather than as collective "labor" and kept, even if benevolently, at a certain distance — the white-collar employees, for instance, in the "Hintergebäude" (31), while the master and his family inhabit the "Vorderhaus" (45). The men around Father Sturm, the one blue-collar character depicted in some detail, are constructed as over-life-size, quasi-mythical giants, remnants of an ancient people. Marggraff seems to have aimed in the same direction as Schweichel when commenting on the kinds of work the novel depicts. The real *Volk* — for him, obviously, workers and craftsmen — would be performing manual work, rather than administrative or service jobs in the national economy or *Volkswirtschaft*.

As most scholars and critics take for granted that *Soll und Haben* is less about specific work than about the social, political, and moral values of the German bourgeoisie, the *Bürgertum,* the above critical voices are important but need to be complemented by the key note on labor issues that reverberates throughout the second half of the nineteenth century and well into the twentieth century, *The Communist Manifesto*. It provides a breathtaking sketch of the very social group and its historical achievements that is also at the center of Freytag's novel.

Comparing the imagery of the first part of the *Manifesto* with passages from *Soll und Haben* reveals some surprising commonalities in the conceptualization of work and its social implications. In this juxtaposition the novel emerges both as the vehicle of an idealized capitalist mode of business presented generically through the means of programmatic realism, in terms of personnel through the patriarchal bourgeois firm, and intertextually as an echo, at times harmonizing, at times ironic, of Marx and Engels's text. In their respective diagnoses of the state of the world at midcentury Marx and Engels and Freytag are not all that far apart. Both texts thematize change and the inevitable losses that modernization entails. But whereas for Marx and Engels these losses appear as a necessary consequence of enlightenment processes, Freytag continuously smoothes over the negatives through poetic harmonizing. The basic common elements — capitalism, the bourgeoisie, trade, the international market — are counterbalanced by contrasting assessments and, of course, by explicit or implicit ideological counterpurposes. In this regard the two texts could hardly be more different. Moreover, some topics do not simply line up along a common axis in the two texts: for instance, the class division of society. There is hardly a sign of class consciousness in *Soll und Haben*. If anything, it is the older *Standesbewusstsein* that informs social divisions, as reflected in the Rothsattels at the upper but also in Father Sturm's thinking at the lower end of the social spectrum of the novel. Sturm thinks still more as a guild member belonging to a fraternity of loaders and shippers than in terms of a working-class consciousness. Generally, it can be said that Freytag's social pie is cut vertically into national slices, rather than into horizontal layers-as-classes. This is different, of course, in the *Manifesto*, which, at least in its rhetorical strategies, has already abolished national borders and "gone global," clearly ahead of its time. Marx's social pie is layered, but not sliced.

Present in both texts is the literary and narrative motive of the quest. The challenges facing the Schröter troupe in the East, first in recovering their goods, then in Anton's efforts on the Polish estate are paralleled in the *Manifesto* in the bourgeois class quest for expanding markets. The *Entwicklungsroman* motif centered on Anton is reflected in the historical ascendance of the bourgeoisie. But there are clear generic differences, too. The *Manifesto*, certainly in its first part, has the compactness that allows it to be carried on the impetus of its own poetic imagery, whereas the novel requires characters and plot. Imagery, therefore — although representing much more than mere rhetorical flourishes — has a more subordinate function in the novel, which makes the unmistakable echoes of the *Manifesto* appear all the more striking and deliberate. Both Marx and Freytag use imagery of connection, flux, (lost) solidity, and stability, even while emphasizing opposite aspects. In analyzing the very intersection of imagery and literary strategies, the fusion of literary means and sociohistorical diagnosis, it appears that in both cases the authors' concern for literary-aesthetic and rhetorical devices far outweighs those for factual-critical representation of contemporary sociohistorical reality. A key difference lies in the novel's rootedness compared to the cosmopolitanism of the *Manifesto*. Not only is Marx's key protagonist the bourgeoisie in the abstract, it is also explicitly not tied to any one place. Freytag, although extolling the values of the same class, represents it in concrete characters, locates it narratively in the institution of the Schröter business and historically and geographically in the specific environment of the East-Elbian *Junkertum* and the Silesian (Breslau) *Bürgertum,* which allows him, for instance, to associate closely the landed gentry and its economic base in agricultural estates.

Both texts — but the *Manifesto* more so than *Soll und Haben* — pursue a "big-picture" approach to work, rather than, say, the "thick description" of specific, concrete professional activities that Marggraff so sorely misses in *Soll und Haben*. In the *Manifesto* work appears in broad outline, as the result as well as the motor of large-scale socioeconomic and cultural-historical changes caused by a whole segment of the population over a long period of time. Thus described, work fits closely its relational description, given above, that links individuals, times, and places in a comprehensive network of class, history, and global exchange.[14] But Freytag rejects Marx's conclusion that the class of people involved in commerce is constantly pulling the rug from under itself and has to reinvent itself time and again. (In the last analysis, even Marx himself believes only in the first part of this scenario, not the second. He sees the proletariat taking over from the bourgeoisie precisely because the latter is no longer able to reinvent itself fast enough to keep up with the chaotic processes of change it has itself set in motion). To slow down "the desperate pace and frantic rhythm that capitalism imparts to every facet of modern life," Freytag drops the Schröter business like an anchor at the center of his narrative, the harbor for seemingly immutable traditions, a backdated and prestabilized harmony as a narrative countermeasure to the Marxian flux that is, thus, but indirectly acknowledged.[15]

Marshall Berman is right to point out the startling fact that Marx in the first pages of the *Manifesto* "seems to have come not to bury the bourgeoisie, but to praise it. He writes an impassioned, enthusiastic, often lyrical celebration of bourgeois work, ideas and achievements" (92). Eleven key paragraphs of the first part of the *Manifesto* begin with "The bourgeoisie" as the subject, followed by some verb of action.[16] Only in three instances is the bourgeoisie not the agent but acted upon by even larger forces: it is "itself the product of a long course of development, of a series of revolutions in the modes of productions and of exchange" (91), a result of the forces of history. And while the bourgeoisie may have initiated the development of its global networks, it is now itself at the mercy of the relentless forces of a "constantly expanding market" that "chases" it all over the globe (93). As a consequence, it has now reached a point where its own creations threaten to evade its control, not unlike — Marx uses a literary reference — "the sorcerer who is no longer able to control the powers of the nether world whom he has called up by his spells" (95). Control is, on the other hand, the defining aspect of Freytag's bourgeois; its loss spells chaos, as can be seen in Poland.

For Marx, "the East Indian and Chinese markets" and the "colonization of America" have provided irresistible impulses "to commerce, to navigation, to industry"; a "world market" has emerged. The guild system has long been replaced by manufacturing, which in turn, thanks to "steam and machinery," is giving way to "Modern Industry" (90). "Production and consumption in every country" have acquired "a cosmopolitan character," so that "old-established national industries have been destroyed or are daily being destroyed" and are replaced by industries that no longer use "indigenous raw materials but raw materials drawn from the remotest zones" (93). Old demands have been replaced by "new wants, requiring for their satisfaction the products of distant lands and climes" (93). In sum, the "bourgeoisie, historically, has played a most revolutionary part" (91). Predictably, this revolution has not stopped at changing industries and trade; it has also profoundly altered human ties and psychological states. It has "put an end to all feudal, patriarchal, idyllic relations." The bourgeoisie has "torn asunder" the "ties that bound man to his 'natural superiors'" and in their place has set up "naked self-interest" (91), the "callous 'cash payment'" (91–92). "It has drowned the most heavenly ecstasies of religious fervor," "chivalrous enthusiasm," and "philistine sentimentalism" and has "resolved personal worth into exchange value." Its only freedom is an "unconscionable freedom — Free Trade." Exploitation, in earlier times "veiled by religious and political illusions," has been replaced by "naked, shameless, direct, brutal exploitation," and the sweeping changes have also "torn away from the family its sentimental veil" and "stripped of its halo every occupation hitherto honored and looked up to with reverent awe." In sum, all "fast-frozen relations, with their train of ancient and venerable prejudices and opinions, are swept away, all new-formed ones become antiquated before they can ossify," and people are forced to reassess the very way they look at themselves and understand their roles: "man is at last compelled to face with sober senses his real conditions of life and his relations with his kind" (92).

With considerably less fury these Marxian winds of change also blow through *Soll und Haben* but are felt, notably by Anton from his firm moorings in the Schröter business, as pleasant breezes wafting in from faraway places. While Freytag agrees with Marx on the existence of an international market, he consistently concretizes, personalizes, and cuts down to size the potentially negative implications for "our hero," Anton. Freytag echoes Marx in insisting on the necessarily transnational character of consumer goods and the effect the demand for them has on local economies. The foreign goods, the *Kolonialwaren,* have begun to replace local products. Even Anton's father, when setting up his son's apprenticeship, had an inkling of this when Schröter treated him at lunch to lapwing eggs and Greek wine, compared to the latter of which the local product appeared as worthless vinegar. But overall, Freytag's world market is still much more circumscribed than Marx's, and business is immediately seen as more risky as it extends, for instance, toward the Turkish border.

As in the *Manifesto,* business life means a constant hustle and bustle, and a confusing, colorful procession of all sorts of people filters through the office; it is true that Anton feels insecure and uprooted and has trouble orienting himself in the first few weeks. But in contrast to the *Manifesto,* where humans and their actions have lost their mooring, a strong element of stability and tradition pervades Freytag's novel. That begins with the proprietor's very name, Traugott ["In-God-We-Trust"] Schröter. Perhaps surprisingly, Schröter warns Anton not about the hectic pace and exhausting speed of trade but about stagnation and boredom, telling him that his life will at times seem monotonous and emphasizing the strict regularity in his firm in particular but also in business in general. Indeed, Anton suffers more from the eternal monotony of the days and hours than from overexcitement or exertion. The tedium of office work will, in combination with a personality entirely unsuited for business life, become Christian Buddenbrook's downfall. Thomas Mann's *Buddenbrooks,* published in 1901, thus rounds off a half-century of discussion of work as business by expanding the debate to work and art. This regularity, tradition, even stiffness is also in evidence in the fact that the Schröter employees are all unmarried young men who live with their employer — a tradition dating back to guild days — and are held to highly regulated social interaction, for instance, over the common meals. Everyone literally knows his place and feels that an insurmountable barrier exists between the clerks of the office and the master's household.

In these circumstances, the introduction to and instruction in the secrets of the commodities — secrets that Marx denies even exist in modern commodities — that Anton receives from Herr Jordan, his mentor, provide much-appreciated distraction. One such lesson parallels issues in the *Manifesto* — trade in foreign goods by members of the European bourgeoisie — but reveals a rather different emphasis. Whereas for Marx the economic, trade, and social developments that the rise of the bourgeoisie has brought in its wake have led to losses, unveiling, denuding, sobering, reducing life to its bare essence, and poetry as the superfluous and nonessential has fled from this reduced reality and migrated into the text that speaks of it, the case is different for Freytag. His world of goods is rich and sensuous and the objects themselves rather than their textual shells provide life's — and the text's — poetry. The hundreds of different things and strange forms that Anton encounters in the Schröter warehouse touch his impressionable mind with an "eigentümliche Poesie" that rests on the fairy-talelike charm that strange and foreign things have on the human soul (47). (The reader will recall that the novel opens with that same "Poesie" in the form of a poetic smell (8), triggered by Schröter's gift of *Kolonialwaren* — coffee and sugar — to Anton's father).

In this key passage the very products and the means of their transportation seem to form a teleology of their own that propels them into the warehouses of the European merchant bourgeoisie. The grand sweep of their gathering in the Schröter basement is markedly different however, from the grand sweep of Marx's world market. The thick, sensuous, object-centered description of these goods, their containers, their origins, their producers, and the anthropomorphized means of transportation that brought them there is in stark contrast to Marx's "thin" structure-oriented description of international trade.[17] Almost all countries of the earth, all races of humankind had worked — final clause — to pile up useful and precious things in front of our hero. The floating palace of the East India Company (Marx's "East Indian market"), the flying American brig, the ancient ark of the Dutch had all circled the globe, and the strong-ribbed whalers had "rubbed their noses on the icebergs of the north and south poles"; black steamers, colorful Chinese junks, light Malayan barges ... all had stirred their wings and fought storms and waves — final clause — to fill Schröter's basement. The next passage links products and producers through some actions the latter perform on the former, which, for emphasis, stand at the head of the sentences: mats had been woven by a Hindu woman; a box had been painted by a diligent Chinese; a rattan weave had been tied around some bale by a Congolese black, and so on. This word order and emphasis continues through the following clauses, where the products stand at the head of each sentence and are the grammatical agents: this tree trunk had rolled down the sand; that square block had stood in a swampy forest in Brazil. Freytag sums up this purposeful gathering of the goods by saying that hundreds of different plants had gathered their wood, their bark, their buds, their fruit, their cores, and the sap of their trunks at this place. Although referring to a different passage, it is these contrived associations that Marggraff criticizes as far-fetched and implausible.

The effect of Herr Jordan's explanations on Anton is such that he remains for hours in the basement in a state of aroused curiosity and wonderment. In the presence of these highly auraticized products, the warehouse turns before his inner eye into a grove of big-leafed palms and the noise of traffic outside into the distant murmur of the sea, which he only knew from his dreams and which he now sees rolling onto the shore on which he stands so safely and securely. This firm stand, as on a rock in the flux of change, is a position unavailable to the humans implied in Marx, the proletarians as the primary victims of the bourgeois-initiated changes, but elusive even to the bourgeois themselves. Anton takes pleasure in the foreign world he has entered so completely without risk. While the Marxian flux and decay are visible in *Soll und Haben* (often associated with specific class or ethnic or national groups — the Rothsattels and the nobility, Itzig and the Jews, Fink and the USA), Schröter's business resists these tidal waves of change. The cashier, for one, is surrounded by iron strongboxes and heavy safes behind his large stone-topped table. Such images of solidity recur; for instance, when Anton returns from the Rothsattels, who have just asked him to become the manager of their affairs. At this decisive moment, with the future up in the air, his vision of the Schröter buildings, with their windows on the ground floor barred, the basement and cellar locked by iron doors, secure and firm in the still of the night, provides "our hero" with a solid and trustworthy base.

Freytag's delivery is generally serious and straightforward. He rarely falls into Stifter's heavy drone of authorial self-righteousness that Russell Berman calls the "authority of address."[18] But Freytag is no doubt aware of the literary models of the *Manifesto*, whose imagery he picks up and plays back. At times he goes to an ironic distance from his characters and their enthusiasm, something not found in Stifter. Thus, when war breaks out in the German border areas in the East, and Schröter's convoy of goods is stuck near the Polish border, this news invigorates Anton as nothing ever before has. Schröter's measured reaction to the perilous situation triggers the younger man's admiration, and Freytag has him exclaim with wild joy:

> Das ist die Poesie, die Poesie des Geschäfts, solche springende Tatkraft empfinden nur wir, wenn wir gegen den Strom arbeiten. Wenn die Leute sprechen, daß unsere Zeit leer an Begeisterung sei und unser Beruf am allerleersten, so verstehen sie nicht, was schön und groß ist. Dem Manne steht in diesem Augenblick alles auf dem Spiel, woran seine Seele hängt, sein Geschäft, der Erfolg eines langen Lebens von rastloser Tätigkeit, seine Freude, sein Stolz, seine Ehre; und er steht kaltblütig an seinem Pult, schreibt Briefe über geraspeltes Farbeholz und gibt sein Urteil über Kleesamen ab, ja, ich glaube, er lacht innerlich. (247–48)

One cannot help but think that Freytag, too, is laughing — at least smiling — at Anton's mock-heroic tirade. This passage is also in indirect answer to Bernhard Ehrenthal's earlier suggestion that business is so prosaic, the passage Marggraff holds up to ridicule. Both instances can be read as examples of (false) romanticizing and poeticizing of business. But Anton contradicts Bernhard heatedly:

> Wir leben mitten unter einem bunten Gewebe von zahllosen Fäden, die sich von einem Menschen zum anderen spinnen. Sie hängen sich an jeden einzelnen und verbinden ihn mit der ganzen Welt. . . . Wenn ich einen Sack mit Kaffee auf die Waage setze, so knüpfe ich einen unsichtbaren Faden zwischen der Kolonistentochter in Brasilien, welche die Bohnen abgepflückt hat, und dem jungen Bauernburschen, der sie zum Frühstück trinkt, und wenn ich einen Zimtstengel in die Hand nehme, so sehe ich auf der einen Seite den Malaien kauern, der ihn zubereitet und einpackt, und auf der anderen Seite ein altes Mütterchen aus unserer Vorstadt, das ihn über den Reisbrei reibt.

"Sie haben eine lebhafte Einbildungskraft und sind glücklich, weil Sie Ihre Arbeit als nützlich empfinden" is Bernhard's reply (181–82). Both passages, focused through Anton, are the effusions of a young man from humble background to whom the bourgeois world of trade appears as the next best thing to chivalry and immortal deeds. Freytag the author keeps himself at an ironic distance.

The accounts of work, as well as the personal interactions among the *Bürger*, aim at creating stability, order, hierarchy, trust — in other words, at building a counterposition to the state of affairs described by Marx and Engels. These accounts are verbally rather close to some of the points in the *Manifesto* — the threads linking people and places, the products from faraway countries, the sheer thrill of being part of a global network — but the resemblance becomes even stronger where Freytag describes the Jewish business practices around the novel's counterhero, Veitel Itzig. In his world of business the dire findings and predictions of the *Manifesto* have already come true and are reflected in Freytag's language.[19] In depicting the thoroughly negatively coded world of Jewish financial business Freytag seems to accept aspects of the *Manifesto* that he denies for the bourgeoisie in a structural bifurcation of representation. This confirms the claim of similar sensitivities and assessments of midcentury trade and business developments by Freytag and Marx: both notice the changes, but they interpret them differently. Thus, when Veitel closes his first shady deal, he brutally destroys the warm feelings that his victim was just beginning to cherish over an unexpected inheritance to which Veitel now makes legal claims. By his ice-cold demand, he beats down all the warm effusions that rise from the heart of the hopeful heir. Veitel's own triumph, however, is severely dampened when his teacher Hippus, the only person toward whom he feels some attachment, behaves in an unfeeling and egotistical manner. As in the *Manifesto*, personal ties are damaged by the rapid changes in the capitalist world; the temperature of human interaction drops.

In references to the other class negatively depicted by Freytag — the nobility — echoes of Marx are also unmistakable. Rothsattel has just received a princely medal of honor that ties him to a grand old tradition. Even in his joy and pride, however, he realizes that the times are changing and notes in outright Marxist language that a new force is emerging in lieu of noble privileges, money.

From his perspective of the class of the future Schröter comments in blunt, almost Darwinian terms on the Rothsattels' dire straits after their sugar-refinery venture fails, arguing that where strength falters in a family or an individual, wealth will naturally vanish and fall into other hands. Continuing with an agricultural metaphor, he adds that the plow shall be taken over by other hands that might guide it more firmly. This image takes up Freytag's geographical and social context of the East Prussian Junker class — nobility, landowners, and agriculturists at the same time. In Freytag it is this class, rather than the peasant of the *Manifesto*, that "sink[s] gradually into the proletariat" (97). Freytag has this in mind in Book 3, chapter 4, where he provides a highly charged account of agricultural work and its ramifications and pronounces happy the man who strides across vast tracts of his own land. Although the life of the farmer is a never-ending struggle, he is tied into the ancient order of nature and has below him the firm ground from which to counter the raw blows of nature — nature cuts both ways. Freytag recognizes that the price of land rises from year to year and maintains that the farmer's influence on others is growing, even as the rugged path across the fields turns into a *Chaussee* and the piece of marshland into a canal and the very market forces that push up the price of land also push the farmer out. Freytag leaves thus unresolved the bind in which agriculture finds itself in an industrializing society that begins to subvert the farmer's firm ground.[20] He recognizes that the successful, modernizing, and technically advanced agriculturist, on whose estate the ancient plowshare and the newfangled steam engine coexist and collaborate, must take note of the changes around him; the farmer is surrounded by the spinning wheels of modern labor and production and increasingly needs a sense for the market as foreigners shake hands with him, tying their advantage to his own. Whereas the farmer earlier was looking at the hustle and bustle of the big cities and the complex interactions brought on by the new era as if at something far away, he has now himself become part of these complex structures and widening circles.

Another echo of the *Manifesto* reaches Anton and the reader from Fink in America, the nation that represents rampant capitalism like no other. Fink is not doing as well as he had hoped; in fact, he finds himself hemmed in by the icy cold of the most terrible speculations — a phrase that could be straight from the *Manifesto*.

By now, the focus on work as a relational field developed in response to the kind of professional activities foregrounded in the novel has come to overshadow somewhat the point of departure of this essay: work as labor, work as a way for an individual to earn a living. No salaries, and no sums other than prices of goods or percentage figures for interest on debts, are ever mentioned. Amounts of mortgages, letters of credit, and other, usually real-estate and investment related, numbers complete the picture. No one earns a specific amount in exchange for putting in a certain number of hours a day or a week. Marx and Engels's notion of the "laborers, who must sell themselves piecemeal" as "a commodity like every other article of commerce" (96) is wholly absent from the novel. Among the bourgeoisie, which the *Manifesto* practically equates with capital, money rarely appears as the just deserts for an individual's work; it appears, instead, as a transactional medium for exchange and conversion, as, for instance, in the haggling between Fink and Schmeye Tinkeles. Only in Anton's conversation with Sturm, the giant packer, is the topic of wages broached, together with issues of laborers' attitudes, a blue-collar work ethic. It is noteworthy that Sturm is financially secure: his house is his own. His thrifty wife, on her death, left him considerable sums stashed away in stockings that fill the whole bottom of her closet. It is not clear how she was able to save that much, although Sturm admits that his income is not bad at all. Money, therefore, not being a problem, Sturm exhibits none of the anxieties and subservience and is completely free from the misery that Marx and Engels allege for their proletariat. What really hurts Sturm and his colleagues is alcohol, specifically beer, of which he consumes forty pints a day — as he announces with a perverse kind of corporate pride rooted in long tradition. Drinking is a professional custom, he assures Anton, as is loyalty; packers must be faithful men. No trace of inferiority or insecurity vis-à-vis the "capitalists" can be detected in this Herculean worker, who is over-life-size, perhaps, in this regard, too.

There is one further aspect of work, its most psychological and individual one: work as an emotional release. Anton uses his job that way when, on the day after his withdrawal from aristocratic society, into which Fink had lured him, he works the whole day like someone bent on numbing himself. He bears the loss of his false higher status with equanimity and, in compensation, launches himself passionately into his work. His reaction is similar when Fink leaves for America. Anton returns sadly to his desk but quickly writes up a business letter to which he appends a list of goods and samples of sugar, as if nothing had happened.

The correspondences between the vastly different texts of *Soll und Haben* and *The Communist Manifesto* are clear: the verbal echoes of the earlier in the later, the comparable perceptions that nevertheless lead to sharply contrasting emphases and programs for the present and the future. Marx and Engels place their bet on the proletariat, Freytag on the bourgeoisie. Universal commerce and trade is a common feature, but the nationalist limitation that Freytag proposes is seen by Marx and Engels as already obsolete. Their bourgeoisie has long exploded national boundaries, and the proletariat operates within them only in a first strategic step. We also note the opposite evaluation of emotions, sentiment, warmth, *Gemütlichkeit,* the imbalances between loss and gain, solidity and fluidity, fixity and mobility, and so forth. In moving on to Stifter, we can put class issues, as such, aside; we only encounter bourgeoisie and nobility (and, indeed, their servants) on the remote country estates of the latter, in pursuit of goals and values that lie entirely in the past yet, by this very fact, do have a utopian dimension as placeholders for Enlightenment promises not yet fulfilled.

2. *Der Nachsommer:* Leisure as Work

What people actually do — or, rather, what they achieve — is in some ways more visible in this novel than in Freytag's with its explicit commitment to the depiction of the people at work. What they do, though, is rarely visible as process, but only as its result. *People* here once again hardly means *Volk*, understood as the general populace. And the relational understanding of work is useful only in one sense: to connect work, concrete manipulations, craft techniques with their appropriate material source, the parts specifically selected for a definite purpose via the use of appropriate tools, the "*Geräte*," with which so many of the novel's rooms are filled. This paramount emphasis on appropriateness, on fittingness, on matching means and ends determines the semantic, as well as the actional, fields of work in this novel. Work as the physical or mental exertion of an individual in pursuit of his or her daily bread or as the collective labor of a social class is largely absent. It appears, instead, as the representative achievement of a social group, reified in its possessions and created not by this group but by others under its command. What Stifter calls "work" is, in fact, the leisure activity of his upper class.[21] *Loisir* is, after all, free time, the time precisely not spent on gainful employment. Such activity, one would assume, ought to give *joy,* to use Campbell's term. There is, however, little evidence for this in the novel, although this may be more a function of the narrative voice and, indeed, of the underlying ideology of order, moderation, appropriateness, mutual assurance, and harmonious conversational exchange than of anything else. This voice is central for maintaining the narrative as a model for the social order it aims to promote. The narrator voices a common purpose, the construction or reconstruction of cultural standards that are seen to be in a state of decadence and decline. Again and again the narrative establishes and proclaims a common understanding among an elite about values and about an order that is, not lastly, aesthetic. Every object or every process that can be moved from the mundane realm of necessity into the realm of deliberateness has the potential to foreground its aesthetic. In this endeavor general cultural, not just artistic, production is aestheticized and imbued with an aesthetic surplus value that propels it from the realm of real work into that of artwork.

In a perfect illustration of the claim made for fiction at the outset of this inquiry, Stifter's Heinrich Drendorf is explicitly and meticulously provided for at the beginning of the narrative. Heinrich's father is, like Schröter, a businessman who continues to work throughout the years the novel covers and sells his business at the end, without the reader ever learning much about it. Heinrich and his sister, Klotilde, inherit money from a great-uncle that is initially administered by their father and then turned over in stages to the children. Heinrich, at eighteen, makes such wise use of the allowance his father gives him that after a short time he receives full power over his inheritance, which provides him with a generous annual income for the rest of his life. The need for work in the sense of getting a job and making money having thus been eliminated, with what sort of activity, presumably more interesting than mere work, is the reader left for the 800 pages of the book?

The first few pages of the novel provide the fixed points for answering this question. After Heinrich has learned the school subjects generally considered basic requirements, he admits that he does not know what to do with his life. At his request for help, his father suggests that he become a "Wissenschaftler im allgemeinen" because he feels a certain leaning in this direction. He anticipates no particular use for this but feels that he ought to pretend that something inwardly valid and important lies ahead. The lack of a clear future use-value for the extensive training and learning process on which he now embarks appears as a monstrosity to his fellow citizens, as they do not fail to point out. They argue that his father should have ordered him to enter a position useful to bourgeois society, some practical profession to which he could dedicate his life so that, in the end, he could leave this world knowing that he had done his part.

The parameters for the decision over Heinrich's future are, thus, individual self-realization versus obligation to society. His father takes a clear position on this choice, saying that man does not exist for society but primarily for his own sake, and as long as everyone exists for himself in the best possible way, he also does so for society at large. This automatism is divinely prestabilized, for God arranges things in such a way that all talent is appropriately distributed, and all work that needs to be done on earth is, indeed, done. Heinrich's father points out that the claims of those who profess to become businessmen, doctors, and public administrators for the benefit of humankind are often not true and only serve to hide a profit motive in that they consider their posts as means to enrich themselves. After Heinrich has outgrown all his — private — teachers, the question about his future surfaces again. He rejects the idea of making a specific plan, instead assuring his parents that he would be his own best teacher and would "die Sache selber... betreiben" (22). This, then, "die Sache" of self-education, is what the novel is about as it follows Heinrich, the "Freund der Wirklichkeit der Dinge" (27) on his way to becoming a "Beschreiber" of the world of objects and nature or an artist.

This self-centered project, however, is not as far out of sync with its time as it might at first appear. Notably, the ideas of Wilhelm Heinrich Riehl resonate in Stifter.[22] In *Die bürgerliche Gesellschaft* (1851) Riehl divides society into four estates: peasantry and aristocracy represent conservative forces of stability, while the

Bürger and the "fourth estate" are seen as progressive forces of movement and change, with the bourgeoisie further subdivided into more progressive and more conservative camps.[23] This is a division with which Stifter implicitly agrees, as he sets the plot of the novel entirely in the countryside among invisible peasants and foregrounded aristocrats on their Austro-Bohemian agricultural estates who befriend conservative bourgeois escaping city life. The key difference with Riehl is that the other two groups — workers and the progressive kind of bourgeois — completely vanish from the novel. It is true that Stifter's Heinrich comes from the *Bürgertum*, but like Freytag's Anton he represents the "right" kind, the conservative, honest, risk-averse type who poses no threat to the existing order by becoming entrepreneurial or innovative. Both figures are guardians of tradition — Anton even a little quaint and philistine, as Fink points out to him. Stifter might also agree with Riehl's formula of "Brot und Bildung," although it was admittedly made to address "the labor question" or "the social question," as the increasingly urgent debate about welfare and the social role of the emerging working class was called.[24] But here, too, he would only deal with one part of it. Taking "bread" as a given, education is left. Without a specific field of application, and absent any material necessity for its use, however, such education becomes self-centered and turns into an elite project. The most idealist, even utopian, elements of the early Riehl's formula that might bear fruit in their application to the working class in the fusion of "*Arbeit*" and "*Geist*," or manual and intellectual labor, are lost; and the formula inevitably is stripped of most of its potential when applied exclusively at a higher social level. All that remains are the parameters for a model, a laboratory experiment.

One important consequence of the disconnection that the Stifterian application of Riehl's formula entails is the way it affects the nature of work. Whereas industrial work, the essential "*Brot*" in Riehl's metaphor, is designed to disappear behind its result, the unrevealing, always identical commodity, the product of the free, unessential work in *Der Nachsommer* is precisely not the commodity but the unique, all-around appropriate and useful aesthetic object. Work thus remains visible not at the moment when it is carried out but in the traces it leaves on its products. Stifter is interested in these traces, not in the work itself. As the novel obsessively emphasizes aesthetic, evaluative disquisition and explanation of such objects over the process of their creation — that is, over the work, the toil, the labor that goes into them — work as process, together with the people that carry it out, remains elusive and opaque. This perspective is reflected in the very language, with its innumerable instances of the passive voice, and in the "had-something-done" stance of the main characters and their position as observers looking at work — for instance, the field work done by their farmhands — as a display.

As work, disconnected from its existential meaning, becomes problematic, so does *Bildung*. It is tempting to short-circuit the *Bildung* that Heinrich acquires and the *Bürgertum*, the class from which he originates, into *Bildungsbürgertum*, the term often used for social categorization in the nineteenth century. But Heinrich is *not* a *Bildungsbürger;* the education, the insights into and understanding of connections he so avidly pursues are precisely not those of the *Bildungsbürger*. The latter's education or culture is text-based, literary in the general sense, representative, socially functional, and often related to a person's profession. What Heinrich seeks is, on the contrary, immediate, nature-based, and not use-oriented. It is an essentialist knowledge, predating and simultaneously transcending its economic application. This self-education combines two key elements: the intellectual component of the natural sciences (geology, physics, geography, meteorology, and so forth) and a practical artisanal element of crafts and skilled manual work. It is nothing that would give him status among, say, *Bildungsbürger*. The latter are urban, are consumers of and often producers for urban cultural and educational institutions; Heinrich is not. The latent tension between urban and rural that permeates the novel is consistently resolved in favor of the countryside.

Historically speaking, Stifter's ideals are based in the Renaissance model of all-around scholarly and scientific, as well as practical, knowledge. Such comprehensive enculturation is inherently class-biased. For Russell Berman, Stifter's "neo-humanist" ideal consists in "reconciling individuality with an overarching order." It will only succeed "if the individual does not engage in excessive specialization but rather mirrors the external order in his own universal education" (112). Heinrich pursues this ideal just as its historical potential is vanishing for good. The realm of still undifferentiated art and science, the Humanist/Renaissance moment of close observation of nature by the artist shading into the close observation of nature by the scientist has passed; specialization is the order of the day. The fragmentation of *Bildung* into separate disciplines is what Stifter fears and fights. The vagueness at the beginning of the novel in determining Heinrich's future activities among becoming a "Wissenschaftler im allgemeinen" (17) or a "Beschreiber der Dinge" or a "Künstler" (28) is not accidental; it is programmatic.

Pedagogically speaking, Stifter's ideals owe much to the thinking of Johann Heinrich Pestalozzi (1746–1827) and his effort to promote an education balanced among "Kopf," "Herz," and "Hand," among the intellectual, moral, and practical engagement of the individual with the topics and tasks at hand.[25]

Stifter is also indebted, at least in theory and as an ideal, to the Enlightenment and the French Revolution, as well as to the bourgeois revolution of 1848, which he initially welcomed but came to reject almost as soon as it occurred. The potential for liberty, equality, and fraternity are present in his project, even if actualized predominantly at the top and horizontally among the ruling class. The vertical, truly emancipatory potential for the lower classes is rarely realized in a discourse confined to equals in the upper class. Interaction with social inferiors is generally instructional. They may improve their professional skills and work procedures — as the stonemasons do in decorating a fountain for Heinrich — but they are never shown to extend and apply enlightened thinking to their own social and political positions. Such talking down, perhaps intended as an expression of benevolent patriarchal attitudes, attempts to obviate the hard issue of the entrenched class system that undergirds the projects of Risach, Heinrich, and Heinrich's father. Stifter's discourse serves to enforce the harmony on Risach's and the other country estates. Heinrich's project of self-realization is conditioned on the existence of the two classes of masters and of servants, helpers, hired hands. As in Hegel, master and servant are linked in a double articulation: between master and servant through instruction and education; between servant and master through the provision of adequate service and appropriate production. The servant's identity and purpose lies in the frictionless performance of his or her assigned duties; that of the master in consumption, representation, and display, notably of an artistic-artisanal kind commensurate with his or her — Mathilde's — social status. The connection between classes follows an input-output model. There exists a concrete, tangible link through the artisanal production processes and their results — the creation or restoration of tools, wainscoting, pieces of marble, drawings and blueprints, buildings, gardens, equipment, and so forth. This production, in turn, is based on the preceding recruitment and, if necessary, training of capable workers for specific tasks.[26]

Overall, the novel's discourse is, both horizontally and vertically, obsessively based on consensus. This tyranny of agreement has a double consequence: in plot, structure, and language the novel becomes monoglot, and work as process vanishes and thins into a mere cipher in upper-class discourse. As it relates to the narrator's own activities, work, lacking the existential dimension of earning a living, is reduced to the self-assigned tasks of an amateur. Insofar as it relates to the lower classes, it appears as reified in the devices and objects, the procedures and setups created or already in place. Work is always in the past, is carried out more often than not on objects of the past (restoration or reconstitution of old things) or, at the least, is based on principles and values of the past, blueprints, sketches, drawings of old objects. *Real* work, the kind Marggraff missed in *Soll und Haben*, work carried out by the major characters — in contrast to the foregrounded leisure and amateur pursuits of the upper class — is hidden here, too. Additionally, as the upper class is also the speaking class, work, as well as those who carry it out, are seen through the distinct evaluative and ordering filter of language itself. The real work is performed by those who do not participate in the novel's discourse. They and their work do not speak but are, instead, spoken to and spoken about. Work thus appears not as part of the plot of the novel, but "only" as the central topic of its discourse.

When Heinrich is let into the Asperhof, for instance, and invited to lunch by Risach on the occasion of their first encounter, he notices that the table is already set: fruit wine, water, and bread are already there; his knapsack has disappeared, and so has his cane. Each instance describes the result of a preceding invisible action, presumably performed by servants. Such a servant is now summoned into the room by Risach's silver bell and appears instantly, but she remains invisible, disappearing behind the *fried* chicken and the *red-flecked* salad she is carrying, the objects rather than the person receiving adjectival treatment. This object-focus dominates later at dinner, too, although the narrator at least notices that *the same* servant is waiting on him and Risach again. As Heinrich is shown the house, including the utility rooms and servants' areas, the kitchen, larder, laundry, bakery, cellar, and fruit and vegetable storerooms, he finds all of these highly useful and practical, as he had expected, but he barely glances at the people populating these parts of the house. When he visits the carpentry shop, the focus is once again on its equipment, the objects it contains, and the general orderliness the room projects. All the reader learns about its crew is that it consists of four workers. The fact that the noise of work only resumes after the visitors have left shows that Marggraff's "real work" takes place as far offstage in Stifter as it does in Freytag.

With work foregrounded in the discourse, its relevance decreases in the plot; with emphasis on the aestheticized product, the labor of the producers, even the producers themselves sink into the background, hidden behind passive and statal constructions. It is true that at the end of the novel the lower classes have a brief moment in the limelight, as it were, as well-wishers and onlookers at Heinrich and Natalie's wedding; but they are named only as a group, the "Volk." And in contrast to Freytag, where *Volk* means the nation, for Stifter it merely means *plebs*.

3. *Pfisters Mühle:* How the Stench Began

Despite having a more openly nostalgic mood than *Soll und Haben*, *Pfister's Mühle*, with its "Ach, noch einmal . . ." opening and repeated "Wo bleiben alle die Bilder?" is simultaneously more modern (the story is set almost contemporaneously with its writing); more realistic (the events described have precedents in reality: the legal proceedings against a refinery at Rautheim); and more resigned (the mill, after all, is being torn down as we read, whereas the Firma Schröter, though anachronistic in its fictional present, remains solid and passes into the hands of the next generation) than Freytag's novel.

The key dichotomy that informs *Nachsommer*, that between city and countryside, each with its own ways of life and kinds of work, is present in *Pfisters Mühle*, too. But it is resolved in the opposite direction: whereas Stifter's younger generation (as well as

Heinrich's city-dwelling parents) retreat to the countryside at the novel's end, Raabe's first-person narrator, Ebert Pfister, and his bride, Emmy, settle in Berlin, where his former tutor, Adam Asche, has already set up shop and where Ebert himself has spent the previous years as a student.

Work has at least three dimensions in this novel: the old, vanishing craft of the miller; the new, research-based laboratory work in which Asche is involved; and the work of the narrator, who is a teacher, a mediator by profession. Each of these strands of work is embedded in its own sociohistorical context: the miller-*cum*-innkeeper has his faithful employees and student guests; Asche's research and founding of a dry-cleaning business is part of the entrepreneurial spirit of the *Gründerjahre;* and the narrator's work reflects typical activities of the *Bildungsbürgertum* of the late nineteenth century.

These three fields of activity are connected along two timelines. There are the four weeks of the narrative present, the time Ebert and his wife spend in his father's mill before it is torn down to make way for a factory. During these last weeks in the condemned old building, where the architect is already spreading out his blueprints, Ebert keeps a diary, the so-called "Blätter" or chapters, numbered 1 through 22, that provide the novel's subdivision. This second timeline leads into the past, covering some twenty or thirty years in the form of the narrator's personal reminiscences. The narrative is loosely chronological but follows its main strands rather whimsically and intersperses them with commentary, often ironic, from the narrative present perspective, including Emmy's sometimes puzzled, sometimes sobering reactions to Ebert's tales. The main strands are the narrator's youth and growing up on his father's mill and his tutoring at the hands of Adam Asche, himself a sort of adopted son of the miller, who becomes a scientist and entrepreneur; Asche's story, which includes his courtship of Albertine Lippoldes and the fate of her family; and, of course, the story of Ebert's father, the old miller and innkeeper. A key part of this last narrative thread is the pollution of the mill creek by a sugar refinery upstream, which leads old Pfister to quit his work and sell the mill, even if, thanks to Asche's research and the lawyer Riechei's legal help, a court case against the refinery is won. The victory is too little too late. Time is up; a new age is dawning; a generation steps back, and with it a way of life and work disappears and a new age of urban encroachment on the land, of industrial production and factory labor, begins.

Der Nachsommer is the only one among the three novels discussed here that provides its hero at the outset with the financial and material basis to free him from work. Anton Wohlfahrt in *Soll und Haben* works up to his station in life and as a reward for his effort becomes Schröter's partner and brother-in-law. Ebert Pfister, like Anton, leaves the professional realm of his father — a royal administrator in Anton's case, a craftsman and independent business owner in Ebert's. But whereas Anton stays within the bourgeoisie, broadly speaking, Ebert leaves a blue-collar environment for a white-collar one. And while Ebert is the first-person narrator and, thus, a crucial force in the text, his personal and professional development, unlike Anton's, is not at the core of the novel. His move away from his father's world into his own seems to have been quite unproblematic. Rather, at the center are Adam Asche's career and the last years of the working life of Ebert's father, together with the social and structural changes that accompany and link both. This is reflected in the fact that the old miller passes on the miller's axe, the symbol of his profession, to Asche rather than to Ebert, his son.

Overall, little is said about the miller's work as such, the daily activities and concrete manipulations or the performance of specific tasks or procedures. If anything, the novel pays more attention to the miller's second job as an innkeeper and holder of a liquor license. Equally little is said about Ebert's course of study and his work as a teacher. The one professional realm that is foregrounded is Asche's, that of the chemist, inventor, *bricoleur*, and, finally, well-to-do entrepreneur and business owner. For the narrative structure this means a double focus. Unlike Heinrich Drendorf, who is both narrator and main character, Eberhard Pfister, rather than occupying the center of the plot, provides the perspective, tone, and moods that dominate the text overall. As a consequence of this separation of content — Asche's story, the miller's tale — and the discursive focus chosen to represent it, *Pfisters Mühle*, the "Sommerferienheft," as the novel's subtitle has it, is a much less monotone and single-voiced novel than *Der Nachsommer*. The narrator is at liberty to be serious, nostalgic, ironic, bantering, and colloquial, as well as literary and learned. *Soll und Haben*, with "our hero" occasionally held up by the authorial narrator for a slightly distanced look or the Schröter clerks, embroiled in some mock heroic quarrel, for gentle ridicule, falls somewhere in between.

In looking back, Ebert notes not only that he had a happy childhood but also that life at the mill, which seemed always full of students and other young people from the city who sought out the place for its beer garden, its singing, and its atmosphere of general good cheer, was much richer and more instructive than a more formal education could possibly have been. In retrospect, Ebert himself seems amazed at all the things one was able to learn and experience in Pfister's mill and garden. He began his career being tutored in Latin by Asche, a philosophy student at the time, in a back room of the mill. That learning Latin could prove to be a perilous first step toward a successful career is pointed out by Asche to the miller at this early stage; Asche does not mind teaching Ebert Latin, but what the latter will be able to put on the table later in life will be entirely up to him. But Ebert moves on into Gymnasium and the university. Asche's career moves are less transparent. What he really studied nobody quite knew, but it was said to be the natural sciences. He did keep the books for the miller for years, in order, as with his Latin teaching, to support himself; but where he lived and what he lived on was open to speculation. As far as his living quarters are concerned, he changed them often and did not always reside in the best neighborhoods. Frequently he could not be found at all for long periods. After the onset of the pollution of the mill creek and the big stink at Pfister's mill that leads to the decline in the number of guests at the tavern and to increasingly unbearable living conditions, Asche is sought out and approached for help and an assessment of the situation. Now *Doctor* Adam Asche, he is finally found in an outlying suburb. Enveloped by an even worse stink than that surrounding the mill and shrouded in vapors that rise from his experiments in a shed behind his rundown tenement, Asche appears to Father Pfister and Ebert more like a medieval alchemist than a modern chemist.

He visits the mill around Christmas and duly notices the stench emanating from the water; he takes note of the milky-green, slimy strands drifting in the creek; he determines under the microscope that the bacteriological culprits are *diatomea*, strands of *melosira*, *encyonema, navicula,* and *pleurosigma,* as well as some *zygnemacea;*

and in an example of the typical, often language-based humor and irony that pervade the novel, he adds toward old Pfister, "Nicht wahr, Meister, die Namen allein genügen schon, um ein Mühlrad anzuhalten?" (93). When, on further careful analysis, he also finds *beggiatoa alba,* he unhesitatingly links this fact with "Krickerode," the sugar refinery upstream, providing the name of that place as a kind of shorthand translation for the name of the bacterium in answer to the miller's uncomprehending question about the meaning of all these Latin terms — another example of spontaneous situational humor arising out of the collision of different linguistic registers. Completing his inquiry in a thorough, professional manner, Asche follows up his findings with a water-sample collection trip along the creek and concludes his efforts on behalf of his friend the old miller by sending the latter his learned report from Berlin. This report, simultaneously published in a professional journal, turns out to be a study of the highest scientific quality and provides the basis for lawyer Riechei's court victory over Krickerode.

There is nothing comparable in either of the other two novels to Raabe's careful outline of a specific professional task, carried out step by step, expressed in the pertaining technical vocabulary, and presented as a central part of the plot. There are further detailed accounts of work and work environments in Raabe — for instance, Asche's workplace at "Schmurky und Kompanie" in Berlin (132). While Ebert notices Asche's surprisingly large and tidy apartment, he is shocked and overwhelmed by his friend's work environment as he passes with him through the smell, noise, and constant motion at his workplace. To Ebert it seems complete chaos, and it exudes the most evil stench that ever overpowered human senses. He stumbles across courtyards and through halls as if caught up and spun around by the big engines, the steam power that moves the machines all around him — the centrifuges, cylinders, rolling presses, colanders, and impregnating, ruffling, stapling, sowing, and folding machines. Moreover, the irony that dry-cleaning is itself a water-polluting business and stinks worse than the mill creek at its worst is not lost on Ebert.

This glimpse of the work of a chemist and the work environment in a modern chemical business leaves out one central aspect of work: human relationships centered on jobs and professional activities. All three novels under discussion here, given the time and social and professional milieus they describe, include servants as part of their narrative personnel. The interaction between masters and servants, a key aspect of work-related issues, is therefore the topic of the next few paragraphs. Servants are, of course, employees, but only a distinction between the two groups will allow a fruitful discussion of labor-related personal interaction in our texts. The clerks in Schröter's office are employees. Their ties to their boss are strictly professional; they owe their superior nothing but their honest and loyal work during certain set periods of time. The fact that they also have board and lodging in Schröter's house creates somewhat more intimate ties, but the spheres of work and family, of the public realm of the job and the private space of the Schröters — that is, the spaces of the employees and their master — are quite strictly demarcated in the front and the back of the house, and the interactions are limited to meals and kept rather formal.

Servants, however — as the term is used here, maids and handymen — are much more intimately tied into the private dimension of their masters' lives. Spatially, they move about in the rooms, the kitchen, the larder, whereas employees have offices, workshops, or gardens where their professions are carried out. But also psychologically and emotionally such servants are at closer quarters with their employers and may have closer bonds to their superiors, bonds that go beyond the cash nexus. Indeed, in many cases their pay may still largely be in kind instead of cash. Especially females — a wet-nurse, for instance — might enter an almost parental or auntlike relationship with the children of the house, and loyalties would sometimes be transferred to the next generation. It is precisely such close personal relations that Marx sees as disappearing in an age where labor is becoming just another commodity sold in the marketplace for cold cash, the only true bond between humans. This rational kind of modern, job-centered, and money-based relationship dominates *Soll und Haben,* although Sabine Schröter has servants, and many older relationships exist, too. In *Der Nachsommer,* in the environment of the agriculture-based large country estates, the divisions are less clear-cut. Are the old gardener Simon and his wife on the Asperhof strictly employees? Among the female house servants, who are generally far in the background and belong more to the novel's object world than to its cast of human characters, there is, nevertheless, Katharine, whom Risach calls "meine Katharine, die das Haus zusammenhält"

(752) and whom the women take into their confidence in domestic matters. *Pfisters Mühle,* on the other hand, is almost all "warm and fuzzy," and the intimate personal and emotional bonds among the secondary characters — the *Gesinde,* to use that now rather obsolete term — and between *Gesinde* and their employers are a key distinguishing characteristic of this novel.[27] These subordinates are recognized as human beings, as friends, and their lives are fully integrated into all aspects of their masters' lives.

The two persons who come immediately to mind are Samse, "unser Samse, ein Drittel Mühlknappe, ein Drittel Ackerknecht, ein Drittel Dorf- und Gartenkellner" (26), a trusty old employee, servant, and friend; and Jungfer Christine Voigt, the old miller's maid, who, after the early death of Ebert's mother, took over this role, too, in addition to running the household. Chapter 18 is largely her chapter, and the narrator admits that there has hardly been enough mention of old Christine, his poor, old beloved guardian and stepmother, as well as, formerly, the last beautiful miller's maid of the town, to do her justice. The shock of her master's death, the end of the milling business, and the impending dissolution of the household, her lifelong *Lebenswelt,* drive her almost over the edge. But Ebert unhesitatingly recognizes and accepts his responsibility for her as part of his father's legacy. He and Emmy take her and Samse with them to Berlin as employees, old friends, and, the reader is led to infer, retirees, helping them, perhaps, as much as being helped by them. Though their life at this late date is thus uprooted, it is simultaneously anchored by a firm strand of human continuity. Nevertheless, on arrival in Berlin, while Christine promises to help Emmy in her new household, Ebert describes her as sobbing, stupefied, and indecisive in facing the bewildering bustle of the metropolis. A few pages later, however, he informs the reader that Samse and Christine now form part of their household, which he and Emmy cannot imagine without the two of them. Long, faithful service and close personal ties do have their just deserts in this case of the young couple of master and mistress and the old couple of maid and servant. But such "feudal, patriarchal, idyllic relations," as Marx and Engels call them (91), are becoming increasingly obsolete at the very time of the novel. Bismarck's social legislation is a first step toward improving the lot of ordinary folks, but it is also, of course, a decisive move of modernization, a step from the personal relation to the "social contract," replacing what Marx and Engels call "the motley feudal ties that bound man to his 'natural superiors'" by the "callous 'cash payment'" (91–92). Samse himself sees a new breed of workers arising who are no longer known and familiar, no longer trustworthy. On their trip up the mill stream to collect Asche's water samples, Samse reminds Ebert not to leave behind the basket containing the bottles: "der Satan trau dem Fabriklervolk da hinter uns, selbst am hochheiligen Festtage. Es treibt sich immer was von ihnen an unserm ruinierten Nahrungsquell im Busch und Röhricht um"; and he calls the factory workers a "Jammervolk" (110).

There is one final work-related issue that needs to be discussed for this novel that so explicitly shows the effects of modernization and industrialization on workplaces, people, and their social, as well as ecological, environment. This issue is summarized most succinctly in the concept of *Heimat* — very much an issue at the time.[28] The ambivalence in the concept of *Heimat* as analyzed by Alon Confino is also present in the novel in its Janus-headedness, looking back nostalgically to the past, yet also trustfully, even enthusiastically — for instance, Asche — toward the future. The sense of the changing times and the necessity of geographical moves so prevalent in late nineteenth-century Germany and, indeed, experienced by the characters in *Pfisters Mühle* leads to feelings of loss of belonging, of roots, of *Heimat* but also, in reaction, to a search for these elements. Confino, who analyzes the *Heimat* movement of the late nineteenth century in terms of local-national mediation, also points to the term's conceptual, temporal, and individual-psychological functions. It is, he argues, taking issue with scholars "who until recently have interpreted the Heimat idea as wholly antimodern," a concept that serves to integrate temporal dislocations, as well as regional diversity. "Instead of viewing modernity and the Heimat idea as oppositional, Heimatlers commonly attempted to strike a modus vivendi between the preservation of national roots and the continuation of modernity and the prosperity it promised.... Heimat thus both glorified the past and celebrated modernity."[29]

This notion ties in well with Asche's sense — he is the quintessential modernizer — of the historical forces tugging at him. He calls himself a potential polluter, a man with the firm intention of fouling up a bubbling source, a crystal-clear stream, a majestic river — in short, any waterway he can get his hands on. But he assures Ebert in the same breath that he would give everything to keep good old Pfister's mill creek clean. He also suspects that Father Pfister might not have called on him to investigate his water problems if the miller had had any idea how much Asche himself was involved with murky waters and strange smells. The dilemma between preservation of the past and participation in modernity and, hopefully, in financial gain, is brought to a point by lawyer Riechei, who promises to win Pfister's case but asks why on earth he himself did not help found Krickerode. Only a few lines further down Emmy, in conversation with her husband, naively restates this question why "poor papa" did not sign up with the big factory and buy its stock. Ebert's answer is brief but goes to the core of the issue: "Weil er nicht anders konnte, Lieb" (121).

The imagery that perhaps expresses most drastically the dichotomies of the age in which Raabe's novel is set — past and future, the tension between nostalgia and utopia, loss and gain, and progress — is that of the factory as a gothic castle, "hoch aufgetürmt, zinnengekrönt, gigantisch beschornsteint — Krickerode!" (103). Ebert alludes to this vision when he describes looking for Asche in Berlin and finding himself outside "Schmurky und Kompanie"; just like at Krickerode, there are gothic gates and walls, behind which, however, are moving things rather different than knights, pages, noble ladies, and so on. The modern city skyline itself blurs elements of old and new, and Ebert, approaching Berlin, notices that nowadays it is no longer the church spires but the smokestacks that appear first on the horizon. This image summarizes what Confino discusses in his analysis of postcards of the "Gruß aus x" type that became popular around that time: the blending of old and new, the representation of an increasingly generic *Heimat*. His most striking example, which is also the frontispiece of his book, is a poster from twenty years after Raabe published his novel. It is a call to sign war bonds and depicts a huge standing figure in medieval armor against the far distant background of a *Heimat* landscape with river, hills, and villages. The hill to the left is crowned by a castle, the other by the smokestacks of some modern factory.

4. Conclusions

Despite the considerable differences among the three novels discussed here, there is one key commonality between them: an asynchronicity between the fictional realities they describe and the historical realities into which they were released. This applies, as well, to the *Communist Manifesto,* which was based not on the German economy of 1848 but on the more advanced industrial capitalism and the much more global trade of the British Empire. The *Manifesto* thus culminates in a vision of a world market that will only be realized in our own time. Freytag's novel, in contrast, is deliberately archaizing, a mock-heroic epic with bourgeois personnel that, among other things, recaptures lost trade goods in a semimilitary action and fights for and from Polish castles. It contains characters, lowly office workers, who are willing to rush into a duel on more than one occasion.[30] At the same time, the novel's nationalist discourse is right on target, in fact predating the historical events that will give substance to its rhetoric in 1871. Conceptually, one could argue that the *Manifesto* is the elegant, poetic, and visionary outline against which Freytag writes. To refute this intoxicating wisp of a text, he has to bring out the complete arsenal of poetic-realist tricks. Only this — the characters, the plots and subplots, the thick descriptions, the authorial voice, the historical and geographical grounding, the conservative bourgeois values — enables him to counter the visionary draft that the *Manifesto* is causing in the political climate, as well as in the literary imagery of the midcentury. *Soll und Haben* obliterates the outlines of the *Manifesto* under its sheer mass of text, but bits and pieces of it are selectively absorbed and peek through the novel's surface.

Soll und Haben is a grand authorially dominated narrative, old-fashioned like Anton's hometown. It resonates with the historical events and the mood of the time after 1848, the combination of awakening German nationalism and conservative Prussian Protestantism, to name just two crucial ingredients both in Freytag's text and its historical context. In its occupational focus on the merchant class the novel also takes up emerging historical developments and pursues, if indirectly, a projected trajectory for that class and its social and professional affiliates: the widening circles, the industrial production (of sugar, for instance), ultimately the global market that the *Manifesto* had conjured up so powerfully. Anton Wohlfahrt is not a local yokel by any means, but it is not his voice and vision, nor Schröter's, nor that of any other character that dominates the novel: it is the narrator's, the powerful voice from outside the story. It is he who ties the bond with the reader, and Anton, "our hero," sometimes pointed to with a touch of bemusement, is no match for him. But in the end it is Anton who takes over the *Handelshaus*. He has earned his wings, and the future is his to win or lose.

Der Nachsommer, too, responds to the revolutionary events of 1848, but to the Austrian version and the possibilities that this historical moment offers — or threatens, as the case may be. The novel's first-person narrator, Heinrich, starts where Anton Wohlfahrt nearly ends up: the son of a businessman. Heinrich's voice, although ever present, is strangely muffled compared to that of Freytag's narrator. What he has to relate is, in essence, a series of travels over the course of many years between his home in the city and places in the countryside, educational trips undertaken to do research and to learn about the natural world through both practical and theoretical approaches; about history as it sediments in objects, tools, equipment of all kinds, and buildings; and about art, mostly painting and sculpture. All knowledge thus acquired is self-serving, circulated only in a small, almost priestlike circle of like-minded friends and acquaintances. It is linked to society at large only tenuously, as expressed early in the novel by Father Drendorf, who claims that if everyone lived for their own sake they would be most useful for society. The extended project of acquisition of both immaterial values — knowledge, skills, and insights — and material ones, such as woods, marbles, furniture, tools, and artworks, culminates in Heinrich's acquisition of the ultimate tool for the perpetuation of his way of life: his beautiful, entirely objectified wife, Natalie, after a protracted, rather boring, and certainly entirely unspontaneous courtship.

Although the novel ends with a wedding fraught with fatherly messages about the centrality of the family, no future trajectory is pointed out that would or should be different from the past. The family is what the age needs. Art, science, human progress, the state rest on the family: that is the core of the parental message. Heinrich is still not sure what his scientific training will do for him, and he does not know whether he will go any further in the sciences. He only knows that with his wedding he has laid the foundation of "das reine Familienleben." He will go on to manage his possessions in the conviction that through his marriage and the founding of a household all enterprises, even scientific ones, now have "Einfachheit, Halt und Bedeutung" (791), the concluding words of the text. Luckily, his education does not need to be put to work: the couple's material future is even more secure now that both their fathers have made over their estates than was young Heinrich's future at the beginning of the novel. There is no need for work, no need for change, no future challenges lie ahead such as Anton surely faces in keeping up his business, or Ebert, who has already left his father's obsolescent profession, or Asche, who is decidedly embracing the future, even inventing it himself in the new business of dry cleaning.

Stifter's narrative, although contemporary with Freytag's, focuses on the nobility that both for Freytag and, of course, for Marx, seems increasingly irrelevant in history. Almost reactionary in its silence about modern industry, technology, and commerce, the novel nevertheless touches on a key modern theme. Alienation, the loss of roots and tradition, the growing unfamiliarity with crafts, skills, and processes, the loss of knowledge about materials and their qualities and origins — all these are distinctly modern themes. The problem is that the attempt at finding and reconstructing such traditions and knowledge occurs anachronistically, with outdated means, and exclusively among the class that least needs emancipation. The novel's suggested remedies are no longer generally applicable, and modern developments are taking a course counter to the one Stifter proposes. His harking back to tradition is inherently class-biased as it splits the intellectual and ideological dimension of work from its material and practical execution. Stifter's project thereby thwarts its own emancipatory potential for unalienated, holistic work that lies in the figure of the general scientist, the describer of things, the artist — in short, in Heinrich's educational program. Instead, Stifter's project reifies existing class divisions and only points from a far distance at its own utopian dimensions. Nevertheless, his notion of the specific and original artisanal product or process is valid to this day, if available only in elitist and exclusive counterproduction to the commodification that the novel fears and positions itself against. *Der Nachsommer* reveals a profound historical aporia, already sensed by Stifter himself. It is this aspect that makes the novel a profoundly melancholic text.

Raabe's broad-based environmental concerns, which include social aspects in addition to natural preservation, appears eminently modern and plausible more than a century after its writing. Not least the ironies and ambivalence, the contradictions between buying shares in new and booming industries that destroy precisely the nature and the ways of life one would like to preserve, are worked out well, and with this comes the inevitably ironic, quintessentially modern *double vision,* the consciousness split between what it knows and what it does with this knowledge. If, as Sheehan suggests, the structure of time, new dimensions of scale, and mobility are three key characteristics of a modern environment, Raabe's is certainly the most modern of the texts discussed here.[31] These elements may be found in the narrative structures, the plot, the imagery, and the discourse, as well as in the historical movements and moments to which the text responds.

It is true that 1884 marks a different moment than 1848, Berlin a different place than Breslau or Austro-Bohemia. But even Freytag in 1855 had responded to the historical challenges more vigorously, and with a clearer orientation toward the future, than Stifter does in 1857 in *Der Nachsommer.* Even if Freytag's reaction to the *Manifesto* was negative, one senses his awareness of a different time. Raabe, in turn, provides Ebert with four weeks of summer vacation, the leisure time to think and write about the past. But after that, Ebert leaves the countryside that is already threatened by urban encroachment and moves to the city and, as it were, into the future. With Stifter time itself, marked by the yearly *Rosenblüte,* is cycling back on itself, the educational project a pipe dream for all but a few. Work, even if conceived as leisure, is thus not shown in a positive light. Its benefits for society are questionable, indirect at best, encapsulated in the countryside, deliberately out of touch with the growing metropoles and the rapidly changing labor and knowledge bases of the "real" and, in most cases, the "realist" world, too.

Notes

[1] A recent and stimulating collection of literary excerpts and commentaries on work and its many aspects is Keith Thomas, ed., *The Oxford Book of Work* (Oxford: Oxford UP, 1999).

[2] Gustav Freytag, *Soll und Haben*, rpt. in his *Werke*, ed. Heike Menges (Karben: Verlag Petra Wald, 1996). References are to this edition.

[3] Adalbert Stifter, *Der Nachsommer* (Frankfurt am Main: Insel, 1982). References are to this edition.

[4] Wilhelm Raabe, *Pfisters Mühle* (Stuttgart: Reclam, 1980). This edition is based on vol. 16 of the Braunschweiger Ausgabe, ed. Hans Oppermann (Göttingen: Vandenhoeck & Ruprecht, 1970). References are to the text-identical Reclam edition.

[5] An indispensable work that summarizes and discusses the many debates about and inquiries into specific aspects of work — social, political, managerial, even artistic and artisanal — is Joan Campbell's *Joy in Work, German Work: The National Debate 1800–1945* (Princeton: Princeton UP, 1989). To this book I owe many insights into the diverse labor debates. For a general historical assessment of the "Culture in the Age of the Bürgertum" see the chapter of that title in James J. Sheehan, *German History 1770–1866* (Oxford: Clarendon P, 1989), 793–852. Sheehan, always integrating cultural and specifically literary aspects into his historical analysis very usefully discusses all three authors in section iii. of the above chapter, 820–36.

[6] For a brief, highly informative general account of *Soll und Haben* see Hartmut Steinecke, "Gustav Freytag: *Soll und Haben* (1855): Weltbild und Wirkung eines deutschen Bestsellers," in Horst Denkler, ed., *Romane und Erzählungen des bürgerlichen Realismus: Neue Interpretationen* (Stuttgart: Reclam, 1980), 138–52. For a calculation of publishing figures for *Soll und Haben* see T. E. Carter, "Freytag's Soll und Haben: A Literal National Manifesto as a Best-Seller," *German Life and Letters* 21 (1967–68): 320–29. Carter's total number of copies sold by 1965 is more than 1.2 million. This does not include the novel's readership through the lending libraries, the main outlet for literature in the second half of the nineteenth century. The number of copies held in such libraries generally far outstripped those of other contemporary novels. See Alberto Martino, "Publikumsschichten und Leihbibliotheken," in Horst Glaser, ed., *Deutsche Literatur: Eine Sozialgeschichte*, vol. 7 (Reinbek bei Hamburg: Rowohlt, 1982), 59–69, esp. 65.

[7] Theodor Fontane, "Gustav Freytag: Soll und Haben," *Literatur-Blatt des Deutschen Kunstblattes* 2 (1855): 59–63; rpt. in Max Bucher et al., eds., *Realismus und Gründerzeit: Manifeste und Dokumente zur deutschen Literatur,*

1848–1880 (Stuttgart: Metzler, 1976), quoted passage, 329. For convenience, contemporary critiques of *Soll und Haben*, unless otherwise noted, are quoted from this collection.

[8] See also Freytag's paraphrase of the motto in his review, "Neue deutsche Romane," from 1853; *Realismus und Gründerzeit*, 73.

[9] Karl Gutzkow, "Ein neuer Roman," *Unterhaltungen am häuslichen Herd* 3 (1855): 558–60; *Realismus und Gründerzeit*, 325.

[10] Hermann Marggraff, "Ein Roman, 'der das deutsche Volk bei seiner Arbeit sucht,'" *Blätter für literarische Unterhaltung* 25 (1855): 445–52; *Realismus und Gründerzeit*, 340.

[11] Robert Giseke, "Soll und Haben," 3 (1855): 311–18; *Realismus und Gründerzeit*, 339.

[12] Gabriele Büchler-Hauschild, *Erzählte Arbeit: Gustav Freytag und die soziale Prosa des Vor- und Nachmärz* (Paderborn: Schöningh, 1987), 86. This is the most detailed study of "work" in Freytag's novel and other realist writings around the midcentury.

[13] Quoted in Frank Trommler, "Die Nationalisierung der Arbeit," in Reinhold Grimm and Jost Hermand, eds., *Arbeit als Thema in der deutschen Literatur vom Mittelalter bis zur Gegenwart* (Königstein: Athenäum, 1979), 107.

[14] For an engaging discussion of the dialectic of building and destroying networks see Marshall Berman's analysis of *The Communist Manifesto* in his *All That Is Solid Melts into Air: The Experience of Modernity* (1982; Harmondsworth: Penguin, 1988), 87–129.

[15] Berman, 91.

[16] Dirk J. Struik, ed., *Birth of the Communist Manifesto: With Full Text of the Manifesto, All Prefaces by Marx and Engels, Early Drafts by Engels and Other Supplementary Material* (New York: International Publishers, 1971). All references are to this edition.

[17] The rest of this paragraph and the beginning of the next is a paraphrasing translation of *Soll und Haben*, 48–49.

[18] Russell A. Berman, *The Rise of the Modern German Novel: Crisis and Charisma* (Cambridge, MA: Harvard UP, 1986), 105.

[19] For a contemporary account that also associates different business practices with specific classes and religious groups see Wilhelm Heinrich Riehl, *Die deutsche Arbeit* (Stuttgart: Cotta, 1861). Riehl's work is discussed in depth in Campbell, esp. ch. 3, "The Bourgeois Ethic of Work," 28–46.

[20] See Sheehan, 747–63.

[21] Where leisure appears as work, real work, which the novel occasionally also presents, appears "as an aesthetic spectacle," for instance, for Risach directing

his servants. For a critical assessment of the "authority of address" see the chapter of that title in R. Berman.

[22] For specifics, see Campbell, esp. ch. 3.

[23] Campbell, 36.

[24] Campbell, 36.

[25] See, for instance, Kate Silber, *Pestalozzi: The Man and His Work* (London: Routledge & Kegan Paul, 1960), for a general introduction to Pestalozzi's life and work. Stifter would certainly agree with the general approach to teaching and learning Pestalozzi took in his school at Stans, the fusion of "das Lernen mit dem Arbeiten." See Ludwig Gurlitt, *Pestalozzi: Eine Auswahl aus seinen Schriften* (Stuttgart: Greiner & Pfeiffer, 1907?), 14.

[26] Risach has a hard time finding skilled carpenters for a restoration project. Finally, he has to first train himself and then hire people who are not carpenters and teach them from scratch. But even then he finds that they lack the drive for excellence he requires and are satisfied with second best (93).

[27] The repressive side of the informal relations between Gesinde and their employers was visible in the Gesindeordnung, a code that was still largely feudal in the limits it imposed on many aspects of servants' lives. It was abolished officially only with the Weimar Republic.

[28] For two careful historical studies of this topic, see Celia Applegate, *A Nation of Provincials: The German Idea of Heimat* (Berkeley: U of California P, 1990), and Alon Confino, *The Nation as a Local Metaphor: Württemberg, Imperial Germany, and National Memory, 1871–1918* (Chapel Hill: U of North Carolina P, 1997).

[29] Confino, 121.

[30] Dueling remains an issue. Theodor Fontane's *Effi Briest* (1895) provides a literary treatment long after midcentury. But the fact that it is available to Freytag for farcical purposes shows that its relevance as a social practice has peaked.

[31] See the discussion in Sheehan, 780–92.

Das Republikanische, das Demokratische, das Pantheistische: Jewish Identity in Berthold Auerbach's Novels

Irene S. Di Maio

BERTHOLD AUERBACH (1812–1882) was one of the most popular and critically acclaimed German authors of the nineteenth century. His oeuvre included novels, literary and cultural criticism, dramas, and stories, but his success rested mainly on his *Dorfgeschichten,* village tales set in his native region of the Black Forest. These tales were celebrated for their social authenticity and for their heightened realism that allegedly captured the German spirit.[1] Prior to the publication of these tales Auerbach, a German Jew, had written two novels about Jewish life: *Spinoza: Ein historischer Roman* (Spinoza: An Historical Novel, 1837), revised as *Spinoza: Ein Denkerleben* (Spinoza: A Thinker's Life, 1854),[2] and *Dichter und Kaufmann: Ein Lebensgemälde* (Poet and Merchant: A Picture of Life, 1840), revised as *Dichter und Kaufmann: Ein Lebensgemälde aus der Zeit Moses Mendelssohns* (Poet and Merchant: A Picture of Life from the Time of Moses Mendelssohn, 1855).[3] The novels' anticipated audience comprised both Jews and non-Jews, and the works were intended to have an integrative function by showing Jewish life at times of transition and making a plea for tolerance based on understanding and the ideal of humanity [*Humanität*]. Auerbach was disappointed by the novels' reception and turned to the genre of the village tales. He never again completed a novel with a Jewish community as its chief subject matter. This is not to say that his turn to a new genre meant that he had turned away from his own Jewish identity.[4] As this study will show, in his post-1848 novels Auerbach places "the Jewish question" — particularly as it is linked with the issues of religious confession, political systems, and social hierarchies — into a contemporary setting and weaves it into the concerns of German realism.

Berthold Auerbach (né Moyses Baruch Auerbacher) was born in Nordstetten, a small town in Württemberg. He remembered relations between the Jewish and Catholic communities of the town, which had a forty percent to sixty percent Jewish-Catholic ratio, as largely peaceful, although interspersed with a few hostile incidents. Auerbach's early education was firmly grounded in Judaism. After attending the first German Jewish elementary school in the state of Württemberg, he went on to a school devoted to the study of the Talmud but was unhappy about the narrow focus of the curriculum there. In Karlsruhe he studied classical languages at a Lyceum before gaining admittance to the Gymnasium in Stuttgart with the intent of preparing for the rabbinate. But he also became interested in the writings of Schiller, Goethe, Herder, and Jean Paul at this time.[5] He assumed the name of Berthold, a sign of his desire to integrate into the larger intellectual community, and expressed doubts about becoming a rabbi.[6] He enrolled as a law student for his first semester at the University of Tübingen but then returned to his original plans. In Tübingen the Protestant theologian David Friedrich Strauss and the Jewish reformer Abraham Geiger helped shape his theological beliefs and his notions about Jewish identity. Auerbach's early interest in becoming a writer is shown by his attendance at a lecture course offered by the poet Ludwig Uhland, in which students submitted their writings for his public criticism.

Auerbach's career path was blocked following his arrest for involvement in a banned student fraternity, "Germania." He had not engaged in revolutionary activities; indeed, anti-Semitic sentiment had kept him in the outer circles of this fraternity. Barred from the university in Tübingen, he continued his theological studies at the University of Heidelberg. Having lost his royal scholarship, he began to write for subsistence. In 1834 he published his first literary work, a history of Frederick the Great, and became a reviewer for the prestigious literary journal *Europa*. The following year was decisive for Auerbach's career. Because his case was still pending, he was denied admittance to the examination for the rabbinate. The development of Auerbach's belief system, his doubts about aspects of Judaism, and his literary talent suggest that he would not have become a rabbi in any case. This fact, however, does not obviate the crushing effects of oppressive and repressive measures during the *Vormärz*. At the end of 1835 Auerbach, along with 200 other young men, was sentenced to serve two months in the Hohenasperg prison. There he worked on *Spinoza* and sold the sketch for *Dichter und Kaufmann*. Although both novels have enjoyed recent scholarly attention because they address issues of Jewish identity, they were only modestly successful in Auerbach's time.

But Auerbach became a sensation on the German — indeed, on the European — literary scene with the publication of a series of *Schwarzwälder Dorfgeschichten* (Village Tales from the Black Forest, 1843).[7] In the village tales, necessity becomes the mother of invention, for they depict "die Ausbildung des Provinciallebens,"[8] the formation and cultivation of provincial life. Comparing regional tales with recent regional histories that lead to an understanding of the nation, "das Bewußtsein der Vereiningung und Einheit" (GS 1:vii), Auerbach claims that such tales also are components of a living whole. Thus Auerbach fashioned something positive out of Germany's lack of a center, an often-lamented factor to which his contemporaries attributed the lack of a satisfactory German realist literature. With respect to religion, Auerbach addresses his own and his educated readers' increasing secularism by justifying the inclusion of religious life in the tales, stating that religion was a fundamental aspect of the life of the German peasantry: "Das religiöse Leben, hier zunächst als kirchliches, bildet ein Grundelement des Deutschen Volksthume" (GS 1:vi), and it would be frivolous and poetically untruthful to ignore it. Scholars today are sometimes at a loss to understand the enthusiastic critical and popular reception of these sentimental tales. Edward McInnes explains the critical acclaim afforded these tales in the context of contemporary critics' despair that German novelists still had not succeeded in creating a novel that grew out of the realities of social existence, that articulated the hopes of ordinary people.[9] According to McInnes, contemporary critics insisted that a national novel "develop out of the experience of the German people and embrace the idealistic impulses which informed the conception of the classical German novel."[10] Auerbach's tales were seen as a crucial breakthrough for realism. They were celebrated for their social authenticity and for depicting the unfolding, the *Bildung*, of an entire community. Auerbach, according to McInnes, presents his protagonists "overtly as representative figures who show the power of the peasant for inner regeneration, his ability to grow in response to the accelerating momentum of historical developments."[11] Of particular interest to my own inquiry is Hans Otto Horch's thesis that in the *Dorfgeschichten* Auerbach seeks to bring all outsiders — the orphans, the physically impaired, and the Jews — home.[12] Auerbach himself was gratified that he, a Jew, had succeeded in revealing something of the inner spirit of the German people and hoped this proof that he was a German would help reduce prejudice against Jews, that they would no longer be viewed as alien.[13]

Auerbach published three more volumes of *Dorfgeschichten*, unsuccessful dramas, volumes of reflections on German literature and culture, and studies of prominent Jews and Enlightenment figures. He continued to write novels that responded to societal problems and political events and issues. Fully in keeping with the dictates of German realism that novels present a comprehensive view of society, Auerbach's novels grew fatter, the characters more numerous, and the plots more complicated. The position of the Jew in German society remained a central, albeit less explicit, concern. Although Auerbach led a peripatetic life, residing in Heidelberg, Vienna, Dresden, and Berlin, interspersed with long sojourns in the Rhineland, he was buried — as he had requested — in the Jewish cemetery of Nordstetten.[14]

The novels *Spinoza* and *Dichter und Kaufmann* are devoted exclusively to the issue of Jewish identity. They express fundamental positions that Auerbach modulated but from which he did not deviate in the course of his life and writing. Both novels are informed by the legal and social status of the German Jews in German lands since the Enlightenment. As Michael A. Meyer explains, prior to the Enlightenment, "in the considerable isolation of the ghetto, Jewish existence possessed an all-encompassing and unquestioned character which it lost to a significant extent only after the middle of the eighteenth century. It is with the age of Enlightenment that Jewish identity becomes segmental and hence problematic."[15] To the extent that the improvement of the political and social condition of the Jews became part of Jewish and non-Jewish Enlightenment projects, the relationship between the minority and majority cultures came into greater flux, and the pressure to change — by acculturation, assimilation, or integration — was always greater on the minority group. Whereas the French Revolution brought about immediate civil emancipation for the Jews in all of France, in German lands the civil status of the Jews remained more problematic. At the beginning of the nineteenth century liberalizing reforms of laws concerning Jews were instituted in some German states by the occupying Napoleonic forces and in others, notably Prussia, as a response to this occupation, so that the state might enjoy the best its citizens, including the Jews, had to offer. But hopes for continuing improvement were soon dashed. The Congress of Vienna swept away much that had been gained, and in the turmoil subsequent to the Napoleonic Wars a virulent form of economic anti-Semitism erupted in several German cities in 1819. In the 1830s hopes for reform were once again dashed as the prevailing powers, under the aegis of Clemens Metternich, invoked increasingly repressive measures not only against the Jews but also against all voiceless German subjects. This crackdown was in response to the 1830 revolution in France, when the bourgeois king, Louis Philippe, acceded to the throne, and to the threat of demonstrations by outlawed student fraternities and other liberals and republicans. On the literary scene the repression included attacks against, and censorship of, German Jewish authors such as Heinrich Heine and Ludwig Börne. It is this context, then, that Auerbach composed *Spinoza* and *Dichter und Kaufmann*.

Using the historical novels of Sir Walter Scott as a model for these two works, Auerbach combined his depiction of the life of two different branches of Jewish people in different time periods with the story of the development of individual characters (12: v). *Spinoza: Ein Denkerleben* treats the Sephardim in seventeenth-century Amsterdam, and *Dichter und Kaufmann: Ein Lebensgemälde aus der Zeit Moses Mendelssohns*[16] treats the Ashkenazim in eighteenth-century Germany during the Enlightenment. Though historical novels, both are *Zeitromane* that address contemporary issues of Jewish identity. The philosopher Benedict (né Baruch) Spinoza of *Spinoza* is depicted as having led an exemplary life, whereas the merchant and minor poet Ephraim Moses Kuh, the protagonist of *Dichter und Kaufmann* is shown to have led a troubled one. The protagonists of both novels clash with their orthodox Jewish communities as they exceed the confines of these communities. The historian David Sorkin considers both novels failures, because in the end the main characters do not integrate into the Jewish community.[17] Sorkin's judgment, I believe, does not appreciate the multiple perspectives on Jewish life both novels provide. Jonathan Skolnik, too, maintains that Sorkin misses the point: "Auerbach's historical novel creates a reading public and presents Jewish and non-Jewish readers with the open-ended drama of modernization: a novel about the limits of communal acceptance in an incompletely secularized society, a novel that itself participates in the creation of a secular Jewish culture."[18] Skolnik's statement also holds true for *Dichter und Kaufmann*.

The main subject of *Spinoza* is the philosopher's intellectual and moral development, presented in the context of the cultural history of the Sephardic Jews. Ismar Schorsch views *Spinoza* in relation to German-speaking Jews' search for a usable past in Sephardic Judaism as they became increasingly critical of the traditions of Ashkenazic Judaism.[19] Auerbach went on to translate Spinoza's works from Latin into German and accompanied his translation with a brief biographical introduction.[20] Being a novel of ideas,[21] *Spinoza* relies primarily on dialogue as characters exchange opinions about issues. Narrative descriptions of selected objects, however, make statements about the history and the rich religious and familial traditions of the Jews. For example, a drawing on yellowed parchment of the holy city of Jerusalem, which Spinoza's father rescued at great peril from the synagogue in Guadalajara, underscores the point that Sephardic Jews were twice exiled: first from Jerusalem and then from their second homeland, Spain. During the Inquisition, Jews were forced to flee, if they could, or to convert to Catholicism and practice their true faith in secrecy, if they could not.

Religious fanaticism, be it on the part of the Spanish Inquisition toward the Jews and the Moors or, to a lesser degree, on the part of the orthodox Jews toward members of their own community, is one of the central themes of *Spinoza*. The fanatical inquisitors, Auerbach's Spinoza reads and hears, forced the Jews, Spinoza's paternal ancestors, and the Moors, his (fictional) maternal ancestors, to convert to Catholicism. Auerbach uses the historical event to assert his views on the issue of conversion in general, especially as it infringed on the life of German Jews from the Enlightenment to his own time. Auerbach maintains that conversion from one religious faith to another should be undertaken only out of inner conviction. Neither persecution nor social pressure should force it. People should remain in the faith into which they are born — not as a matter of religious confession but out of loyalty to their heritage. Despite Spinoza's and the Christian Olympia's fictional mutual love,[22] Spinoza renounces the possibility of marriage because it would require his conversion, and he could never swear a false oath and convert to a faith in which he did not believe (11: 94–95). According to Auerbach's Spinoza, we have no choice about the life or the faith into which we are born; the test of our strength is how we endure them and become either resigned or liberated within them (11: 93).

Name changes may result when two cultures intersect. During the Inquisition in Spain the change from a Hebrew to a Christian name was imposed at the time of forced conversion. Some Marranos, however, retained their Jewish names within the Jewish community. Christian names might also be regarded as a protective device, for they concealed Jewish identity. Name changes also occur during the process of assimilation. The imaginative scene depicting Spinoza's name change reveals Auerbach's strong identification with Spinoza, as well as the novel's assimilative trajectory. Olympia mocks the gloomy sound of the fictional Spinoza's Hebrew name — "Bahruhch! Nein, das geht nicht" (10: 194) — and "baptizes" him with its Latin equivalent, Benedictus. Olympia maintains that since Spinoza is a scholar and will be famous one day, he must have a Latin name. Here the name change signifies that Spinoza's scholarship will take him beyond the confines of Judaic studies. Because Auerbach and Spinoza shared the same Hebrew name, this passage also suggests that Auerbach assumed the name Berthold in anticipation that he himself would reach beyond the confines of the Jewish community. Horch considers this novel "a masked and wishful autobiography."[23]

As Auerbach's Spinoza matures, he engages with the entire Jewish tradition before turning to Cartesian philosophy. Spinoza's interpretations of the writings of Maimonides, the medieval rabbi and physician who was one of the greatest Jewish philosophers, serve as turning points. Early on, Spinoza recalls Maimonides' teaching that the pious of all religions will achieve eternal bliss (10: 101); he gains this theological insight at the same time as he reaches a conclusion about secular life: that the Jewish people and their teachings are no longer the center of the world.[24] Although the novel dwells on the wealth of Sephardic Jewish history, tradition, and learning, it also touches on the constraints imposed by narrow-minded members of the community. Through their religious practices Jews themselves have separated from other people (11: 130). Auerbach's Spinoza grows to believe that the Jews' mission has been fulfilled and that only the hatred of nations continues to sustain it. The horrifying consequences of fanatical sectarianism is one of the reasons Auerbach argues here for religious tolerance, more specifically for a faith in God that transcends the narrow confines of all positive religions. Reflecting on the hatred and chaos and destruction borne of fanatic sectarianism, Spinoza envisions a transcendent ideal of humanity that warrants that those of all faiths will attain eternal bliss.

After challenging Maimonides for lacking the courage to separate the teachings of Scripture from those of reason, Spinoza follows that path of reason in his own scholarly pursuits. He interprets human relationships in terms of mathematical principles and arrives at his fundamental concept that nothing exists that is not in and of God, a pantheistic worldview based on principles of unity and harmony that became Auerbach's own understanding of God. Brought before the synagogue court, Spinoza professes the deepest love of God but places more credence in the power of reason than in the Bible. Just as Mosaic law did not lie in heaven, according to the Bible, Sinai now lies in reason, on the height of pure, godly thought (11: 193–94).

Auerbach's next novel demonstrates that this reign of reason, with its promise of religious tolerance and its vision of all-pervasive godliness, would remain in the realm of the ideal. *Dichter und Kaufmann*[25] offers a sweeping survey of the Ashkenaznic German Jewish community[26] as it experiences one of the most tremendous upheavals in Jewish history: the impact of Enlightenment thought. The protagonist, Ephraim Moses Kuh, asserts that the Jews are the barometers of humanity (13: 38), meaning that the position and the condition of the Jews in a nation is the measure of the extent to which that nation and its society have achieved the ideals of the Enlightenment: emancipation, tolerance, friendship, mutual cooperation, and brotherly love. Auerbach repeats this statement in *Studien und Anmerkungen zu Lessings Nathan der Weise* (Studies and Notes on Lessing's *Nathan the Wise*, 1858). Like *Spinoza*, the novel contains an early chapter describing with reverence the solemn rituals at the home of the protagonist and in the synagogue on the Sabbath. These harmonious scenes are preceded, however, by the depiction of a rag-tag group of homeless Jews cursing, jostling, and crowding as they stand in line for their meal ticket, dependent on the organized charity of the more fortunate members of the Jewish community. The novel begins, then, by showing the consequences of centuries of persecution and expulsions and the deleterious effects of homelessness and poverty. Further, here and elsewhere the novel reproaches the ruling powers for not attending to the well-being of the Jewish people. Although the system of Jewish charity is laudable, the extensive need for it is deplorable. According to Sorkin, of the 60,000 to 70,000 Jews who lived in 1750 in the areas that were to constitute Imperial Germany, more than half endured a marginal existence of petty trading, begging, and thievery. It was extremely difficult to gain the right of residence.[27] When the narrator notes that the Jews must provide for the schooling of their children, he does not appreciate the Jewish community's autonomy over its own affairs, a special relationship between the Jews and political rulers going back to medieval times, but castigates the prevailing powers for neglecting the Jewish people in their midst. Once again, Auerbach reveals his integrative perspective. Sorkin notes that by the 1770s some Enlightenment writers, including Lessing, "began to promote the environmentalist argument that the Jews' faults — so obvious among the poor — were the result of discrimination and disabilities rather than of national character or religion." This argument, according to Sorkin, was always tempered by the notion that "toleration and emancipation were made contingent upon regeneration."[28] Sixty years later a form of this debate about whether the integration of the Jews into Germany should be predicated on regeneration, which includes the process of *Bildung* [acculturation, education], or on civil emancipation continued. Even though Auerbach was a vociferous advocate of *Bildung,* passages such as the one above demonstrate that if made to chose between the gradual process of regeneration and the immediate effect of emancipation, Auerbach would chose emancipation. I will explore this point in my analysis of *Das Landhaus am Rhein* (The Villa on the Rhine, 1869)[29] below.

Auerbach depicts the attitude toward their Jewish identity of a broad range of characters from the poorest beggar, the debased Jewish toll collector, the marriage broker, and the disaffected rabbi to the great philosopher Moses Mendelssohn. The fate of Ephraim Moses Kuh, a merchant and the first Jewish poet to publish in German, although historically accurate, is also emblematic of his time. Auerbach adheres closely to known events in Kuh's life[30] but casts them in such a way as to underscore his own worldview. Having grown up in a closed Jewish community, Kuh confronts societal changes, is unable to find a metaphoric home, and suffers a crisis of identity. His schizophrenia reflects the schizophrenic position of the Jew in Germany during an era of attempted emancipation. Ritchie Robertson surmises that "in portraying Kuh's slow descent into madness, Auerbach may well be projecting and thus exorcising his own anxieties about unsuccessful integration.[31] There are some general parallels between Spinoza's life and Kuh's that serve Auerbach's ideology: the initial rabbinical studies, the turning to a life of practical work combined with secular study and writing, the clashes with the orthodox Jewish community. But both in life and in the fiction Spinoza is the exception because of his genius and because his independence embraces isolation from society in general, whereas Kuh is closer to the rule for a Jew who seeks a home but cannot or will not be integrated either into the Jewish or the non-Jewish community.

The stories of Ephraim Kuh's family members display both the continuing prejudice against the Jews and the rapid changes that transpired within the Jewish community during the Enlightenment. Kuh's uncle, Veitel Ephraim, historically one of the richest Jews in Berlin, is denigrated as a commercial Jew and vilified as a minter of shaven coin. That he is afforded no more dignity than the *Trödeljude* demonstrates that just treatment through the privilege of exception is not true justice. Kuh's father, Moses Daniel Kuh, is a dignified family patriarch and highly charitable member of the Breslau Jewish community. He finds deep joy in Judaic tradition and views the Enlightenment as a threat to the Jewish people. His exemplary life, however, does not spare him from being the victim of prejudice; indeed, jealousy may make him a target. The fictional Moses Daniel is accused of the age-old "blood libel"[32] of killing a Christian and using his blood in the Passover ceremony. He is imprisoned and threatened with torture. Even though the true murderer is found out, Moses Daniel dies a broken man, and his wish for God to call him before he has to experience the apostasy of his children is fulfilled.

Two salon scenes in the home of Moses Mendelssohn,[33] placed at the novel's center, serve as a counterpoint to the genre scenes. Prominent figures of the Enlightenment, the most important of whom is Gotthold Ephraim Lessing, are guests in Mendelssohn's home. The Lessing who is portrayed by Auerbach in various chapters is the author of the drama "*Die Juden*," who professes to have made a conscious effort to divest himself of acquired prejudice about class, religious beliefs, and the Jews (12: 136). Lessing claims that what is learned can be unlearned; the best way to overcome prejudice against Jews is to get to know them (GW, 12: 137). The scene *de amicitia* contains a discussion on the nature of friendship that culminates in Mendelssohn's observation that friendship must be based on equality and in Lessing's epigram, "Wer Freunde hat ist sie zu finden werth; / Wer keine hat, hat keinen noch begehrt (12: 219). As they take their leave, one character remarks to Ephraim that Lessing and Mendelssohn — two intellectual heroes — may be added to the list of great friends among the Ancients, for these two men of different confessions stand at the portals of the new era (12: 219). Noting this scene, George L. Mosse discusses the critical importance of the eighteenth-century cult of friendship for *Bildung* or self-cultivation, the process through which German Jews sought to integrate themselves into German society. Mosse explains that the cult of friendship went hand in hand with the emancipatory process.[34] Friendships were important to Auerbach throughout his life. His visits and correspondence with people at all levels of society suggest that he regarded himself as an ambassador of the German Jews.

During the second evening at Mendelssohn's home Lavater attempts to persuade Mendelssohn to convert, and Lessing and Mendelssohn engage in a friendly debate over the role of religion in the development of mankind. Both the fictional Mendelssohn and the fictional Lessing draw on Lessing's Ring Parable in *Nathan der Weise*. Mendelssohn contends that a revelation claiming exclusivity is not the true one, and Lessing then draws on the moral of the Ring Parable to claim that, ultimately, deeds will reveal the true religion. Auerbach's own belief in a progressive historical development of religion was more in keeping with Lessing's thought than with Mendelssohn's. Ephraim Kuh's outburst about his position on conversion condenses Auerbach's life-long position on his own Jewish and German identity:

> Abgesehen von allem Andern . . . könnte ich kein Christ werden, wie ich als Deutscher kein Franzose oder Engländer werden kann, wenn ich auch diese Völker für mächtiger und glücklicher hielte; ich könnte auch meine innere Sprachreligion nicht ändern; ich muß ein Deutscher bleiben und ich bin ein Jude, und würde ich ein Ausreißer aus dem Judenthum, meine Lebenswurzeln wären mir zerschnitten und ausgerissen. (13: 42)

The issue of what constitutes Jewish identity is conflicted in Auerbach's writings by the fact that Jews were not fully integrated into German society and did not enjoy full civil rights in 1840. This fact colors any discussion of what it means to be a Jew. In *Das Judenthum und die neueste Literatur* (Judaism and the Most Recent Literature, 1836) Auerbach asserts, "Sie nennen uns 'Volk,' und ärgern sich nur ein wenig, wenn wir ihnen die richtige Behauptung entgegenstellen, daß wir schon längst nur Confession sind."[35] One of his role models, Gabriel Riesser, whose early works Auerbach summarizes in *Gallerie der ausgezeichneten Israeliten aller Jahrhunderte, ihre Porträts und Biographien* (Gallery of the Most Outstanding Israelites of All Centuries, Their Portraits and Biographies, 1836), stressed that Judaism was a *confession;* with respect to national identity, German Jews were *Germans.*[36] In his own discussion in the pamphlet Auerbach argues against the exclusion of Jews from the life of the German state on the ground that they had at heart the interests of a Jewish state, interests that conflicted with those of the state in which they resided. Such diverse thinkers as Mendelssohn and Maimon had already proved that with the fall of the Jewish state, religion and the state were separated. Auerbach also points out repeatedly that Judaism is in a constant state of development, although he will not presume to predict what forms it will take.[37] Even though Auerbach became disaffected from the life of the synagogue, and his attendance at services seems to have been motivated by a desire to maintain a sense of religious fellowship,[38] he felt himself to be a Jew and advocated on the Jews' behalf to the end of his life. Despite strategic protestation to the contrary, being a Jew meant to Auerbach not only adherence to the creeds and rituals of Judaism — for him this was, perhaps, least important — but also rootedness in a specific group with its own cultural history. Auerbach sought to reconcile the two parts of his identity: the Jew and the German.[39]

Critics interested in the issue of Jewish identity state that Auerbach seldom treats Jews in his later novels; some even claim — erroneously — that there are no Jewish characters in these works. What they fail to note is that Auerbach's Jewish identity is *the* definitive experience that shapes his views on many social and political issues, so that even if certain topics in the novels are not overtly about Jewish issues, Jewish identity is the subtext. M. I. Zwick's claim that Auerbach never changed his core belief systems and that his Jewishness was at the heart of his concerns still holds true.[40] But the extent to which Jewish authors address issues perceived as emanating from their "Jewishness" is vexed. Horch informs us, for example, that B. Saphra (Benjamin Segel) claims in the Jewish journal *Ost und West* that "all of Auerbach's books were Jewish, 'the most Jewish being those that weren't about Jews.'" This statement was later quoted in the anti-Semitic *Semi-Kürschner.*[41] For the anti-Semites, Auerbach was too Jewish. In our post-Holocaust era he is, for some, not Jewish enough. In an article on the Jewish historical novel Nitsa Ben-Ari lists Auerbach with the German authors Raabe, Freytag, and Gutzkow, not with the Jewish authors Bernstein, Kompert, and Franzos, and then dismisses both groups for their tendency "to describe traditional Jewish figures and customs in caricature-like fashion, which enjoyed a certain amount of success among assimilated and non-Jewish readers."[42] Ben-Ari focuses on Jewish historical novels written in German that were not meant for a German public. Ben-Ari is correct insofar as Auerbach was not aligned with the latter ghetto novelists but, rather, with authors such as Gutzkow and Freytag in seeking in his post-1848 novels accurately to depict a broad spectrum of German society and to capture its ethos. Just as he had turned from the early Jewish novels to the village tales, Auerbach now did not want to parody himself and restrict his focus to the peasantry, having found new material in the conflicts among the middle classes and the aristocracy, "die Conflicte, die in den tapezirten wie in den getäferten Zimmern daheim sind."[43]

Bildung, a value upheld by the German-Jewish community long after it had lost its centrality for the rest of the German middle class in the nineteenth century, and which is a significant theme in *Dichter und Kaufmann,* is retained as a key concept in Auerbach's post-1848 novels. *Ein neues Leben*[44] (1851) concerns the education of the peasantry; *Auf der Höhe* (1865) revolves around the inner development of characters representing a broad spectrum of society, from peasants to the royal couple; *Das Landhaus am Rhein*[45] (1869) has as its premise the best pedagogical method for educating a middle-class heir to wealth; and in *Waldfried*[46] (1874) Martella, who grew up hidden in the forest, becomes domesticated.

The main theme of *Ein Neues Leben* is the effort of a nobleman, who, after escaping prison and the firing squad for his participation in the revolution, assumes the identity of a village teacher to construct an educational system that will improve the lot of the peasantry. Some of the peasants participated in the 1848 revolution and are bitter about the defeat. Although Leo Tolstoy paid Auerbach a visit a decade after the novel's publication because the work had inspired him to found a free school on his estate, contemporary critics severely criticized the novel for its tendentiousness and its hodge-podge themes. In his *Grenzboten* review Auerbach's friend Gustav Freytag[47] offered him well-meant advice to choose material for which he could not possibly indulge in epigrammatic conversations, to work according to a strict plan, and to keep the language simple and the representation true.[48] In these respects, Auerbach was always more successful in the shorter village tales.

Recently Freytag's own best-selling novel, *Soll und Haben* (Debit and Credit, 1855), has received renewed critical attention because of its negative depiction of Jewish financial manipulators. Much cited in the late nineteenth and the twentieth centuries by anti-Semites, it left a fateful legacy. But Auerbach was among the many contemporary critics to laud what they considered the first successful realist German novel because it depicted the work ethos and the economic success of the German middle class. According to Margarita Pazi, Auerbach did note the predominance of corrupt Jewish figures, which he regarded as an aesthetic imbalance.[49] Jeffrey L. Sammons's observation in the chapter "Raabe and the Jews" in his *Wilhelm Raabe and the Fiction of the Alternative Community* (1987) that "social, class, ethnic, and national typology is virtually universal in nineteenth-century literature"[50] helps us to understand why Jewish authors were not as sensitive to Jewish stereotypes as we might expect. Sammons does not offer this as an excuse but, rather, provides us with an insight that explains why Auerbach was able to praise the novel, and another German-Jewish contemporary, Fanny Lewald, could claim that Freytag was the only German realist author who knew how to construct a novel.

Auerbach's subsequent novel, *Auf der Höhe: Roman in acht Büchern* (On the Heights: Novel in Eight Books, 1865)[51] is a bridge between the *Dorfgeschichten* and the post-1848 realist novel. Contrasting country life with life at a royal court and drawing in middle-class characters, as well, the novel is Auerbach's idiosyncratic version of the "Schloß oder Fabrik?" phenomenon of German realism. I adapt this term from Patricia B. Herminghouse, who sees an assimilationist tendency in German literature written between 1848/49 and 1870. Feeling a threat from below, the educated middle class sought support through rapprochement with the aristocracy. According to Herminghouse, by criticizing the aristocracy for moral degeneracy and frivolity, while depicting in detail aristocratic codes and customs, this bourgeois literature avoided direct political confrontation with the aristocracy.[52] To this point I would add that descriptions of beautifully furnished castles, lovely gardens, and elaborate gowns — the nineteenth-century version of "Lives of the Rich and Famous" — also satisfied the reader's voyeuristic taste and helped sell more novels. The two realms of court and country are connected by Walpurga, the wetnurse fetched from a mountain village to suckle the royal couple's first-born son. In keeping with the opposition of these two spheres, key issues — conversion, social strata, politics, values, and human relations — are also posed in terms of opposites. Much of the plot at court revolves around the king's vacillating feelings for the queen and mother of his infant and for Countess Irma von Wildenstein, with whom he eventually has an affair.

Conversion, a key issue in Auerbach's first two novels, is a secondary theme in *Auf der Höhe*. Nonetheless, the issue's inclusion indicates that it remained a central concern. It is framed in the context of the religious differences of the Catholic king and the Protestant queen. After her son's birth and baptism, the queen wants to convert so that nothing will separate her from her husband and child. Arguments representing several points of view are made to dissuade the queen. The king places the issue in its political context, pointing out that acts of royalty are never private but have universal ramifications. The king's middle-class advisor, Gunther, views the issue from a rationalist perspective with arguments found in the two early novels. He does not disapprove of conversion out of conviction, which is not the case here. But when we convert to another religion, we relinquish our freedom of thought, for we must adhere to the dictates of the new confession, whereas we are free to question the faith into which we are born. Finally, the advisor argues that tolerance for religious diversity benefits a country and its people, for it wards off fanaticism. One can be an upright human being within any religious confession and even without professing and adhering to the practices of a particular faith. Walpurga, who represents the *Volk*, gives the concluding argument. Her deceased father maintained that in a world where the least portion of human beings were Christians, it would be a vile God, indeed, who damned the others to hell for not being born into Christianity (1: 195). Her father's final thoughts on the subject of confessional differences were prompted by the harmonious singing of a chorus: "Die Kirchen alle, die unsrig', und die evangelisch und die jüdisch, und die türkisch, und wie sie all heißen — da ist jedes so eine Stimm' im Gesang, und da singt ein Jedes, wie es seine Kehle hergiebt, und das stimmt doch zusammen und giebt einen guten Chor" (1: 198–99). Because the queen seeks unity and harmony, this argument comforts her the most, and she remains in her faith. In *Auf der Höhe* Auerbach transposes many of the arguments against conversion from Judaism to Christianity in *Spinoza* and *Dichter und Kaufmann* into arguments against conversion from one Christian denomination to another, and he reiterates his plea for tolerance and humanity.

In contrast to *Ein neues Leben*, whose peasantry is bitter about the defeat of the 1848 revolution, in this novel the peasantry is little concerned about politics. There is in the background a political struggle at court between constitutional monarchy and royal absolutism. The queen is associated with the liberal opposition, whereas the king convenes a reactionary cabinet strongly supportive of the Catholic Church. The king cynically deems advantageous his employment of the middle-class Gunther as privy councilor and royal physician, for Gunther's assertion that he is a freethinker lends the king a veneer of liberalism. Some doubts may be cast on Gunther for associating with a royal court at all, but his wife is beyond reproach. From a well-off and well-educated Swiss — and therefore democratic — family, Frau Privy Councilor Gunther is free by disposition.

She is independent, is active in the household, and participates in all public institutions that are open to women. She respects her husband yet relies on her own judgment. Disdainful of the folderol of court hierarchy and favoritism, she never sets foot in court but provides her husband a secure home base to which to return from the slippery and unsafe ground of court life (1: 216–17). Democratic ideals, including the notion of full citizen participation in public life, underlie the novel's belief system but cannot be realized in this petty German state. The ideals are reaffirmed only in that Gunther chooses to remain an independent scholar after the king invites him to return to the court following his initial dismissal.

Although the backdrop of the novel is court and country, the values it promulgates are the nineteenth-century middle-class ones of honesty, loyalty, fidelity, level-headed thinking, hard work, productivity, and the wise investment of money — values that Ernest K. Bramsted calls the middle-class ideology of "the gospel of labour" that finds literary expression in the works of Auerbach, Freytag, Friedrich Spielhagen, and Gottfried Keller.[53] Walpurga may amuse some aristocrats with her fresh, seemingly naive utterances, but she has agreed to go to the court to help her family get ahead and to provide it with security. Her letters constantly admonish her husband, Hansei, to be on guard against duplicitous villagers, lest they part him from the gold coins the couple received as an initial payment. Despite the comforts at court, Walpurga finds that activities there lack purpose, and she looks forward to working in the fields again. On her return home Walpurga and Hansei invest her earnings in a neglected but fertile farm. Their upright character and hard work earn them invaluable advice from the most prosperous but misanthropic peasant in the village.

The marital trials of the king and queen are also based on bourgeois notions of fidelity, for in aristocratic circles it is acceptable for the king to take a mistress. For his part, Hansei, desperately lonely while Walpurga is away at court, shows that he is morally superior to the king, for he resists the powerful temptation of Black Esther. Her corruption is attributed, in turn, to the fact that an aristocrat had seduced and abandoned her when she was a girl.

Despite the middle-class values stressed in this novel, however, Auerbach's ideal of humanity reinforces social and political stasis. Characters move around a great deal, but there is little sign of the social mobility that is often found in realist novels. Early on, Gunther tells Irma that human beings can enjoy equal rights without the dissolution of class distinctions (1: 122–23). Egalitarianism, then, is posited in terms of a common humanity and human dignity, not of equal social status. In comparison, in two novels by Auerbach's German Jewish contemporary, Fanny Lewald, *Wandlungen* (Changes, 1853) and *Von Geschlecht zu Geschlecht* (From Generation to Generation, 1864–66), characters ranging from working-class to aristocratic are not bound by class lines as they go through the process of realizing their talents and potential. Indeed, in the later novel the baron's bastard son, who has made his fortune in America, and the son's Jewish wife become the owners of the baronial estate. Auerbach's ideology of humanity, in contrast to Lewald's indomitable faith in progress, reinforces the conservative status quo. Even the invocation of Auerbach's icon of the Enlightenment reinforces this status quo when Frau Gunther cites Lessing's Nathan the Wise: "Mittelgut wie wir, findet sich überall in Menge" (3: 423). She means that most misery is created when people of intellect and education, who have a modicum of talent, consider themselves to be superior and overstep customary boundaries and duties.

Toward the end of the novel we find the central characters engaged in self-examination and atonement. As they gather on the high mountain meadow, where Irma dies in anorexic transfiguration, they forgive one another. The novel's final message is that virtue and loyalty are qualities of an upright life, but compassion is a quality of humanity. In her discussion of Auerbach's next novel, *Das Landhaus am Rhein,* Nancy A. Kaiser cites Franz Röhse's analysis of "the central concept of a harmonious, inclusive order for Auerbach's oeuvre, a concept derived from the traditionally religious principle of an encompassing, divine *ordo* in the world."[54] This pantheistic harmony, which is in consonance with the orderly axioms of Spinoza's worldview, is even more prevalent in *Auf der Höhe*. It manifests itself in the novel's structure, plot, and ethos and culminates in its harmonious resolution, where all characters, having worked through their individual problems, are gathered in. Both Röhse and Werner Hahl[55] understand the German realist authors' effort to harmonize the form of their novels to be an expression of the increasing difficulty of reconciling the ideal with reality. This holds true for Auerbach, as well. Nevertheless, in

Auerbach's case the harmonies of plot and form in his post-1848 novels are just as much an expression of his religio-philosophical views as they are of his sociopolitical beliefs. Enjoying the best reception of all his novels, *Auf der Höhe* was an immediate popular success, and Auerbach was particularly gratified by the critic Friedrich Theodor Vischer's praise in the *Augsburger Allgemeine Zeitung*.[56] Vischer thought that the combination of village tale with the story of court and state was "pragmatisch eine wohlgeschlungene und wohlgelungene."[57]

A scene in *Auf der Höhe* in which the advisor's wife presents the queen with a book on slavery serves as a link to *Das Landhaus am Rhein*. The latter is a novel about America set on German soil, but it is equally about German lands when the setting shifts to the United States.[58] The broad strokes of its canvas depict a common theme in the nineteenth-century European novel: the rise of the middle classes and the decline of the aristocracy. The specific subject matter of the novel, however, is unusual for a German work whose author did not sojourn in the United States: the cruelties of slavery and the slave trade, and the abolition of slavery as a result of the American Civil War. Among the characters are two Jews. These seemingly disparate aspects are explicitly linked in Erich Dournay's shorthand assessment of the times in a letter from America: "Dem Monarchischen, dem Aristokratischen und Monotheistischen gegenüber steht das Republikanische, das Demokratische, das Pantheistische; es sind drei verschiedene Namen für drei Regionen desselben Princips" (3: 285). Erich's statement makes clear that a nation's or an individual's choices with respect to form of government, class system, and religious credo are governed by a core principle and that one manifestation of a given principle is related to the others. To Nancy A. Kaiser's observation of a divine order in Auerbach's works I would add that there are two opposing orders in *Das Landhaus am Rhein* — one liberal and liberatory, the other conservative and repressive. Only one can emerge triumphant.

In the Bildungsroman[59] within this *Zeitroman*, both tutor and tutee are protagonists. As the novel opens, Erich Dournay, a Huguenot who left the military to pursue the study of classical antiquity (he did not want to continue training men to kill), has just been awarded his doctorate. Erich grew up in a loving and cultured environment. His recently deceased middle-class father was a scholar and court tutor to a prince, and his mother, of aristocratic origin, lives as an educated middle-class citizen and is referred to as "die Frau Professorin." Although Erich is content to live in scholarly isolation, the family's future has become uncertain. After losing out to an aristocrat for a position as museum director, Erich becomes a tutor at Villa Eden, a sumptuous country estate on the Upper Rhine. Erich's pupil is Roland Sonnenkamp, the son of a man who made a fortune in America. Herr Sonnenkamp's origins and the source of his wealth are, at first, a mystery, but gradually Erich — and the reader — learn that he owned great plantations built by slaves and that he had previously engaged in the illegal slave trade. On his final voyage he threw his cargo of slaves overboard alive to avoid capture by a British ship. Described as the most infamous slave trader in the American South, he even published defenses of slavery to demonstrate that not all Germans were softened by the sentimental ideal of humanity (3: 21). These pamphlets infuriate Dr. Fritz, a Forty-Eighter émigré to the United States who supports the abolitionist cause.

Roland proves an eager pupil once Erich figures out an appropriate pedagogical method and discourages the distractions of spa and court society.[60] Being himself a novice, Erich is assisted by several older middle-class characters who hover about him in a manner that echoes the Tower Society that guides Wilhelm in Goethe's *Wilhelm Meisters Lehrjahre* (Wilhelm Meister's Apprenticeship, 1795–96) and provide aid and advice in moments of crisis. These characters include an estate owner whose sons founded prosperous enterprises using modern techniques of mining, forestry, and manufacturing; a retired military officer; a newspaper editor; a physician; and various professors and tutors. Professor Einsiedel suggests that the best one can do in educating pupils from aristocratic or wealthy families is to guide them to act ethically and on their own initiative. Einsiedel encourages Erich to continue his own studies; doing so will benefit both himself and his pupil. All agree that Roland must be prepared to manage his father's estate and his fortune.

Auerbach cannot resist providing his readers an annotated bibliography of liberal readings by summarizing the ideas of works central to Roland's education, which include Benjamin Franklin's autobiography and a book on slavery by the American Unitarian theologian and social reformer Theodore Parker. A commentary on

Franklin written by Erich's father convinces Erich to begin Roland's instruction with the autobiography. Erich's father lauds Franklin for being the first self-made man, a model human being for the modern era. He praises Franklin's industriousness, his inventiveness, and, above all, his civil, political, scientific, and ethical good sense (1: 264–65) and implies that a modern German citizen would be well served if he possessed Franklin's qualities. (Auerbach translated and edited Franklin's autobiography,[61] and Jeffrey L. Sammons states that he continued to revere Franklin at a time when Franklin "came to be misunderstood as the avatar of soulless pragmatism and naked greed for profit."[62] E. K. Bramsted cites Auerbach's reference to Franklin in his discussion of the middle-class ideology of the virtues of labor.[63]) Roland's discovery of Parker's text creates a dilemma for Erich. By this time he is aware that Sonnenkamp owned plantations, and he has some trepidations about permitting Roland to read an antislavery book. But Roland has read deep into the night, and Erich is proud of his pupil's desire for knowledge. Indeed, Roland's questions about slavery in antiquity, which Erich is unable to answer, motivate Erich to begin his own systematic study of slavery from antiquity to the present. Roland is struck by Parker's statement referring to the compromises on slavery during the drafting of the United States Constitution, quoted several times, that all great documents of humanity are written in blood (2: 12; 3: 248). This reading also releases in Roland repressed memories of blacks carrying him when he was a child, and he has nightmares about slave drownings (2: 180, 185).

When Erich learns of the full horror of Sonnenkamp's past, he concludes that it is good that he is there to guide a youth with such a fateful heritage. Knopf, tutor to the Russian prince Valerian, comments that Roland must do something for the Negro slaves when he reaches his majority, just as his own pupil must be taught to lead the freed serfs in his homeland.[64] Roland's later readings on slavery include *Uncle Tom's Cabin* (1852), which he criticizes for promising the tortured slaves their reward in heaven. *Vormärz* writers frequently criticized eschatological promises offered as a substitute for the immediate amelioration of earthly misery. Roland finds the German Friedrich Kapp's *Geschichte der Sklaverei in den Vereinigten Staaten von Amerika (*History of Slavery in the United States of America, 1861) more satisfactory reading because of its painstaking scholarship, although he is deeply disturbed to learn that Germans were among the exclusively foreign owners of slave ships and disillusioned to read about the compromises on slavery made by Franklin and other founding fathers. Above all, Roland is profoundly moved by Abraham Lincoln's Cooper Union address, quoted at length in German, which ends: "Recht gibt Macht. In diesem Glauben laßt uns handeln wie die Pflicht es gebietet bis zum Ende unserer Tage" (3: 249).

A common theme of realism — middle-class upward mobility — is displayed by Sonnenkamp's efforts to become a member of the aristocracy. Prancken, an impoverished aristocrat who seeks the hand of Sonnenkamp's daughter, Manna, to obtain Sonnenkamp's millions, serves as the intermediary. Because Sonnenkamp is a grandiose villain, and Prancken is a slimy opportunist, upward mobility is cast in a negative light. Prancken introduces Sonnenkamp at court and advises him to make a gift of a villa to an influential baron to ingratiate himself. Just as Sonnenkamp believes he is about to receive the prized title, his past is exposed in a newspaper editorial. When Sonnenkamp appears at court, Adams, the African king he had enslaved and who was the sole survivor of the slave drowning at sea, rushes into the room in a rage and identifies him. The humiliated Sonnenkamp will soon return to America and attempt to establish a monarchy in the South, but he does not leave before assembling a jury comprised of his middle-class neighbors.[65] He cynically seeks exoneration by narrating his life story and expressing contempt for the hypocritical aristocracy that had rejected him. He argues that his slave trading was no worse than the German rulers' sale of their subjects to fight in the American Revolution.

Many characters, and through them Auerbach, question the whole enterprise of middle-class people seeking to become aristocrats. Expressing a view "from below," even Sonnenkamp's servants remark on their employer's efforts to gain a title, finding it preferable to remain the richest citizen than to become the newest aristocrat. Whereas Sonnenkamp tries to buy a title with his wealth, some aristocrats seek to obtain middle-class wealth through their titles, as in Prancken's case. Frau Weidmann maintains that when a healthy, middle-class girl marries an aristocrat, she alienates the fruits of her people's labor and betrays both her ancestors and her descendants (3: 7). Chlodwig, the most sympathetic nobleman in the novel, also regards the middle-class acquisition of titles as betrayal and renegadism. He points out that the nobility is a dying institution in this age of equality under the law. Science, art, and business are the main preoccupations of the times; the power of the state is no longer based on land ownership, and the nobility has become superfluous in this industrial age with its market economies (2: 293). What holds true for the majority culture is all the more applicable to a Jew, Chlodwig continues. A Jew who becomes a nobleman is a foppish anachronism (2: 294), for he already descends from nobility. There is no older, purer race (2: 293), and it is the right and the duty of all Jews to become members of the developing middle class (2: 294). Chlodwig himself is the ultimate example of the literally dying aristocracy. He has lived in isolation, devoted to the study of archaeological remnants (the past), but dies without issue (the future).

The novel criticizes the opportunistic alliance between the Catholic Church and the aristocratic forces of legitimacy. It cast these allies in an equally negative light when they vie for power and money, although some nuns and priests do address the suspicions about their venality and declare that their concern is for souls, not money. In general, however, Auerbach treats the Catholic Church as a defender of the status quo. His opposition to the Catholic Church here and in *Auf der Höhe* must be understood in the context of liberal nationalism that led to the misguided *Kulturkampf* in the early years of the Second Empire. Protestant denominations, too, are seen as derelict in their moral obligation to ameliorate human suffering. Prince Valerian criticizes those who preach love and brotherhood yet stand aside and observe slavery and serfdom (3: 129), a criticism also found in *Uncle Tom's Cabin*.

There are only two, relatively minor, Jewish characters: the banker and Fräulein Milch. Yet what is said about them in a few passages addresses key questions debated since the Enlightenment about how the Jewish minority culture may be integrated into the German majority one. Further, they provide unique insights into the issue of slavery and prejudice. Because the banker is never named and is referred to only by his occupation, he remains a type. He functions to counteract an age-old stereotype of the Jew who profits from the misery and misfortune of the Gentile or, in the case of the court Jew, from the power of local rulers, for he is scrupulously correct in his business dealings (3: 241). At seventy he still possesses a youthful restlessness (a quality the Jewish convert to Catholicism, Annette, in Auerbach's next novel, *Waldfried,* overcomes), intellectual curiosity, and communicativeness. In the nineteenth-century context, however, restlessness is a negative stereotype that distinguishes the quick-minded Jew from his deep, contemplative German counterparts. (Critics have sometimes commented on Auerbach's own restlessness, attributing it to his Jewishness.) Although Professor Einsiedel is put off by the banker's restlessness, he does praise the man's appreciation of learning, which he considers to be a positive Jewish characteristic (2: 283). The banker's large home library decorated with statues signals that its Jewish owner possesses the *Bildung* to merit integration into the majority community. Finally, the case of this elite, exceptional individual serves as commentary on the upward mobility of middle-class Jews. While the reader never learns why the banker sought a title in the first place, his *withdrawal* from that endeavor is the point the novel wishes to make.

Fräulein Milch illustrates a different Jewish fate. Throughout most of the novel all know her as the Major's housekeeper and confidante. Only after Sonnenkamp's crisis do she and the Major reveal they are husband and wife and that she is Jewish. She recounts her story of leaving her close-knit family and the community in which her father was a respected rabbi. Refused permission to marry, she and the Major, her fallen brother's comrade, eloped and were wed civilly. Partly to atone for leaving and partly to disprove her father's accusation that she was seeking recognition from the world, Fräulein Milch did not assume the honor of being recognized as "die Frau Majorin." The young couple lived in a quiet union [*Einigkeit*]. Longing to pray with a community, Fräulein Milch attended a Christian church, reciting from the prayer book her father had written, as well as from the one her brother had carried on the battlefield. Fräulein Milch's story highlights the Jewish people's centuries-old story of oppression. They may celebrate annually their passage out of Egyptian bondage, but the average Jewish villager still views himself as a member of an oppressed minority. Jews may chose to live as an isolated community in order to preserve their religion and their family traditions; yet, prejudice against Jews is also a factor in this self-isolation. Fräulein Milch does not renounce the man she loves for the sake of her Judaism and her community. She makes a conscious choice to pass from the confines of the Jewish community into what she calls the wider world. That she passes over on Passover suggests that she views her former life to be a kind of bondage. But she also finds comfort in the familial and cultural tradition of Jewish prayers — reciting them, however, within a larger community to a God who transcends sectarian separation. Auerbach suggests here that it is possible to adhere to the specificity of one's heritage and simultaneously be a member of the majority society.

Fräulein Milch's story, however, is inherently problematic. Because she keeps her marital and religious/ethnic identity a secret and nevertheless finds acceptance, the novel implies that the appropriate basis of societal acceptance is character. In contrast to some in the Jewish community, she has a strong sense of self-worth; she is her own affirmation. But what does it signify that Fräulein Milch is accepted by the majority community but is not recognized to be a Jew? Auerbach here lays himself open to the same criticism that has befallen one of his icons, Lessing's *Die Juden* (The Jews, 1755), whose lauded protagonist has no identifiable traces of being Jewish.

The central link between the struggle for the abolition of slavery in the United States and the issue of Jewish identity is the Jews' own historical past: the fact that their ancestors were once slaves. An old rabbi once explained to Chlodwig that the Jewish people's memory of their own oppression, of their enslavement by the Egyptians, planted in them aspirations for the highest achievements, the ability to withstand oppression and — most important, with respect to this novel — the ability to recognize all forms of injustice and the sufferings of others. Out of the Jews' own experience arose a historically incomparable compassion (2: 294).

A later passage somewhat deflates this lofty view of the Jewish people in order to elaborate on minority/majority relations. When the Jewish banker expresses sorrow that some Jews profit by selling munitions to the Confederate army, Erich responds in a letter: "Warum verlangen Sie, daß alle Juden auf Seite des sittlichen Princips stehen? Es soll sich zeigen und es zeigt sich, daß keine Religion auserwählt zur Sittlichkeit ist" (3: 282). In addition to reiterating Auerbach's often-voiced point that no religion is superior to another, Erich implicitly argues here that a minority group need not be morally superior to a majority to gain equal status. Further, referring in passing to a historical figure, D. E. Twiggs, a Jewish general who fought in the Mexican War and turned over his army, fortress, and munitions to the rebels, Erich explains that a Jew may support his native state out of patriotism: "Die Juden, die so lange und so grausam ausgestoßen aus staatlicher Gemeinschaft und zu einem traurigen Kosmopolitismus verdammt waren, bewähren sich in der Befreiung als Eingeborene der verschiedenen staatlichen Gemeinschaften und halten sich zunächst an den Patriotismus" (3: 282). This single sentence encapsulates Auerbach's response to many European nations' resistance to accepting the Jews among their people based on the suspicion that Jews were "cosmopolitan," that they would always put the interests of their own people above those of the state in which they resided. Indeed, this suspicion frequently flourished — and among some, still flourishes — as the prejudiced notion of a "worldwide Jewish conspiracy." Then, likening the Huguenots to the Jews, Erich challenges the very notion that citizenship be solely based on "blood," that is, ethnicity, and sees unity in a nation's diversity (3: 282). He comes full circle and concludes with the assurance that many Jews are fighting bravely and selflessly for the Union's cause, and that the banker's monetary contribution to the war is being used conscientiously.

As he treats the issues of slavery, race, and prejudice, Auerbach, the Jewish German, appears to embrace African-Americans far more than do some liberal German authors who oppose slavery but find blacks personally repugnant. The text is not devoid of unpleasant depictions of blacks — in particular Adams, who tends to rage and foam at the mouth in the presence of his tormentor, Sonnenkamp. Adams discomfits some of the characters, but Fräulein Milch observes that if one is not acquainted with a particular group of people and has no favorable preconceived notions about them, then one may easily ascribe the characteristics and the faults of an individual to the whole group. Adams was first a slave, then a lackey, and did not need to provide for himself; therefore, he does not want to learn and work. But according to Fräulein Milch, it would be unjust to believe that all blacks are like Adams. Her close identification with the blacks as an oppressed people is evident when she muses on whether they will ever be completely free unless they liberate themselves, unless a Moses arises from their midst. In any case, it might take another generation before they reach the land of freedom. Oblivious to the nuances of Fräulein Milch's argument, not comprehending that her own Jewish experience gives her such keen insight into the nature of prejudice, Einsiedel voices a commonly held notion that the black race has no culture, that its liberation will be the acquisition of *Bildung*. This majority-culture view of the black has some affinity with its view of the Jew. When Jewish emancipation became an issue during the Enlightenment, one train of thought — as I have discussed in connection with *Dichter und Kaufmann* — was that the dirty, repugnant, morally and ethically depraved Jew could only gradually become assimilated into German society through the process of *Bildung*.

At Weidmann's estate, the locus of experiments to improve the peasantry's conditions, where all the characters bound for America learn useful skills, Adams rehabilitates himself to a degree for which even Fräulein Milch would not have hoped. Adams is ashamed of his idleness after he observes everyone else's industriousness. He does hard physical labor during the day, and at night he and Prince Valerian sit side by side as Knopf tutors them. Adams practices penmanship, while the prince continues his study of history and mathematics (3: 243). Roland's studies continue, as well, for Weidmann wants to be absolutely sure that he comprehends the full horror of slavery, noting that even beneficent people gloss over the inhumanity of the slave trade. Roland must understand that there is *no* justification for treating as objects human beings with the gift of language and reason (3: 245).

In America, Adams wants to fight for the liberation of his people; but Lincoln will not yet allow black units, explaining to Roland (!) that he considers the Civil War to be a war among brothers with reconciliation — not annihilation — as its goal (3: 275). Erich writes that in the United States patriotism has not yet become fused with humanity; that is, there is a strong faction in the North that wants to preserve the Union by defeating the South, not by abolishing slavery. Erich, too, addresses the reluctance to abolish slavery — the prime factor being the slaves' monetary value — and the deeply rooted prejudice underlying the fear of the consequences of emancipation. Erich asserts that self-interest greatly exaggerates the vices of the blacks. Those whom slavery benefits argue that the slaves are not worthy of emancipation. But, Erich maintains, whatever vices they may have are directly attributable to their harsh treatment and the ignorance to which they have been condemned (3: 280). Education, again, is the solution to integrating the emancipated black fully into society. Erich cites the example of a black man who had been a slave for twenty-two years but now had acquired "eine vollkommene wissenschaftliche Bildung" (3: 280). There can be no doubt that the blacks' integration into American society, of the minority into the majority culture, is the novel's ideological fundament. Having attended the burial of an old slave woman, Manna, who is now Erich's wife, laments that blacks have segregated burial sites: "Noch im Tode die Ausscheidung" (3: 282). Even though Erich — who, after all, is a teacher — advocates education as the means to ease the blacks' entrance into political and social life, he is fighting for the Union for the abolition of slavery (not just to preserve the Union). For Erich, and Auerbach, who brings to bear a discussion that had its counterpart with respect to Jews during the Enlightenment, *gradual* emancipation of the blacks predicated solely on regeneration is out of the question.

Adams's desire to fight for his people's emancipation is fulfilled, and Fräulein Milch's vision of the blacks' self-liberation is realized, when blacks are called to serve in the military. Erich and Roland join the black regiment, an implicit manifestation of the ideal of brotherhood. The battles take heavy tolls; included among the many casualties are Erich, who is severely wounded, and Roland, who is captured. Although Auerbach was a pacifist, he shows that this war is worth waging for the sake of emancipation, unity, and humanity. Lincoln's fear of the blacks' vengeance is belied when the wounded Adams finds the mortally wounded Sonnenkamp on the battlefield and fetches Erich instead of giving the death blow. In a bizarre scene of partial reconciliation Adams fulfills Sonnenkamp's dying wish by tearing out bunches of heather for his grave (3: 293–94).

Das Landhaus am Rhein, which interrogates its leitmotif — Goethe's verse motto "Amerika, du hast es besser" — is about Germany and America. Its ethos is an egalitarian, transcendent view of the possibilities for humanity with respect to race, ethnicity, religion, class, and nation. Through this novel Auerbach aspires to a unity that does not abnegate difference, and the struggle for unity is framed here in the context of nationhood on American and German soil with attention to Germans' roles in hindering or achieving nationhood. During the American Revolutionary War, Erich writes, the German petty rulers sold their subjects to fight for the British. In contrast, now German Forty-Eighters are fighting to emancipate the slaves and to uphold the American Union. But what the Germans help to bring about on American soil — emancipation and unity — remains a desideratum on German soil. Nevertheless, Erich and Manna's return to Villa Eden, and the historical events at the time of the novel's publication, suggest that German unification may soon be realized.

Many of Germany's liberal Jews advocated unification because they believed that it would result in uniform laws affecting the status of the Jews in all German lands. Indeed, German Jews were finally granted full rights of citizenship in 1871. Auerbach's next major novel, *Waldfried: Eine vaterländische Familiengeschichte* (1874),[66] is a first-person account of three generations in one German family. Written and published after the German Empire was founded, it covers a time period from the end of the Napoleonic Wars to German unification and celebrates unification by bringing all generations home: emigrants and exiles, Germans and Jews. The idyll, unfortunately, would be brief, and Auerbach despaired when the old forms of anti-Semitism, compounded by a new "scientific" racial anti-Semitism flared up in Europe, North Africa, and America. As is already evident in *Waldfried*, Auerbach's creative and imaginative powers had begun to fail, and he was unable to respond by writing a novel about the history of the Jews that he had contemplated decades earlier. Instead, he attacked anti-Semitism in letters, petitions, and articles — which he believed would, in any case, have a more immediate impact than a work of fiction. Among the letters was one to Friedrich Kapp, whose antislavery book was such an influential text in *Das Landhaus am Rhein*, concerning an incident in Saratoga, New York, when a hotelier would not permit a Jewish banker to lodge at his establishment. Auerbach advised that such a moral pestilence must be exterminated swiftly. But there is a slight shift, already incipient in *Das Landhaus am Rhein*, when he stresses that such anti-Semitism is a problem with which Christian preachers must deal. He addresses, as does Fanny Lewald in *Jenny* (1843) and *Familie Darner* (1887), the issue of Jewish ostentation, but he sees it as a manifestation of the nouveau riche class rather than an ethnic issue.[67] Having treated the blood-ritual myth in *Dichter und Kaufmann* in 1840, he despaired at the Russian blood-ritual trial in 1879. In his article "Kannibalische Ostern" in *Die Gegenwart* he again emphasizes that it is the responsibility of Christians, right up to the pope in Rome, to explain that there had never been one iota of truth in this accusation. He invokes his early heroes, Spinoza and Mendelssohn, claiming they would never have remained in a religion where such practices occurred.[68] He again invoked Mendelssohn while listening to debates in the Reichstag concerning the Jews that arose from resentment toward Jewish stockbrokers.[69] In his last published letter, dated 7 August 1881, he thanked Josef Ignaz Döllinger[70] for delivering a speech against fanaticism and the persecution of the Jews. The letter ends with a quotation from Sophocles' *Antigone* — "Nicht mitzuhassen, mitzulieben bin ich da"[71] — that sums up Auerbach's lifelong personal and literary project.

Notes

[1] Edward McInnes, "Auerbach's *Schwarzwälder Dorfgeschichten* and the Quest for 'German Realism' in the 1840s," in Mark G. Ward, ed., *Perspectives on German Realist Writing* (Lewiston, Queenstown & Lampeter: Edwin Mellen P, 1995), 95–111.

[2] *Berthold Auerbach's gesammelte Schriften,* 20 vols. (Stuttgart: Cotta, 1857–58), vols. 10–11. Cited in the text by volume and page number.

[3] *Gesammelte Schriften,* vols. 12–13.

[4] See, for example, *Marbacher Magazin Sonderheft* 36 (1985): 1: 1–2, and Lothar Kahn and Donald D. Hook, *Between Two Worlds: A Cultural History of German-Jew Writers* (Ames: Iowa UP, 1993), 40.

[5] Jakob Auerbach, introduction to *Berthold Auerbach: Briefe an seinen Freund Jakob Auerbach,* 2 vols. (Frankfurt am Main: Rütten & Loening, 1884), 1: xv.

[6] Letter to Bernhard Frankfurter in Anton Bettelheim, *Berthold Auerbach: Der Mann — Sein Werk — Sein Nachlaß* (Stuttgart & Berlin: Cotta, 1907), 56–57. Bettelheim points out similarities between Auerbach's letter and that of his eponymous protagonist, Ivo der Hajrle, who is studying for the priesthood in one of the early *Schwarzwälder Dorfgeschichten*. See also Hans

Otto Horch, "Berthold Auerbach's First Collection of Dorfgeschichten Appears," in Sander L. Gilman and Jack Zipes, eds., *Yale Companion to Jewish Writing and Thought in German Culture 1096–1996* (New Haven & London: Yale UP, 1997), 159.

[7] The first set of *Dorfgeschichten* is published in *Berthold Auerbach's gesammelte Schriften*, vols. 1–2.

[8] Berthold Auerbach, "Vorreden spart Nachreden," *Berthold Auerbach's gesammelte Schriften*, 1:vii. For Auerbach's attempt to speak to the nation through regional stories see Wolfgang Seidenspinner, "Oralisierte Schriftlichkeit als Stil: Das Literarische Genre Dorfgeschichte und die Kategorie Mündlichkeit," *Internationales Archiv für Sozialgeschichte der deutschen Literatur*, 22:2 (1997 [1998]): 36–51.

[9] McInnes, 96.

[10] McInnes, 99.

[11] McInnes, 108. McInnes believes, however, that Auerbach's liberal ideology, which emphasized the combined efforts of individuals to reform society, led to his "failure to record the full severity of the poverty affecting the rural communities." This was not only a humanitarian failure, as Moses Hess suggested, but an artistic failure; McInnes, 110.

[12] Horch, 161.

[13] Letter to Ferdinand Freiligrath, cited in *Marbacher Magazin Sonderheft* 36 (1985): 49.

[14] In addition to Bettelheim and Jakob Auerbach, sources for this biographical synopsis are M. I. Zwick, *Berthold Auerbach's sozialpolitischer und ethischer Liberalismus: Nach seinen Schriften dargestellt* (Stuttgart: Kohlhammer, 1933); Nancy A. Kaiser, "Berthold Auerbach," in James Hardin and Siegfried Mews, eds., *Dictionary of Literary Biography*, vol. 133: *Nineteenth-Century German Writers to 1840* (Detroit: Gale Research, 1993), 114–19; and Horch, 158–63.

[15] Michael A. Meyer, *The Origins of the Modern Jew: Jewish Identity and European Culture in Germany, 1749–1824* (Detroit: Wayne State UP, 1967), 8.

[16] I only have the revised editions of the collected works at my disposal. This is not unduly problematic for my analysis, however, because the mature Auerbach believed his revisions clarified his ideas.

[17] David Sorkin, "The Jewish Community: Emancipation, Secular Culture, and Jewish Identity in the Writings of Berthold Auerbach," in Jehuda Reinharz and Walter Schatzberg, eds., *The Jewish Response to German Culture* (Hanover & London: UP of New England, 1985), 107.

[18] Jonathan Skolnik, "Writing Jewish History between Gutzkow and Goethe: Auerbach's *Spinoza* and the Birth of Modern Jewish Historical Fiction," *Prooftexts* 19 (1999): 107. Skolnik uses Spinoza's fantasized encounter with

the Wandering Jew, Ahasuerus, in the epilogue as his point of departure: "The death of the Wandering Jew in Auerbach's historical novel marks the beginning of something new: the birth of a secular Jewish literature in a Western language," 104.

[19] Ismar Schorsch, *From Text to Context: The Turn to History in Modern Judaism* (Hanover NH & London: Brandeis UP, published by UP of New England, 1994), 71–82.

[20] Berthold Auerbach, trans., *B. de Spinoza's sämmtliche Werke aus dem lateinischen mit einer Lebensgeschichte Spinoza's,* 2nd rev. ed., 2 vols. (Stuttgart: Cotta, 1871).

[21] Horch states that Auerbach remained aesthetically indebted to the Young German novel of ideas, 161.

[22] The account of Spinoza's love for Olympia is not historical, although when Auerbach wrote the first edition of this novel based on a biography by Jean Colerus, he believed it to be true. B. Auerbach, trans., *B. De Spinoza's Sämmtliche Werke,* xxviii.

[23] Horch, 160.

[24] Commenting on this passage, Schorsch maintains that Auerbach portrays Spinoza as a reincarnation of Maimonides, 81–82.

[25] In my previous study, "Berthold Auerbach's *Dichter und Kaufmann:* Enlightenment Thought and Jewish Identity," *Lessing Yearbook* 19 (1987): 267–85, I make several of the same points. The current study, however, emphasizes the relationship between Auerbach's novels.

[26] Ashkenaz is "the medieval Jewish designation for the world between Cologne and Strasbourg that expanded as the Jews from this area moved south toward Rome, east toward Vienna and Lvov," *Yale Companion to Jewish Writing and Thought in German Culture 1096–1996,* xviii.

[27] David Sorkin, "Jews, the Enlightenment and Religious Toleration — Some Reflections," *Yearbook for the Leo Baeck Institute* 37 (1992): 7.

[28] Sorkin, 8–9.

[29] Auerbach, *Das Landhaus am Rhein* (Stuttgart: Cotta, 1869). Cited in the text by volume and page number.

[30] M. Kayserling, *Der Dichter Ephraim Kuh* (Berlin: Springer, 1864), and Hans Rhotert, "Ephraim Moses Kuh" (Diss. U of Munich, 1927).

[31] Ritchie Robertson, *The "Jewish Question" in German Literature 1749–1939: Emancipation and its Discontents* (London & New York: Oxford UP, 1999), 89.

[32] Deeply shaken when Ephraim tells him about his father's persecution, Moses Mendelssohn underscores the tenacity of this libel by recalling that Rabbi Menasse ben Israel had taken a solemn oath that a Jew could never carry out

such a practice before the English Parliament during Cromwell's era (13: 43–44). Salomon Maimon's grandfather may have served as the model for Moses Daniel, for Auerbach incorporates several anecdotes from Maimon's autobiography — *Lebensgeschichte*, 2 vols., ed. K. P. Moritz (Berlin: Vieweg, 1972) — into this novel. Heine also depicts a "blood-libel" scene in his novel fragment "Der Rabbi von Bacherach" (The Rabbi from Bacherach, 1840).

[33] Alexander Altmann characterizes the historical Mendelssohn as "the patron saint of German Jewry." He was revered as the first Jew to identify himself with the cultural concerns of Germany and as the first Jewish philosopher in modern times. He was steadfast in his allegiance to the Jewish faith, and fought for civil rights. "Moses Mendelssohn as Archetypical German Jew," in *The Jewish Response to German Culture*, 17–31.

[34] George L. Mosse, *German Jews beyond Judaism* (Bloomington: Indiana UP / Cincinnati: Hebrew Union College, 1985), 10.

[35] Auerbach, *Das Judenthum und die neueste Literatur* (Stuttgart: Brodhag, 1836), 22.

[36] "Gabriel Riesser," in Auerbach and N. Frankfurter, eds., *Gallerie der ausgezeichneten Israeliten aller Jahrhunderte, ihre Porträts und Biographien* (Stuttgart: Brodhag, 1836), 5–42.

[37] Auerbach, *Das Judenthum und die neueste Literatur*, 51.

[38] Jacob Katz, "Berthold Auerbach's Anticipation of the Jewish Tragedy," *Hebrew Union College Annual* 53 (1982): 225.

[39] For an analysis of Auerbach's nonfiction writings on Jewish identity see also Heidi Thomann Tewarson, "Die Aufklärung im jüdischen Denken des 19. Jahrhunderts," *Forum Vormärz Forschung Jahrbuch* (1998): 44–51.

[40] Zwick, *passim*, but esp. 13–25.

[41] Horch, "Auerbach's First Collection of *Dorfgeschichten*," 158.

[42] Nitsa Ben-Ari, "The Jewish Historical Novel," in *Yale Companion to Jewish Writing and Thought*, 147.

[43] Letter to Heinrich König cited in *Marbacher Sonderheft*, 65.

[44] Berthold Auerbach, *Ein neues Leben, Gesammelte Schriften*, vols. 14–16.

[45] Berthold Auerbach, *Das Landhaus am Rhein*, 4th ed., 3 vols. (Stuttgart: Cotta, 1874). Cited in the text by volume and page number.

[46] Berthold Auerbach, *Waldfried: eine vaterländische Familiengeschichte*, 6 vols. (Stuttgart: J. G. Cotta, 1874).

[47] Both Horch, "Gustav Freytag and Berthold Auerbach — eine repräsentive deutsch-jüdische Schriftstellerfreundschaft im 19. Jahrhundert," *Jahrbuch der Raabe-Gesellschaft* (1985): 154–74, and Margarita Pazi, "Wie gleicht man

auch ethisch Soll und Haben aus?" *Zeitschrift für deutsche Philologie* 106, no. 2 (1987): 204–5, discuss Auerbach's and Freytag's friendship, although they interpret its dynamic differently.

[48] Bettelheim, 238–39.

[49] Pazi, 204–5.

[50] Jeffrey L. Sammons, *Wilhelm Raabe and the Fiction of the Alternative Community* (Princeton: Princeton UP, 1987), 76.

[51] Auerbach, *Auf der Höhe: Roman in acht Büchern,* 4th ed., 3 vols. (Stuttgart: Cotta, 1866). Cited in the text by volume and page number.

[52] Patricia B. Herminghouse, "Schloß oder Fabrik? Zur Problematik der Adelsdarstellung im Roman des Nachmärz," in Leslie Adelson, Peter Uwe Hohendahl, and Paul Michael Lützeler, eds., *Legitimationskrisen des deutschen Adels 1200–1900* (Stuttgart: Metzler, 1979), 245–61.

[53] Ernest K. Bramsted, *Aristocracy and the Middle-Classes in Germany: Social Types in German Literature 1830–1900,* 2nd rev. ed. (Chicago & London: U Chicago P, 1964), 109.

[54] Kaiser, "Berthold Auerbach: The Dilemma of the Jewish Humanist from *Vormärz* to Empire," *German Studies Review* 6:3 (1983): 414, citing Franz Röhse, *Konflikt und Versöhnung: Untersuchungen zur Theorie des Romans von Hegel bis zum Naturalismus* (Stuttgart: Metzler, 1978), 161–75.

[55] Werner Hahl, *Reflexion und Erzählung: Ein Problem der Romantheorie von der Spätaufklärung bis zum programmatischen Realismus* (Stuttgart: Kohlhammer, 1971), 200–42, esp. 206.

[56] Bettelheim, 308.

[57] *Marbacher Magazin Sonderheft,* 79.

[58] Cf. Sammons, *Ideology, Mimesis, Fantasy: Charles Sealsfield, Friedrich Gerstäcker, Karl May, and Other German Novelists of America* (Chapel Hill & London: U of North Carolina P, 1998), 258–59.

[59] Kaiser finds *Erziehungsroman* a more applicable term. "Berthold Auerbach: The Dilemma of the Jewish Humanist from *Vormärz* to Empire," 413. I consider it a partial Bildungsroman because the *tutor* is going through a process of *Bildung*.

[60] The novel presents the reverse of *Neues Leben,* whose theme is the education of the peasantry. David Friedrich Strauss wrote Friedrich Theodor Vischer that he did not find the education of an over-rich youth to be a well-chosen subject and thought Auerbach was losing foot with the novel's didacticism.

[61] Kaiser, "Berthold Auerbach," 15.

[62] Sammons, *Ideology, Mimesis, Fantasy,* 259.

[64] Bramsted, 110–14. Bramsted considers Freytag's *Soll und Haben* more successful in terms of realistic observation because Auerbach reflects, whereas Freytag describes. More recently, Robert C. Holub has disputed that this novel — lauded for its depiction of German people at work — actually shows business dealings: *Reflections of Realism: Paradox, Norm, and Ideology in Nineteenth-Century German Prose* (Detroit: Wayne State UP, 1991), 180.

[64] Fanny Lewald, too, equated the liberation of the serfs in Russia, the emancipation of the slaves in the United States, and the emancipation of the Jews as the three liberatory events of the nineteenth century.

[65] The concept for this jury might be derived from Friedrich Gerstäcker's *Die Regulatoren in Arkansas* (The Regulators of Arkansas, 1846).

[66] Auerbach, *Waldfried: Eine vaterländische Familiengeschichte*, 6 vols. (Stuttgart: Cotta, 1874).

[67] Bettelheim, 375.

[68] Bettelheim, 375–76.

[69] Bettelheim, 376.

[70] Döllinger was a former Catholic bishop who had been excommunicated for his refusal to conform to the doctrine of papal infallibility, Gordon A. Craig, *The Germans* (New York & Scarborough, Ont.: New American Library, 1982), 93.

[71] Bettelheim, 376. I am deeply grateful to my writing group, Katherine A. Jensen, Michelle Massé, and Anna Nardo, for reading portions of this study, for their many helpful suggestions, and for their encouragement.

E. Marlitt: Narratives of Virtuous Desire

Kirsten Belgum

E MARLITT WAS A CONTEMPORARY of the male authors typically considered German realists. She was born in the middle of the generation of realist writers, within ten years of Keller, Freytag, Meyer, Storm, Raabe, Spielhagen, and Fontane, and her writing career (spanning the 1860s, 1870s, and 1880s) overlapped with that of most of those authors. Like many of the works of her male contemporaries, Marlitt's novels are set in her day; most of them explicitly thematize specific contemporary social and political issues, such as the stock-market crash of the 1870s, Bismarck's "*Kulturkampf,*" and technological innovation. Her narratives depict plausible characters and are occasionally based on actual events. Her settings and scenes are described in extensive detail, and almost all of her novels take place in a clearly identifiable Thuringian landscape that Marlitt knew intimately, often in her hometown of Arnstadt. Yet, despite these similarities, Marlitt's works have not generally been included in the canon of nineteenth-century German realism. With a few exceptions, Marlitt has for most of the last 100 years been a rather peripheral figure in scholarship on realism.[1]

This study examines that peripheral status and analyzes what other scholars have overlooked in Marlitt's work. In the process, it also aims to contribute to our understanding of realism and how it functions in a variety of ways. Works of German realism have traditionally been evaluated according to two measures. On the one hand, they are seen as adhering more closely than other literature to the stuff of real life, striving for verisimilitude. On the other hand, scholars have noted the tendency in works of German realism to harmonize or, as Otto Ludwig proposed for a "poetic realism," to idealize the details of the real world.[2] I contend that a third, but less acknowledged, aspect of realist fiction is the powerful element of fantasy and wish fulfillment. Although this is typically seen as a marker of popular literature, I hope to show that it is closely tied to other realist characteristics. To do this I will turn to Marlitt and examine one of her novels in detail. This is not an attempt to "rescue" Marlitt from the label of popular literature, but rather an attempt to show what a serious reading of her novels can tell us about realism and its relationship to desire.[3]

Marlitt and Her Reception

Friederike Henriette Christiane Eugenie John, who later took the pen name E. Marlitt, was born on December 5, 1825, to a small businessman (her father ran a lending library) and a woman from a well-to-do family. She first came on the literary scene in 1865 as the author of a short story published in the popular family magazine *Die Gartenlaube*. The following year both a second story and her first novel, *Goldelse*, were serialized in the same magazine, and from that point on E. Marlitt was touted as a star author by the magazine's editors and its audience alike. During the next two decades, Marlitt published eight more novels in *Die Gartenlaube* and subsequently in book editions.[4] The interesting story of who Marlitt was and how she came to write has been told and retold by many scholars and chroniclers.[5] I would like to tell it here in the form similar to the one Marlitt used: that of the romance narrative. My purpose in doing so is both to show the autobiographical quality of Marlitt's work and to point out that the heroines of her novels, who patiently and diligently struggle against social barriers and malicious enemies, are modeled on Marlitt's own experiences. Here is her story:

Our heroine, E. Marlitt, early in life exhibits intelligence and artistic talent and is encouraged by her father to consider a life beyond the confines of the home. Supported by teachers, she dreams of becoming a singer and, especially after her father experiences a severe financial crisis, of helping to support her family. Her dream takes off when Princess Mathilde von Schwarzburg-Sondershausen agrees to finance her study at a music academy in Vienna. Marlitt's training is good and her singing future promising; she performs in several cities until stage fright and a hearing ailment cut short her career. A few years later she receives a second "chance" as the social companion of and reader to the princess, an occupation that introduces her to the life (and bitter jealousies) of the nobility. After a decade of service, Marlitt is released when the princess, who has been divorced, has to reduce her expenditures. In 1863 our heroine thus returns to her Thuringian hometown to live in tight quarters with her brother's family. Nearing age forty, Marlitt, who is already suffering from severe arthritis, seems to have failed in her aspirations of pursuing a professional career and becoming financially independent. Her future seems bleak, and she turns inward. Soon, however, she renews another creative interest: writing. In 1865 one of her first submissions to Ernst Keil's *Die Gartenlaube* is accepted for publication, and within a year her fiction earns her an unprecedentedly large audience through that periodical. Our heroine becomes a national sensation and is soon on her way to being the most popular author of her day. Every installment of her subsequent novels is awaited by an unprecedented number of devoted readers with intense anticipation. Marlitt, who never marries, becomes wealthy, builds a villa for herself and her extended family, and, most important, becomes a household name and role model for millions of Germans. She dies in June 1887 at age sixty-one, having lived the story of victory over adversity; hers is a tale of the triumph of a strong will and a large heart.

Following her own life, Marlitt's fictional stories generally recount the tale of a young woman overcoming hardship, maintaining her virtue and moral standards in the face of a society filled with fraudulence, greed, and even lust. Each story begins with a girl or young woman who is limited by some external force, such as a rigid guardian or lack of money. This problem serves as the backdrop for a characterization of the heroine's strength of will, determination, and moral stamina. Through the ensuing confrontation with other characters, the protagonist achieves important victories that demonstrate her virtues, as well as her undaunted activism on behalf of less-fortunate individuals (the downtrodden). The struggle is not brief; her successes are interspersed with apparent failures, including, most importantly, her own inability to understand her desire for the man who gradually emerges as her counterpart. The heroine's persistence, however, eventually triumphs, *and* in the arms of a man she finds happiness she presumed she would never attain.

The most noticeable aspect of Marlitt's reception was her unprecedented popularity. Ernst Keil, editor and publisher of the *Gartenlaube* from its beginning in 1853 to his death in 1878, was, from his first encounter with Marlitt's work, an unwavering fan.[6] To be sure, Keil's literary interest in Marlitt cannot be distinguished from his financial interests. After the resounding success of her first novel, *Goldelse* (Gold Elsie, 1866), the first novel by any author serialized in the *Gartenlaube,* Keil pushed Marlitt to produce more novels as fast as she could. But if we are to take him at his word, he sincerely appreciated both her style and her political commitment to liberalism and German unification.

Without Keil's support, Marlitt would certainly never have found the audience she gained so quickly. Given his early encouragement, she remained committed to publishing only in his magazine even after his death. The size of Marlitt's readership and, thus, the extent of her popularity can be deduced from several factors: the circulation of the *Gartenlaube,* the presumption that each of these issues was generally read by several individuals, and the editions of her novels, which were quickly published as independent volumes.[7] At the very least, her devotees numbered in the hundreds of thousands if not more than a million. Beyond the statistics, anecdotal evidence such as readers' letters to the *Gartenlaube* and fan mail to Marlitt herself suggests that her readers in Germany spanned the middle and lower middle classes and included mostly women, but also many men, from a wide range of age groups, from young household servants to the elderly (*Gartenlaube,* 1868, 208).

Several literary contemporaries of Marlitt praised aspects of her style. The critic Rudolf Gottschall, who also contributed to the *Gartenlaube,* noted Marlitt's gift of narration, as well as a talent for depiction.[8] Levin Schücking, who as a young man had worked with the respected Annette von Droste-Hülshoff, wrote, perhaps comparatively: "Die Marlitt ist ein Erzählertalent, wie es noch keine Frau in Deutschland entwickelt hat, sie ist in manchen Dingen wirklich gross. Namentlich in zwei Dingen, in der Psychologie des Frauenherzens und in dem, was ich Kolorit nenne."[9] Their praise, however, was not unequivocal. Gottschall saw a repetitive pattern, what he called a Cinderella motif in all of Marlitt's early novels,[10] and Schücking noted that, although he took his hat off to such a genius, he had his reservations.[11] By the 1880s critical voices became increasingly audible. Friedrich Friedrich (himself the author of more than seventy volumes of popular literature) attacked Marlitt as immoral and incapable. Gottfried Keller ridiculed this "knabenhafter Angriff" proclaiming Marlitt a hundred times better than her critic.[12] The most vocal and public rebuttals to this criticism came from Marlitt's family and the *Gartenlaube*, which included testimonials from common readers such as a letter from "a worker" to Marlitt's brother shortly after her death: "ich habe die Geistesgaben unserer Dichterin stets mit Andacht gelesen und mich in den verschiedenen Lebensaltern daran erbaut und aufgerichtet."[13]

It can thus be supposed that negative reviews and moralizing criticism of Marlitt's works had little impact on her status in the eyes of her readers. Yet, the dominance of negative evaluations of Marlitt's work among literary scholars can be seen in the lack of any serious treatment of Marlitt in literary histories throughout the first half of the twentieth century. In the forward to her 1926 dissertation Bertha Potthast apologetically emphasizes that she selected E. Marlitt as the subject for analysis because of the popular author's cultural-historical significance, not because her works possess any intrinsic aesthetic value.[14]

The renewed interest in Marlitt in the 1970s and 1980s came in the context of growing attention to popular literature or "*Trivialliteratur*."[15] Scholars acknowledged that the canon of German literary history did not overlap with what most of the readers in the past 200 years had read. In an attempt to give voice to those readers' choices, while not necessarily revising the literary canon, many tried to come to terms with what they labeled "trivial" literature. This frequently meant finding categories that explained the characteristics of such literature and accounting for its popularity, while continuing to ridicule it for its inferior language and structure. For George L. Mosse, the popular fiction of Marlitt is a dream world that had little to do with reality. As such, it exemplifies the provincial nature of nineteenth-century Germany and German culture.[16] Michael Kienzle's condemnation of Marlitt's works barely acknowledges the "female" interests represented in them. Rather, Kienzle cites Marlitt as an example of "middle-class experiences and petit-bourgeois mentality" reproducing itself in popular literature.[17] Borrowing from Marx and Althusser, Kienzle argues that popular literature as entertainment plays a key function in the process of the conceptual reproduction of existing social relations (86). Jochen Schulte-Sasse and Renate Werner also view Marlitt's work as a paradigmatic subject for an examination of *Trivialliteratur* because of its popularity, and, like Kienzle, they aspire to make the social function of such trivial texts transparent.[18] This function, they argue, consisted in presenting a conservative, backward looking utopia that could reassure lower-middle-class readers who had been made insecure by processes of modernization (408–9). This utopia was defined by the moral victory of positive (that is, family-oriented, community-minded, antimaterialist) characters over negative ones who value social climbing, money, and themselves more than concern for others. While allowing her novel a small element of protest, Schulte-Sasse and Werner conclude that the compensatory and conservative function of Marlitt's *Im Hause des Kommerzienrates* (At the Councillor's, 1876) allowed readers to experience their existence and relationship to the larger social order as meaningful (428–29).

Several scholars began to pay attention to Marlitt and her works in the context of assessing the formula that made the nineteenth-century middle-class family magazine *Die Gartenlaube* extraordinarily popular by the 1870s.[19] Additionally, in the wake of a growing interest in feminist criticism in German literary scholarship there was a renewed interest in Marlitt both as a woman author and as an author of the so-called *Frauenroman*, a topic first investigated in 1926 by Potthast, whose subtitle read "Ein Beitrag zur Geschichte des deutschen Frauenromans." Gabriele Strecker included Marlitt in her 1969 work on the German woman's novel that focused on the astonishing continuity of form and material in popular women's texts.[20] More recently, feminist scholars of literature have incorporated works by Marlitt into their investigation of the nineteenth century, and several dissertations have been devoted to Marlitt's works and her role as a female author.[21] Another approach to Marlitt that has emerged recently might best be described as a renewal of her regional relevance. As a kind of "*Heimatautor*" Marlitt has become the focus of a support group [*Interessengemeinschaft*] in her hometown of Arnstadt, Thuringia, over the last fifteen years.[22] This is part of a movement to rescue her from the label of popular literature and acknowledge her importance alongside other nineteenth-century Thuringian authors, such as Otto Ludwig and Willibald Alexis.[23]

Reevaluation of Marlitt Based on *Die Frau mit den Karfunkelsteinen*

The most common criticism of Marlitt is that her characters are schematic, black-and-white characterizations. They are either good (and then all good) or bad (and then consistently mean-spirited, cruel, selfish, self-absorbed).[24] Even some scholars, such as Astrid Bazzanella, who have looked to Marlitt as a creator of positive, strong, and emancipated female role models, have seen her female characters as divided between the disappointing alternatives of satanic witches or spotless saints.[25] Yet, because such standard readings, including feminist explorations of Marlitt's female characters, focus mainly on the division between positive and negative characters, they miss the narrative development that is central to her novels. Indeed, I argue that the success and appeal of Marlitt's novels lies not in the static oppositions between good and evil but, rather, in the works' dynamic. This dynamic consists (in most of the novels) of a gradual evolution in a few key characters. The character who is typically the least predictable (that is, the least easy to define and pinpoint at the outset) is the male hero, the eventual love interest of the heroine. In the course of the novel he comes into ever sharper relief as an appropriate and desirable partner for the morally upstanding heroine. Although he may not actually change, the heroine's perception of him shifts dramatically. This shift is usually preceded by the narrator's increasingly favorable view of the hero in a move to encourage the reader's sympathy. In doing so, the narrator alerts the reader to the gradually emerging desire of the heroine for this male character. The conclusion of the novel rests on the heroine's own complete recognition of her attraction to him and on her eventual acceptance of him as deserving of her love.

To make this case I have chosen to focus on *Die Frau mit den Karfunkelsteinen* (The Lady with the Rubies, 1884), a novel that has received less scholarly attention than other works of Marlitt's.[26] It was also the last novel that Marlitt was able to finish before her death. In other words, although it may not be judged her most popular work, it was, by definition, her most mature one. For that reason, I pay particular attention to elements of this novel that differ from earlier works, such as the independence and future activity of the heroine after her "engagement" to the hero at the end of the novel.[27]

Die Frau mit den Karfunkelsteinen was Marlitt's ninth novel in fewer than twenty years. It bears similarities to her other works in that its protagonist is a strong-willed young daughter in an upper-middle-class family. When the novel begins, Margarete is nine and living in a large house with her father, younger brother, maternal grandmother, her stepuncle (the stepbrother of her deceased mother), and Aunt Sophie, whose exact relation to the other members of the family remains vague — "die letzte einer Seitenlinie der Familie" (8). It soon becomes clear that Margarete is at odds with many of her own family members. She seems to have a good relationship with her father and her maternal grandfather, and her loyal supporter and ally is Aunt Sophie. But her young brother is willful and malicious in his treatment of her, her grandmother is highly critical of all she does and of what she is, and her stepuncle, Herbert, a gymnasium student preparing for his exams, appears insulted by his niece and condescending toward her.

From the beginning of the novel Margarete is a resolute, independent-minded character. She pays little heed to typical feminine conventions: she is outspoken, thrills in racing a small wagon pulled by two goats against her father's steed, and cares nothing for fancy dresses and fragile clothes.[28] She is decidedly not superstitious, finding several rational explanations for supposed "sightings" of a ghostly "lady with the rubies" in the abandoned part of the family's house. Most significant, in my view, is the fact that she rejects the traditional feminine education of a boarding or finishing school for girls and, instead, eventually leaves home for five years with her great-uncle, who is an archaeologist, and great-aunt, traveling as far abroad as Greece and Egypt learning about ancient cultures and art.

Margarete (backed by Sophie) stands in sharp contrast to her grandmother's ambitious adoration of nobility and power. Even as a child she is as liberal-minded and compassionate toward others (in particular, toward the lower-class individuals who work for her father) as she is independent. She stands by the Lenz family, the elderly porcelain painter and his wife, who live in the packing house, a back house attached to the villa. She adores their beautiful daughter, and years later, when their young grandson appears apparently from nowhere, she treats him like a younger brother. She speaks out against the superficiality of the nobility and resents her grandmother's adulation of local aristocrats. She rejects a noble suitor for herself, arguing, against her grandmother's insistence, that she is not yet ready for marriage. When her father dies suddenly, having hinted to her alone about a dark secret he has carried with him, her main charge seems to be moderating her younger brother's ruthless new management of the firm and the household. Her search for truth ultimately uncovers her father's secret: that he had been clandestinely married to the beautiful young woman from the packing house, who had been perceived, on her frequent trips to his rooms via an abandoned wing of the villa, as the ghostly "lady with the rubies," and that the Lenzes' grandson is thus, indeed, her stepbrother. Through this whole process the attentions and attraction of her stepuncle Herbert, ten years her elder, have grown. He has become increasingly struck by her charm, honor, and nobility of soul.

Before we examine this concluding love interest more closely, let us consider the key themes of this novel that not only helped to account for Marlitt's great popularity with a broad middle-class readership but also link her to other realist writers of her age. As I have already mentioned, Marlitt was proud of her connection to the liberal politics for which the *Gartenlaube* stood. This liberalism was in part a critique of the increasingly outdated nobility, but it was also an enlightened stance that defined middle-class values in opposition to social prejudice, provincialism, and irrationality in any form and in any social class. Marlitt's commitment to these values emerges in three themes that are central to *Die Frau mit den Karfunkelsteinen*. The first two themes are also common to the novels of male realist authors; the third unites Marlitt with the generation of early German feminist authors.

The first theme presented in this last novel (as in many of her others) is the struggle of rational thought and reason against ignorance and superstition. The narration begins with images of Aunt Sophie's bleaching day and the attendant motifs of sunlight, whiteness, cleanliness, and enlightenment. The brilliant sun and the activity of bleaching linens in the open air contrast with the closed rooms with curtained windows in the back wing of the house, which holds a dark family history: in 1795 the beautiful young wife of Herr Justus Lamprecht died in childbirth. The cause of her death, according to local legend, was the ghost of Lamprecht's first wife. This wife, it seems, had on her deathbed forced an oath from her husband never to remarry. This oath thus came back to haunt him and his second wife. Ever since her death, even into the time of Justus's great-grandchildren, townspeople and the servants in the Lamprecht household had believed and "seen" the sad phantom of the second wife, the "lady with the rubies," float past windows, rustle curtains, and so forth. The enlightened Aunt Sophie, the woman of sun and bleached whiteness, rejects this superstitious chatter. The same holds for her protégé, Margarete, who, when told by the housekeeper, Bärbe, that one should not even look toward those windows, counters that seeing is knowing: "Abergläubische alte Bärbe. . . . Erst recht muß man hinsehen! Ich will wissen, wer das gewesen ist!" (25). Unlike her brother, who is easily frightened by spooky tales, Margarete looks for rational explanations and eventually for solutions. The novel concludes on this same theme, with a nervous Bärbe worried about the future of the last Lamprecht heir. Marlitt thus shares the exploration of superstition in nineteenth-century society with canonical realist authors such as Keller and Storm.

The novel's central theme, one common to all of Marlitt's novels, is the victory of human kindness and considerateness over prejudice and social convention. While the lower-class characters, such as domestic servants, are the most susceptible to superstition, it is the upper-middle-class characters who are most harshly criticized for bearing prejudices against the lower middle class and mindlessly following the standards established by the nobility. Margarete consistently rejects the formality of courtly etiquette and feels that her grandmother is demeaned by her groveling attempts to curry favor with the local aristocracy. She ridicules her stepuncle, Herbert, as a man solely in pursuit of political influence and power, suspecting him of seeking an aristocratic wife in order to further his career. As an adult she is outraged by her brother's stinginess and obsession with guarding the family's wealth. Even her father, whom she adores and admires as a child, is revealed to have been bound by the class prejudice of high society.

Margarete's rebellion against social convention begins in childhood and persists into adulthood. She rejects a marriage proposal by a northern aristocrat, preferring to remain independent and unfettered. She refuses, contrary to her grandmother's wishes, to be introduced to the local nobility. In contrast to many of those around her, her actions are uniformly motivated by attempts to help those who are less fortunate than herself. She knows the workers in her father's porcelain factory and dares to maintain contact with the Lenz family in defiance of her grandmother's and brother's orders. When she learns of Mrs. Lenz's illness, she sneaks through the ghostly back wing to bring food to the woman. Margarete summarizes the problems of upper-middle-class society in tirades against the negative aspects of modern life: "der Servilismus, die Machtanbetung, das ungenierte Buhlen um die Gnade einflußreicher Persönlichkeiten, das waren jetzt die Gespenster im Lamprechtshause, gegen die sie sich ihres Leibes und Lebens zu wehren hatte!" (101).

As this quotation from the end of chapter 8 reveals, the social criticism of the novel is connected to the aforementioned motifs of enlightenment and superstition. The figure who ties them together is Blanka Lenz, the daughter of the porcelain painter. Blanka's name (meaning "white") corresponds to her dress, her attraction to white roses, and her idealized purity. She appears initially as the schoolboy love interest of Margarete's stepuncle, Herbert. Later, we learn that the apparent arrogance of Margarete's father toward the Lenzes and their house was his attempt to hide his own love for Blanka from the public eye. It turns out that the two were married, and that Blanka's presence in the unused wing of the main house was the actual cause of the mysterious "sightings" of the "lady with the rubies." Thus, ironically, Margarete's father has been perpetrating a modern "superstition": as Margarete later describes it, he was blinded by social prejudice; he acted unkindly and inhumanely out of servility, a fear of failing in the eyes of high society. Because of this fear, he never openly acknowledged his love for Blanka, their marriage, or their son (who was born abroad after Blanka left home). Thus, the "dark powers" that are mentioned on the last page of the novel, which allude to continued superstition, are also Marlitt's name for the ruthlessness of social convention (326). This concern links Marlitt to realists such as Fontane or Raabe, whose novels also condemned the harsh and at times inhuman rigidity of social conventions.

The third theme of *Die Frau mit den Karfunkelsteinen* is less common in works by male realist authors but, rather, has its predecessors in such feminist novels of the 1840s as Fanny Lewald's *Jenny* (1843) and Louise Aston's *Aus dem Leben einer Frau* (Out of the Life of a Woman, 1847). Marlitt's novel practically preaches women's independence, and by beginning when the protagonist is only nine years old it even depicts a scenario for independent female development. Margarete first learns under the tutelage of Aunt Sophie. Then, against her father's and grandmother's wishes, she chooses her own educational path, rejecting the traditional finishing school for girls and electing instead, at age fourteen, to learn as an apprentice from a scholar of archaeology and ancient history, her great-uncle. Together with him and her great-aunt she travels the world. This education not only affects her view of her former surroundings, opening her eyes to architectural and historical detail (85).[29] It also causes a change in her appearance; she explains (in the face of her grandmother's recriminations) that she cut her hair because it interfered with her archaeological work (105). Style and fashion give way to utility and convenience for this modern woman; she boasts: "Ich hätte mich kahl geschoren, wenn es nötig gewesen wäre" (106).[30]

Many critics have noted this initial independence in Marlitt's heroines, only to see them apparently renounce this self-reliance at the end of the novel, as soon as they find their men. Indeed, in *Im Hause des Kommerzienrates* Käthe, the young woman who has been running the family mill on her own throughout the novel, is asked by the doctor she is about to marry to close her account books for good. The novel achieves a certain closure when she accedes. Yet, placing too much emphasis on this element does a disservice to the extensive and undeniably liberating images of independence (both financial and intellectual) that each of Marlitt's heroines provides for 300 to 400 pages. In these novels marriage is the appropriate reward (desirable for the time) for the woman's strength of character. There is nothing in the novels to lead the reader to think that these strong women will cease speaking their minds, standing up for what they believe in, and fighting courageously for liberal causes as they have all along. Their outspokenness and self-reliance is vindicated in these marriages to likeminded men, not taken back.

This criticism of Marlitt's heroines based solely on the novels' conclusions ignores the substance of each story; her female protagonists manage to save lives (*Goldelse*), expose sinister authorities, be they Jesuit priests or aristocrats (*Die zweite Frau* [The Second Wife, 1879]), and assist the poor and needy (*Im Hause des Kommerzienrates*) not because they are passive women waiting to be rescued from maidenhood by manly husbands but because they are determined and undaunted, even in the face of personal danger (*Das Haideprinzeßchen* [The Little Moorland Princess, 1872], *Die zweite Frau*). In the process, they frequently take on the task of convincing a skeptical man that an intelligent, rational, outspoken, active, and determined woman is the best partner for an enlightened and moral man.

Furthermore, in Marlitt's last novel there is no mention of the heroine's withdrawal from her public role. Margarete has achieved lasting victories: she has persuaded her ailing grandfather (her longstanding ally) to move back into the house, while her grandmother (who disapproves of the marriage and of the Lenz boy's inclusion in the family) retreats to Berlin. The final scene of the novel portrays a new, idealized, and unconventional family: the grandfather; his son, Herbert; Aunt Sophie; the housekeeper, Bärbe; the Lenz grandparents and grandson; and Margarete. Rather than being absorbed by a man and domesticated, the heroine has succeeded, thanks to her activism throughout the novel, in creating an open, cross-class and multigenerational family of like-minded souls. Margarete is, indeed, engaged to Herbert by the end of the novel, but it seems that this impending marriage will leave her at the head of this new family she has created.

More important, to read Marlitt's novels as paeans to marriage by overemphasizing the narrative closure is to misread much of the rest of each work. In *Die Frau mit den Karfunkelsteinen* love is, indeed, a complicated and at times tragic thing for most of the characters. One of the main points of the novel, and its initial premise, is that a dying wife can doom her husband to unhappiness by obliging him to promise to remain faithful to her after her death. According to local superstition, Margarete's ancestor lost his second wife and child in childbirth because of his dead wife's revenge. But in Margarete's eyes, the unhappy fate of her father, Balduin Lamprecht, and his second wife turns out to be no less painful. Both unnecessarily die separately in grief and isolation. The marriage of Margarete's grandparents is also depicted as less than perfect: her grandfather does not even live in the main house, because his supercilious wife (and her parrot) drive him to distraction. At best, the partnership of Margarete's great-aunt and great-uncle, who collaborate in the archaeological trips and research, is a kind of model marriage, but it plays a minor role in the narrative.

Indeed, the happiest, most contented character in the novel is the confident, cheerful, supportive, liberal, and fiercely independent Aunt Sophie, who has never been and never plans to be married. Her tie to the family and reason for living in Balduin Lamprecht's house is not nearly as important in the logic of Marlitt's narrative as her forceful character, rational approach to life, and unlimited moral support of the young heroine. For the reader, this older woman is a model of optimism, rationality, good humor, and feminine independence. When the grandmother, upset by Margarete's stubborn support of the Lenzes, threatens to throw her granddaughter out of the house, Sophie counters that she has enough savings to afford a small cottage and that, of course, Margarete could live with her there (287). Although it never comes to this pass, clearly Margarete's safety net remains this older single woman.

Each of Marlitt's novels has such a figure. Since many of the heroines' mothers are absent, these older, occasionally socially isolated women function as advisors for the young protagonists. These are, perhaps, the truly radical feminist role models who have been neglected by previous Marlitt scholarship. They are independent and dismissive of social norms and prejudices, they possess strong minds and outspoken characters, and they are, above all, effective through their assistance to the female protagonists. Indeed, as much as Marlitt depicted aspects of her own life in her young heroines, the older female characters embodied her later role in life and hoped-for influence. By the age of forty-five she had achieved her childhood dream of being able to care for her family financially: her brother's family and her father moved with Marlitt into the villa she built with her earnings.[31] As a popular author she was able to be a mentor to thousands (if not millions) of young female readers, all potential heroines, many of whom no doubt looked to her stories for advice and guidance.[32]

But ultimately, it is the narration itself that provides these willing readers with the most profound lesson that Marlitt had to offer. Through the stance of the narrator, we come to see Marlitt's heroine develop and the potential hero grow in response. The female protagonists, who for the most part are consistently outspoken, independent, and fearless, change only in their ability to see their own desirability. The main male character eventually softens in the presence of this heroine and comes to see her as desirable precisely because of her moral rectitude and her behavior that is untraditional for a woman.

In *Die Frau mit den Karfunkelsteinen* Marlitt's partisan narrator supports the young female protagonist in her struggle against social injustice and prejudice. From the beginning of the novel Margarete clearly enjoys the sympathy of the narrator. She is described in typically unfeminine yet decidedly affectionate terms as "wild," "ungezügelt," "geradeheraus," "unverblümt," "närrisch," "streitlustig," "bestimmt," "scharfsinnig," and "mutwillig."[33] By contrast, her younger brother is characterized disparagingly as "weinerlich," "blaß und schmal," "ängstlich," "nervös," "unruhig," and "schlotterich."[34] The strengths of the heroine are also highlighted by an ironic narration. After Margarete has returned home a young, educated, and widely-traveled woman, she encounters skepticism on the part of Herbert to her extensive knowledge and liberal opinions about politics and society. "Und ich, ein Mädchen! Ein Mädchen, das acht Lot Gehirn weniger hat, als die Herren der Schöpfung, wie sollte ich mir darüber ein eigenes Urteil bilden und meinen eigenen Weg gehen wollen!" (139). This ironic reference to contemporary male underestimation of women's intellectual capacities is accentuated by Margarete's and Sophie's devious facial expressions.

Marlitt undercuts not only the stereotype of the unthinking, feeble-minded woman but also preconceptions about women's narrative traditions. Early in the novel, when Margarete insists to her father that she encountered a woman in the abandoned wing of the house, Balduin condescendingly accuses her of participating in "Fraubasen- und Spinnstubengeschichten" (50). The reader, however, already knowing Margarete to be a reasonable and rational girl, can disregard this attack as a defensive maneuver (50). A much later remark by Margarete's grandfather, that Margarete could have been switched at birth with a princess, can be seen as Marlitt's humorous allusion to critics' view of her work as "fairy tales." Unlike the stereotype of the Marlitt heroine as a "Cinderella," Margarete does not come into a fortune she never had; she is not revealed at the last minute to be a princess or of noble lineage. Rather, her evolution comes from a gradual recognition that her attraction to Herbert and her passionate love for him are not at odds with her political ideas and social commitment.

Thus, although Margarete's rationality and goodness do not change throughout the novel (a static aspect that many scholars have deprecated about Marlitt's characters), she does undergo a significant change in the course of the narration. As a young girl, Margarete is curious about the power of both the beautiful Blanka Lenz and the ghostly "Lady with the Rubies." Yet, as a naïve girl, naïve especially in love and about her own attractiveness, she cannot comprehend the role that Blanka and this spooky figure play for the male characters — even for her father, to whom she is very close. When she returns to her home as a young woman, however, she begins to enter the role of the "Lady with the Rubies": first examining her picture, then on a whim putting on her clothes and jewels. She also enters the space of Blanka (in the side wing of the house and eventually through increased contact with the Lenz family). Margarete's assertiveness and stubborn rationality will protect her from the fate of her ruby-wearing ancestor and the lovely Blanka Lenz. As an enlightened and confident young woman, she will not fall victim to the secretiveness born of superstition in which Justus Lamprecht and her father engaged. And yet, despite her intelligence and reason, Margarete cannot unlock the secret of these characters' stories. Until she is introduced to her own attraction to a man, she remains uncomprehending. The awakening of her sexual desire arrives with the help of the narrator.

If the narrator was Margarete's strong ally from the beginning of the novel, she begins to distance herself from Margarete as the novel progresses in order to give the reader signs of Herbert's attraction to his stepniece (which is synonymous with his growing respect for her). When her grandmother fears that Margarete's strong will and liberal ideals will scare off any appropriate male suitor, Herbert reproaches her, but only in Margarete's absence: "ein Mädchen wie Margarete wird begehrt werden, auch wenn ihr Vermögen noch so sehr zusammenschmilzt" (252). Aunt Sophie recognizes dramatic changes in Herbert: "er ist so herzlich, so zutraulich" (226). Toward the end of the novel Margarete begins to revise her opinion of Herbert as he helps her defend the rights of the poor Lenz family (268). With Herbert's assistance she solves the puzzle of her father's second marriage; yet, she proves more capable than he in opening the desk that houses the paper evidence of the marriage (300).

Despite his apparent adoption of her values, Margarete remains convinced that Herbert's career interests and socializing with the local aristocrats must lead to his engagement to a beautiful young noble lady. Increasingly, as the actions of Herbert toward Margarete change, the otherwise rational and competent Margarete becomes distracted and confused. She avoids his gaze (226), she comes close to tears with frustration about him (229), she turns her head away in silence (243). Toward the end of the novel her preoccupation with Herbert and his activities in the local palace is like a dream from which she awakens embarrassed (314). She wanders dazedly through a snowy landscape, imagines the happiness of the other woman, and is uncharacteristically paralyzed by the fear of being discovered "Einen Augenblick stand die Lauscherin wie gelähmt vor Schrecken" (318). In the moment Herbert discovers her, he teasingly forces her to admit her love for him and pledges his love for her. The novel ends at this point, because the purpose of the narrative has been achieved: the heroine has understood and accepted her desire for the hero.

That Margarete's gradual realization of her desire for Herbert coincides with a growing disorientation and insecurity of her character is not contradictory. Rather, I would contend that female desire is the most radical topic that Marlitt addresses in her novels. While the women's movement of the 1860s had begun to popularize ideas of women's education and even women's work, female sexual desire was still a taboo topic.[35] I argue that Marlitt's heroines are not weakest when confronted by a man; indeed, each of Marlitt's heroes must first prove himself worthy of love by openly adopting the heroine's political and social values. Margarete is confused not about Herbert but about her own desire. The resolution of Marlitt's novel resides not in the domestication of the heroine but in the release of tension in acknowledging this powerful force in her. Thus, Marlitt's appeal to her contemporary readers can be traced only in part to her depiction of moral, confident and principled young women. The other component that must have attracted her readers again and again was the opportunity they provided to live out the experience of desire.

Accepting Marlitt as a Realist, Feminist, and Popular Icon

As we have seen, many of Marlitt's characters (both the young heroines and their older unmarried mentors) bear close similarities to the historical Eugenie John who wrote and corresponded under the name E. Marlitt. In other words, despite the alleged fairy-tale element of her novels, Marlitt's own life proved that her tales were possible; the young, not traditionally attractive, yet talented girl with immense determination could make it on her own and become an influential advisor and a supporter of good and just causes. But beyond this testament to the verisimilitude and realism of Marlitt's novels, it seems indisputable that their staying power is linked to their ability to encourage and fulfill fantasies of desire in nineteenth-century readers.

E. Marlitt has long been acknowledged as a popular author, a star with a mass following of eager readers. She has also been celebrated as a woman who (against the odds) managed to establish herself as an important role model and icon; through her writing she became financially independent and more famous and influential than most middle-class women of her time could even imagine. Marlitt and her works are seldom included in discussions of realism, however, because realism has traditionally not been defined to include female fantasy. German realism has traditionally been a literature of male authors and their male bourgeois heroes. The ideals and goals articulated by Stifter's Heinrich Drendorf, Freytag's Anton Wohlfahrt, and Keller's Heinrich Lee have always been considered the central concerns of mid-nineteenth-century German letters, if not of German society as a whole. German literature did not have a Brontë or Sand, an Eliot or Austen who regularly depicted the lives and struggles of female characters in the same detail as those of male protagonists. Although Fontane included many women in his stories, even as title figures, rarely does one get a sense of these women being empowered by his plots; rather, they suffer in silence and denial (Lene Nimptsch) or die from struggling for freedom of movement (Effi Briest).

What does E. Marlitt do differently? To be sure, her works adhere to a clear pattern; all of her heroines are variations on a theme.[36] The pattern in her novels is consistent: a youthful heroine full of energy and enthusiasm is challenged by one or more selfish, mean-spirited opponents. She prevails, defying their apparent power and authority and ultimately finding her reward — sometimes in money, but always in love. What is less often mentioned, however, especially by those interested in condemning Marlitt as a trivial writer, are the crises that occur in all of her works: the realistic traumas (death, illness, betrayal, ruthless aggression) that the heroine must overcome before she can succeed. What Marlitt spent her life depicting was the female fantasy that spoke to her contemporaries, a counterpart to the male fantasy of success in business and careers that male authors depicted. Of course, today it can be viewed as feeding into the conservation of the image of women as primarily domestic creatures.[37] Yet, these heroines are not passive; they struggle against the nineteenth-century ideal of women as weak, inactive, and unthinking. The fact that Marlitt rewarded her female protagonists with men who love them and seek them out precisely for what they do, rather than for a passive and exterior beauty, can be considered an emancipatory fantasy.

I argue for a broad definition of realism, one that includes the perceived importance of desire on the part of nineteenth-century readers, female as well as male. The fact that these fantasies would not be fulfilled in the lifetime of most middle-class readers has never prevented the positive fate of Heinrich Drendorf or Anton Wohlfahrt from being considered part of the realist hero. Why should female fantasy and ideals be treated any differently, other than in the interest of perpetuating a male-centered, misogynist culture?

If we recognize the importance of reader fantasy in the literature of realism, rather than merely evaluating it as a measure of "triviality," I believe that we will not only gain a better, more subtle understanding of what women's literature was about but will also be better attuned to the diverse and often unnoticed function of canonical realist texts: the awakening and vicarious satisfaction of middle-class dreams. Marlitt's enthusiastic readers long understood the root of her appeal; it was predominantly literary critics and scholars who chose to label that appeal "trivial." I suggest that we return to our realist texts as enthusiastic and desiring readers. In doing so, I contend, we will become better, more perceptive scholars.

Notes

[1] Some scholarly works on German realism that include work by Marlitt are Horst Denkler, ed., *Romane und Erzählungen des bürgerlichen Realismus: Neue Interpretationen* (Stuttgart: Reclam, 1980); Margret Rothe-Buddensieg, *Spuk im Bürgerhaus: der Dachboden in der deutschen Prosaliteratur als Negation der gesellschaftlichen Realität* (Kronberg/Ts.: Scriptor, 1974); Kirsten Belgum, *Interior Meaning: Design of the Bourgeois Home in the Realist Novel* (New York: Peter Lang, 1991). More recent works that argue for comparing Marlitt to her realist contemporaries include Cornelia Brauer (Hobohm), "Eugenie Marlitt: Bürgerliche — Christin — Liberale — Autorin" (Diss. University of Erfurt, 1993), Hans Arens, *E. Marlitt: Eine kritische Würdigung* (Trier: Wissenschaftlicher Verlag, 1994), and Cornelia Hobohm, "Geliebt; Gehaßt; Erfolgreich: Eugenie Marlitt (1825–1887)," in Karin Tebben, ed., *Beruf: Schriftstellerin: Schreibende Frauen im 18. und 19. Jahrhundert* (Göttingen: Vandenhoek & Ruprecht, 1998), 244–75.

[2] Otto Ludwig, "Der poetische Realismus," in Gerhard Plumpe, ed., *Theorie des bürgerlichen Realismus* (Stuttgart: Reclam, 1985), 148–50. Ludwig's essay was first published posthumously in 1874.

[3] Inspiration for this analysis comes from the groundbreaking work of Nancy Armstrong on English domestic novels of the eighteenth and nineteenth centuries. Armstrong suggests convincingly that the expression of desire, especially female desire, in literature was perceived at times as a threat to middle-class stability. *Desire and Domestic Fiction: A Political History of the Novel* (New York: Oxford UP, 1987). The realization that passionate and sexual desires of literary characters are a central aspect in some German realist texts has been thoughtfully understood by recent scholars. See, for example, Robert C. Holub, "The Desires of Realism: Repetition and Repression in Keller's 'Romeo und Julia auf dem Dorfe,'" in his *Reflections of Realism: Paradox, Norm, and Ideology in Nineteenth-century German Prose* (Detroit: Wayne State UP, 1991), 101–31, and Peter van Matt, "Conrad Ferdinand Meyer: Die Richterin (1885): Offizielle Kunst und private Phantasie im Widerstreit," in Denkler, ed., 310–24. Desire in realist fiction is not always exclusively sexual. Russell Berman has identified the bourgeois desire for commodities as a key component of Gustav Freytag's fiction and aesthetic theory. See his *The Rise of the Modern German Novel: Crisis and Charisma* (Cambridge: Harvard UP, 1986), 55–105.

[4] Marlitt's works were all initially published serially in the *Gartenlaube*. Her collected works also appeared in separate volumes published by the Verlag von Ernst Keil's Nachfolger in Leipzig and later by the Verlag der Union, Deutsche Verlagsgesellschaft in Stuttgart, which published a total of eight different inexpensive "*Volksausgaben.*" In 1917, thirty years after the author's

death, six additional reprint editions were published, including a ten-volume "Illustrated Edition" by the Verlag A. Weichert in Berlin. This information appeared in a flier commemorating the 100th anniversary of Marlitt's birth: Karl Robert Vogelsberg, "Der Lebensgang und das Werk der Dichterin." I received this pamphlet from Günter Merbach of the Intreressengemeinschaft Marlitt in Arnstadt, and I do not believe that it has been reprinted elsewhere.

[5] For a succinct version see Brent O. Peterson, "E. Marlitt (Eugenie John)," in James Hardin and Siegfried Mews, eds., *Dictionary of Literary Biography*, vol. 129: *Nineteenth-Century German Writers, 1841–1900* (Detroit: Gale Research, 1993), 223–28. Marlitt's androgynous pen name stems from 1865, when she submitted her first work to Ernst Keil for consideration. One recently published assumption suggests that the pseudonym stands for "Meine ARnstadter LITTeratur." Hobohm, "Geliebt," 249.

[6] Keil accepted every one of her works with the exception of one of her first two submissions, the short story "Schulmeisters Marie," which he rejected, as others had, because of its apparent similarity to the *Dorfgeschichten* of Berthold Auerbach, which many writers were seeking to imitate at the time. Alfred John, "Eugenie John-Marlitt: Ihr Leben und ihre Werke," in E. Marlitt, *Gesammelte Romane und Novellen*, vol. 10 (Leipzig: Ernst Keil's Nachfolger, 1890), 405.

[7] The year after Marlitt's first novel was published in the *Gartenlaube* the magazine's circulation increased approximately fifty percent (from 142,000 in 1866 to 210,000 to 230,000 in 1867). This increase continued until 1875, when the circulation peaked at 382,000. Kirsten Belgum, *Popularizing the Nation: Audience, Representation, and the Production of Identity in* Die Gartenlaube, *1853–1900* (Lincoln: U of Nebraska P, 1998), 200. Beginning as early as 1869, Keil's publishing house also printed book editions of Marlitt's works, some of them appearing in up to six editions by 1890. John, 422.

[8] Arens, 14.

[9] John, 428.

[10] John, 418. Gottschall's judgment has been frequently repeated in the scholarship and survived into the late twentieth century. Bertha Potthast, "Eugenie Marlitt: Ein Beitrag zur Geschichte des deutschen Frauenromans" (Diss. U of Cologne, 1926), 37; Gabriele Strecker, *Frauenträume — Frauentränen: Über den deutschen Frauenroman* (Weilheim/Oberbayern: Otto Wilhelm Barth, 1969).

[11] Arens, 15.

[12] Keller presumed that the article had been written by Hermann Friedrichs (as the author was listed in *Das Magazin für die Literatur des In- und Auslandes: Organ des Allgemeinen Deutschen Schriftsteller-Verbandes*), but it was, in fact, written by the director of the Allgemeiner Deutscher Schriftsteller-

Verband, Friedrich Friedrich. Gottfried Keller, *Gesammelte Briefe,* ed. Carl Helbling, vol. 3, 1 (Bern: Benteli, 1952), 251, 536. Among other things, Friedrich condemns Marlitt for telling stories full of "lüsterne Sinnlichkeit" (Arens, 16–18). What Friedrich describes from a hypothetical male reader's perspective as teasing about male sexual conquest is, I contend, a gross misreading of Marlitt, who consistently writes about desire from the female protagonist's point of view.

[13] Quoted in John, 443–44.

[14] Potthast, 1.

[15] Although the most common English equivalent for *Trivialliteratur* is "popular literature," the German term has a decidedly more pejorative connotation.

[16] George L. Mosse, "Was die Deutschen wirklich lasen: Marlitt, May, Ganghofer," in Reinhold Grimm and Jost Hermand, eds., *Popularität und Trivialität* (Frankfurt am Main: Athenäum, 1974), 116.

[17] Michael Kienzle, *Der Erfolgsroman: Zur Kritik seiner poetischen Ökonomie bei Gustav Freytag und Eugenie Marlitt* (Stuttgart: Metzler, 1975), 57 and 68.

[18] Jochen Schulte-Sasse and Renate Werner, "E. Marlitts 'Im Hause des Kommerzienrates': Analyse eines Trivialromans in paradigmatischer Absicht," in E. Marlitt, *Im Hause des Kommerzienrates* (Munich: Fink, 1977), 389–434.

[19] Heide Radek, "Zur Geschichte von Roman und Erzählung in der *Gartenlaube* (1853 bis 1914): Heroismus und Idylle als Instrument nationaler Ideologie" (Diss. U of Erlangen-Nuremberg, 1967); Hazel E. Rosenstrauch, "Zum Beispiel: *Die Gartenlaube,*" in Annamaria Rucktäschel and Hans Dieter Zimmermann, eds., *Trivialliteratur* (Munich: Fink, 1976), 169–89; Belgum, *Popularizing,* 199–41.

[20] Strecker, 8.

[21] Carol Diethe, *Towards Emancipation: German Women Writers of the Nineteenth Century* (New York: Berghahn, 1998), 119–27; Ruth-Ellen Boetcher Joeres, *Respectability and Deviance: Nineteenth-Century German Women Writers and the Ambiguity of Representation* (Chicago: U of Chicago P, 1998), 219–55; Astrid Bazzanella, "Das Frauenbild in den Romanen Eugenie Marlitts: Zwischen Emanzipationsbestreben und 'weiblicher Bestimmung'" (Diss. U of Trento, 1994); Brauer; Hobohm, "Geliebt"; and Todd Kontje, *Women, the Novel, and the German Nation 1771–1871: Domestic Fiction in the Fatherland* (Cambridge: Cambridge UP, 1998), 183–201.

[22] To date, two issues have been published of *Jahrbuch der Interessengemeinschaft Marlitt* (Wandersleben: Gleichen Verlag, 1997 and 2000). See also Günter Merbach, *E. Marlitt: Das Leben einer großen Schriftstellerin* (Hamburg: Martin Kelter, 1992), 183–86.

[23] Alexis was born in Breslau but moved to Arnstadt in the early 1850s after the onset of health problems and he died and was buried there. He is celebrated in the city museum as a local author. Cornelia Hobohm, *Das literarische Arnstadt* (Wandersleben: Gleichen, 1997), 23–29.

[24] Schulte-Sasse and Werner, 389–434.

[25] Bazzanella, 73–76.

[26] Those works that have been the focus of scholarly interpretations include *Goldelse* (1866), her first novel; *Die zweite Frau* (1874); and *Im Hause des Kommerzienrates* (1876). For the first see Belgum, *Popularizing;* for *Die zweite Frau* see Joeres; for the last Schulte-Sasse and Werner and Belgum, *Interior Meaning.* *Die Frau mit den Karfunkelsteinen* is, of course, discussed along with all of Marlitt's works in Potthast and more recently, yet cursorily, in Arens. I do not make the claim of revising Marlitt's reputation by treating all of her works, as Arens does. Indeed, contrary to Arens, I think that the detailed discussion of one work can be an important contribution to a serious reconsideration of an author. All quotes from *Die Frau mit den Karfunkelsteinen* taken from the second book edition, E. Marlitt, *Gesammelte Romane und Novellen,* vol. 6 (Leipzig: Ernst Keil's Nachfolger, n.d.).

[27] Some scholars have overstated the pattern of Marlitt's works: the heroine of Marlitt's last novel cannot be accurately described as renouncing her achievement at the conclusion. See Peterson, 222.

[28] In particular, Margarete's cart driving would have established her as decidedly "unfeminine" for standard nineteenth-century realist texts, as my recent comparison of Freytag's *Soll und Haben* (Debit and Credit, 1855) and Berthold Auerbach's *Das Landhaus am Rhein* (The Villa on the Rhine, 1869) has shown. "Tracking the Liberal Hero," in Steven Brockmann and James Steakley, eds., *Heroes and Heroism in German Culture: Essays in Honor of Jost Hermand* (Amsterdam: Rodopi, 2001), 15–34.

[29] This experience is similar to the educational awakening experienced by Heinrich Drendorf in Stifter's *Der Nachsommer* (Indian Summer, 1857).

[30] The image of Margarete with short hair (as illustrated by Carl Zopf in the early book editions) is remarkably similar to Marlitt's own appearance; as documented in the two existing photographs of Marlitt, her hair hangs loose in tight curls and does not quite reach her shoulders.

[31] For information about Marlitt's last will and testament see Merbach, 186–90.

[32] For several passages from admiring readers, see "Ein Marlitt-Blatt," *Gartenlaube* (1875): 68–80. See also Belgum, *Popularizing,* 138–39.

[33] 12, 15, 15, 26, 137, 147, 165, respectively.

[34] 13, 27, 27, 93, 93, 202, respectively.

[35] Already in the 1870s the *Gartenlaube* had respectfully reviewed the activity of the "Allgemeiner Deutscher Frauenverein," founded in 1865. See Belgum, *Popularizing*, 126–27.

[36] This constancy in itself is not grounds for condemning her work. Indeed, basic plots and a happy resolution are repeated in the works of canonical authors such as Jane Austen and Charles Dickens.

[37] The predominance of this view even among feminist scholars of German literature can be seen in the various entries of a recent feminist reference work: Susanne Kord and Friederike Eigler, eds., *The Feminist Encyclopedia of German Literature* (Westport, CT: Greenwood P, 1997). Several contributors call Marlitt's work "trivial and non-emancipatory serial love stories" (288) that propagate "female virtues such as passivity and modesty" (336) and "the princess motif" in which "characters lose their mothers early on in the story, then struggle through life until a charming man saves them in holy matrimony" (416). I argue that such charges arise from a limited notion of female emancipation and an, at best, cursory reading of Marlitt's works.

The Appeal of Karl May
in the Wilhelmine Empire:
Emigration, Modernization,
and the Need for Heroes*

Nina Berman

IN HIS RECENT monograph on German novelists of America, Jeffrey L. Sammons describes his strong disinclination to include a discussion of Karl May:

> On the one hand, the contour of my subject seemed to require his inclusion; on the other, I remained unproductively baffled that an author whom I found silly and tedious should be, by a gigantic margin, the best-selling fiction writer in his homeland and not only a favorite of children, as one might expect, but an object of veneration and solemn contemplation by many adults and even scholars. Few features of the German culture that is supposed to be my life's work have contributed so much to my sense of strangeness from it than the phenomenon of Karl May.[1]

Sammons's ambivalent attitude toward May results in a relatively brief investigation of the author's reception in the United States. He shows that May's work has generally received scant attention there, suggesting that the personal puzzlement of the literary critic regarding May's success in Germany is quite in line with the reaction of his fellow Americans. As Sammons argues convincingly, May fails to portray North America in ways that could generate a significant interest among larger sections of that society. Most Americans simply cannot identify with May's novels, for even though May drew heavily on James Fenimore Cooper and other sources popular in the United States, he used this material in ways that must alienate American readers. A generally anti-American current pervades most of May's novels staged in North America. But, as Sammons argues, even more than the presence of this bias in May's writings, the novels' lack of appeal can be explained in terms of the author's inability to represent "what makes America significant in the course of human affairs: the great experiment in creating a democracy, in balancing the often conflicting claims of liberty, equality, and justice...."[2] This ignorance of issues central to Americans' self-image convincingly explains the absence of May from the U.S. popular-culture canon, much more than the stylistic deficiencies on which Sammons elaborates, quite amusingly, with loathing and bewilderment.[3]

However, May's success elsewhere is a fact, in spite of or (however unfortunate it may be to some) even because of the aesthetic dimensions of the texts. While May cannot speak to Americans for the reasons Sammons proposes, Germans and substantial audiences outside of the German-speaking world have found the novels tremendously appealing since they were first published. In Germany, more than 70 million volumes have been printed since 1892, in addition to the original publications in widely circulated journals and calendars.[4] This staggering figure points to an even larger number of readers: over the last 120 years few Germans have not read at least one or part of one of the novels, and many have read scores of texts by May. May's novels and short stories were collected in many editions; the largest, the Bamberger Ausgabe, comprises 74 volumes. The critical edition, currently being prepared by Hermann Wiedenroth and Hans Wollschläger, promises to encompass 102 volumes.[5] May's work has been translated into at least thirty-two languages.[6] Even non-English immigrant communities in the United States were interested in May's novels, as is documented by the number of translations that were made at the turn of the twentieth century into, for example, Finnish, Slovenian, and Czech and published by immigrant publishing houses in the United States.[7] To first-generation U.S. immigrants May's novels were evidently appealing.

What, then, accounts for the success of May's novels? I will not attempt to explain the writer's popularity outside of the German-speaking world, or over the entire period of his publishing history. With regard to German-speaking audiences during the period of Wilhelmine Germany, the focus of my exploration, however, I suggest that the appeal of the texts lies in their ability to address contemporary concerns. This is to a large degree owing to May's reliance on his sources and to the manner in which he used this material. Scholarship on May's novels has revealed the extent to which the author depended on contemporary sources. Franz Kandolf's study from 1922, for example, demonstrates that for his novels set in the Middle East, May drew extensively on Austen Henry Layard's accounts of his journeys and archaeological expeditions.[8] Kandolf's analysis is but one in a long series of articles documenting May's use of historical sources. The autobiography of Johann Gottlieb Krüger, who deserted from the Prussian army in 1833 and led an adventurous life in North Africa, first as a soldier in the French army in Algeria and then (deserting once more) at the court of the Bey of Tunis, was the blueprint for May's figure Krüger-Bei. This character plays a crucial role in three texts: the narrative "Der Krumir" (1882), the novel *Deutsche Helden — Deutsche Herzen* (German Heroes — German Hearts, 1885–87), and the travel narrative *Krüger Bei* (part of *Satan und Ischariot* [Satan and Iscariot], 1894–95).[9] That is, May recycled his own literary texts, which were, in turn, based on other source material. Often May's writings follow the original sources so closely that entire passages can be identified as reworked versions of the model, as is evident, to mention another instance, in his use of Alfred Edmund Brehm's *Reiseskizzen aus Nord-Ost-Afrika* (Travel sketches from Northeast Africa, 1855).[10]

While May's dependence on sources is quite extensive, it is even more relevant to understand *how* he used this material. May often employed contradictory primary texts at the same time, and this explains many of the inconsistencies in his writings. A decidedly positive image of Native Americans, for example, emerges slowly in the course of a couple of decades. Initially, Winnetou, the fictional Apache chief central to countless of May's America novels who has become emblematic for May's (and Germany's) romanticized idea of the Native American, was not the noble savage the reader encounters in the later texts. While May began in the late 1870s to use material from George Catlin's studies of Native Americans, he only gradually adopted Catlin's ideological position, namely his sympathetic portrayal of his subject. Earlier texts, such as the bloody "Old Firehand" (1875–76), follow prevalent racist portrayals, while the later *Winnetou* novels (volumes 1–3, 1893; volume 4, 1909–10) are famous for their idealization of American Indians.[11]

Since May drew on his earlier writings ("Old Firehand," for instance) for the second and third volumes of the *Winnetou* series, however, the later texts reveal a great deal of inconsistency in their representation of Native Americans. Petra Küppers elaborates on these inconsistencies with regard to the image of Winnetou and shows that, although he is generally thought to be a positive figure, the Apache contains aspects of stereotypical representations of cultural and racial difference that mark Indians as inferior and dubious characters.[12] This phenomenon is noteworthy because the extreme dependence on contemporary material makes May's work a mirror of diverse views that were widespread at the time. To paraphrase the effect of this eclectic composition style, one could say that it allows contemporary discourses to speak through May. For this reason May's writings, especially those texts composed up until about 1900, make for an excellent case study of conflicting and simultaneously existing discourses in Wilhelmine Germany.[13]

In fact, May's success was largely due to this specific appropriation of diverse sources. His unique accomplishment is that he picked up the crucial issues of his times and presented his material in a suspense-filled style, even if the content did not always convey a coherent message. In the contemporary context, May's novels spoke to many concerns central to the lives of the ordinary people who were his original audience.[14] In May's work something was to be found for everybody. In addition, May wrote in linguistically accessible ways that allowed for a large audience to identify with the texts, and they appealed even to people who were still learning to read.[15]

Elsewhere I have discussed May's *Orientzyklus* (Orient Cycle, 1881–88) and placed the six novels in the context of colonial and imperial aspirations of the Wilhelmine Empire to show how they reverberate with widespread views about attitudes toward other cultures.[16] In the following discussion I will focus on texts set in North America to show how May's protagonists highlight issues central to Germans attempting to cope with the effects of a modernizing society. In particular, I will explore questions of emigration, modernization, and the position of the subject in the changing world.

German Emigrants in May's Novels

One of the contemporary issues reflected in May's novels is the large-scale emigration that was transforming German society in the nineteenth century. Between eighty-five and ninety-two percent of these German emigrants went to North America.[17] During the period "from 1816 to 1914, about 5.5 million Germans emigrated to the United States."[18] At various times most of the immigrants coming to the United States were Germans, and today they make up the largest group of European immigrants in the country. While earlier emigration movements were inspired by hopes for greater religious or political freedom, the nineteenth-century emigration was mostly a result of economic pressures.[19] The highest number of emigrants is recorded for the period 1880 to 1893; during these years about 1.8 million Germans came to the United States.[20]

In light of these figures, the repercussions for German society in general cannot be overstated. Between 1872 and 1913 the German population grew from 40 million to 67 million; during this period approximately 3 million Germans emigrated overseas. One should also not forget the influx of approximately one million immigrants into Germany, mostly from Eastern Europe, during this period.[21] These figures document a high level of mobility. With regard to overseas emigration, the number of Germans leaving was noticeable to everyone. A significant percentage of young and energetic Germans packed up, said goodbye to friends and family, and embarked on a journey to the Promised Land. Everyone had family members or knew someone who had emigrated. At a time when moving was not as common as it is today, and distances were not yet shortened by airplanes and telecommunication, this large-scale emigration had tremendous effects on German society as a whole.

May's popular novels, I want to argue, became one of the main vehicles for processing the concerns associated with emigration. His many novels and shorter narratives set in the United States are a testimony to the impact German emigration to North America had on German society. For one thing, May's novels gave the relatives and friends of emigrants, who might also have harbored the desire to depart, a surrogate of sorts, a chance to travel to the New World in the realm of fantasy. At the same time, readers were validated in their decision to stay at home because the protagonist, who was in most cases the first-person narrator and assumed to be identical with Karl May, always returned to Germany. In both cases, however, the main appeal of the texts lies in their ability to speak to the contemporary effects of emigration to the United States.

Some scholars have argued that May did not write emigration novels per se, but that his novels fulfilled certain expectations of an audience largely familiar with the topic of emigration.[22] While it is true that May never devoted an entire volume to a discussion of the issue of emigration in particular, his novels feature important characters who are identified as emigrants. In an article that includes detailed historical data on German emigration, Elisabeth Gohrbandt discusses emigrants and settlers in May's North American novels.[23] She shows that these characters are quite distinctly drawn and embody a range of types of emigrants who left Germany for different reasons (although she does not sufficiently distinguish German from other national groups of settlers and emigrants; thus, the ideological distinctions among May's characters remain largely unexplored). Through these characters May articulates the contemporary interest in emigration, and he raises questions about the motivation and the success or failure of emigrants. A closer look at these emigrant characters sheds light on May's portrayal of the German emigration to the United States and on the appeal of fictional emigrant characters to the German audience.

One such emigrant character, Klekih-Petra, features prominently in the first of the *Winnetou* novels. Early in the novel the protagonist and first-person narrator, Old Shatterhand, is working for a land-surveying company. He has gotten into an argument with one of a group of men accompanying the surveying team for their protection and is about to shoot his opponent when a stranger suddenly interferes: "Wir . . . sahen einen Mann hinter einem Baume hervortreten. Er war klein, hager und buckelig und fast wie ein Roter gekleidet und bewaffnet. Man konnte nicht recht unterscheiden, ob er ein Weißer oder ein Indianer war."[24] This man, who might pass for an Indian, is Klekih-Petra, "der berühmte Schulmeister der Apachen," who is accompanied by Winnetou and Winnetou's father, Intschu tschuna (*Winnetou I*, 99–100).

In the course of the narrative the reader learns that Klekih-Petra is a German who left his homeland after the 1848 revolution. In fact, he had been an active leader of the revolution but, as he explains to Old Shatterhand, had grown to realize how wrong the rebellion was. In a passionate speech he blames himself for having been a thief and a murderer (116). He describes how he came to see that his revolutionary activities had brought only pain and misery for simple people who, despite their poverty, had been content with their lot (117). To find a new life and inner peace the former political activist decided to abandon civilization for the wilderness. He also wanted to remain involved with people, however, and is acting now according to his newly found spirit. During his stay in the United States, Klekih-Petra learned about the plight of the Indians and decided to help them. The Apaches accepted him into their ranks and gave him his Apache name, which is said to mean "weißer Vater" (290). As he explains to the narrator, he realized that he was not going to be able to prevent the decline of the Indians, but his goal was "ihm den Tod erleichtern und auf seine letzte Stunde den Glanz der Liebe, der Versöhnung fallen lassen" (118).

Klekih-Petra is especially dedicated to Winnetou, and he voices his confidence that had the Apache been born to a European sovereign, he would have become a great general and "ein noch größerer Friedensfürst" (118). In moving words he expresses his wish to be able to give his life for Winnetou. And sure enough, only two pages later Klekih-Petra dies in the exact manner he has just described to Old Shatterhand: protecting Winnetou with his body, he catches a bullet meant for the young Apache and is mortally wounded (121–23). Before he dies, however, he asks Old Shatterhand to continue his mission and stay faithful to Winnetou, thus creating a continuity between himself and Old Shatterhand and giving legitimacy, as well as a sense of calling, to the ensuing relationship (122).

What does May tell his readers through this character? Klekih-Petra represents the type of German who left his home country for political reasons. Unlike most German political emigrants after the 1848 revolution, who left because their liberal ideals had not been materialized, however, Klekih-Petra condemns the revolution. As May describes the former revolutionary's story of faithlessness and rebellion against the state, he suggests a connection between Klekih-Petra's initial renunciation of the Christian faith and his ensuing political activities. Klekih-Petra's renunciation of his religion led to his abandonment of the state order (116). Thus, his emigration comes as a sort of penance for the revolutionary activities unequivocally condemned by May.

Klekih-Petra's nickname, "the schoolmaster," also has important implications. As Klekih-Petra embarks on his mission to support the Indians, his intent is not to help them organize a large-scale rebellion against the white settlers (which would mirror what he considers a failure, the German revolution of 1848) but to alleviate their suffering and to educate them. Klekih-Petra's greatest wish is to convert the Apache Winnetou to Christianity (118). He calls Winnetou "mein eigenstes Werk," "mein geistiges Kind" (118). This influence of Klekih-Petra on Winnetou implies that the exceptional character by which Winnetou is distinguished results from his Christian upbringing at the hands of his first German mentor, who is succeeded by his second German mentor, Old Shatterhand. With so much emphasis on his education by Germans, the characteristics that make the greatest Apache so noble are, in fact, behavior in keeping with ideas of ideal Germanness and Christian spirit. In effect, Winnetou is much less a "noble savage" than a "noble German."[25]

Another type of emigrant appears in the figure of Old Firehand. May wrote a shorter narrative about this character in 1875–76 ("Old Firehand," 1876) and drew on this story in *Winnetou II* and in *Der Schatz im Silbersee* (The Treasure in the Silver Lake, 1890–91), which was written for a youthful audience. Old Firehand bears some of the same characteristics as Klekih-Petra: he is German, and he also left the country as a consequence of the revolution, although not for political reasons. He is a close friend of Winnetou's; in fact, both men had once wooed the same woman, the Indian Ribanna, but Winnetou abandoned his courtship because of his deeper bond to Old Firehand. Old Shatterhand admits to the reader that the intensity of Winnetou's friendship with Old Firehand almost made him jealous.[26] Old Firehand comes across as another representation of the noble German. The reader learns about the reasons that compelled Old Firehand to emigrate through an account by his son, Harry:

> Vater war Oberförster da drüben im alten Lande und lebte mit seinem Weibe und einem Sohne in ungetrübtem Glücke, bis die Zeit der politischen Gärung kam, welche so manchen braven Mann um seine Ziele betrogen hat und auch ihn in den Strudel trieb, welchem er sich schließlich nur durch die Flucht zu entziehen vermochte. (*Winnetou II*, 431)

In this description of events leading up to Old Firehand's emigration, the 1848 revolution is again rendered as a calamitous episode with devastating repercussions for ordinary people. Old Firehand, who led a peaceful life until the revolution, is forced to emigrate to save his family. As in the case of Klekih-Petra, May suggests that Germany lost a valuable man because the ill-fated actions of democrats and liberals had a detrimental impact on society at large.[27]

While the figures of Klekih-Petra and Old Firehand link emigration to political events, two other German emigrants acknowledge economic plight as a motivation for emigration. In *"Weihnacht"* (Christmas, 1897) May prefaces an adventure novel set in North America with a story about an impoverished family named Hiller. The young first-person narrator (who has not yet advanced to become Old Shatterhand) and a friend encounter grandfather, mother, and son Hiller on a hiking trip in the mountains. The husband and father had emigrated to the United States three years earlier; in fact, he had had to flee because of crimes he had committed when faced with financial problems. After establishing himself in the new country, he had sent tickets for the journey across the Atlantic to reunite the family. The grandfather had gotten sick on the journey to the port city, and the family, held up for months, had finally run out of money. The two young travelers arrange a Christmas party for the Hillers and afterward confer on them all the money they themselves have saved for their travels. Years later the adult Old Shatterhand meets the father during one of his stays in the United States. Hiller has become a dubious character who has lost faith in the Christian religion and in the core teachings of his ethical upbringing, only to be converted again to Christianity and returned to civilization at the end of the novel.

In *Winnetou III* May offers a highly positive image of a German emigrant community. On one of his rides through the country he comes upon a German settlement in a valley. The scene is reminiscent of life in a German agrarian community, with fields, grazing animals, German-style farmhouses, and a chapel over which towers a giant cross with a carved figure of Jesus. As Old Shatterhand approaches the settlement with Winnetou and another companion the congregation sings an "Ave Maria" written by the first-person narrator himself![28] The hamlet, Helldorf Settlement, and its inhabitants convey the image of a peaceful agrarian utopia.

Originally from the Bavarian Fichtelgebirge, the villagers had emigrated collectively to Chicago, saved up to buy a farm, and moved together to found and build up the settlement. In May's narrative the positive image of this community is largely owed to the fact that they preserved their Germanness and their belief in Christianity. May draws a comparable image of a German emigrant community in *Der Ölprinz* (The Oil Prince, 1893–94).

The Hiller family and the Helldorf community highlight contrasting types of emigrants. While May only marginally acknowledges the economic hardship that led to displacement, he emphasizes the social context of emigration. The Hiller family faces several challenges brought on originally by the father, who left the family behind and whose ethical corruption is further advanced by the negative aspects of life in the American West. The Helldorf community, on the other hand, acted as a group, clinging to ideal German values (family, solidarity, community) and their Christian faith.

Finally, Old Shatterhand himself is a type of emigrant. Because of his guaranteed return back home at the end of his novels, one could call him a kind of eternally returning migrant. As is the case with some of the other emigrant figures, Old Shatterhand does not inform the reader in much detail about the reasons for his departure from Germany. He only mentions that he was motivated by "unpleasant circumstances" back home and by an inborn thirst for action. He also stresses that when he first crossed the Atlantic, the conditions for the advancement of young people were far more auspicious (*Winnetou I*, 16–17). The narrator does not elaborate on the nature of the "unpleasant circumstances," although he concedes that emigration can open up new possibilities. His remark that things used to be better for young emigrants can, however, be seen as an attempt to discourage young people from following in the footsteps of their hero. The importance of May's guaranteed return to his home country after every journey is also the key to the enormous uproar he faced when his audience found out that his novels were not based on his own experiences but were drawn from other sources and were ultimately a product of his imagination. When it became clear that he had, indeed, never left Germany until his journey of 1899–1900 (he traveled to the United States for the first time only in 1908), his return — that is, the return of the first-person narrator —, was rendered less valuable.[29]

May offers his reader not one but a number of diverse images of German emigrants to America.[30] While he certainly takes a conservative stance when it comes to discussion of the revolution of 1848, he does acknowledge the economic plight that led many Germans to leave their country. The economic problems in Germany, however, are in some cases presented as repercussions of activities that go against the state, agrarian life, and Christianity. In North America, emigrant Germans are allowed to live as traditional Germans, if they choose to do so. May stresses the need for them to stick together as emigrant communities and the importance of holding onto Christian and German values. For the readers at home, then, the ideal is not an exotic life in the New World, one promising the freedoms of modernity, but rather the true life of the Old World. May's emigrants do not aspire to gain political, religious, or personal freedom but, instead, reflect the fact that most actual emigrants were driven by socioeconomic motives. While May often presents emigration as the result of personal circumstances, such as a broken heart or problems with the law or with superiors, economic motives play at least a partial role in most of his scenarios.[31]

Many of the situations aspired to by the emigrants in May's novels are reminiscent of an idealized premodern life in Germany: a life of peasants and God-fearing Christians. The vision of society as communicated through May's German emigrants in the United States is that of a preindustrial, agrarian community, one grounded in patriarchy, Christianity, and a belief in authoritarian structures. It inherently favors a feudal order through its critique of democratic movements. Also, because his main protagonist always returns home, and the economic problems that led many to emigrate are associated with the past, May sends a message to his readers that actual emigration to the United States is no longer either desirable or necessary. Beginning in the early 1890s, this perspective mirrored the declining emigration rates.

To some degree, May's image of emigration reflects the motivations of actual emigrants; even more, however, it appeals to the audience at home in that it counters the changes brought on by political and economic modernization with images of an idealized past, erasing the plight of peasants and workers employed in the traditional sectors of the old economy. At the same time, May avoids an explicit discussion of the hardships his contemporaries encounter.[32] As we have seen in the case of emigrant characters in the novel, however, the absence of elaborate direct references to historical events does not preclude the relatedness of the novels to their political and socioeconomic context. Indirectly, the reader is, nevertheless, exposed to some of the questions he or she confronts on a daily basis.

The Lure of May's Superheroes

May's adventure novels further appealed to Germans during the Wilhelmine era in that they focus on the actions of an individual who faces and masters exceptional challenges. These challenging situations are staged in a preindustrial landscape that bears few signs of the modernizing world that was the readers' lived reality. The protagonist's actions, however, especially the manner in which he solves the problems he encounters, as well as the physical backdrop against which these actions are set, speak to developments under way in late nineteenth-century Germany.

Mobility is the word that best expresses the plethora of transformations occurring during the Wilhelmine era. Germany transformed, in the words of Klaus Bade, from an "agrarian society with a powerful industry to an industrial society with a strong agrarian base."[33] While the agrarian sector remained strong until the First World War, millions of Germans found work for the first time in the industrial sector and in the emerging tertiary sector. The birthrate rose dramatically after 1870; the German population increased by more than fifty percent between 1871 and 1910.[34] Especially after 1890, however, the booming economy was able to absorb most of this growing workforce, the pressure of which had until then been to some extent alleviated by the large-scale emigration. Many of the workers employed in the new industries and the tertiary sector came from the big cities, but millions also left the countryside searching for a better life.[35] Moreover, although the proportion of women working for pay remained at around thirty percent, an increasing number of women joined the workforce in these newly developing sectors.[36]

Within one generation, the traditional security network that had been in place for most people living outside of the cities — the support extended by family, kin, and the village community — was no longer able to provide fully the protection it had traditionally offered, especially to those who migrated. Anthony Giddens, who conceptualizes the impact of modernization processes in his *The Consequences of Modernity*, describes this change affecting kinship relations and local communities. He argues that abstract systems were introduced that were able to cross indefinite spans of time and space, thus granting the stability that had been disrupted by modernization.[37] The social-insurance legislation implemented by Bismarck's government exemplifies such abstract systems. It ensured social security for workers and indicates a shift away from traditional to state-regulated support systems. Health insurance was introduced in 1883, accident insurance in 1884, and old-age and invalid insurance in 1889. In addition, individuals encountered entirely new modes of production through the innovations occurring in the industrial sector. Schivelbusch, for instance, has shown how the industrialization of light in the nineteenth century permitted independence from working patterns determined by the availability of natural light and thus made it possible for work hours and cultural life to be extended much later into the night.[38]

Other significant changes occurred in transportation. Landscapes were dramatically altered by the building of new roads, railroad tracks, daring bridges, and tunnels. The condition of roads constantly improved with such innovations as the introduction of concrete pavement, facilitating a further increase in transportation speed.[39] An ever-expanding system of railroads, trams, and subways cut passages between places to a fraction of the time previously necessary. At the end of the century the first automobiles and airplanes were built. Elevators, escalators, parachutes, the abandonment of toll systems, and even skiing added to the increase in physical mobility.

At the same time, people left their familiar contexts and moved away from families and friends to places that promised work. While distances could now be crossed in less time, people were also uprooted and displaced. Changes in what Giddens calls "time-space distanciation — the conditions under which time and space are organised so as to connect presence and absence" — deeply affected social relations.[40] Kinship ties and the relations between the sexes required redefinition. Rising crime rates and homicide statistics are additional signs of a transforming and destabilized society.[41] The extent and the pace of these developments presented great challenges for individuals.

May's original readership consisted largely of people who benefited "only in a very limited way" from the economic boom of the Wilhelmine era.[42] These people were also the most uprooted; while vertical social mobility was still quite limited, horizontal mobility (that is, into new labor markets) and physical mobility (to places where work was available) was necessary for these people to survive.[43] But May's texts also appealed to people who belonged to more-privileged groups, because his protagonists addressed concerns connected to modernization processes shared by most people in the Wilhelmine Empire.

Apart from some of the ideological contradictions that are revealed by closer analyses of May's texts, the author's heroes offer a coherent worldview in a period marked by upheaval. The protagonists of the adventure novels constantly resolve conflicts and restore order. While the individual leading characters, such as Old Shatterhand and Kara Ben Nemsi Effendi, the hero of novels set in the Middle East, differ in their abilities and achieve their goals by somewhat contrasting means, their function in the novels is consistent. Old Shatterhand is a true superhero characterized by physical prowess, as is signaled by his name. His strength is enormous; using only his right arm, for example, he lifts up adult men with ease (*Winnetou I*, 20). In endless situations he demonstrates his physical vigor. In *Winnetou I* the reader sees the "greenhorn" Old Shatterhand master a life-threatening confrontation with a herd of bison (57–63), eat three pounds of the best meat from the bison he successfully shot (72), chase wild mustangs and tame a mule in a most dramatic scene (73–85), and kill a tremendous grizzly bear with his knife (91–95). In the course of only forty pages Old Shatterhand proves beyond doubt his seemingly supernatural strength and courage.

But his power is not based only on physical might: Old Shatterhand is also skilled and resourceful. Even in his first encounter with the Wild West, he can shoot better than any other gunman (26) and is able to outsmart even the most seasoned opponent. Tricks play a crucial role in assuring Old Shatterhand's superiority. In one suspenseful scene, for example, he and his companions face almost certain death by torture for their presumed complicity in the killing of Klekih-Petra. Old Shatterhand is able to convince the Apache leaders to give him a chance at a fair fight. Should he win, his companions (except for the true villain) will go free, as well. In a one-on-one battle Old Shatterhand fools Winnetou's father, Intschu tschuna, with a sequence of tricks. Of course, he does not kill Intschu tschuna when he finally defeats his challenger. As a result, the Apache people of May's novel respect Old Shatterhand and accept him into their ranks. The welcoming words of Winnetou, "Mein Bruder Old Shatterhand mag mit mir kommen," are registered by Old Shatterhand with pride and affection: "Dies war das erste mal, daß er mich 'mein Bruder' nannte" (317).

This success brings up the next component constitutive of the protagonist's superiority, his use of knowledge. Not only did Old Shatterhand undergo intensive training in riding, gymnastics, wrestling, and fencing but he also studied arithmetic, geometry, and geography (*Winnetou I*, 21–22). His physical strength is thus matched by his intellectual capacity. Old Shatterhand constantly confounds his fellow travelers and his opponents with his comprehensive knowledge of every aspect of life in the Wild West, even situations he has not before encountered but has read up on. He is mocked when he refers to the books he has consulted (*Winnetou I*, 68, 88), but his erudition always pays off. Often, his bookish knowledge proves to be more accurate than the judgment of experienced trappers or cowboys, who are baffled by the greenhorn from Saxony.

The learned side of Old Shatterhand is not only useful when it comes to mastering adverse situations; it is also a central trait defining the protagonist's position vis-à-vis the other characters. He is always keen to teach whomever he encounters. When facing white settlers or trappers, he lectures them on the false use of violence (*Winnetou I*, 196) or on the right notions of justice (127–28). In dealing with Indians, he preaches the key tenets of Christianity and civilized behavior (340–43). Of course, in the end the lectures are really for the reader. At times he addresses the reader directly, for instance, as when he laments the deplorable situations of the Indians in the introduction to *Winnetou I* (9–13).

Old Shatterhand has a clearly defined moral position among the characters, and his closest friends are those who act according to his principles, such as Winnetou and Old Firehand. Consequently, Winnetou's conversion to Christianity is one of the central themes of the novels. The dying Klekih-Petra, Winnetou's original German mentor, confides to Old Shatterhand that he hopes ardently that the Apache will become a Christian (*Winnetou I*, 118). Winnetou's moral education is thus completed when the dying Apache chief utters his last words 1,400 pages later: "Schar-lih, ich glaube an den Heiland. Winnetou ist ein Christ. Lebe wohl!" (*Winnetou III*, 419).

In some ways, Old Shatterhand bears resemblance to the traditional trickster, such as Till Eulenspiegel, or confidence man, such as Baron von Münchhausen. Like these figures, Old Shatterhand survives by using his brains, manipulating the strong, and displays almost supernatural powers. But May's superhero is physically even more robust, has an additional aspect of grandiosity, and has clear aspirations for real power. He interferes not from the margins, like the jester, but wields power at the center of the action. In comparison to Kara Ben Nemsi Effendi, however, Old Shatterhand is certainly much more defined by his physical strength. Old Shatterhand is perhaps a blend of Rambo and the young Obi-wan Kenobi.

Given the outlandish nature of some of his adventures, it is surprising that his original audience believed the stories to be authentic events that the first-person narrator had encountered (until, beginning in 1899, a series of press articles and lawsuits put an end to the legend).[44] But this aspect only validates the allure of the image of an empowered individual, which was appealing to various audiences: economically struggling individuals found this role model attractive as a fantasy of the ideal self, while members of upwardly mobile social groups identified with Old Shatterhand's style of leadership and informed behavior. Old Shatterhand's ability to master difficult situations is the key factor: he models character traits and essential modes of behavior for the audience back home. The hero emphasizes certain qualities, such as initiative, self-confidence, physical strength, and strict ethical norms, and he places a challenge to self-imposed authorities while asserting a need for leadership. Old Shatterhand conveys a sense of law and order, of stability and empowerment — attributes that must have had a strong appeal in a period defined by constant change.

The figure of Old Shatterhand reflects a dream of omnipotence in the face of overwhelming economic and social transformation. An important feature of the novels is the first-person perspective of the narrator. This stylistic means allows the reader an even more direct experience of empowerment. In many ways, Old Shatterhand and his Middle Eastern alter ego, Kara Ben Nemsi Effendi, express not only the upheaval but also the growing self-confidence of the booming empire. While these characters served as utopian role models in the 1870s and 1880s, when the economy went through a series of crises (although historians today agree that this period was nevertheless one of retarded growth[45]), the actions of May's protagonists gradually also grew to reflect the increasingly dominant role played by the German empire in world affairs.

Even though women have always made up a significant segment of May's readership (and might have looked for inspiration in the texts for the same reasons as did men), his writings were much more crucial to men. Questions related to men's self-image can be found everywhere in the texts, and themes of male bonding are given prominence in all the novels. While female figures occasionally play important roles, and individual women at times represent an ethically superior order (such as Marah Durimeh, who figures prominently in the Orient Cycle and in texts such as *Ardistan und Dschinnistan* [1907–1909]), relations between men are at the center of the novels. (In this regard, May's works do not correspond to the reality of emigrant communities; the percentage of male emigrants ranged between fifty-five and sixty-six.[46] The percentage of female emigrants was thus much higher than is conveyed by the number of fictional female characters in May's novels). Homoerotic fantasies are undoubtedly contained in many situations involving Old Shatterhand and Winnetou, but the overall message of the novels appeals more to homosocial desire, where erotic desire is not acted out but might still underlie and define male-male relations.[47]

In his exploration of the socio-psychological function of May's novels in Wilhelmine Germany, Jochen Schulte-Sasse argues that May's texts about the United States function to provide guidance for a disoriented population.[48] Schulte-Sasse does not elaborate, however, on the specific kind of guidance May offers his readers, particularly in light of modernization processes. May suggests an image of masculinity that is modern and traditional at the same time. It is traditional because it affirms a male identity based on physical strength and operates almost exclusively within a realm of authority solely defined by men. This may be a response to the challenges posed by the concurrent emergence of the women's movement and the transformation of gender relations. On a more general level, however, it reflects the need for the restoration of order and guaranteeing of agency for men. Regarding the overall worldview, May's ideal man affirms authoritarian structures and stresses the central role of an adherence to Christian beliefs.

At the same time, May's image of the ideal man responds to the reshaping of the economy from primarily agrarian to industrial structures. In this sense, May's exemplary man is modern because he is distinguished by notions of *Bildung* and expertise. He is skilled and educated and consistently points out the value of learning (*Winnetou I*, 137). May's protagonists are for the most part opposed to senseless violence, and May grew consistently more pacifist, becoming quite critical of colonialism. While this attitude is only developed in his later writings, which never gained the public recognition won for him by his earlier adventure novels, it retains definite signs of paternalism. Altogether, May's heroes display an incoherent blend of modern and traditional characteristics, which again facilitate the identification with these models for quite diverse members of the audience.

From Old Shatterhand to Luke Skywalker

May's adventure novels set in the United States appealed to Germans during the Wilhelmine Empire because they succeed in articulating concerns relevant to large sections of Germany's population. With regard to emigration, the novels function on two levels: they allow for an imagined emigration and exploration of unknown territory, but they also validate the situation of the German citizens who, for whatever reason, did not emigrate. The figure of the returning protagonist and the portrayal of specific types of emigrants relegate emigration to the past, which makes it (for the most part) less appealing to the contemporary audience. In the context of the Wilhelmine Empire, May's male protagonists fulfill another function in addressing questions related to social, economic, and political behavior. The identification with the powerful protagonists of May's novels enables readers to try out in their imagination attitudes deemed necessary in a changing world.

The preindustrial scenario serves as the backdrop for staging the encounter between the civilized and the savage, the modern and the traditional. But the world of adventure is less a world in contrast to reality than a reflection of the same reality from which the heroes seem to escape. However indirectly, the novels explore questions related to emigration and mobility, and the fictional travel to a different world contemplates behavior that is necessary to master the challenges of daily life at home. In his essay "Das Abenteuer," Georg Simmel suggests that modern man escapes into the simplicity of the premodern world hoping to find guidance for life in the modern world, a world that does not offer sufficient orientation.[49] In essence, the longing for the familiar premodern landscape mirrors the longing for the (presumably) stable self-confidence of the premodern self. While the wilderness in May's novels is a return to the premodern self, however, it also provides a more reliable (because familiar) testing ground that allows the exploration of behaviors and attitudes necessary for success in the modern world.

Since the Wilhelmine Era, German society has undergone large-scale political, social, and economic transformations; May's popularity, however, has never decreased. This persistence of May's success is, indeed, puzzling. A glance at the websites available on May quickly illustrates his omnipresence in the German cultural sphere. Some of the key aspects that distinguish the novels and that also continuously play a role in German societies since the time of the Wilhelmine Empire are the centrality of *Bildung*, male-male relations, an anti-American current, the idealization of premodern cultures, and a reluctance to change. Other aspects, such as the role of religion, are more marginal today, although the scholarship on May never tires in its attempts to elaborate on this topic.

Much like George Lucas's *Star Wars* (1977), which over the past twenty-five years has offered (and most likely will continue to offer for many years to come) a narrative containing elements crucial to the self-image of Americans, May's works and their reception provide a key to understanding late nineteenth- and twentieth-century German culture. More comprehensive analysis of both the changing and the consistent functions of May's novels over time remains to be pursued.

Notes

* I would like to thank Marike Janzen for her excellent work in updating my bibliography on May. I am also grateful to Peter Siegenthaler for his editorial comments.

[1] Jeffrey L. Sammons, *Ideology, Mimesis, Fantasy: Charles Sealsfield, Friedrich Gerstäcker, Karl May, and Other German Novelists of America* (Chapel Hill: U of North Carolina P, 1998), x.

[2] Sammons, 254.

[3] Sammons, 229–45.

[4] Jürgen Wehnert, "Der Karl-May-Verlag," in Ueding and Tschapke, eds., *Karl-May-Handbuch,* (Stuttgart: Kröner, 1987), 684. See also Reinhard Tschapke, "Der literarische Markt im 19. Jahrhundert: Verlag, Vertriebs- und Verbreitungsformen," in Ueding and Tschapke, eds., 39–56.

[5] An outline of the edition and an overview of the already published volume can be seen at < http://karlmay.uni-bielefeld.de/kmg/primlit/histkrit.htm>.

[6] Hans-Dieter Steinmetz, "'Es werden hier deutsche Werke massenhaft nachgedruckt': Zeitgenössische finnische, tschechische und slowenische Karl-May-Übersetzungen in Einwanderer-Verlagen der USA," *Jahrbuch der Karl-May-Gesellschaft* (1994): 313. According to Ulrich von Thüna, May's works have been translated into thirty-nine languages. "Übersetzungen," in Ueding and Tschapke, eds., 646.

[7] See Steinmetz, 312–37.

[8] Franz Kandolf, "Kara Ben Nemsi auf den Spuren Layards: Ein Blick in die Werkstätte eines Schriftstellers," *Karl-May-Jahrbuch* (1922): 197–207.

[9] Mounir Fendri, "Neues zu Karl Mays Krüger-Bei: Das Manuskript des Muhammad ben Abdallah Nimsi alias Johann Gottlieb Krüger," *Jahrbuch der Karl-May-Gesellschaft* (1992): 277–98.

[10] See, for example, Helmut Lieblang, "'Der Inhaber dieses Buiruldu...': Alfred Edmund Brehms Orient in Karl Mays Frühwerk," *Jahrbuch der Karl-May-Gesellschaft* (1997): 232–71. See also Wolfgang Hammer, "Karl Mays Novelle 'Leilet' als Beispiel für seine Quellenverwendung," *Jahrbuch der Karl-May-Gesellschaft* (1996): 205–30.

[11] Gregor Seferens, "'Immer... wenn ich an den Indianer denke': Eine Studie zur Entwicklung des Indianerbildes bei Karl May," *Jahrbuch der Karl-May-Gesellschaft* (1994): 86–103.

[12] Petra Küppers, "Karl Mays Indianerbild und die Tradition der Fremddarstellung: Eine kulturgeschichtliche Analyse," *Jahrbuch der Karl-May-Gesellschaft* (1996): 315–45.

[13] Several leading scholars on May, it should be added, ardently reject recent approaches that focus on intertextuality and discourses in the author's work. See Hans Wollschläger's polemical introduction to the 1998 *Jahrbuch der Karl-May-Gesellschaft* (7–8) and Helmut Schmiedt's article in the same volume, "Karl May gibt es gar nicht: Beobachtungen und Überlegungen aus neuerer literaturwissenschaftlicher Sicht," 152–63. Wollschläger calls these recent approaches "blödsinnig und gottverlassen" (8). Wollschläger and Schmiedt fail to see that analyses of the interdependency of texts raise questions that underlie both May *and* his sources.

[14] See Andreas Graf, "Literarisierung und Kolportageroman: Überlegungen zu Publikum und Kommunikationsstrategie eines Massenmediums im 19. Jahrhundert," *Jahrbuch der Karl-May-Gesellschaft* (1999): 191–203.

[15] "Nach optimistischen Schätzungen konnten um 1830 nur etwa 40 Prozent, 1870 ungefähr 75 Prozent und 1900 nahezu 90 Prozent der Bevölkerung lesen." Reinhard Tschapke, "Der literarische Markt im 19. Jahrhundert: Verlag, Vertriebs- und Verbreitungsformen," in Ueding and Tschapke, eds., 55.

[16] "Karl Mays Orientzyklus," in my *Orientalismus, Kolonialismus und Moderne: Zum Bild des Orients in der deutschsprachigen Kultur um 1900* (Stuttgart: Metzler, 1997), 41–164. Part of the chapter appeared as "Orientalism, Imperialism, and Nationalism: Karl May's *Orientzyklus*," in Sara Friedrichsmeyer, Sara Lennox, and Susanne Zantop, eds., *The Imperialist Imagination: German Colonialism and Its Legacy* (Ann Arbor: U of Michigan P, 1998), 51–67.

[17] Klaus J. Bade, "Die deutsche überseeische Massenauswanderung im 19. und frühen 20. Jahrhundert: Bestimmungsfaktoren und Entwicklungsbedingungen," in Bade, ed., *Auswanderer, Wanderarbeiter, Gastarbeiter: Bevölkerung, Arbeitsmarkt und Wanderung in Deutschland seit der Mitte des 19. Jahrhunderts*, vol. 1 (Ostfildern: Scripta Mercaturae, 1984), 270.

[18] Bade, "From Emigration to Immigration: The German Experience in the Nineteenth and Twentieth Centuries," in Bade and Myron Weiner, eds., *Migration Past, Migration Future: Germany and the United States* (Providence, RI: Berghahn, 1997), 5.

[19] On the various phases and repercussions of emigration to the United States, see Agnes Bretting et al., "Deutsche in den USA," in Bade, ed., *Deutsche im Ausland, Fremde in Deutschland: Migration in Geschichte und Gegenwart* (Munich: Beck, 1992), 135–85.

[20] Bade, "From Emigration to Immigration: The German Experience in the Nineteenth and Twentieth Centuries," 7.

[21] Volker R. Berghahn, *Imperial Germany, 1871–1914: Economy, Society, Culture and Politics* (Providence, RI: Berghahn, 1994), 43.

[22] Gudrun Keindorf, "Formen und Funktion des Reisens bei Karl May: Ein Problemaufriß," *Jahrbuch der Karl-May-Gesellschaft* (1996): 294.

[23] Elisabeth Gohrbandt, "'Selbst bei einem drei Jahre langen Urbarmachen einer Wildnis wird man nur ein Settler, aber kein Westman': Auswanderer und Siedler in Karl Mays Nordamerikaerzählungen," *Jahrbuch der Karl-May-Gesellschaft* (1995): 165–205.

[24] Karl May, *Winnetou I* (Zurich: Haffmans, 1996), 97. All translations from the German are mine.

[25] See also C. Lindemann, "Verdrängte Revolutionen? Eichendorffs 'Schloß Dürande' und Karl Mays Klekih-Petra-Episode im *Winnetou*-Roman," *Jahrbuch der Eichendorff-Gesellschaft* 34 (1974): 24–38; Claus Roxin, "Vernunft und Aufklärung bei Karl May: Zur Deutung der Klekih-Petra Episode im *Winnetou*," *Mitteilungen der Karl-May-Gesellschaft* 28 (1976): 25–30. I disagree especially with Roxin's and Gohrbandt's (footnote 23, 179–81) interpretations of Klekih-Petra; both downplay the antidemocratic message of the figure.

[26] May, *Winnetou II* (Zurich: Haffmans, 1996), 396.

[27] A possible source for Old Firehand might be Carl Beyschlag's narrative "Die Prairien: Erlebnisse eines deutschen Flüchtlings," *Gartenlaube* (1859): 460–64. See Helmut Schmiedt, "Winnetou I–III," in Ueding and Tschapke, eds., 210–11.

[28] May, *Winnetou III* (Zurich: Haffmans, 1996), 368.

[29] For an account of the construction and dismantling of the legend, see Christian Heermann, *Der Mann, der Old Shatterhand war: Eine Karl-May-Biographie* (Berlin: Verlag der Nation, 1988), 238–358.

[30] A comprehensive analysis of all emigrant characters remains to be written; Gohrbandt's essay is a step in this direction. One such additional type is Tante Droll, a cross-dressing trapper character, who — like May — is from Saxony and shares some biographical details with the author. Tante Droll appears in several texts, for example, *Der Schatz im Silbersee*.

[31] Gohrbandt, 182–84.

[32] In "Karl Mays Amerika-Exotik und deutsche Wirklichkeit: Zur sozialpsychologischen Funktion von Trivialliteratur im wilhelminischen Deutschland," Jochen Schulte-Sasse argues that pulp fiction is distinguished by the indirect nature of its aesthetic elements. In Schmiedt, ed., *Karl May* (Frankfurt am Main: Suhrkamp, 1983), 110.

[33] Bade, "Transnationale Migration und Arbeitsmarkt im Kaiserreich: Vom Agrarstaat mit starker Industrie zum Industriestaat mit starker agrarischer Ba-

sis," in T. Pierenkemper and R. Tilly, eds., *Historische Arbeitsmarktforschung: Entstehung, Entwicklung und Probleme der Vermarktung von Arbeitskraft* (Göttingen: Vandenhoeck & Ruprecht, 1982), 182–211.

[34] Berghahn, 310–11.

[35] "In 1871 some 63.9 percent of the population still lived in communities of under 2,000. By 1890, this figure had declined to 53 percent and, by 1910, to 40 percent." Berghahn, 47.

[36] See tables in Ute Frevert, *Women in German History: From Bourgeois Emancipation to Sexual Liberation*, trans. Stuart McKinnon-Evans et al. (Oxford: Berg, 1990), 328–34. Berghahn cites slightly differing statistics (308–10).

[37] Anthony Giddens, *The Consequences of Modernity* (Stanford, CA: Stanford UP, 1990), 79–111.

[38] Wolfgang Schivelbusch, *Disenchanted Night: The Industrialization of Light in the Nineteenth Century*, trans. Angela Davies (Berkeley: U of California P, 1995).

[39] Installation of the first concrete street pavement is recorded on July 13, 1891, in Bellefontaine, Ohio. Leonard C. Bruno, *On the Move: A Chronology of Advances in Transportation* (Detroit: Gale Research, 1993), 137.

[40] "The problem of order is seen here as one of time-space distanciation — the conditions under which time and space are organised so as to connect presence and absence. . . . In conditions of modernity, the level of time-space distanciation is much greater than in even the most developed of agrarian civilisations." Giddens, 14.

[41] Berghahn, 248.

[42] Berghahn, 9. See also Wolfgang J. Mommsen, *Imperial Germany, 1867–1918: Politics, Culture, and Society in an Authoritarian State* (London: Arnold, 1995), 113.

[43] On patterns of social mobility, see Berghahn, 50–55.

[44] See note 30.

[45] Berghahn, 12.

[46] Gohrbandt, 178.

[47] See my discussion of homosocial relations in May's *Orientzyklus* in *Orientalismus, Kolonialismus und Moderne*, 69–84.

[48] Schulte-Sasse, 119, 124–26.

[49] Georg Simmel, "Das Abenteuer," in his *Philosophische Kultur: Über das Abenteuer, die Geschlechter und die Krise der Moderne. Gesammelte Essais* (Berlin: Wagenbach, 1986), 33.

Making Way for the Third Sex: Liberal and Antiliberal Impulses in Mann's Portrayal of Male-Male Desire in His Early Short Fiction

Robert Tobin

IT MAY SEEM odd to include Thomas Mann in a study of realism, considering that he wrote the majority of his novels and short fiction in the twentieth century, long after the age of realism. Indeed, some of his greatest literature appeared after the Second World War, when the movement had already found a final resting place in the lexica and encyclopedias of literary history. Nonetheless, Mann considered himself a nineteenth-century writer, heavily indebted to such masters of realism as Dickens and Dostoyevsky. With respect to male-male desire, one of the primary concerns of his works, he is even more thoroughly a product of the late nineteenth-century realist imagination than he himself admits.[1] Deeply entrenched in Mann's early short fiction is one of the major constructions emerging from the late nineteenth-century German-speaking world that produced realism: the modern homosexual, who was discovered — some would say invented — by liberal sexologists, jurists, and activists in Germany and the Austro-Hungarian empire. Admittedly, Mann's essayistic writings actually endorse a subsequent politics of male-male desire that came to be popular with antiliberal modernist thinkers at the end of the century, but the late nineteenth-century realist view of the "third sex" fundamentally shapes his literature. Thus, Mann's fiction promotes a liberal medico-legal vision of same-sex desire that emerges from the same roots as late nineteenth-century German realism, although his nonfiction writing flirts with a modernist, early twentieth-century understanding of male-male sexuality.

The "Third Sex"

The progressive vision of same-sex desire espoused by the late nineteenth-century medical community and the homosexual emancipation movement is aptly summed up by the term "the third sex." It is the view that men who love men and women who love women are characterized by gender inversion. In other words, members of the third sex are actually female souls dwelling in male bodies or male souls in female bodies. Karl Heinrich Ulrichs (1825–95) coined the term and articulated this conception of same-sex desire most influentially. Ulrichs can be considered the founder of the homosexual emancipation movement in Germany, the first such movement in the world.[2] A classically trained lawyer, he openly argued for the rights of men who loved men, going so far as to appear in person at a congress of 500 lawyers in Munich in 1867 to call for the decriminalization of consensual sexual acts between adult men.

The first recorded use of the term "the third sex" is in an 1862 letter from Ulrichs to his family in which he "came out" as a man who loved other men.[3] In the brochure *Vindex*, which was published in 1864, he identifies *das dritte Geschlecht* as a specific kind of human being, comparable to but different from the other two sexes; he labels these beings *Urninge* [urnings].[4] The identifying characteristic of this third sex is gender inversion: members of the third sex have female souls although they possess male bodies. His initial discussion of female souls trapped in male bodies rapidly expands to include female "urnings," and he eventually assumes that there are as many female urnings as male ones.[5] At times he refers to the female urnings as the fourth sex, but in common usage both male and female urnings came to be grouped together under the category of the third sex.

Fundamentally, the model of the third sex has the important effect of putting homosexual men and lesbian women together as a single class of individuals. It is, to use Eve Kosofsky Sedgwick's vocabulary, minoritizing instead of universalizing.[6] That is to say, it argues that a discrete subgroup of humans loves members of its own sex; it thereby rejects the possibility that every person might have the capability of loving homosexually. Rather than allowing for a broad spectrum of sexualities and frequent changes in orientation, it favors a strict taxonomy of separate classes of sexuality. Ulrichs is typical of, and perhaps in part responsible for, the late nineteenth-century European belief that the homosexual is not simply a person who happens to commit a homosexual act but, in Foucault's famous words, "a personage, a past, a case history, and a childhood, in addition to being a type of life, a life form, and a morphology, with an indiscreet anatomy and possibly a mysterious physiology."[7] The nature of the urning is not likely to change, because his or her sexual identity is innate and immutable, largely for biological reasons: in the book *Memnon,* published in 1868, Ulrichs gives a detailed account of the development of embryos into males, females, and urnings.[8] The ideology of the third sex is thus closely bound up with assumptions of fixed sexual categories.

Ulrichs believes that science and medicine can be harnessed for his vision of love and desire. In what was intended to be the inaugural issue of a journal devoted to the third sex titled *Uranus,* Ulrichs expresses the hope that more physicians will read the journal.[9] In fact, those involved in the homosexual emancipation movement actively sought out the assistance of the medical community, many of whose members shared the movement's liberal goals of decriminalizing consensual sexual acts among adults.[10] While Ulrichs's belief that sexuality is set in the embryo does not permit culture to have a large effect on desire, he is willing to speculate on the ability of medical science to change desire: he imagines that a blood transfusion from a nonurning (a "dioning," in his terminology) could change the urning's sexual orientation, although probably only for a fortnight.[11] So staunch is Ulrichs's faith in the medical world that he is willing to accept the possibility that medicine could some day cure all urnings and thus remove them from the face of the earth. He asserts that because same-sex desire is a medical and biological condition, it should not be penalized. Instead, if society cannot live with it, physicians and scientists should be encouraged to find ways of removing it by medical, rather than legal, means.[12] That much of his statement is made in the subjunctive indicates that he does not really want to see a world cleansed of homosexuality, but the fact that he is willing to entertain such possibilities shows the extent to which Ulrichs is ready to trust medical science.

This biologistic understanding of the third sex as an innate and immutable part of identity, changeable only by such physiological interventions as blood transfusions, makes it possible to see the third sex not only as comparable to males and females but also as analogous to racial categories, which the nineteenth century was also increasingly prone to seeing as a physical fact. In particular, the third sex was compared to Jews, who, as Sander Gilman notes, were regarded more and more as a racial rather than a religious group as the nineteenth century progressed.[13] Ulrichs repeats the comparison between urnings and Jews insistently and with a strong biological intonation. In his most striking statement on this subject he declares that male urnings only act the man's role, just as the Jew born in Germany only enacts Germanness or the German born in France only performs Frenchness.[14] The gender inversion that Ulrichs believes is key to the understanding of same-sex desire is firmly linked to the innate national status attributed to Jews and Germans. Like the urnings, neither of these groups can escape their identity. A biological understanding of both sexuality and nationality makes the comparison between homosexuality and Jewishness almost inevitable in the German context.[15]

Some of the connection between Jewishness and homosexuality is attributable to the traits of orientalism and exoticism in German culture. As Gilman has demonstrated, Jews in Germany were regarded as an increasingly feminized Other within German society.[16] For many Germans — from Goethe and Winckelmann to the photographer Gloeden and Thomas Mann — the Mediterranean was a realm in which same-sex desire was permitted and practiced, and in the cultural fantasy of Germans the appeal of the Jew was similar to the appeal of the Southern Italian or the North African.[17] But while both Jews and homosexuals could be seen as exotic outsiders within the German populace, neither group could be easily distinguished, respectively, from non-Jewish or heterosexual Germans. With the assimilation of the Jews into nineteenth-century German society, it became increasingly difficult to differentiate Jews from Germans on the basis of external characteristics.[18] Similarly, it was generally not possible to tell homosexuals from heterosexuals on the basis of mere appearance. Thus, in both cases biologically trained, scientifically schooled physicians claimed to be able to provide the diagnosis that would alert the public to the otherness of these groups by giving the final word on who was an outsider and who was not.

As appalling as this mixture of race, sexuality, and pathology sounds to twenty-first-century sensibilities, the general thrust of this medico-biologistic racializing view of sexuality was a liberal effort to build on the model of the emancipation of the Jews, which progressed intermittently from Enlightenment theories and Napoleonic reforms to the ultimate removal of all legal distinctions between Jews and non-Jews in Germany in 1871.[19] A large element of Ulrichs's identification of urnings with Jews consists in the affirmation of minority politics. Minority groups should stick together and fight for their rights, according to Ulrichs, whether they be Poles, Catholics, Hanoverians, Jews, or illegitimate children.[20] He demands freedom for minorities, castigates politicians who call themselves liberal while not defending minorities, and speaks a language redolent of human rights.[21] In keeping with his progressive agenda — and, perhaps, also because his view of male-male desire is predicated on the presence of female souls in male bodies — Ulrichs avoids misogynistic discourses.

Following this liberal paradigm, nineteenth-century homosexual rights activists such as Ulrichs wanted to construct a strong sense of identity within the third sex and demanded a series of rights for that group. Ulrichs tirelessly sought to unify urnings within cities by serving as a clearinghouse for contact requests; he then attempted to put these communities throughout Germany, Austria, and the world in contact with each other. His efforts at establishing a publication for urnings were unprecedented, as was his attempt to create legal funds for urnings who got into trouble with the law. His willingness to demand that even urnings accused of atrocities such as the mutilation and murder of children be granted full due process in courts of law is noteworthy even today.[22] Many of his other proposals are literally a century ahead of their time. Most notably, Ulrichs wanted urnings to have the right to marry, and he envisioned the day that unions between men would be sanctioned in St. Hedwig's Church in Berlin.[23]

In short, Ulrichs sets forth a remarkably coherent view of same-sex desire that has proven extraordinarily resilient. Such important sexologists as Magnus Hirschfeld followed it closely, and it still informs liberal discussions of homosexuality. In the third sex theory, male and female homosexuals are brought together in a single fixed category, which is characterized by gender inversion. This gender inversion has a biological basis, which allows for comparisons to racial categories. The purpose of these comparisons is to promote minority rights as part of a larger liberal platform supported by, among others, progressive members of the legal and medical communities.

Emancipated Women and the Third Sex in Mann's Early Fiction

The attentive reader of Mann will have noted many possible connections between the late nineteenth-century legal and medical analysis of same-sex desire and Mann's writings. The interest in same-sex desire is, of course, a starting point, as is Mann's fascination with disease and pathology. Mann's curiously ambivalent relationship with Jewishness, which spans his marriage to the daughter of a prominent Jewish family and the anti-Semitic asides in many of his early writings, provides an important parallel to the complexities of his portrayal of male-male desire both as pathological and as central to his project. Along these lines, the orientalism and exoticism inherent in the connection between Jewishness and homosexuality show up in Mann's constant fetishization of the erotic appeal between North and South.[24]

Mann's early short fiction demonstrates that the late nineteenth-century model of the third sex underlies his approach to the treatment of same-sex desire. The most explicit evidence for this supposition comes from a depiction of an emancipated woman in an obscure early novella, "Gerächt." Mann is not famous for the emancipated women in his fiction, nor does he seem to have wanted such renown: "Gerächt," which was published in the literary journal *Simplicissimus* in 1899, was, unlike almost all of his other early short fiction, which generally appeared both in magazines and in story collections, never republished in his lifetime.[25] Perhaps Mann subsequently realized the extent to which the figure of the third sex is featured in this story and, therefore, wanted to take it out of circulation.

Ulrichs established a precedent for Mann by comparing male homosexuals to emancipated women, arguing at one point that male urnings are not effeminate males, as is typically assumed, but, rather, are like emancipated women in that they are actually "virilized": that is to say, they are, in fact, real women who, under the effects of society, have assumed a masculine role.[26] While this is obviously not an entirely positive view of the emancipation of women, it provides for the possibility of using the figure of the liberated woman to theorize about the homosexual man. Mann's "Gerächt" takes advantage of this opportunity. The narrator describes a friend named Dunja Stegemann, who is explicitly presented as a product of "Emanzipation."[27] Perhaps modeled on Lou Andreas-Salomé, Dunja speaks Russian, French, and German fluently, lives as a "Philosophin und Junggesellin," and publishes literary and musical critiques in obscure journals (176). What specifically links this emancipated woman to the third-sex model is the narrator's description of her as a "Weib mit vollkommen männlich gebildetem Hirn" (177). Dunja thus presents a classic case of gender inversion. Like many such cases reported in the medical journals of the time, her "masculine brain" also affects her female body: tall, with small breasts and hips, she looks like a boy.

For a time the narrator enjoys his buddy-style relationship with Dunja Stegemann. A relationship between the masculine narrator and this person with the masculine brain could have a homosexual tendency, at least on the mental and spiritual level. To ensure that this male-male relationship remains asexual, the narrator claims to regard Stegemann's body with disgust; he tells her at one point that the charm of the relationship lies in the tension between their intellectual affinity and the pronounced distaste he has for her body. The logic here is typical of homophobia among certain groups of men in times of sexual uncertainty: it must be made explicit that the male-male friendship is not sexual in nature. References to Wagner and his opera *Tristan,* which the two characters discuss, however, suggest forbidden sexuality, as Wagner was, like the poet Walt Whitman, something of a code word in late nineteenth-century Continental homosexual subcultures.[28] These allusions imply that the novella is not only about the sexual tensions inherent in a relationship with an emancipated woman but also about the potentially frightening possibility of a relationship with a member of the third sex.

The novella turns on the revelation that Dunja had a love affair with an attractive young man in the past. Although the narrator hastens to reassure himself that it was Platonic, Dunja insists that it was, indeed, physical. The narrator ponders the fact that a man has embraced Dunja's allegedly so unattractive body (179). The thought spurs his own fantasy about a sexual relationship with Dunja, an idea that she rejects. Although no sexual acts take place between the two characters, Mann uses the figure of the emancipated woman to tell a story that could certainly be about a man coming to terms with his desire for a member of the third sex.

Queer Men and the Third Sex

As one of his earliest published works, "Gerächt" sets the tone for the depiction of boyish women and sexually uncertain men as Mann prepares the way for the third sex. While there are some somewhat emancipated women in Mann's subsequent fiction, the short stories that he published in 1898 in the collection *Der kleine Herr Friedemann* (Little Mr. Friedemann) showcase a series of queer men who exhibit many of the features of the third sex. All six of the stories in this collection feature peculiar men, generally afflicted with health problems, who are somehow stunted in their ability to love. While Mann does not make an explicit issue of gender inversion in these stories, he links biological infirmities with sexuality in a way that clearly points to the late nineteenth-century view of the third sex. One example from this collection is "Der Wille zum Glück" (The Will to Happiness), which was initially published in *Simplicissimus* in 1896. Young Paolo Hofmann, a talented artist from a well-to-do family, cannot marry because of his weak heart. His will to happiness, however, keeps him alive until he is finally allowed to get married — whereupon he dies in his wedding bed. Although the story is ostensibly about heterosexual love, many of its constructs relate it to the discursive tradition surrounding the third sex.

To begin with, Paolo is sickly, which immediately makes his case a medical matter. Moreover, his particular sickness is metaphorically significant: because "matters of the heart" are, traditionally, love affairs, it is not hard to conclude that Paolo's ailment has to do with his secret passion. These desires are further overdetermined as forbidden because they are directed at a Jewish woman, Baroness Ada Stein. The question of the Steins' Jewishness is thematized from the moment they are first mentioned. Mr. Stein is not Jewish, but his wife is "eine häßliche kleine Jüdin in einem geschmacklosen grauen Kleid" (47). The anti-Semitism in the description of the mother is unmistakable, but it serves a function in the novella: given the strong analogy between Jews and homosexuals in the tradition of the third sex, Paolo's medically forbidden love for a Jew might be comparable to homosexual love. In addition, the Jewish theme belongs to a related discourse involving mixed racial heritage. Paolo is himself only half German: his father married a native woman while making a fortune on South American plantations. Paolo is, thus, like many of Mann's characters with questionable sexualities in that he is in part foreign. His beloved Ada Stein, too, belongs to a third intermediary category of race, if not of sexuality. Both she and Paolo are, therefore, clearly marked with the erotic appeal of the Other. Thus, "Der Wille zum Glück" can be read as a depiction of the forbidden love between members of intermediary sexual categories, as well as intermediary racial ones.

Paolo travels to escape his forbidden love, saying that traveling must replace drinking, smoking, and loving (52). This is one of the most explicit statements of the connection, recurring repeatedly in Mann's oeuvre, between travel and illicit desire. Furthermore, the places to which he travels add a specifically homoerotic coloring to this forbidden desire. First he goes to Munich, which was regarded in the nineteenth century as the German city most tolerant of male-male sexuality; Ulrichs repeatedly refers to Munich and Bavaria as the areas of Germany that are most tolerant of urnings.[29] Then he moves to Italy, which had no laws against sodomy and was, therefore, a beloved travel destination for well-to-do homosexual men from northern European countries such as England and Germany that did have antisodomy laws. Like so many of these men who eventually lived in exile in the South, Paolo declares that he feels at home in Italy (52). Thus, the particular patterns of flight that this artist chooses reinforce the notion that his forbidden desire may have to do with exotic taste for something like the third sex.

Curiously, Mann's narrator always happens to be traveling in the same areas as Paolo, and he also moves to Italy. Not only does the narrator have the same escape mechanisms as Paolo but he also repeatedly describes Paolo as attractive. Indeed, when he runs into Paolo in Munich, he compares him to an Italian model (43). Paolo's transitional racial status thus turns out to have the same appeal for the story's narrator as Ada's does for Paolo: the narrator is, perhaps, in love with Paolo, the representative of the intermediary type between German and South American, just as Paolo is in love with Ada, who is an intermediary between German and Jew. Here, then, the racial categories stand in for sexual ones, in a way typical of late nineteenth-century discourse on the third sex. "Der Wille zum Glück" easily lends itself to an interpretation emphasizing the biological and medical nature of the third sex.

The title story of *Der kleine Herr Friedemann,* which was first published in the *Neue Deutsche Rundschau* in 1897, also operates with the iconography of the third sex. It, too, relies on the notion of a sickly individual whose illness prevents him from following the customary patterns of heterosexual love. Although Johannes Friedemann denies to Gerda von Rinnlingen that he was born with his malady, the fact that it befalls him when he is an infant in his nursery makes it into a lifelong affliction in keeping with the late nineteenth-century medical and legal view of the third sex (92). That the cause of the affliction is the inattentiveness of a drunken nurse is a touch of naturalism that, with that movement's interest in pathology, is thoroughly in keeping with the spirit of the medical and political discourses surrounding the third sex.

The accident in the nursery not only stunts Friedemann's growth but also results in his inability to engage in heterosexual relations. After a failed love affair at sixteen, he renounces amour forever (69). It is, on the one hand, significant that Friedemann thereby declares his lack of sexual interest in women. But on another level, the use of the vocabulary of renunciation is itself telling, for Mann consistently views renunciation as one of the mandates of same-sex desire — a man cannot, in Mann's opinion, act on his love for another man. On two different levels, then, Friedemann looks like a candidate for being one of the third sex, and, indeed, the narrator describes him as filled with unsatisfied desires (71). Moreover, he develops many of the secondary characteristics of members of the third sex. He educates himself beyond the call of duty, has a peculiar literary taste, and is acquainted with foreign cultures. Above all, he is devoted to the theater, pointing in the direction of the sexual ambiguity that turn-of-the-century medicine attributed to actors.[30] To sum it all up, the narrator declares that he is an epicurean, suggesting the decadent, hedonistic sensuality that was attributed to members of the third sex (70).

When Friedemann meets Gerda von Rinnlingen, the wife of the military man who has just moved to town, he discovers in her what he hopes will be a soul mate. There is in fact evidence that she too belongs to the third sex. By her own account, she has also been sickly throughout much of her life (84). And in her own way, she is as emancipated a figure as Dunja Stegemann. Just as Friedemann has many of the characteristics of male members of the third sex, Gerda has many of the masculine characteristics of a gender-inverted female. She smokes, rides, and is generally boyish (73). For the medical thinking of the day, it is not at all surprising that her marriage is childless.[31] When Johannes meets Gerda, he can, therefore, hope that he has at last met another member of the third sex. As so often in Mann's stories about the third sex, Wagner's music plays a significant role: at a performance of *Lohengrin* Johannes becomes aware of his erotic attraction to Gerda. As he grows increasingly emboldened by his love for her, the narrator's query, "War sie nicht eine Frau und er ein Mann?" becomes something other than rhetorical. Perhaps the question needs to be taken seriously — perhaps Friedemann is hoping to find in Gerda Rinnlingen another sexual intermediary. Her refusal to return his love links her once again to Dunja Stegemann and points to the difficulties Mann sees for lasting relationships between members of the third sex. And his suicide fits only too well with the prognosis often offered to members of the third sex by medical thinkers.

The Third Sex, Irony, and "Life": *Tristan*

While the stories in *Der kleine Herr Friedemann* feature a series of lonely men with problematic sexualities (one could continue the analysis given above with the other stories in the collection, including "Enttäuschung,"[32] "Der Tod," "Der Bajazzo," and "Tobias Mindernickel"), Mann's next collection, *Tristan,* which appeared in 1903, contrasts these members of the third sex more explicitly with the heterosexual order. Generally, the stories expose the queer men to ridicule and present the heterosexuals as *Leben* in opposition, presumably, to the *Geist* of the third sex. But while Mann seems to endorse a submission of spirit to life, he reveals in the *Betrachtungen eines Unpolitischen* (Reflections of a Nonpolitical Man, 1918) that the surrender of spirit to life is always slightly ironic.[33] Thus, in this collection he gives the third sex a masochistically inflected centrality through his depiction of its ironic submission to heterosexuality.

It is worthwhile to begin with the explanation of the relationship between spirit and life that Mann gives in the *Betrachtungen*. This relationship is explicitly not comparable to gender, although it is eroticized (570). Because the genders of these two spheres are not fixed, the erotic relationship between them can be either homo- or heterosexual. Mann adds, however, an analysis of the power dynamics of this relationship that is definitely gendered. Specifically, the subordination of spirit to body that he endorses is, in his words, no longer really masculine, because it is too submissive. It is also typical of artists (25). Thus, the artist — and Mann is generally thinking of male artists — takes on a nonmasculine, feminine approach to a powerful body, most likely represented by someone such as a young soldier. The male artist, with his feminine attitude toward masculine life, takes on the role of the third sex, with its gender inversions that Mann generally finds distasteful. Indeed, Mann can scarcely imagine a fully masculine artist, "so bar aller Ironie . . . so männlich befriedigt . . . so bürgerlich standfest" (578). This is because for him, masculinity is typical of enlightened didactic rationality with its moralistic directness, which stands in opposition to the irony and ambivalence that is so important for Mann's view of art (404). Thus, despite the submission of spirit to life, spirit remains dominant in the realm of art. Although in art the spirit subordinates itself to life, there is triumph and superiority in this surrender.

The ironic submission of the spirit to life and the ambiguous role of the third sex show up in "Luischen," which first appeared in *Die Gesellschaft* in 1900. Typically for Mann, the story centers on a freakish man — in this case, the monstrously overweight lawyer Christian Jacoby. He seems to have no erotic appeal for his wife, and no one knows why they married in the first place. The marriage is childless. Like Johannes Friedemann, Jacoby is filled with self-hatred. When he dies on the stage at his wife's party, dressed up in red satin baby clothes and grotesquely dancing for the audience, a Jewish doctor ascertains his death, linking Jewishness with the medical treatment of his condition.

Jacoby's wife, who was baptized Anna Margarethe Rosa Amalie but goes by the acronym of her given names, Amra, is closely integrated into society, in contrast to her outsider husband. With the musician Alfred Läutner, with whom she is having an affair, she organizes a party that seems to showcase sexuality: it features African dancers, about as sensually erotic a spectacle as provincial Germany at the turn of the century could imagine. Amra and Alfred perform piano music for four hands while Christian dances himself to death. "Making music" is often a substitute for "making love" in Mann — Johannes Friedemann also wants to play the piano with Gerda Rinnlingen. In "Luischen" the connection between music and sex is clear, because it is only while watching them perform together as he dances in front of the audience that Christian realizes that his wife is having an affair with Alfred. This realization leads to his death and seems to suggest the weakness of the third sex in the face of heterosexual life.

The irony of the story becomes apparent, though, in Amra's character. The narrator mentions the exoticism of her nickname, which goes hand in hand with her dark skin. This exoticism has the tendency to position her away from the heterosexual majority. It turns out that she and Alfred are both sickly — admittedly, not seriously so, but sickly nonetheless (the narrator asserts that they are just ill enough to enjoy their ailments; *Wille*, 151). In her sickliness and childlessness, she resembles Gerda von Rinnlingen, who is also a potential soul mate for a member of the third sex. Thus, Amra turns out to be a better match for her husband than at first seems to be the case. The story centers on Christian's humiliation and death, but the victory of Amra and her lover is less clear-cut than expected and thus reveals the irony of Mann's degradation of the third sex.

The title story of the *Tristan* collection provides further evidence of this pattern of both subordinating and exalting the third sex. Detlev Spinell, the writer who demonstrates that what distinguishes a writer from all other people is the amount of difficulty he has with writing, is cut out of the cloth of the third sex. The novella is set in Einfried, a sanatorium filled not only with consumptives but also with men suffering from the effects of venereal diseases, which thematizes the medical contribution to the construction of sexuality. Spinell is no exception, as he is marked as sickly. His bad teeth are mentioned repeatedly, but his real sickness seems to be a lack of discipline. He says that he has come to the sanatorium because of its sleek Empire style, which does not allow for lascivious ornamentation. He gets up early at Einfried because he usually likes to sleep in late. Only under the medical auspices of the sanatorium can he control himself. The fact that he is also notably lacking in manliness — he does not need to shave, as he only has a few eccentric tufts of facial hair — suggests that this lack of self-control, this need for a medically supervised self-overcoming, is related to issues of gender. His lack of masculinity, a signifier of the third sex, is part of a generally undisciplined nature that needs medical control just like the members of the third sex.

In all of this Spinell is depicted as clearly in opposition to Anton Klöterjahn, a monument to testicular masculinity. Spinell and Klöterjahn are in competition for the love of Gabriele Klöterjahn. In a sense, Anton has won from the outset, for Gabriele has already chosen him. But she, like so many of the other women in Mann's early short fiction, has many traits of the third sex. She is truly ill with tuberculosis, much more so than Spinell. She has an artistic sensibility that renders her suspicious in Mann's works, given Mann's understanding of the gender inversion of the artist. That she and Spinell share a love of Wagner's opera *Tristan,* which gives the story its title, further links her fate to that of the third sex, given Wagner's importance in homosexual discourses. Anton and his son may survive as representatives of "life" at the end of the story, but Spinell has, indeed, managed to pull Gabriele over to his side of the battle, sorely undercutting the triumph of life over the third sex.

"Tonio Kröger," which also appeared in the *Tristan* collection, not only deals more explicitly than the other stories with the question of the third sex but also thematizes the irony in the submission of the third sex to heterosexuality. In this story there is no need to read between the lines regarding the protagonist's gender and sexuality. In what was certainly a bold move in 1903, the narrator bluntly announces in the first pages of the story that Tonio is in love with Hans. Although he goes on to fall in love with Ingeborg Holm, the male-male attraction makes the first and most lasting impression in the story. Following the tradition of the third sex, Tonio's desire for Hans is linked to his inadequate manliness. Not only is Tonio unable to keep up with the boys in such gender-specific activities as horseback riding, at which Hans excels, but he cannot even stick with his sex while dancing. Because he ends up dancing the woman's part in dance class, his instructor, the unforgettable Herr Knaak, teases him as "Fräulein Kröger."[34]

The medical factors of the discussion of gender inversion in the third sex come to the fore in the references to Kröger's poor health. Like many of Mann's male protagonists, Kröger is of mixed blood, having a Prussian father but an exotic mother, thus making his intermediary sexual status also a racial issue — which again is a mainstay of the discourses around the third sex. In contrast to the dark-complexioned Kröger, Hans Hansen and Ingeborg Holm are presented not only as having sexualities that are straight as an arrow but also as blond and blue-eyed, thus belonging to the Germanic national ideal. Here, too, heterosexual and homosexual are mapped onto a model that pits the Germanic in opposition to the foreign.

When Kröger is older, he brings up the issue of gender inversion when discussing the inadequate masculinity of artists. In Munich he denies to his friend Lisaweta Iwanowna that artists are men and compares them to the papal castrati (40). The gender inversion of artists, though, is related to their irony. Kröger concludes that artists should not try to change the Hans Hansens of the world, real men who prefer books with pictures of horses to poetry. While this can be seen as a generous recognition of difference, it also has an elitist side, keeping poetry only for those who understand it. Here, too, Kröger is quite explicit, explaining to Lisaweta that pure, unadulterated feeling produces an artistic fiasco because it is sentimental and lacking in irony (39). The true artist always undercuts his love with irony. Thus, in the last lines of the novella, Kröger's love of Hans Hansen and Ingeborg Holm is a product not only of desire and bliss but also of envy and "ein klein wenig Verachtung" (81).

Like "Luischen" and "Tristan," "Tonio Kröger" documents the submission of the third sex to heterosexuality, while it ironizes that submission. From the beginning the narrator makes clear that he who loves suffers, and Kröger does, indeed, love. Thus, while Mann places Tonio Kröger's suffering into ironic context, he nonetheless keeps this suffering as the central aspect of the story. The ironic but real submission of the third sex's mind to the life of the first and second sexes, then, becomes the leitmotif of the stories published in the collection *Tristan*.[35]

The Antiliberal Reaction

"Die erotische Ironie des Geistes" is Mann's definition, however improbable that might seem in the contemporary political arenas of North America and Europe, of conservatism in the *Betrachtungen*. And, indeed, with "Tonio Kröger" one approaches the antiliberal Mann who flourished in the first two decades of the twentieth century. To understand this antiliberal position, it is important to consider the view of male-male sexuality that emerged in reaction to the late nineteenth-century liberal scientific and political view. Writers and theorists such as Benedict Friedlaender (1866–1908), Adolf Brand (1874–1945), and Hans Blüher (1888–1955) rejected the theory of the third sex with its medical grounding and legal ramifications.[36]

These thinkers owe a heavy debt to Nietzsche, using language of asceticism, self-overcoming, and *ressentiment*. While Nietzsche himself may not often have written directly about same-sex desire, there are elements in his writing that allow for possible connections to a theory of male-male sexuality. Sedgwick sees these links: (1) Nietzsche wrote in the same linguistic and cultural arena in which homosexuality was being redefined; (2) both Nietzsche and male homosexuality have been implicated in certain analyses of fascism; (3) Nietzsche writes for and about men, particularly the union of such masculine forces as Apollo and Dionysus; and (4) Nietzsche had an interest in decadence, a phenomenon that is often seen to include homosexuality.[37] One could add to this list Nietzsche's rejection of medicine and psychology as overarching explanatory discourses and his support for an elite individualism of warriors. Thomas Mann himself found many appealing elements in this view of male-male sexuality, which stand roughly in the same contrast to the liberal medical view of sexuality as modernism does to realism.

The architects of this modernist view of sexuality, Friedlaender, Brand, and Blüher, originally worked with the sexologists and activists of the homosexual emancipation movement, such as Magnus Hirschfeld, but eventually parted ways with them. In 1904 Friedlaender published a massive defense of his understanding of homosexuality, *Renaissance des Eros Uranios: Die physiologische Freundschaft, ein normaler Grundtrieb des Menschen und eine Frage der männlichen Gesellungsfreiheit*. Brand edited a journal, *Der Eigene: Ein Blatt für männliche Kultur*, which extolled the beauty of German masculinity from 1897 until it was eliminated by the National Socialists in 1933. Brand, who had been imprisoned for outing prominent personalities in Wilhelmine Germany, was kept under observation by the Nazis and prohibited from publishing during their reign but avoided incarceration. The most influential of these men was Blüher, who first outraged Germany in 1912 with his critique of the homoerotic basis of the youth movement and later achieved prominence with his discussion of homoeroticism throughout society in his two-volume work *Die Rolle der Erotik in männlichen Gesellschaft,* which appeared in 1918 and 1919.[38] Despite his self-acknowledged conservatism and his anti-Semitic glorification of Germans, Blüher's support for erotic male-male friendship made him dangerous to the Nazi regime, which banned his books and prohibited him from publishing.

Like Sigmund Freud, who had specifically rejected those "homosexual men who in our era have undertaken energetic actions against the legal limitation of their sexuality" and spoke against their attempts to categorize themselves "as a sexual intermediary step, as a 'third sex,'"[39] these thinkers weigh in vehemently against what Blüher calls the "banal" category of the third sex. Although Blüher prefers the term "invert" to "homosexual," he has no truck with the concept of gender inversion. For him, men who love men, far from having female souls, are actually more "masculine" than men who love women — an opinion that he shares with Friedlaender and Brand.

In rejecting the category of the third sex these theorists make a radical attack on sexual classifications in general, much as Freud does. For Friedlaender ancient Greek culture was laudable because of its apparent fluidity of sexual boundaries. It was a "trivial truth" in that culture, according to Friedlaender, that men are capable of sexual desire for both women and men.[40] Friedlaender claims that "so-called homosexuals" represent merely an extreme case of the normal condition of masculine desire for other men. He speculates that most men are capable of sexual desire for other men, that they have, so to speak, a "homosexual vein," and that they are, therefore, fundamentally bisexual (86). It is only the colossal sexual oppression of the modern era that prevents men from living out this bisexuality openly. In some of his more explicit borrowings from Nietzsche, Friedlaender asserts that this oppression comes to a great extent from women and from priests, who attempt to clip the wings of the soaring men (19, 33).

According to Blüher, too, all men are inherently bisexual. He assumes that most inverts get married and produce children. Conversely, he praises ancient Greece as a culture in which it was "self-evident" that a happily married man might occasionally have sex with an attractive male youth.[41] The category of "friendship," especially important in Germany, is not hermetically isolated from sexuality — here, too, Blüher imagines fluid and frequently changing boundaries between the sexual and the nonsexual realms. This changeability is the most important distinction between the theories of the third sex and the opposing theories. While the category of the third sex implies that sexual identity is constant and fixed, the assumption of basic bisexuality in human nature leads to the highly destabilizing conclusion that sexual orientation might change frequently. While Ulrichs and his followers assure readers that there is little danger that heterosexuals could become homosexual by seduction or contact, Friedlaender and Blüher open up precisely that possibility.

The rejection of sexual identity in the sense of the "third sex" goes hand in hand with a denunciation of the medical institutions that seek to prove the existence of these sexual categories. Friedlaender concedes that there are some strategic benefits to the use of medicine as a mouthpiece for decriminalization of male-male relationships, but he otherwise has little use for the medical establishment (57). Blüher roundly decries what he calls "Die Katastrophe der Psychiatrie," which — he asserts — works hand in hand with the law (*Rolle*, 1: 226). Blüher haughtily repudiates the notion that homosexuals are in need of healing, asking why it never occurs to heterosexuals that *they* need to be healed (1: 135). Unfortunately, he argues, society has become so twisted that men who feel a desire for other men think that they have no other choice than to go to the physicians and request advice.[42] This is a tragic mistake, because male-male desire is not degenerate or pathological in any way (1: 121). Blüher concludes by arguing that the damage done by medical approaches to sexuality must be overcome if German male bonding is to recover (1: 212).

In rejecting the medico-biological explanation of sexual identity, these conservative thinkers pursue a majoritizing, rather than a minoritizing, strategy. Arguing that all men could be bisexual, they come to see the attainment of this goal as a patriotic objective. Brand's journal *Der Eigene* regularly featured attractive Germanic youths. A typical issue from 1920 shows a young man on its cover with the caption, "Deutsche Rasse." In the majoritizing perspective, homosexuals are no longer identified with the Other, the comparatively small group of Jews in Germany, but, rather, with the population of non-Jewish Germans. A denigration of the minority accompanies this identification with the majority: anti-Semitism is a decided element in this antiliberal view of male-male desire. Indeed, the one race that is alleged to be unlikely to exhibit homosexual tendencies is the Jewish race. Friedlaender frequently quotes with admiration the virulent anti-Semite Eugen Dühring, although Dühring would have nothing to do with Friedlaender's speculations about male-male desire. Following Nietzsche, Friedlaender attributes the decline of male-male bonding to the priestly class; he specifically holds Judaism and Christianity (along with Buddhism) responsible for this new moral order that has strangled the masculine Eros.

Blüher is even more extreme in his statements regarding Jews, although he admits to finding Jewish men especially attractive (1: 212). At a time when liberals were pushing to open the army to Jews, Blüher, who believed that the adhesive that holds the military together is the erotic appeal of its young soldiers, insisted that only the young German soldier, and not the young Jewish soldier, could unite the armed forces with his sexual attractiveness (2: 173).[43] He approvingly notes the strident anti-Semitism of the fraternities, which he also believes are unified by their homoerotic appeal (2: 203). Not only does Blüher celebrate the anti-Semitism of his male-bonding Germans; he also argues that Jews are the one group that is incapable of male bonding in this erotic way. His basic thesis is that while the family consists of men and women and is heterosexual in nature, the state consists exclusively of men and is homosexual (1: 7). Blüher thus claims that because Jews are a stateless people, they do not have the opportunity to develop their male bonding and masculine homosexuality (2: 170).[44] Blüher mitigates his anti-Semitism slightly by asserting that Zionism offers hope for the Jews to resuscitate the masculine side of their erotic life (2: 170). He basically believes, though, that homoeroticism is a particularly Germanic virtue.

Following Nietzsche, these antiliberal thinkers set up ancient Greek culture in opposition to Jewish culture. For them, part and parcel of the project of encouraging the development of the bisexuality of German men is an identification with ancient Greece, a culture in which they believe most upper-class men had sexual relations with male youths, as well as with women. Friedlaender cites a classicist, Emil Bethe, who argues in a 1907 article, "Die dorische Knabenliebe: Ihre Ethik und ihre Idee," that at least the Dorian aspects of Greek culture were dominated by ritual pederasty in which male youths physically ingested the semen of older men as part of coming-of-age rituals.[45] By the end of the nineteenth century ancient Greece had undergone an astonishing transformation in the German cultural imagination from being the birthplace of democracy to being the model of an utterly illiberal, antibourgeois society.

While in the nineteenth century bourgeois society had established the asexual sanctity of childhood, and the progressive bourgeois model of homosexuality codified by Ulrichs had pursued such normative projects as marriage between urnings of more or less equal age, these antiliberal thinkers tended to support pederastic relationships on the ancient Greek model. Friedlaender envisions a future Germany in which older men will have a series of relationships with younger men, many of whom will go on to marry heterosexually. Blüher is also convinced that every young man goes through a phase of leaving the mother and needing a sexually intimate relationship with a father figure (*Rolle*, 1: 242). This pederastic vision of male-male desire goes along with the fluidity of sexual identity that these antiliberal thinkers endorse, for it is part of their philosophy that sexuality changes at various point in a man's life.

In rejecting the bourgeois version of the third sex, writers such as Blüher also reject the liberal politics that accompany such a view. Blüher mocks liberalism's support of women at the university and its rejection of racial politics (2: 204). Friedlaender emphasizes ancient Greece's rejection of the credo that all men are created equal and calls for a return to aristocratic ideals. While both Blüher and Friedlaender go along with the liberal bourgeois in hoping for the decriminalization of sexual acts between consenting adults, they disagree with many of the other objectives of the emancipation movement. They have no interest in establishing a sense of community with those males who think they have female souls; if there is going to be community, it should include all — and only — masculine men. They also reject aspirations for some kind of homosexual marriage, arguing, as Friedlaender puts it, that true social progress would consist not in more marriages but, rather, in looser, less binding structures of interpersonal relationships allowing for bisexual activity (182).

The antiliberal reaction to the third sex, which shares with modernism a common origin in Nietzschean thought, thus rejects the notion of a separate medically identifiable category consisting of men who love men and women who love women. It thereby also rejects a minoritizing view of sexuality and denies the claim that homosexuals and Jews have an analogous relationship. Instead, it looks to its view of ancient Greece, with its majoritizing approach to male-male desire and its pederastic tendencies. The proponents of this view reject the liberal political aims of the sexologists and activists in the homosexual rights movement, including their alliance with women's movements.

Thomas Mann's Antiliberal Views

While many aspects of the liberal understanding of the third sex have resonances in Mann's writings, Mann explicitly endorses this antiliberal view in his nonfiction. Like Friedlaender and Blüher, he is under the sway of Nietzsche and, thus, open to the radical individualism, the rejection of socially constructed categories, and the glorification of a nonhumanistic vision of ancient Greece that these antiliberal thinkers propose. Point for point, Mann's essayistic writings and letters to friends overlap with the antiliberal perspective.

In a letter about *Der Tod in Venedig* (Death in Venice, 1912) to Carl Maria Weber on July 4, 1920, Mann mentions the fascination that Blüher's ideas hold for him.[46] The year 1920 is shortly after the publication of Blüher's most important work, *Die Rolle der Erotik*, and still within the period in Mann's life when he saw himself as conservative. Although Mann quickly adjusted to the Weimar Republic and became a spokesperson for liberal causes, his most explicit support for the antiliberal point of view on homosexuality is in his essay "Über die Ehe" (On Marriage) written in 1925.[47] There he directly cites Blüher and fully concurs with his notion that, while the family is a heterosexual institution, society is a male homoerotic one. Homoeroticism is aesthetic, according to this essay, while heterosexuality is prosaic.[48] In "Über die Ehe" Mann emphasizes more than Blüher the importance of self-overcoming and renouncing the homoerotic sphere in order to do one's duty in the family sphere, but he clearly adheres to Blüher's basic worldview.[49]

In his essayistic writings Mann rejects the idea that male-male desire is the product of gender inversion. He declares that in male homosexuality masculinity is so paramount that it even dominates the erotic realm. His belief, to some commentators incomprehensible, that his most ferociously antiliberal work, *Betrachtungen eines Unpolitischen*, expresses his own inverted tendencies has to do with the connections he sees between masculinity and male-male desire.[50] While he does not explicitly address same-sex desire at great length in this nearly 600-page polemic, he does glorify the male bonding that war produces, which he fears will permanently destroy the soldier's small, narrow, pedantic home life with women (461–62). As Anthony Heilbut notes, Mann "is 'intoxicated' by the warriors freed from the bonds of matrimony. Whatever his conservatism protects, it's not the nuclear family" (295). Even after Mann embraced liberalism in the early 1920s, however, he continued to see male homosexuality as a masculine phenomenon, rather than as a case of gender inversion. In his essay *Von deutscher Republik* (Of the German Republic, 1923) he insists that many of the believers in "this eros" are militarists.[51] In published memoirs from the early 1930s he repeats the claim that male homosexuality, rather than being the product of a female soul in a male body, is, in fact, a matter of hypermasculinity and belongs in the sphere of warriors and heroes.[52]

A fundamental part of Mann's antiliberal thinking is his claim that he is hostile to pathologizing medical views of sexuality. Some skepticism with regard to this claim is justified, given the obvious relish with which Mann depicts such illnesses as cholera, typhus, tuberculosis, and syphilis in his writings. In 1897, however, when one of the confidants of Mann's youth, Otto Grautoff, revealed that he was seeing Albert Moll, the famed sexologist, presumably about his sexual orientation, Mann wrote that he had never had much respect for this branch of medicine.[53] In his letter to Weber about *Der Tod in Venedig* Mann claimed that he was "forced" by the era's naturalistic mindset to regard Aschenbach's situation in a "pathological" light, implying that in the 1920s he would no longer have done so.[54]

Mann's *Betrachtungen* are filled with vituperative attacks on the medical understanding of human nature. He mocks efforts at understanding politics in terms of sexual pathologies (317). He sarcastically notes that literary psychologists love to find sex at the basis of everything; for their explanations of events they turn to Krafft-Ebing, the sexologist whose *Psychopathia sexualis* (1886) dominated late nineteenth-century understandings of sexology and introduced concepts such as masochism and sadism (334). The sexological diagnosis of masochism particularly incenses Mann, since it was used to label German obedience a sickness. Given that Mann is clearly highly interested in the erotics of hierarchies of power in, for instance, the military, it is not surprising that he wants to remove such issues from pathologizing scrutiny. As he is similarly anxious to avoid medical analyses of same-sex desire, he attacks "psychologism" in a wide variety of his writings, including the *Betrachtungen* and *Der Tod in Venedig*.

Like Friedlaender and Blüher, Mann links same-sex desire to the German character. In his diaries he ridicules Hitler's campaign against the SA leader Ernst Röhm, who was accused of homosexuality and assassinated in 1934. According to Mann, Röhm's homosexuality is an integral part of being a warrior and a German.[55] In published memoirs from the early 1930s he repeats the claim that homosexuality is particularly suited to a country such as Germany, because the German people are homoerotic in nature.[56] Although in the rest of his political outlook Mann had abandoned conservatism and embraced liberalism, here he retains the antiliberal view of male homosexuality.

This claim to a particular German affinity for male homosexuality accompanies a variant of the anti-Semitism that antiliberals such as Blüher had promulgated. In the *Betrachtungen* Mann clearly regards the Jews as a foreign element in the German body politic, but he attempts to portray the presence of this foreign element somewhat positively. He asserts that the difficult encounter between Germans and Jews has given Germany a particularly acute moral sense (471). Because of the incorporation of the Jews into the German *Volkskörper*, the German psyche has become so finely attuned that it allegedly hurts to study the products of German intellectuals (471). Mann means this as a compliment, although it is clearly not an unmixed one. Nonetheless, he defends Jews against Dostoyevsky's claim that they will betray their homelands, pointing out that the German Jews were patriotic through the bitter end of the First World War (530). Despite these measured compliments and defenses of Jews, Mann, like Blüher, cites with approval the bonding that goes on between the German soldiers as they utter anti-Semitic epithets on their way to the front (112). It is, therefore, clear that he also carries on the tradition of associating male bonding with anti-Semitism.

Accompanying Mann's understanding of a certain anti-Semitic slant to German male homoeroticism is his grecophilic emphasis on the youthfulness of the male object of desire. Even near the end of his life, as he watched an Argentine play tennis in Switzerland on August 6, 1950, he was taken by the attraction of male youth, which he considers incomparable and unsurpassed by anything in the world.[57] Watching his own son, Klaus, he reports in 1920 that he is falling in love with the fourteen-year-old. Of course, it is not surprising that a father should love his son, but Mann's diaries add a physical dimension to this emotion that points in the direction of homoeroticism along Greek models. The sight of Klaus's "naked brown torso" in bed "confuses" Mann on July 25, 1920.[58] On October 17 of that year his son's adolescent body again perturbs Mann.[59] While Mann was presumably no child abuser, his awareness of the beauty of male youth fits into the antiliberal, Greekist model of same-sex desire.

Generally, Mann eschews the progressive political agenda of the proponents of the third sex. The thrust of his essay on marriage concerns the importance of overcoming one's homosexual desires and doing one's duty in heterosexual marriage, so he certainly does not call for the legal possibility of homosexual unions. While even the most ardent antiliberals called for the decriminalization of same-sex activity between consenting adults, Mann wavered in his public support for the removal of Paragraph 175, the article in the German Basic Law that penalized male-male sexual acts. He first signed Magnus Hirschfeld's petition for the repeal of the paragraph, then withdrew his signature "for reasons best known to himself," as Charlotte Wolff reports.[60] In any case, it seems unlikely that he had any legitimate fear about taking this stand, as more than 200 prominent intellectuals, writers, and artists, including Albert Einstein, Gerhart Hauptmann, Frank Wedekind, Rainer Maria Rilke, Hermann Hesse, Stefan Zweig, Mann's brother Heinrich, Käthe Kollwitz, and Georg Grosz, had also signed the petition, as had many physicians and sexologists, such as Richard von Krafft-Ebing, Albert Eulenberg, Paul Näcke, and Albert Moll. Rather than fear, it seems that a consciously antiliberal agenda motivated him to remove his endorsement from the petition.

Mann's Antiliberal Turn and *Der Tod in Venedig*

Generally, then, in his public and private writings on homosexuality Mann aligns himself with the antiliberal understanding of male-male desire, rejecting the notion of gender inversion and the analogy to Jewishness, instead favoring a Greek model with an emphasis on masculinity and the beauty of male youth and, furthermore, avoiding most concrete political assertions. This view is consistent in his nonfiction writings throughout his life, well into the twentieth century. Nowhere in his fictional works is Mann's antiliberal turn more apparent than in *Der Tod in Venedig*, which appeared in 1912 in *Die neue Rundschau* and came out as a book the same year. Gustav von Aschenbach, the protagonist of *Der Tod in Venedig*, expressly gives allegiance to the antiliberal view of sexuality, identifying with the majority, rejecting medical approaches, and turning to classicism. Yet, the poet Stefan George, who clearly ascribed to the antiliberal view of male-male sexuality, nonetheless condemned the novella for associating male-male love with degeneration and sickness.[61] George has a point: ultimately, the biological, pathological views of sexuality that have their root in late nineteenth-century German liberalism prove more accurate than Aschenbach's beliefs, which turn out to be self-deluding. Even when Mann's characters give explicit support to an antiliberal position on sexuality that is part of the modernist package, Mann's narrative retains a legacy of liberal realism.

The foundation of Aschenbach's antiliberal views on male-male desire is his rejection of gender inversion. He insists that both his career as an artist and his erotic desire for the young Pole, Tadzio, are manly and military (*Schwere Stunde*, 245–46). Like other post-Nietzschean antiliberals, he rejects the medical and particularly the psychological understanding of sexuality. Repeatedly, the novella mentions Aschenbach's disgust with the psychologizing of his era, which certainly would include efforts to classify people according to sexual orientation (196–97). Instead, Aschenbach turns to classicism and ancient Greece, a move that the narrator mirrors as he includes references to Greek mythology and even metric patterns from Greek poetry in his account. The turn to Greece is notably Nietzschean, heavily infused with the spirit of the Dionysian, which is further typical for the antiliberal theorists of homosexuality in the late nineteenth century.

One of the repercussions of the interest in ancient Greek culture on the field of sexuality is the apparent endorsement of pederastic relationships.[62] Aschenbach rejects the many queer adult men who cross his path on his way to Venice, some of whom are clearly homosexual, such as the aging fop who takes the ship from Pola to Venice, and the others who can at the very least be read as possibly homosexual.[63] Instead, following the ancient Greek models, he falls in love with a young man and even explicitly compares his relationship with the relationship between Socrates and Phaedrus. Finally, in keeping with the antiliberal tradition of same-sex relationships, Aschenbach does not identify himself with minority groups. Instead, he is proud to be part of the establishment: recently ennobled, he is a world-famous author included in the textbooks read in schools throughout the country.

Aschenbach's consciously antiliberal view of sexuality is undercut by the novella as a whole, however, for biologistic views of the late nineteenth century reassert themselves in the end. Although Aschenbach does not identify with a minority group, he is, in fact, of mixed blood. While he hopes to live up to the heritage of his Prussian father, he still has the legacy of his Bohemian maternal line. Thus, the liberal tendency to compare sexual orientation with exotic national identity returns. This is repeated again and again in the case of the queer men who approach Aschenbach on his way to Venice, from the man in the cemetery in Munich to the entertainer at the hotel, all of whom are marked as foreigners either by their looks, their clothes, or their accents. In general, the novella's extended discussion of the connections between sexual desire and wanderlust reinforces the racializing tendencies of late nineteenth-century approaches to sexuality. Aschenbach's residency in Munich and his trips to Italy add a geographical dimension to the depiction of his sexuality, which is also quite in keeping with the late nineteenth-century tradition that had seen both of these locales as places where homosexual men were to be found, as noted in the discussion of "Der Wille zum Glück."[64]

The racializing tendency is a product of the biological approach to sexuality, which often views same-sex desire as analogous to a pathology. In *Der Tod in Venedig,* of course, Aschenbach's desire for Tadzio appears simultaneously with the appearance of cholera. It is made explicit that the city's relationship to the plague is identical with his relationship to his desire, in that neither the city nor he wants to eliminate the source of their problems (*Schwere Stunde*, 242). To connect the illness with the racializing tendencies even more, the cholera in *Der Tod in Venedig* is specifically labeled "Indian cholera" and is described as originating in tiger-infested bamboo swamps that could not be geographically farther from Europe's cultural understanding of itself (253–54).

All of these tendencies work toward the disruption of the most fundamental effort of the antiliberal homosexual thinkers: breaking down the connection between homosexuality and gender inversion. Ultimately, Aschenbach must concede that, as manly as his art and his Eros are, he is nonetheless like a woman (263). As he falls entirely victim to his disease and succumbs completely to the exotic orientalist fantasies associated with it, he gives up his pretence of manliness. Thus, in the end, the late nineteenth-century view of homosexuality based on gender inversion, with its roots in liberal medicine and the realist era, outlasts the antiliberal, post-Nietzschean modernist view to which Mann consciously subscribed.

In his letter of July 4, 1920, to Carl Maria Weber, Mann disavows the connections to illness in the novella, saying that he only includes them because of the "naturalistic" attitude of his generation, which could only view such desire pathologically.[65] In fact, there were writers of his generation, such as Stefan George, who resisted such pathological views, and Mann found their ideas captivating. Setting aside George's evaluation of the two models, it is nonetheless possible that George's critique of the novella as denigrating a high form of love is more astute than Thomas Mann's own stated understanding of his story. Although Mann's protagonist, Gustav von Aschenbach, speaks the language of a modernist vision of male-male desire, Mann's portrayal of that desire, even as late as *Der Tod in Venedig*, is formed by the late nineteenth-century understanding of sexuality emerging out of liberal medicine, political activism, and the Zeitgeist of realism.

Notes

[1] It is now generally accepted that male-male desire is an important element in Mann's fictions. See, for instance, Hans Mayer, *Thomas Mann* (Frankfurt am Main: Suhrkamp, 1980), 260–61, as well as many of the sources cited in this essay. In two essays Marcel Reich-Ranicki makes the point that the publication of the diaries made clear what an essential issue male-male desire is for Mann: "Die ungeschminkte Wahrheit" (1978) and "Die Geburt der Kritik aus dem Geiste der Epik" (1986), in his *Thomas Mann und die Seinen* (Stuttgart: Deutsche Verlags-Anstalt, 1987), 29–49, 63–81. Until the publication of Mann's diaries, however, there was considerable resistance to studying homoeroticism in his works. Even when the diaries were published, many early reviews managed to avoid a single reference to the allusions to homoeroticism in them. See for instance, Rudolf Hartung, "Mensch und Werk: Zu den Tagebüchern 1933–34 von Thomas Mann," *Neue Rundschau* 89, no. 2 (1978): 285–91; Herbert Lehnert, review of Thomas Mann's diaries, *Orbis litterarum* 39 (1984): 79–88; Peter de Mendelssohn, "Dichtung und Wahrheit in den Tagebüchern Thomas Manns," *Ensemble 15: Internationales Jahrbuch für Literatur* (1984): 7–28.

[2] Important background information on this movement can be found in James Steakley's classic, *The Homosexual Emancipation Movement in Germany (1862–1945)* (New York: Arno, 1975). For further background on literary manifestations of same-sex desire, see James W. Jones, *"We of the Third Sex": Literary Representations of Homosexuality in Wilhelmine Germany* (New York: Peter Lang, 1990).

[3] Karl Heinrich Ulrichs, *Forschungen über das Räthsel der mannmännlichen Liebe,* ed. Hubert Kennedy, 4 vols. (Berlin: Verlag rosa Winkel, 1984); vol. 1, "Vier Briefe," 45. The *Forschungen* consist of twelve pamphlets and books that have been collected into these four volumes without being repaginated. Thus, references will be to the volume in which the work appears, the title of the individual work, and, when there are page numbers, to the page number in the named work.

[4] Ulrichs, vol. 1, "Vindex," 5.

[5] Ulrichs, vol. 4, "Prometheus," 4.

[6] Eve Kosofsky Sedgwick, *Epistemology of the Closet* (Berkeley: U of California P, 1990), 82–86.

[7] Michel Foucault, *History of Sexuality,* volume 1: *An Introduction,* trans. Robert Hurley (New York: Vintage, 1978), 43.

[8] Ulrichs, vol. 2, "Memnon," 3.

[9] Ulrichs, vol. 4, "Prometheus," 72. The first issue was also the last. The issue was titled *Prometheus* and, for financial reasons, Ulrichs's hopes for the journal *Uranus* were abandoned.

[10] Klaus Müller, *"Aber in meinem Herzen sprach eine Stimme so laut": Homosexuelle Autobiographien und medizinische Pathographien im neunzehnten Jahrhundert* (Berlin: Verlag rosa Winkel, 1991).

[11] Ulrichs, vol. 1, "Formatrix," xviii.

[12] Ulrichs, vol. 2, "Gladius furens," 22.

[13] Sander Gilman, *The Jew's Body* (New York: Routledge, 1991), 22.

[14] Ulrichs, vol. 1, "Inclusa," 13.

[15] Sedgwick discusses the comparison between Jews and homosexuals, 75–82, as does George L. Mosse, *Nationalism and Sexuality: Middle-Class Morality and Sexual Norms in Modern Europe* (Madison: U of Wisconsin P, 1985), 36–37, 138–43.

[16] Gilman, 76.

[17] Robert Aldrich, *The Seduction of the Mediterranean: Writing, Art, and Homosexual Fantasy* (London: Routledge, 1993).

[18] Gilman, 99.

[19] For a review of this history, see Shulamit Volkov, *Die Juden in Deutschland 1780–1918,* trans. Simone Gundi, Enzyklopädie deutscher Geschichte 16 (Munich: Oldenbourg, 2000).

[20] Ulrichs, vol. 4, "Prometheus," 9.

[21] It is perhaps worth mentioning here that the term *liberal* refers fairly specifically to those progressive bourgeois political parties that defined themselves as such; it is, of course, not being used in the current American fashion as a loose synonym for left-wing politics. Similarly, the term *antiliberal* does not necessarily overlap with current meanings of *conservative*.

[22] Ulrichs, vol. 3, "Incubus" and "Argonauticus." These works were both first published in 1869 and deal primarily with the case of Carl Friedrich Wilhelm von Zastrow, who was accused of the brutal anal rape of a five-year-old boy who subsequently died. Zastrow denied committing the crime and identified himself as a member of the third sex. In his publications Ulrichs insists on due process of law, despite the widespread public revulsion felt for Zastrow.

[23] There are many references to the right to marry in the *Forschungen*. Some of the more prominent are vol. 1, "Ara Spei," 79; vol. 3, "Argonauticus," 101; vol. 4, "Prometheus," 33, 40.

[24] For more on Mann's parallel treatment of Jews and homosexuals, see Gerhard Härle, *Männerweiblichkeit: Zur Homosexualität bei Klaus und Thomas*

Mann (Frankfurt am Main: Athenäum, 1988), 149, and Anthony Heilbut, *Thomas Mann: Eros and Literature* (New York: Knopf, 1996), 26–28, 75.

[25] The other comparable example is "Gefallen," which appeared in *Die Gesellschaft* in 1894 and was never republished in Mann's lifetime. It deals explicitly with the sexual emancipation of women, and though the main female character does not read well as a member of the third sex because of her explicit female sexuality, some of the men who sit around discussing her fate do seem to fit the bill.

[26] Ulrichs, vol. 1, "Formatrix," 23.

[27] Thomas Mann, *Der Wille zum Glück: Erzählungen 1893–1903* (Frankfurt am Main: Fischer, 1991), 177. Hereafter cited parenthetically in the text.

[28] For the connections between homosexuality and Wagner's music, see Hans Fuchs, *Richard Wagner und die Homosexualität* (Berlin: Barsdorf, 1903). For sexological references to the appeal of Wagner's music among homosexual patients, see Havelock Ellis, "Sexual Inversion," in his *Studies in the Psychology of Sex* (New York: Random House, 1905), 131-32. See also Paul Näcke, "Über Kontrast-Träume und speziell sexuelle Kontrast-Träume," *Archiv für Kriminal-Anthropologie und Kriminalistik* 28 (1903): 1-19. For a more recent discussion, see Mitchell Morris's article in Lloyd Whitesell and Sophie Fuller, eds., *Secret Passages: Music and Modern Transitional Queer Identity, 1880-1940* (Bloomington: U of Indiana P, forthcoming).

[29] For instance, Ulrichs, "Gladius furens," 5.

[30] Many sexologists were convinced that homosexuals were particularly gifted in the theatrical world: Albert Eulenburg, *Sexuale Neuropathie: Genitale Neurosen und Neuropsychosen der Männer und Frauen* (Leipzig: Vogel, 1895); Douglas McMurtrie, "Die konträre Sexualempfindung des Weibes in den Vereinigten Staaten von Amerika," *Archiv für Kriminal-Anthropologie und Kriminalistik* 55, nos. 1-2 (1913): 141-47. Paul Derks traces the stereotype of the homosexual actor back at least to Iffland in his *Die Schande der heiligen Päderastie: Homosexualität und Öffentlichkeit in der deutschen Literatur 1750-1850* (Berlin: Verlag rosa Winkel, 1990).

[31] For a description of smoking, horse-riding lesbians, see August Forel, *Die sexuelle Frage: Eine naturwissenschaftliche, psychologische, hygienische und soziologische Studie für Gebildete* (Munich: Reinhardt, 1909), 287.

[32] For a queer analysis of this story, which is set in Venice and features a blasé, cynical, single man who could well be homosexual, as a predecessor to *Der Tod in Venedig*, see Härle, 168, and Heilbut, 80-81.

[33] Thomas Mann, *Betrachtungen eines Unpolitischen* (Frankfurt am Main: Fischer, 1983), 25. Hereafter cited parenthetically in the text.

[34] Thomas Mann, *Schwere Stunde: Erzählungen 1903-1912* (Frankfurt am Main: Fischer, 1991), 29. Hereafter cited parenthetically in the text.

[35] For recent scholarship on another story, "Gladius Dei," that appeared in the collection *Tristan* in 1903, see Y. A. Elsaghe, "'Herr und Frau X. Beliebig'? Zur Funktion des Vornamensinitiale bei Thomas Mann," *German Life and Letters* 52, no. 1 (1999): 58-67. Elsaghe links the artwork that so enrages the protagonist of "Gladius Dei" to Baron von Gloeden's homoerotic photography.

[36] Although most in this antiliberal camp identify themselves as politically conservative, there are some, notably the novelist John Henry Mackay, who situate themselves on the radical anarchist left wing of the political spectrum.

[37] Sedgwick, 132.

[38] Among the authors who discuss Blüher and male bonding are Julian H. Schoeps, *Leiden an Deutschland: Vom antisemitischen Wahn und der Last der Erinnerung* (Munich: Piper, 1990) and Hans Wisskirchen, "Republikanischer Eros: Zur Welt Whitmans und Hans Blühers Rolle in der politischen Publizistik Thomas Manns," in Gerhard Härle, ed., *"Heimsuchung und süßes Gift": Erotik und Poetik bei Thomas Mann* (Frankfurt am Main: Fischer, 1992), 17-40.

[39] "Eine Kindheitserinnerung des Leonardo da Vinci." In Freud, *Gesammelte Werke* (Frankfurt am Main: Fischer, 1999), 8: 168. See also Freud's famous claim that "all people are capable of homosexual object choice and have actually made such a choice in their unconscious" in a footnote to his "Drei Abhandlung zur Sexualtheorie," *Gesammelte Werke*, 5: 44.

[40] Benedikt Friedlaender, *Die Renaissance des Eros Uranios: Die physiologische Freundschaft, ein normaler Grundtrieb des Menschen und eine Frage der männlichen Gesellungsfreiheit* (Berlin: Renaissance, 1904), 6. Hereafter cited parenthetically in the text.

[41] Hans Blüher, *Die Rolle der Erotik in der männlichen Gesellschaft*, 2 vols. (Jena: Diederick, 1917, 1919), 1: 169. Hereafter cited parenthetically in the text.

[42] Blüher, *Familie und Männerbund* (Leipzig: Der neue Geist, 1918), 26.

[43] See Gilman, 40-48, for an extensive discussion of the arguments around including Jews in the German and Austro-Hungarian militaries.

[44] See also Blüher, *Deutsches Reich, Judentum und Sozialismus* (Prion: Anthropos, 1920), 9.

[45] Emil Bethe, "Die dorische Knabenliebe: ihre Ethik und ihre Idee," *Rheinisches Museum für Philologie*, n.s. 62 (1907): 438-75, specifically 471.

[46] Thomas Mann, *Briefe: 1889-1936*, ed. Erika Mann (Frankfurt am Main: Fischer, 1962), 177.

[47] Klaus Werner Böhm, "Die homosexuellen Elemente in Thomas Manns 'Der Zauberberg,'" in Hermann Kurzke, ed., *Stationen der Thomas-Mann-Forschung: Aufsätze seit 1970* (Würzburg: Königshausen & Neumann, 1985), 145-65.

[48] Esther Lesér, *Thomas Mann's Short Fiction: An Intellectual Biography*, ed. Mitzi Brunedale (Rutherford, NJ: Farleigh Dickinson UP, 1989), 172.

[49] Ignace Feuerlicht, "Thomas Mann and Homoeroticism," *Germanic Review* 57, no. 3 (1982): 89-97. See also Mayer, 267.

[50] Heilbut mentions some of the critics, including Erich Heller, who are unable to make heads or tales of this remark (296).

[51] Thomas Mann, "Von deutscher Republik," in his *"Von deutscher Republik": Politische Schriften und Reden in Deutschland,* eds. Peter de Mendelssohn and Hanno Helbling (Frankfurt am Main: Fischer, 1984), 154-55. See also Mayer, 267, as well as Wisskirchen.

[52] Thomas Mann, "Leiden an Deutschland: Tagebücher aus den Jahren 1933 und 1934," in his *An die gesittete Welt: Politische Schriften und Reden im Exil,* eds. de Mendelssohn and Helbling (Frankfurt am Main: Fischer, 1986), 57-58.

[53] Thomas Mann, *Briefe an Otto Grautoff 1894-1901 und Ida Boy-Ed 1903-1928,* ed. de Mendelssohn (Frankfurt am Main: Fischer, 1975), 88.

[54] Mann, *Briefe: 1889-1936,* 177.

[55] Thomas Mann, *Tagebücher 1933-1934,* ed. de Mendelssohn (Frankfurt am Main: Fischer, 1977), 470.

[56] Thomas Mann, "Leiden an Deutschland," in *An die gesittete Welt,* 58. For more on the question of male bonding as a specifically German problem, see also Mayer, 317-18, as well as Schoeps and Wisskirchen.

[57] Thomas Mann, *Tagebücher 1949-1950,* ed. Inge Jens (Frankfurt am Main: Fischer, 1991), 239.

[58] Thomas Mann, *Tagebücher 1918-1920,* ed. de Mendelssohn (Frankfurt am Main: Fischer, 1979), 454.

[59] *Tagebücher 1918-1920,* 470.

[60] Charlotte Wolff, *Magnus Hirschfeld: A Portrait of a Pioneer in Sexology* (London: Quartet, 1986), 43.

[61] Quoted by Karl Werner Böhm, *Zwischen Selbstzucht und Verlangen: Thomas Mann und das Stigma Homosexualität* (Würzburg: Königshaus & Neumann, 1991), 21. For a good analysis of George's approach to homosexuality see Mosse, 60.

[62] From the very beginning Mann referred to this novella as a story of "Knabenliebe," or the love of boys. Letter to Philipp Witkopp, July 18, 1911. Cited in T. J. Reed, *Thomas Mann: The Uses of Tradition* (Oxford: Clarendon P, 1974), 150.

[63] See my essay, "Why is Tadzio a Boy?" in Thomas Mann, *Death in Venice: A New Translation, Backgrounds and Contexts, Criticism,* trans. and ed. Clayton Koelb (New York: Norton, 1994), 220, 225.

[64] For more on the relationship between exoticism and homoeroticism in *Der Tod in Venedig,* see Härle, 174.

[65] Mann, *Briefe: 1889-1936,* 177.

Effi Briest and the End of Realism

Russell A. Berman

THE FINAL SCENE of Theodor Fontane's *Effi Briest* (1895) recapitulates the agenda of literary realism, while exposing its limits, as well. As this novel, surely the most recognized and among the best achievements of German realist fiction, draws to a close, it reviews the fundamental elements of its aesthetic program, savoring it one last time, before announcing its conclusion: the end of *Effi Briest* and the end of realism. The idyllic setting of the garden at Hohen-Cremmen and the casual domesticity of the exchanges — hallmarks of the literary movement as a whole — stand in stark contrast to the substance of the fictional moment. For it has only been a month since the single child of the house, the heroine of the novel, has died, and a marble gravestone has just been set to mark her final resting place in a round flower bed. It was here that Effi, as a spirited young woman full of fantasy and adventure, had been introduced to the reader at the outset of the novel; and it is here that Fontane buries that same youthful romanticism. Realism in German literature had, in effect, always represented an effort to control, to bridle, and to dismiss the romantic legacy of the beginning of the century, with its capacity for imagination in art, as well as in politics. Realism operated as the repression of the romantic past, designed explicitly to assert the order of nature and society after the suppression of the revolution of 1848. Effi's grave buries that past one more time: hence the narrator's satisfied observation that putting in the stone had not even required disturbing the heliotropes; and hence, also, the placid and unmoved tenor of the parental discussion. This is a world where emotions are as orderly as a well-tended garden, even if one's only child is buried in it.

The scene highlights a second aspect of realism, as well: its systematic prohibition of certain classes of speech. For when Briest, the father, ventures a speculative comment, his wife reprimands him and breaks him off. His language has always been too ambiguous for her strict taste, and she is prepared to blame his robust linguistic registers and frequent wordplays for Effi's adultery and, by implication, her death, as well. The concern that semantic ambiguity could generate moral ambivalence is, however, only one example of an imperative of linguistic disciplining that would, in the name of "realism," — understood somehow as focused solely on all that is hard and fast — prohibit speculative speech and, in particular, philosophical discourse. True to character, Luise von Briest reserves room, of course, to ponder guilt and assign blame, but even this accusatory questioning is not permitted to go too far. In the regime of realist discourse, it is the *realia* of the world that demand concern, not abstract speculation. For the realist theory of the mid-century, the dismissal of philosophical idealism and romantic imagination went hand in hand, along with the suppressed aspirations for revolutionary change. In this final scene of the realist novel Fontane brings this program to the fore, but in a context in which he makes its repressive substance painfully clear. Where Briest would ponder the possibility of natural love — he points to the loyalty of the dog lying by the grave — his wife silences him in order to insinuate and accuse.

Yet, Briest gets the last word, in a famous rejoinder that represents the culmination of realism and its failing at the same time. In response to his wife's recriminations and self-blame, he utters his leitmotific dictum "das ist ein *zu* weites Feld."[1] Just as she has interrupted his speech a moment earlier, blocking his ruminations, now he breaks her off, preventing her from reconsidering their own responsibility for Effi's fate. He declares her topic out of bounds, not because it is insignificant or obscure, but, on the contrary and quite explicitly, because of its magnitude. Realism indicts itself as the literary language that proscribes treatment of ultimate questions, even in the face of death. By drawing attention to the severity of this repression, however, the text at the same time calls it into question and points beyond it. In his final novel, *Stechlin* (1899), Fontane would break with the inherited conventions of realism, dissolving the world even further into conversation than is the case already in *Effi Briest*, and draw close to the formal features of literary modernism.

The assertion that Luise von Briest's questions go too far is based on a metaphor of distance and constriction that pervades the novel and that pertains, in particular, to questions of geography and nationhood, preferred tropes in the realist register. It is, however, in the very nature of Briest's objection to the presumed breadth of Luise's remark that his implied priority of narrowness is not only foregrounded but also revealed to be untenable. Briest's evident privileging of the narrow, as the region to which proper discourse should be restricted, necessarily stands accused of complicity in the repression of the past. Luise's query, after all, points to a potential recognition of parental error, which momentarily raises the prospect of a notional change of course within the specific ontology of the work of art: if Luise were to admit her guilt, then Effi could be vindicated and redeemed. That faint promise, however, is held at bay by Briest's realism, his directive to Luise to cease the speculation and to return to the present. The constellation is uncannily reminiscent of the deliberation on the fate of another young woman, seduced out of a narrow world and then abandoned: Faust's Gretchen, whom Goethe explicitly saves from judgment. No such leniency for Effi: facing their daughter's gravestone, each parent turns out to be quite capable of initiating a process of mourning through the questions they pose in this brief conversation. Yet, each blocks the other from getting very far, insuring that the discussion will never call established opinion and convention into question. It is this mandated constriction that *Effi Briest* explores in several permutations. At one and the same time, it is a realistic novel, in the sense that it comments directly on its society, its class composition, and the nature of contemporary conventions, while it also examines the very possibility of realistic narration, its implied epistemology, and its aesthetic philosophical standing.

The novel begins, as already noted, where it concludes, in the garden of the Briest estate at Hohen-Cremmen in the Havelland region of Brandenburg. The opening chapter sets the realist stage by announcing a conventional register of tropes and images: the domestic scene, populated by aristocrats with a "von" in the family name. Realism tended to prefer the middle class, but the von Briests hardly belong to the aristocracy of the highest order. Indeed, here and in the course of the novel Effi is repeatedly positioned outside of or even against core elements of the nobility. While it would be wrong to read *Effi Briest* as primarily an indictment of aristocratic society, somehow contrasted with a bourgeois world, neither is the Junker upper class portrayed as in any way particularly appealing. Whatever their class pedigree, the Briests lead a bourgeois life. In the first scene mother and daughter are introduced embroidering; later, Effi performs gymnastics and play with her friends. This is the unheroic, everyday life of realism.

The text is, moreover, realistic in the perspective and structure of the description of the scene. The narrator provides a landscape architect's overview of the house, its park, and the wall beside it. The description closes in on the mother and daughter and then zooms in even closer to examine the yarn and the needles. This is the standard realistic effect of order and precision, elaborating a world full of material facts but an always ordered fullness, in the center of which the narrator positions the human subject, at home in the world: here, the mother and her increasingly bored daughter. Effi is restless not only because sitting in the garden with her mother is tedious. On the contrary, she is outgrowing the whole limiting life in Hohen-Cremmen, and it is this affective situation that underpins her imminent engagement to her suitor, Geert von Innstetten. She is anxious to leave but will not say so. Such is the realist regime that, having overcome romanticism, prefers the indirect detail to a direct expression of emotion. For all of Fontane's use of conversation, *Effi Briest* remains a novel about what is not said.

On one level the scene, like the novel as a whole, can be read as social description, thereby meeting the conventional expectation for realistic writing. The front of the Briest villa is, for example, bathed in sunlight, but the family chooses to escape the heat and enjoy the shade of the park. The distinction between light and dark here marks the social artifact of a distinction between public and private space. It demonstrates, furthermore, the realistic preference for a domestic (and, therefore, unheroic) life, no matter how much public matters, including political rank, may penetrate it. Bismarck's power to pull Innstetten away from his young wife later in the novel may be taken as an indication of an imminent postrealist dissolution of the distinction between public and private, as the arm of the state reaches increasingly into the intimacy of the family. Yet, that, too, is an example fully consonant with the hypothesis that the realist novel is concerned with contemporary society and its description. Public and private spheres, Bismarck and dirty dishes, are all appropriate topics for realistic discourse.

Yet, the generic markers of realism — the family bliss, the everyday activities, the ordered spatiality — are simultaneously undermined by a network of allegorical signifiers, a rich set of symbols that stands very much at odds to the ontology of realism. A situation of dual power prevails, with two distinct modalities of representation inhabiting the same textual space. The garden in Hohen-Cremmen is not merely a matter of human subjects in a harmonious setting, occupied with needlework and small talk. Effi and Luise are framed by another order of meaning altogether, one that stands in an ultimate antagonism to the realistic world. The shaded yard is overlaid with an allegorical — indeed, religious — significance that points far beyond realism. The churchyard appears to set a spatial limit to the life of the family, just as the playful mock funeral at the end of the first chapter, an innocent game for Effi and her friends, foreshadows the death of the adulteress. Social space, in which the private life of the family transpires, is, therefore, simultaneously an epitaphic space, overshadowed by death. The scene that commenced as a realistic description of social types — Prussian aristocrats at home — takes on an allegorical character. Effi and her mother, sitting in the shadow, embroidering an altar cloth while looking out to the churchyard, constitute a mythic image of the fates at work. That Effi is so anxious to interrupt this labor anticipates her own trajectory and its premature termination. The end of the novel, Effi's end, and the end of realism are all prefigured in the opening scene.

The aspiration of literary realism to generate narratives capable of placing human subjects in a cosmos of sensuous objects and purposeful action presumed the obsolescence of the older, otherworldly discourses of Romanticism and idealism, as well as traditional religion and popular superstition. Nineteenth-century historical optimism and a growing faith in the bounty of industry and science underpinned the realist agenda. Yet, for Fontane, writing in the last decades of the century, much of that optimism had been tempered by the disappointments of personal and historical experience. A hesitant, sometimes pessimistic predisposition undercuts the realist aspiration to master the world with order and reason. While Romanticism in the strict sense had come to an end, its claim on a central role in human affairs returns repeatedly in modernity, competing with the rationality of scientific description and social realism. Within the cultural process of modernization unleashed by the Enlightenment, the irrational reasserts itself not simply as a vestige of a past somehow inadequately eradicated but as a dialectical component of the social condition itself. Life takes place in the shadow of death, and the past remains present, even in the shape of ghosts: denying the specters would itself be profoundly unrealistic.

For *Effi Briest* the consequence is the dual regime of realism and allegory, a fault line that runs through the novel, always threatening to erupt. For example, the opening scene not only announces a realistic space; it also defines a historical and political temporality by declaring that the Briest family had occupied the home since the early seventeenth-century reign of Georg Wilhelm, Elector of Brandenburg. Once that reference establishes a calendar, other political allusions allow for a more precise dating within Fontane's contemporary history (and this device is characteristic of Fontane's other novels, as well: private lives measured in terms of political history). Yet, there is a second temporality, as well, evidenced by the sundial, a cosmic time; and it is, significantly, the sundial, the order of nature, that will be removed to make room for the gravestone, pointing to the temporality of eternity that challenges the secular calendar of the state.

While realism and allegory compete in the temporal understructure of the novel — is *Effi Briest* about Germany in the Bismarck era or is it about life and death? — the tension between the two literary registers is equally evident in a second example, the use of networks of symbols that, seemingly integrated into realistic description, simultaneously point beyond it. In a novel of a fatal love triangle, the frequent use of the number three stretches the limits of realistic plausibility: the wedding date is the third of October, Annie is born on the third of July, the shipping accident that distracts Innstetten takes place on the third of January, Roswitha reports losing her child after three days, and the telltale letters were hidden in the third compartment of the sewing basket. The realist obsession with precision is put to use here in the interest of the allegorical principle.[2] Similarly, Fontane color-codes the novel: red as the conventional signal of danger and yellow as sign of aging and death. Crampas's letters are old and yellowed, and they, therefore, imply the question of a statute of limitations: should not Innstetten just overlook the transgression from the past? Yet, the letters are also bound with a red ribbon, signaling danger. Similarly, the flowers at the duel site are red and yellow; and so are the leaves on the trees at Hohen-Cremmen in the late-September final scene.[3] In this matter, as well, the realist convention of providing concrete detail supports the separate allegorical order of meaning.

The distance between realism and allegory is evidenced in a third manner when the text doubles back on itself, calling its own account into question. The naïve epistemology of realism, the notion that its literary language provides a transparent window on the world, becomes untenable when the textual structure foregrounds the necessarily artificial character of the literary object. At such points realism is robbed of its deceptive appearance of naturalness, further highlighting the nonrealistic and, therefore, allegorical character of the text. Thus, during the Christmas festivities at the Rings' the aristocratic Sidonie von Grasenabb complains to the Pastor about the declining morality of the age and the weakness of the flesh just as she is serving herself a healthy portion of roast beef. The point is not merely to undercut her hypocritical moralism by gesturing to her gluttony but, more important, to highlight the materiality of language: when she says "flesh," the meat appears. The realistic portrayal of conservative values in the Prussian aristocracy is thus tempered by a visual pun that draws attention to the constructedness of the text.

A more poignant example involves the repetition, across nearly the full span of the novel, of the call "Effi, come": at first her girl friends' exhortation that she return to their games, but later her father's welcoming his suffering daughter back to her family home. What had been a mere incident is revealed to be prefiguration within a complex textual network. A related effect of doubling is achieved in chapter 31: we read excerpts from Luise's letter to Effi announcing her sorry fate after the discovery of the adultery, a severe and brutal text, but it is immediately juxtaposed with fragments from Frau Zwicker's letter to a friend, a trivial and gossipy contrast but at the same time a demonstration of a more pragmatic and humane sensibility. Zwicker's first name, Sophie, may indicate a fundamental wisdom, or it may be intended to underscore the absence thereof. The judiciousness of Fontane's ambivalence is such that both may be true. The doubling of epistolary texts in the wake of the discovery of the hidden letters, however, surely underscores the constructed textuality of the narrative, undermining the claim to objectivity on which realism is based. In a comparable way, Fontane parodies the seeing-is-believing epistemology of realism when Luise — who, having traveled to Berlin to visit an eye clinic, is able to spend time with Effi — later reports to her husband that their daughter is getting along better with Innstetten. "Sie hat mir so was gesagt, und was mir wichtiger ist, ich habe es auch bestätigt gefunden, mit Augen gesehen" (232). Visual description, one of the fundamental elements of a realistic aesthetic, turns out to be deceptive and unreliable.[4]

Effi: Transgression, Nationality, and Imperialism

It would be tempting to map the competition between realistic and allegorical registers onto the two central figures: Effi, associated with a Romantic otherworldliness and lyrical innocence, and Innstetten, the stern and pedantic bureaucrat. In fact, this hybrid character of the literary work echoes standard philosophical-aesthetic characterizations of the novel as genre since Hegel: the synthesis of poetic fantasy and a prosaic world.[5] In literary historical terms *Effi Briest*, as a novel of adultery, is typically grouped with *Madame Bovary* (1857) and *Anna Karenina* (1873–76), although these novels were written considerably earlier. The question has, therefore, been posed whether *Effi Briest* may not have more in common with contemporary works of the 1890s, works by Schnitzler and Wedekind, let alone Freud, that explicitly address issues of gender and that are imbued with a modernist (rather than realist) psychological sensibility.[6] In that case, *Effi Briest* would have to be treated more properly as part of fin-de-siècle culture than as an example of realism.

Yet, what marks *Effi Briest* as a realist novel is the extensive exploration of national identity. Despite the indisputable importance of the allegorical and irrational components, the text retains a social historical component that cannot be marginalized: whatever else the novel may achieve, it provides a textured study of the Bismarckian Wilhelmine world and its relationship to the substance of the newly formed German state. There is, of course, a much larger question to be posed with regard to the relationship of literary realism (and not only in Germany) to the topic of nationhood: was there a necessary linkage, a constitutive and defining interconnection between the realist novel and the modern nation-state, or was it only an accident of time, a function of the shared nineteenth-century context, in which both realistic aesthetics and nation-building loomed large? In either case, the fact remains that realism and nationhood inhabited the same cultural space, and the realist novel was a particularly effective vehicle to explore nationality and disseminate its expectations. *Effi Briest* is no exception in this regard. A closer look at its treatment of nationhood, however, uncovers unexpected connections that go to the heart of the aesthetics of the text and the judgment on the figures. In other words, the problem of national identity is interesting here not primarily in order to determine, for example, Fontane's political position on Bismarck or the Junkers. Instead, the deployment of political material pertinent to German nationality and the Wilhelmine social structure within the novel is relevant to the relationship between Effi and Innstetten and, therefore, to the knotty intertwining of realism and its alternatives.

Fontane based Effi's story on a contemporary case: Elizabeth Freiin von Plotho married Armand Leon von Ardenne in 1873; she was nineteen, he twenty-four. His career took them first to Berlin, then to the far west, Metz and Düsseldorf, where she began a liaison with a district judge, Emil Hartwich. The relationship with Hartwich continued after the Ardennes returned to Berlin. The correspondence between the lovers was discovered; Ardenne shot and killed Hartwich in a duel and divorced his wife, retaining custody of the children.

Both differences from and similarities to Fontane's fictionalized version are striking. The enormous age difference between Effi and Innstetten is a novelistic invention, as is the lover's social status (Fontane transforms the bourgeois judge into the aristocrat Crampas and moves him into the military). Yet, the adultery itself, the discovery of letters, the duel, and the divorce all follow the trajectory of the Ardenne case. Hartwich, by the way, like Crampas, was active in artistic and theatrical circles, which is where the affair presumably began to develop. That Fontane has Effi die young is, by way of contrast, a literary decision, consonant with the conventions of novels of adultery. Elizabeth von Ardenne herself was able to remain active as a caregiver (Effi discovers that she is shunned and barred from charitable activity) and died in 1952 at ninety-nine.[7]

Fontane's transformations of the Ardenne material point to a concern with questions of time. Inventing the age difference between Effi and Innstetten, he suggests a source of their marital difficulties, while allowing for the particular history between Innstetten and Luise: for Innstetten to have courted Luise, he, of course, has to be old enough to be Effi's father. In addition, the affair between Ardenne and Hartwich was still very much alive when they were discovered. In contrast, Fontane has allowed Effi to terminate the connection to Crampas through the move to Berlin, thereby underscoring the particular moral challenge facing Innstetten: how to respond to this injury from a relatively distant past.

Yet, the spatial transformation of the Ardenne material is more important for the status of *Effi Briest* as a realist novel addressing the structure of national identity. Instead of a story that would have spanned Germany from the far west, including sites of the Franco-Prussian War, to Berlin, the novel unfolds primarily in Hohen-Cremmen, Kessin, and Berlin — distinct locales, to be sure, but all in the Prussian northeast. This territorial shift of the Ardenne material away from the west corresponds to Prussian ascendancy in unified Germany; in other words, narrowing the geographical focus makes the fiction all the more emblematic of the Wilhelmine state, with its Junker hegemony. In particular, the displacement to the northeast allows for the important role that the shadow figure of Bismarck can play in the novel: Kessin is described as close to Varzin, one of Bismarck's historical estates, and it is to Varzin that Innstetten would be summoned, leaving his wife alone and, consequently, susceptible to her youthful fears and romantic imagination.

That she is left alone or with little companionship is a consequence both of Bismarck's proximity but also, and perhaps more importantly, the provincial limitations of Kessin. Instead of the large city and artistic center of Düsseldorf, where the Ardenne affair commenced, Fontane conjures up a small port and vacation resort (based in part on the memories of his own childhood in Swinemunde) with little opportunity for a social life. This cultural and social narrowness, which resonates in the cramped character of the Innstetten residence, is emblematic of the constraints of Wilhelmine society: Effi has left the small world of Hohen-Cremmen, but although she has married an ambitious and promising career civil servant, she has not at all arrived in a grand world of glamour and social opportunity. On the contrary, Kessin and Pomerania represent an existential narrowness and a specific rejection of any greater horizons. In that regard, there is an unmistakable, if unexpected, consonance between the substance of the province and — despite all differences of mood and predisposition — Briest's final admonition against topics too wide. To be sure, the idyllic glow of Hohen-Cremmen is worlds apart from the dreary emptiness of Kessin, but on a deeper level they both exemplify a mode of local particularity, the retreat from universalistic frameworks, that imbues German nationality with its specific flavor, sometimes provincial and sometimes federalist. Precisely for this reason, the move from Düsseldorf to Kessin makes the narrative more national.

The semiotics of local particularity functions as the alternative to any topic "too broad," and its most prominent political articulation takes place at the Christmas celebration, when Baron von Güldenklee delivers his spirited toast in honor of the head forester, Ring. He begins with puns on the name, listing various sorts of rings, leading to the prediction that an engagement ring would soon grace the finger of one of the daughters of the house. He then proceeds to a literary allusion, the parable of the ring from Lessing's play *Nathan der Weise* (Nathan the Wise, 1778), an Enlightenment-era plea for religious tolerance. Fontane has Güldenklee speak of it derisively as a "eine Judengeschichte, die, wie der ganze liberale Krimskrams, nichts wie Verwirrung und Unheil gestiftet hat und noch stiftet. Gott bessere es" (167). This is clearly the voice of the conservative aristocracy, hostile to Jewish emancipation, as well as to the larger program of nineteenth-century liberalism. It is, moreover, an emphatically particularist speech: while appealing to local Pomeranian identity, he never employs the term "German," which would presumably be too national, inclusive, and broad. Similarly, he is quite prepared to invoke the king, the legitimate monarch of Prussia, but he never refers to him as *Kaiser,* the German emperor.[8] This political commentary, comparable to the remarks on Jewish emancipation, is symptomatic of conservative ideology. Its inclusion in the novel is a further example of the manner in which the text meets the expectation that the realistic novel provide a variegated description of the social hierarchy.

Of special note, however, is the manner in which his ideological particularism determines the very form of Güldenklee's oratorical rhetoric. He moves from the playful imagery of many rings (the unlimited semantic ambivalence of the term) to Lessing's three rings (a narrower set but very much implicated in a universalistic vision) to a concluding celebration of a single ring — Ring, the host: for it is this one Ring who, so says the toastmaster, has united the traditional loyalists and royalists of Kessin, bringing them together around his table. Moving from the many to the one, Güldenklee's speech is a celebration of narrowness, even at this festive occasion. In a characteristic move, however, Fontane immediately repositions the same content — narrowness and constraint — in the subsequent plot, where it takes on a quite different coloration. Güldenklee's exuberant panegyric to a narrow way of life is metamorphosed into a disheartening, and then a highly ominous, tight fit. On the ride home Effi is first trapped into sharing a sleigh with the dreary Sidonie, which is unpleasant enough. Yet, when some local flooding halts the party and Sidonie returns to the comfort of her carriage, Effi is trapped again — this time alone in the sleigh with Crampas, her seducer.

Does Effi's fall result from the loosening of moral standards, as the conservative voices in the novel would have it? Güldenklee's toast might be taken to prefigure the seduction in the sleigh, blaming it on the excessive liberalism of the *Reich* or even on Lessing and the Jews. Crampas himself is, in fact, not above using Heine in his seduction strategy. Yet, the danger to Christian morality comes from a quite different source: Ring's home stands on the site of an ancient heathen temple; and the flooding, which holds up the homeward journey and leaves Effi alone with Crampas, is buried beneath the sand. "Alles geht nämlich unterirdisch vor sich" (172). The threat to morality is archaic and subterranean, not, as Güldenklee would have it, modern and public. Close attention to the structure of space in Kessin and in Güldenklee's speech demonstrates how Germany is not at all "too wide a field" and certainly not too liberal. On the contrary, it is limited and limiting, bound by tight rings of convention and allowing minimal room for individual growth. It is endangered by its own archaic and pre-Christian predispositions. Trapped in this social, cultural, and even architectural straitjacket, Effi falls prey to Crampas's advances. In the narrow world of Germany there is little alternative to succumbing, as little for Effi as there had been for Gretchen a century earlier.

Yet, both the psychology of the heroine and the organization of space are considerably more complex. Provincialism is not the only tendency in the dynamic organization of space in the novel, nor is Effi's role only that of a victim.[9] On the contrary, she plays an important part in opening up the fictional map, pushing at the borders, and expanding the structure of space to take on national and international dimensions. Güldenklee's particularism and Briest's closing denigration of wide fields represent a repressive predisposition toward a self-enclosed and restrictive spatiality, which undoubtedly burdens Effi, whose exuberant preference for motion was evident in the opening chapters. This is not the only structuring force at work in the geography of the novel, however. *Effi Briest* is also marked by a particular effort to project a national map of the united Germany in the full proud expanse of the Wilhelmine *Reich*. If Kessin marks an eastern extreme, identified through the Trippelli material, as a stopover on the way to St. Petersburg, the western antipode is Bad Ems, the famous spa in the Rhineland not far from Koblenz. It is to Ems that Effi travels for reasons of health with her companion, Frau Zwicker, and it is there that she receives the decisive letter from her mother announcing Innstetten's discovery and decision. (Like Varzin in the east, Bad Ems also points to Bismarck, since it was his publication of the Emser telegram, an account of a meeting between Wilhelm I and the French ambassador, that helped precipitate the Franco-Prussian War. Fontane's choice of Ems as the site for epistolary ambiguity — the contrast between the letters by Luise and Frau Zwicker — may be intended to point toward the dubious textual status of the telegram, which Bismarck notoriously edited precisely to provoke calls for war.) In addition, the national map traces a North-South vector. After Effi and Innstetten move to Berlin, their initial summer vacation plans to visit Oberammergau in the Bavarian south come to naught because of Innstetten's work schedule, and they travel instead to the far north, the isle of Rügen on the Baltic. It is as if the geography of the novel were designed to stake out the borders of the Bismarckian state.

In this expansive map Effi continues to feel a constant pull to the idyllic home in Hohen-Cremmen, and it is there that she returns in response to the adversities that she must face. Nonetheless, she is not a weak and victimized character seeking shelter or retreating into a dogmatic provincialism, as does Güldenklee. On the contrary, from the start she perpetually seeks wider horizons and pushes against the borders; traveling to Ems, traveling to Rügen, and from there to Denmark, and while she and Innstetten miss Oberammergau, they have, in fact, already gone much farther than Bavaria on their Italian honeymoon. Despite the pull of the provinces, Effi's world unfolds as much larger than Hohen-Cremmen or Kessin.

Effi's appetite for new experiences and adventure runs counter to the predominant discourse of constraint, both social and spatial. We find her at the start giving up the minutiae of embroidery and choosing, instead, to perform calisthenics. She does not object to the engagement to Innstetten; he is quite right for her, because he provides her with the prospect of pursuing her ambitions for wealth and stature.[10] While Kessin later turns out to be disappointing, she is at first animated both by the promised cosmopolitanism of the port, with its connections to distant lands, and by the associated exoticism that she is likely to encounter there. She reprimands Innstetten for presenting Kessin as a backwater, since she anticipates a new world of excitement: "Eine ganz neue Welt, sag ich, vielleicht einen Neger oder einen Türken, oder vielleicht sogar einen Chinesen" (49). This push for qualitatively new experience, coupled with the expansive geographic space, represents the countermovement against the emphatic provincialism of Briest and Güldenklee. Despite her attachment to her childhood home, Effi is the figure most associated with new places and a desire for an expansive space. She is, therefore, able to call the repressive moderation of her mother into question. Simultaneously, her instinct to cross borders anticipates her willingness to transgress against conventions, a different sort of border-crossing.

Effi's predisposition toward an expansion of space poses the question of imperialism and its standing within the novel, exemplified particularly in the story of the Chinese servant. The figure of the "China voyager" Thomsen alludes to the German pursuit of commercial advantages in the China coastal trade in the midcentury, leading eventually to German military interventions. Peter Utz has pointed out that many of the names in *Effi Briest* — Anna, Hertha, Luise, Vineta — were also the names of German battleships deployed against China, suggesting that Fontane intended to invoke the real history of imperialism as a frame for the reading of the novel. In fact, the economy of imperialism maintains a shadow existence in the background, with the emerging agricultural competitors, Russia and America, invoked at a distance, while Briest worries about the price of crops, which Bismarck would come to support with a protectionist trading policy. Yet, it is, above all, the figure of the Chinese ghost that points most starkly to German imperialism. German engagement in China was well underway at the time Fontane was working on *Effi Briest*, and it would lead a decade later to Germany's leadership role among European nations collaborating to suppress the Boxer rebellion.

Critics have argued that Effi, as a victim of the patriarchal social code in Germany, is positioned against the imperialist expansionism. In this sense, Utz has claimed that the incorporation of references to imperialism in *Effi Briest* takes on a critical, antiimperialist character only through the ghost material and the link to Effi. The imperial references would be little more than historical background, were it not for the fact that they are linked to Effi's situation through the ghost narrative. Hence, Utz suggests that the ghost is a vehicle for Innstetten intentionally to educate his young bride by manipulating her fears. We will turn to Innstetten's relationship to the ghost in a moment; here another matter is at stake. In the novel's semiotics of space Effi is the primary force behind expansionism through her search for new experience, her adventuresome character, and her desire for the romantic and the exotic. She was, after all, looking forward to "Negroes, Turks, and Chinese" even before she arrived in the port of Kessin. Rather than figuring as a collateral victim of imperialist ideology, Effi herself enfigures the program of spatial expansionism: imperialism. *Effi Briest* surely disallows any comfortable linkage between a heroine victimized by patriarchy and the presumed victims of overseas adventures. On the contrary, her exuberance and desire for wider horizons and distant lands are the very motor of imperial adventure.

This imperial expansionism is the diametrical opposite to conservative particularism, a dialectic that sheds important light on the construction of political discourse in Wilhelmine Germany. Imperialism was, more often than not, a progressive discourse associated with science and technology and one, moreover, that could have a particular appeal to women hoping to escape the limitations of the social order in Germany.[11] Contemporary with Fontane, Frieda von Bülow worked as the premier author of *Kolonialliteratur* — literary fiction about life in the German colonial empire — one of the important themes of which was the role of women in the colonies and the opportunities that they would find there. To be sure, much of that colonial representation was propaganda, marketing, and a recruitment strategy. Nonetheless, Effi's inexorable drive toward the new, including new spaces, points to a paradoxically progressive substance within the imperialist agenda, the conquest of the "wide fields," from which Luise had been held back by Briest. Effi's imperialism is, however, deeply tragic, since the desire to transgress borders also implies the willingness to flout convention that leads to her demise. On an allegorical level this expansionism would tend to link her with the navy, a predisposition announced by her description of her own outfit in chapter 2 as that of a midshipman. Yet, we soon find out that Effi, so elementally associated with air, is always endangered by water — recall the flooding as the scene of seduction — which suggests a fundamental ambivalence within the imperial project: an opportunity for new experience, and, at the same time, a threat that could become fatal.

Innstetten's Ghost

From Romanticism, which realism attempted to suppress, Effi inherits a *Fernweh*, a desire for faraway lands. Her expansionist search for the exotic and the will to challenge the constraints of conventional boundaries merge with the thrust of German imperialism within the novel's array of cultural references. Innstetten, too, is an heir to Romanticism, but his is a different legacy: wounded love and a fixation on the past. This fundamental irritation with time is as important for an understanding of Innstetten and the novel in general as is the problem of space for Effi.

The opening scene of *Effi Briest* announces the complexity of time, as has already been discussed: historical time in the reference to the Elector of Brandenburg, cosmic time with the sundial, and the foreshadowing of immortality beside the churchyard. The simple present of the mother and daughter engrossed in needlework is, in fact, a penultimate moment, for the suitor, Effi's future, is about to call; but he is a suitor who, strangely, also signals the mother's past. The present marks the border between aspiration and memory, the thin line where future possibilities run up against the mandates of history. On the level of realist descriptivism the age difference between Effi and Innstetten can be read as a comment on inequality in the social institution of marriage (although it is a gross exaggeration of the reality of the Ardenne marriage). It also poses, however, the conceptual problem of asynchronicity: the present is never only present, the past is never fully past. This temporal complexity tends to undermine the aesthetic of realist referentiality, with its need to assume and assert an unproblematic presence of things.

It is tempting to suggest that this obsession with time is a defining feature of German literature in the broadest sense, with its recurrent focus on the past, the repression of the past, the redemption of the past, as well as utopian and lyrical invocations of the future. In *Effi Briest,* despite the insistence on linking the central plot to contemporary politics, an archaic past erupts into the present. The Christmas celebration with Güldenklee's speech takes place at the site of an ancient pre-Christian temple: a reference to a distant past that parodies the orator's reactionary stance, while setting the stage for the seduction. It is at Rügen, when Effi and Innstetten visit the Herthasee, however, that they confront ancient Germanic ruins, sacrificial altars replete with grooves for the blood of the victims. Effi chooses to leave, reluctant to be reminded of the guilt she is carrying. The significance of the episode is heightened by the connection to the preferred vacation goal that they had been forced to abandon, Oberammergau and the Passion Play. That, too, would have conveyed a scene of guilt and sacrifice, albeit a Christian one. While conservatives such as Sidonie and Güldenklee fret over the declining morality of the age, the text describes a time in which archaic calls for sacrifice reach into the present and demand their due. What Effi was able to avoid in Bavaria confronted her on Rügen and caught up with her in Ems.

Effi may flee the relics at the Herthasee because of a fear of sacrifice as retribution. For Innstetten, by way of contrast, sacrifice takes a modern form: self-sacrifice. Effi herself introduces him in the account that she provides to her friends in the first chapter as representing a "Geschichte mit Entsagung" (11), a sort of narrative that she explicitly endorses. He carries within him the scars of an enormous loss, the failed pursuit of Luise nearly two decades earlier. His love for Luise was so great that he came close to suicide, and the personality structure he subsequently developed, with its particular combination of eccentricity, pedantry, and awkwardness, derives directly from that pain. It is a psychological profile comparable to that in Thomas Mann's *Der Tod in Venedig* (Death in Venice, 1912), in which Gustav von Aschenbach is portrayed as having overcome his romantic youth through the assertion of a repressive discipline and a rigorous Protestant Ethic. Yet, the resemblance does not go much further, for while Aschenbach discovers an unexpected love, Innstetten appears nearly incapable of loving at all.

Now, however, he is returning to marry Luise's daughter, and that marriage withers in the shadow of the pain Luise meted out two decades earlier. His "inhibited behavior toward Effi reflects ... the fear of emotional involvement of someone who had his fingers badly burnt in the past."[12] Effi names the problem in her deathbed confession to her mother: Innstetten is "ohne rechte Liebe" (318). The scene is so stunning because these final words are followed immediately by a subtle redirection of the reader's attention to Luise. Effi may be attempting a final self-vindication, laying blame at Innstetten's cold doorstep. His inability to love denied her the emotional fulfillment that she would have needed and that could have prevented her from succumbing to Crampas. Yet, the textual gesture of the shift to Luise proposes a quite different argument: Effi points to Innstetten, but the text points at Luise. Her daughter is dying because Innstetten could not love her, but his inability derives, so the text suggests, from an internalization of the denial he had experienced years ago at her hands. His behavior surely contributes to Effi's fate, but only because he, too, has been mutilated within an ineluctable network of harm and a ubiquitous reluctance to love: if Innstetten is guilty, so is Luise.

Innstetten's return to Luise in order to marry her daughter interrupts natural time. The past reaches into the present. He is, in a particular sense, a *revenant,* a ghost, who himself cannot escape the past. His weird attachment to the gloomy house in Kessin is not at all a matter of careerism or public obligation (as he suggests to Effi) but an expression of a deep psychological attachment because of its past. Like Innstetten, the house has a hidden history. It had belonged to the China trader Thomsen, whose granddaughter's wedding celebration took place in the mysterious room upstairs just prior to her unexplained disappearance; their Chinese servant died soon after. The facts are never fully clarified, to be sure, and the status of the ghost is left open.[13] Yet, it is not difficult to patch together the narrative congruence between the two failed love affairs: Innstetten lost Luise in the same way that he could imagine the servant, the secret lover, losing the bride, engaged to another man. Innstetten fails to explain away the ghost to Effi not, as Crampas would have it, because he manipulates the fiction and her fear in order to keep her under control. Quite to the contrary, he harbors a deep affinity for the ghost story, perhaps even a belief in the ghost itself, which represents the memory of his crushed love and his own repressed Romanticism.

Innstetten's life is haunted by the ghost because he cannot escape his past, the loss of his love and the trauma he has endured. The result is "a deeply troubled personality and a morbid imagination which, as is shown on other occasions, is also responsive to the music of Wagner and to the eerie and desolate beauty of the landscape around Kessin."[14] The intrusion of the past into the present takes the form of a ghost, perpetually recalling what was lost but also underscoring its absence. It represents the repression of love, while keeping the memory of love alive. What is at stake here is both realistic and allegorical: the ghost of the Chinese lover as the psychological projection of Innstetten's pain, and the marker of the repression of Romanticism. It is the constant, critical reminder of the price Innstetten had to pay to accommodate the reality principle and renounce his youthful aspirations. It is, therefore, the (ghostly) body of a critique of realism. For if the realist program insisted on a secularized real world, with concrete details and an orderly space, the ghost story should have no place at all in the novel. As much as one can read the ghost as a plausibly psychological phenomenon, its standing as the marker of the past in the present represents a profound revision of realistic temporality. The sundial and the churchyard, light and dark, in the halcyon first chapter already set the stage for the ghost as the return of the repressed romantic. It is telling that Fontane would comment that he wrote *Effi Briest* with little effort, as if with a "psychograph," a device that spiritists would use to invite ghosts to write and to which Trippelli refers in her conversation with Effi.[15]

To understand Innstetten's character as a consequence of his past, and to treat the ghost as a marker of asynchronicity, the past haunting the present, run counter to conventional approaches to *Effi Briest,* which simply cast Effi as the victim of an oppressively domineering husband. Yet, to argue that Innstetten manipulates the ghost story to terrorize his wife means, in effect, adopting the interpretation provided by Crampas, who is not credible.[16] No matter how a modern reader might withhold approval from Innstetten, it is not clear why the hardly admirable Crampas should be trusted. He was, after all, attempting to seduce Effi, and accusing her husband of abusing her was an effective tactic, as the text makes quite clear. That Effi might lend credence to Crampas's insinuations is psychologically plausible, but why readers remain equally susceptible to the seducer's melodramatic account of an evil husband and a helpless victim is less clear. The adultery in *Effi Briest* lacks any utopian glow, and there is no glamorous lover who might be seen as speaking an unquestionable truth. The affair does not rank as a true and authentic, genuinely romantic love, which might stand in stark contrast to the mundane and routinized life with the bureaucratic husband. Crampas is no Tristan offering an otherworldly beauty. On the contrary, the liaison has a sordid feel to it, and Crampas comes off as nothing more than a rogue. Perhaps Innstetten, despite his sense of responsibility and order, is no better than Crampas. Critics have suggested that the two correspond to twin evils of the Bismarck era: Innstetten's rigorous adherence to principles and Crampas's equally distasteful disregard for principles.[17] It is, however, surely not the case that Crampas is a better man than Innstetten. The opposite claim would have greater plausibility.

Innstetten's standing becomes clearer in comparison with both Crampas and the other key male figure, Gieshübler, the pharmacist in Kessin who dotes on Effi with a platonic admiration. The distinction between the rogue seducer and the kindly neighbor needs no commentary: the good friend and the bad friend. It is, therefore, all the more striking to discover what these opposites share. Both carry physical deformities: Gieshübler has a hunchback (to which he attributes his bachelor status and loneliness) and Crampas has been shot in a duel, pursuant to a previous amorous affair, leaving him with an impaired arm. For all their differences, wounds tied to love mark the two men. Innstetten is physically unscathed, but he has a much deeper wound, the legacy of the love for Luise. All the men bear injuries, external or internal, signaling a ubiquity of suffering, in which the Chinese servant took part, as well. They all face cruel constraints on the possibility of happiness in the present because of the disappointments of the past, which are not past at all.

Time is treacherous in *Effi Briest*. Archaic strata can erupt to the surface, and the conclusion of the novel is evident in the opening scene. Love might promise to outwit time and last forever, but it is precisely love in the present that is impaired by the failed love of the past. The former pain has made Innstetten realistic, incapable of giving in to his own need for tenderness, which Effi astutely recognizes. She would have the power to break the spell, and there are moments when a gradual warming of the relationship begins. Yet, Fontane tells a particularly bitter story. It is after Annie's birth, when Innstetten can begin to see Effi more as a women and less as a child, that he begins to show greater affection; but by that time she has already fallen under the sway of Crampas. If Effi married too early, Innstetten's love for her has come too late: asynchronicity.[18]

Religion and Realism

Literary realism participated in the larger movement of nineteenth-century culture toward secularization, critical not only of the philosophical idealism of the period around 1800 but also of orthodox and traditional forms of religion. Ironically, the mortal enemies of the eighteenth century, religion and philosophy, suddenly faced common enemies, a celebration of scientific success and the dynamic productivity of a capitalist economy that was transforming the material world. The new sensibility of the age found its literary expression in realism. In *Effi Briest*, as in Fontane's other novels, the fate of the characters is played out in a natural environment of flowers and trees, sand and sea. The reconstitution of the world as a site of sensuous experience is the hallmark of realism and the this-worldly orientation of the emerging posttraditional culture. The joke of serving Sidonie the platter of roast beef just when she is indulging in a denunciation of the flesh exemplifies the realistic rejection of dogmatic religion.

The preference for the natural life determines the evaluation of the major characters, as well: Innstetten is associated with paperwork and, at best, a pedantic interest in art history, while Effi, from the start, performs calisthenics and plays on a swing. Luise underscores this priority of a natural life by presenting Effi to Innstetten "noch erhitzt von der Aufregung des Spiels, wie ein Bild frischesten Lebens" (18). In contrast to Innstetten's stiff awkwardness, Effi is described as a "Tochter der Luft" (9), and this difference contributes to the reader's predisposition toward her.

Yet, there is more at stake in Effi's association with the air, which takes on two quite distinct meanings. On the one hand, it lodges Effi in a network of elemental signs. Just as she thrives in the air, she is threatened by water: in Kessin, on Rügen, even at the spa Ems. Her desire for air attracts her to the evening window in Hohen-Cremmen at the conclusion, but it is the night dampness that exacerbates her illness and leads to her death. The natural register of realistic language not only describes a physical environment; it also inserts Effi into a mythological cosmos of primitive physical forces, as her fate hangs in the balance between water and air. On the other hand, her very orientation to the air and, therefore, to the heavens points to a countermovement, a spirituality, no matter how naive, that strives for a higher being that might overcome a merely natural life. In her prayer at the window in the final chapter she expresses her desire to return to a celestial paradise, a final border crossing into a wider field. Her simultaneous confession that she does not know if there truly is an afterlife may confirm her self-assessment as a poor Christian. This lability of faith is all the more urgent, given the threats to Christianity inherent in both the archaic heathen strata and the secularizing impact of the Enlightenment, denounced by Güldenklee in his attack on Lessing. For the archconservative Junker the parable of the ring is merely part of the liberal erosion of value. Yet, one can also treat the parable as fully compatible with the basic religious sensibility of Effi's prayer, the insistence on the urgency of belief as an alternative to the discipline of dogma. The novel, therefore, stages the contemporary conflict between orthodox and modernizing forms of belief. Strikingly, the novel positions certainty — be it realistic or dogmatic — as part of a habitus of constraint, while authentic religious temperament and allegory reserve the possibility of grace and redemption.

Thus, the landscape of *Effi Briest* is as much religious as it is natural, despite the secularizing predisposition of the realist program. Even in terms of the specific historical referent (let alone the status of allegory), religion protrudes as a primary issue. The novel describes the world of state Protestantism that characterized Wilhelmine Germany, and it is significant that Innstetten describes Kessin has "also" having a Catholic church. His intent is surely to demonstrate how the small town is growing but, more importantly, it serves as a marker of the historical moment, Germany in the wake of the *Kulturkampf,* the extended hostility between the newly formed state and the Catholic Church. The religious conflict is played out in the contrast between Johanna, the proper but disciplinarian Protestant, and Roswitha, Annie's nurse and, eventually, Effi's companion. Roswitha is surely the more interesting figure: undogmatic, as evidenced by her casual disregard for confession, yet somehow better attuned to human needs. It is difficult not to read the novel as tilting toward a Catholic position; this is, at least, Innstetten's self-critical judgment when he comes to regard the poor Catholic servant as a better person than himself and his friend, the paragons of success as career civil servants in the Protestant state. In the eyes of one critic, Roswitha is nothing less than the antipode of Bismarck in the novel.[19] To read the novel in relation to the *Kulturkampf* is especially compelling, since a central theme in the historic conflict was precisely the question of civil marriage. Interestingly, Fontane passes over the wedding of Effi and Innstetten with hardly a word: we learn much more about the festivities before and afterward, as if the ceremony itself had lost any significant sacramental status. Viewed in this light, the novel conveys an adversarial criticism of the triumphalism of state Protestantism in Germany.

Yet, the religious question in *Effi Briest* goes much further than social-historical commentary on the reverberations of the *Kulturkampf.* The very aesthetic fabric of the work involves a conflict between alternative modes of representation that map onto confessional differences. Innstetten and Wullersdorft especially, but the Briests, too, and most of the upper class are trapped in a quandary of Protestant semiotics, the iron cage of which Max Weber would write.[20] Searching for signs of grace in the world, modern sensibility experiences a disappearance of immanent meaning. All that can remain is the duty to adhere automatically to conventional behavior, to play comedy (a phrase that recurs repeatedly in the novel), to live a perfunctory life, and to rely on "Hülfskonstruktionen"

(312), claims that are devoid of substance or credibility but accepted blindly. Hence the rigorous self-discipline, as well as the nearly mechanical obedience with which Innstetten feels compelled to carry out a verdict no one required except himself. His irrepressible drive toward the duel betrays a compulsion to execute a verdict that anticipates Georg Bendemann's self-destruction two decades later in Kafka's "Das Urteil" (The Judgment, 1912).

Roswitha signifies a different relationship to the world and a quite different aesthetic principle. In place of disciplined faith in empty constructs, she exemplifies the role of love and good works. The two orientations, Innstetten's and Roswitha's, cross in the final scene at Effi's grave. Instead of the natural time of the sundial, the grave now marks the eternity of death and, simultaneously, the conclusion of the novel: indeed, the simple inscription on the stone is the same as the title of the book — *Effi Briest*. The end of the fiction is comparable to the end of the figures and, hence, a death of sorts. Yet, the imagery establishes a deeper connection: this realistic writing has an epitaphic quality; it is a response to a dying world in which meaning is disappearing. Realism hereby indicts itself for participating in this terminal reification. The novel buries realism, as it buries Effi. At the same time, however, the realist novel can thrive precisely as a fiction, an "auxiliary construction," the untruth that allows life, in all its emptiness, to continue. This is a stark and self-doubting characterization of literature as the disciplined effort to represent a world that is forever slipping away into the shadow of death.

Defining literature as a leap of faith in the face of death is, however, only one side of the final image. Literature, and realism in particular, is not only epitaphic. An alternative is implied by the image of the dog lying by Effi's grave. This is the topic of Briest's brief speculation, which Luise interrupts. Yet, Briest's designation is theologically compelling: the animal, he claims, represents the mourning of the "creature," expressing the solidarity of all creation, a fundamental love of things of the cosmos, precisely as part of a creation. This is quite distinct from Innstetten's theory of fiction as an accommodation to a meaningless world ruled by death. Its focus is, instead, community in the face of a creator; the literature that has the specific capacity to incorporate the plenitude of creation — realism — has a mission to save it. The enduring viability of realist writing, which continues to remain the staple of most literature, derives precisely from this embracing capacity to recreate creation and to imbue the descriptive mandate of "realism" with allegorical knowledge of an alternative. *Effi Briest* addresses the end of realism not primarily by being the termination of a literary movement or period (to be followed by some other literary-historical phase) but, rather, by showing that realism can point so emphatically beyond the limits of any merely mundane "reality." It is a kind of writing that, by virtue of its descriptive function, locates material in a time and place, and it is, therefore, "realistic." At its best, however, as in *Effi Briest*, it can escape the constraining grip of those determinants and break the spell of nature. It can redeem the fallen things of the world, bringing them to another order and an eternal life. "Effi, come."

Notes

[1] Theodor Fontane, *Effi Briest*, in *Fontanes Werke in Fünf Bänden*, vol. 4 (Berlin & Weimar: Aufbau, 1969), 319. Subsequent references to this volume are incorporated into the text.

[2] Detlef Kremer and Nikolaus Wegmann, "Wiederholungslektüre(n): Fontanes *Effi Briest*: Realismus des wirklichen Lebens oder realistischer Text?" *Deutschunterricht* 47, no. 6 (1995): 69.

[3] Kremer and Wegmann, 70–71.

[4] Valerie D. Greenberg, "The Resistance of *Effi Briest:* An (Un)told Tale," *PMLA* 103 (1988): 775.

[5] Wilhelm Solms, "Effi und Innstetten: 'ein Musterpaar'? Zum poetischen Realismus Fontanes," *Germanisch-Romanische Monatsschrift* 35 (1984): 202.

[6] Solms, 200–201.

[7] Jean Leventhal, "Fact into Fiction: *Effi Briest* and the Ardenne Case," *Colloquia Germanica* 24 (1991): 181–83.

[8] Henry H. Remak, "Politik und Gesellschaft als Kunst: Güldenklees Toast in Fontanes *Effi Briest*," in Jörg Thunecke, ed., *Formen realistischer Erzählkunst: Festschrift for Charlotte Jolles* (Nottingham UK: Sherwood P, 1979), 551.

[9] Greenberg, 770.

[10] Solms, 195–96.

[11] Cf. Marcia Klotz, "White Women and the Dark Continent: Gender and Sexuality in German Colonial Discourse from the Sentimental Novel to the Fascist Film" (Diss. Stanford U, 1994).

[12] Brian Holbeche, "Innstetten's 'Geschichte mit Entsagung' and Its Significance in Fontane's *Effi Briest*," *German Life and Letters* 41 (1987): 23.

[13] Greenberg, 774.

[14] Holbeche, 24.

[15] Frances M. Subiotto, "The Ghost in Effi Briest," *Forum for Modern Language Studies* 21 (1985): 139.

[16] Holbeche, 41.

[17] Leventhal, 187.

[18] Holbeche, 27.

[19] Clifford Albrecht Bernd, "Die Politik als tragendes Strukturelement in Fontanes *Effi Briest*," in Gabriela Scherer and Beatrice Wehrli, eds., *Wahrheit und Wort: Festschrift für Rolf Tarot zum 65. Geburtstag* (Bern: Lang, 1996), 70.

[20] Max Weber, *The Protestant Ethic and the Spirit of Capitalism*, trans. Talcott Parsons (Los Angeles: Roxbury, 1996), 181.

Works Cited

Adorno, Theodor. "Extorted Reconciliation: On Georg Lukács' *Realism in Our Time*." In his *Notes to Literature*. Vol. 1. Trans. Shierry Weber Nicholsen. New York: Columbia UP, 1991. 216–40.

Aldrich, Robert. *The Seduction of the Mediterranean: Writing, Art, and Homosexual Fantasy*. London: Routledge, 1993.

Alexis, Willibald. *Ruhe ist die erste Bürgerpflicht*. 1852; Frankfurt am Main: Ullstein, 1985.

Alker, Ernst. *Die deutsche Literatur im 19. Jahrhundert (1832–1914)*. 3rd ed. Stuttgart: Kröner, 1969.

Altmann, Alexander. "Moses Mendelssohn as Archetypical German Jew." In Jehuda Reinharz and Walter Schatzberg, eds. *The Jewish Response to German Culture*. Hanover, NH & London: UP of New England, 1985. 17–31.

Amann, Klaus, and Karl Wagner, eds. *Literatur und Nation: Die Gründung des deutschen Reiches*. Vienna: Böhlau, 1996.

Anderson, Alexander Robinson. "Spielhagen's Problematic Heroes." Diss. Brown U, 1962.

Anderson, Benedict. *Imagined Communities: Reflections on the Origin and Spread of Nationalism*. London: Verso, 1983; rev. ed., 1991.

Anonymous. Review of Friedrich Spielhagen's *Sturmflut*. *Atlantic Monthly* 40 (1877): 383.

Applegate, Celia. *A Nation of Provincials: The German Idea of Heimat*. Berkeley: U of California P, 1990.

Arens, Hans. *E. Marlitt: Eine kritische Würdigung*. Trier: Wissenschaftlicher Verlag, 1994.

Armstrong, Nancy. *Desire and Domestic Fiction: A Political History of the Novel*. New York: Oxford UP, 1987.

Auerbach, Berthold. *Auf der Höhe: Roman in acht Büchern*. 4th ed. 3 vols. Stuttgart: Cotta, 1866.

———. *Berthold Auerbach: Briefe an seinen Freund Jakob Auerbach*. 2 vols. Frankfurt am Main: Rütten & Loening, 1884.

---. *Berthold Auerbach's gesammelte Schriften*. 20 vols. Stuttgart: Cotta, 1857–58.

---. *Das Judenthum und die neueste Literatur*. Stuttgart: Brodhag, 1836.

---. *Das Landhaus am Rhein*. 3 vols. 4th ed. Stuttgart: Cotta, 1874.

---. *Waldfried: Eine vaterländische Familiengeschichte*. 6 vols. Stuttgart: Cotta, 1874.

---, trans. *B. de Spinoza's sämmtliche Werke aus dem lateinischen mit einer Lebensgeschichte Spinoza's*. 2nd rev. ed. 2 vols. Stuttgart: Cotta, 1871.

---, and N. Frankfurter, eds. *Gallerie der ausgezeichneten Israeliten aller Jahrhunderte, ihre Porträts und Biographien*. Stuttgart: Brodhag, 1836.

Auerbach, Erich. *Mimesis: Dargestellte Wirklichkeit in der abendländischen Literatur*. Bern: Francke, 1946. Trans. Willard R. Trask as *Mimesis: The Representation of Reality in Western Literature*. Princeton: Princeton UP, 1953.

Aust, Hugo. *Literatur des Realismus*. Stuttgart: Metzler, 1977.

Bade, Klaus J. "Die deutsche überseeische Massenauswanderung im 19. und frühen 20. Jahrhundert: Bestimmungsfaktoren und Entwicklungsbedingungen." In Bade, ed. *Auswanderer, Wanderarbeiter, Gastarbeiter: Bevölkerung, Arbeitsmarkt und Wanderung in Deutschland seit der Mitte des 19. Jahrhunderts*. Vol. 1. Ostfildern: Scripta Mercaturae, 1984. 259–99.

---. "From Emigration to Immigration: The German Experience in the Nineteenth and Twentieth Centuries." In Bade and Myron Weiner, eds. *Migration Past, Migration Future: Germany and the United States*. Providence, RI: Berghahn, 1997. 1–37.

---. "Transnationale Migration und Arbeitsmarkt im Kaiserreich: Vom Agrarstaat mit starker Industrie zum Industriestaat mit starker agrarischer Basis." In T. Pierenkemper and R. Tilly, eds. *Historische Arbeitsmarktforschung: Entstehung, Entwicklung und Probleme der Vermarktung von Arbeitskraft*. Göttingen: Vandenhoeck & Ruprecht, 1982. 182–211.

Bakhtin, Mikhail M. *The Dialogic Imagination: Four Essays*. Ed. Michael Holquist. Austin: U of Texas P, 1981.

Bamler, Friedrich. "St. Thomas." *Mitteilungen für die Gesellschaft der Freunde Wilhelm Raabes* 29 (1939): 107–12.

Barthes, Roland. "L'Effet de Réel." *Communications* 1 (1968): 84–89.

---. *S/Z: An Essay*. Trans. Richard Miller. New York: Hill & Wang, 1974.

Baumann, Christiane. "Angstbewältigung und 'sanftes Gesetz': Adalbert Stifter: *Brigitta* (1843)." In Winfried Freud, ed. *Deutsche Novellen: Von der Klassik biz zur Gegenwart*. Munich: Fink, 1993. 121–29.

Bazzanella, Astrid. "Das Frauenbild in den Romanen Eugenie Marlitts: Zwischen Emanzipationsbestreben und 'weiblicher Bestimmung.'" Diss. U of Trento, 1994.

Belgum, Kirsten. *Interior Meaning: Design of the Bourgeois Home in the Realist Novel*. New York: Peter Lang, 1991.

———. *Popularizing the Nation: Audience, Representation, and the Production of Identity in* Die Gartenlaube *1853–1900*. Lincoln: U of Nebraska P, 1998.

———. "Tracking the Liberal Hero." In Steven Brockmann and James Steakley, eds. *Heroes and Heroism in German Culture: Essays in Honor of Jost Hermand*. Amsterdam: Rodopi, 2001. 15–34.

Bennett, E. K. *A History of the German Novelle from Goethe to Thomas Mann*. 2nd ed. Rev. H. M. Waidson. New York: Cambridge UP, 1961.

Berghahn, Volker R. *Imperial Germany, 1871–1914: Economy, Society, Culture and Politics*. Providence, RI: Berghahn, 1994.

Berman, Harold. "Friedrich Spielhagen: The Novelist of Democracy." *Twentieth Century Magazine* 4 (1911): 347–49.

Berman, Marshall. *All That Is Solid Melts into Air: The Experience of Modernity*. 1982; Harmondsworth: Penguin, 1988.

Berman, Nina. *Orientalismus, Kolonialismus und Moderne: Zum Bild des Orients in der deutschsprachigen Kultur um 1900*. Stuttgart: Metzler, 1997.

Berman, Russell A. *Enlightenment or Empire: Colonial Discourse in German Culture*. Lincoln: U of Nebraska P, 1998.

———. "An Imagined Community: Germany according to Goldhagen." *German Quarterly* 71 (1998): 63–67.

———. *The Rise of the Modern German Novel: Crisis and Charisma*. Cambridge, MA: Harvard UP, 1986.

Bernd, Clifford Albrecht. *German Poetic Realism*. Boston: Twayne, 1981.

———. *Poetic Realism in Scandinavia and Central Europe 1820–1895*. Columbia, SC: Camden House, 1995.

———. "Die Politik als tragendes Strukturelement in Fontanes *Effi Briest*." In Gabriela Scherer and Beatrice Wehrli, eds. *Wahrheit und Wort: Festschrift für Rolf Tarot zum 65. Geburtstag*. Bern: Lang, 1996. 61–71.

Bertschik, Julia. *Maulwurfsarchäologie: Zum Verhältnis von Geschichte und Anthropologie in Wilhelm Raabes historischen Erzähltexten.* Tübingen: Niemeyer, 1995.

Bethe, Emil. "Die dorische Knabenliebe: ihre Ethik und ihre Idee." *Rheinisches Museum für Philologie,* n.s. 62 (1907): 438–75.

Bettelheim, Anton. *Berthold Auerbach: Der Mann — Sein Werk — Sein Nachlaß.* Stuttgart & Berlin: Cotta, 1907.

Beyschlag, Carl. "Die Prairien: Erlebnisse eines deutschen Flüchtlings." *Die Gartenlaube* (1859): 460–64.

Bieber, Hugo. *Der Kampf um die Tradition: Die deutsche Dichtung im europäischen Geistesleben 1830–1880.* Stuttgart: Metzler, 1928.

Blackbourn, David, and Geoff Eley. *The Peculiarities of German History: Bourgeois Society and Politics in Nineteenth-Century Germany.* Oxford: Oxford UP, 1984.

Blackwell, Jeannine, and Susanne Zantop, eds. *Bitter Healing: German Women Writers 1700–1830. An Anthology.* Lincoln: U of Nebraska P, 1990.

Bleibtreu, Carl. *Revolution der Literatur.* Ed. Johannes J. Braakenburg. Tübingen: Niemeyer, 1973.

Blüher, Hans. *Deutsches Reich, Judentum und Sozialismus.* Prion: Anthropos, 1920.

———. *Familie und Männerbund.* Leipzig: Der neue Geist, 1918.

———. *Die Rolle der Erotik in der männlichen Gesellschaft.* 2 vols. Jena: Diederick, 1917, 1919.

Blumenberg, Hans. *The Legitimacy of the Modern Age.* Trans. Robert M. Wallace. Cambridge, MA: MIT P, 1983.

Böhm, Klaus Werner. "Die homosexuellen Elemente in Thomas Manns 'Der Zauberberg.'" In Hermann Kurzke, ed. *Stationen der Thomas-Mann-Forschung: Aufsätze seit 1970.* Würzburg: Königshausen & Neumann, 1985. 145–65.

———. *Zwischen Selbstzucht und Verlangen: Thomas Mann und das Stigma Homosexualität.* Würzburg: Königshaus & Neumann, 1991.

Boeschenstein, Hermann. *German Literature of the Nineteenth Century.* London: Arnold, 1969.

Bonaventura. *Nachtwachen.* Ed. Wolfgang Paulsen. Stuttgart: Reclam, 1964.

Bovenschen, Silvia. *Die imaginierte Weiblichkeit: Exemplarische Untersuchungen zu kulturgeschichtlichen und literarischen Präsentationsformen des Weiblichen.* Frankfurt am Main: Suhrkamp, 1979.

Brahm, Otto. "Der Schlußband von Freytag's 'Ahnen.'" *Deutsche Rundschau* 26 (1881): 315–17.

Bramsted, Ernest K. *Aristocracy and the Middle-Classes in Germany: Social Types in German Literature 1830–1900.* 2nd rev. ed. Chicago: U of Chicago P, 1964.

Brauer (Hobohm), Cornelia. "Eugenie Marlitt: Bürgerliche — Christin — Liberale — Autorin." Diss. University of Erfurt, 1993.

Brenner, Peter J. "Die Einheit der Welt: Zur Entzauberung der Fremde und Verfremdung der Heimat in Raabes 'Abu Telfan.'" *Jahrbuch der Raabe-Gesellschaft* (1989): 45–62.

Bretting, Agnes, et al. "Deutsche in den USA." In Klaus J. Bade, ed. *Deutsche im Ausland, Fremde in Deutschland: Migration in Geschichte und Gegenwart.* Munich: Beck, 1992. 135–85.

Brewster, Philip J. "Onkel Ketschwayo in Neuteutoburg: Zeitgeschichtliche Anspielungen in Raabes 'Stopfkuchen.'" *Jahrbuch der Raabe-Gesellschaft* (1983): 96–118.

Brinker-Gabler, Gisela, and Sidonie Smith, eds. *Writing New Identities: Gender, Nation, and Immigration in Contemporary Europe.* Minneapolis: U of Minnesota P, 1997.

Brinkmann, Richard. *Wirklichkeit und Illusion: Studien über Gehalt und Grenzen des Begriffs Realismus für die erzählende Dichtung des neunzehnten Jahrhunderts.* Tübingen: Niemeyer, 1957.

———, ed. *Begriffsbestimmung des Literarischen Realismus.* Darmstadt: Wissenschaftliche Buchgesellschaft, 1969.

Brown, Marshall. "The Logic of Realism: A Hegelian Approach." *PMLA* 96 (1981): 224–41.

Bruno, Leonard C. *On the Move: A Chronology of Advances in Transportation.* Detroit: Gale Research, 1993.

Bucher, Max, et al., eds. *Realismus und Gründerzeit: Manifeste und Dokumente zur deutschen Literatur, 1848–1880.* Stuttgart: Metzler, 1976.

Büchler-Hauschild, Gabriele. *Erzählte Arbeit: Gustav Freytag und die soziale Prosa des Vor- und Nachmärz.* Paderborn: Schöningh, 1987.

Campbell, Joan. *Joy in Work, German Work: The National Debate 1800–1945.* Princeton: Princeton UP, 1989.

Carter, T. E. "Freytag's *Soll und Haben*: A Literal National Manifesto as a Best-Seller." *German Life and Letters* 21 (1967–68): 320–29.

Caudwell, Sarah. *The Shortest Way to Hades.* New York: Dell, 1984.

Collingwood, R. G. *The Idea of History.* Oxford: Oxford UP, 1946.

Confino, Alon. *The Nation as a Local Metaphor: Württemberg, Imperial Germany, and National Memory 1871–1918*. Chapel Hill: U of North Carolina P, 1997.

Conrady, Karl Otto, et al. *Germanistik — eine deutsche Wissenschaft*. Frankfurt am Main: Suhrkamp, 1967.

Cowen, Roy C. *Der Poetische Realismus: Kommentar zu einer Epoche*. Munich: Winkler, 1985.

Craig, Gordon A. *The Germans*. New York & Scarborough, Ont.: New American Library, 1982.

Crane, Susan A. *Collecting & Historical Consciousness in Early Nineteenth-Century Germany*. Ithaca NY: Cornell UP, 2000.

Damerau, Burghard. *Literatur und andere Wahrheiten: Warum wir ohne Bücher nicht sein wollen*. Berlin: Aufbau, 1999.

David, Claude. *Zwischen Romantik und Symbolismus 1820–1885*. Gütersloh: Mohn, 1966.

de Mendelssohn, Peter. "Dichtung und Wahrheit in den Tagebüchern Thomas Manns." *Ensemble 15: Internationales Jahrbuch für Literatur* (1984): 7–28.

Demetz, Peter. *Formen des Realismus: Theodor Fontane. Kritische Untersuchungen*. Vol. 88. Munich: Hanser, 1964.

———. "Über die Fiktionen des Realismus." *Neue Rundschau* (December 1977): 554–67.

———. "Zur Definition des Realismus." *Literatur und Kritik* 2 (1967): 333–45.

de Morsier, Edouard. *Romanciers allemands contemporains*. Paris: Perrin, 1890.

Denkler, Horst. *Neues über Wilhelm Raabe: Zehn Annäherungsversuche an einen verkannten Schriftsteller*. Tübingen: Niemeyer, 1988.

———. *Wilhelm Raabe: Legende — Leben — Literatur*. Tübingen: Niemeyer, 1989.

———. "Das 'wirckliche Juda' und der 'Renegat': Moses Freudenstein als Kronzeuge für Wilhelm Raabes Verhältnis zu Juden und Judentum." *German Quarterly* 60 (1987): 5–18.

———, ed. *Romane und Erzählungen des Bürgerlichen Realismus: Neue Interpretationen*. Stuttgart: Reclam, 1980.

Derks, Paul. *Die Schande der heiligen Päderastie: Homosexualität und Öffentlichkeit in der deutschen Literatur 1750–1850*. Berlin: Verlag rosa Winkel, 1990.

Dickens, Charles. *David Copperfield*. 1850; New York: Modern Library, n.d.

Diethe, Carol. *Towards Emancipation: German Women Writers of the Nineteenth Century.* New York: Berghahn, 1998.

Di Maio, Irene Stocksieker. "Berthold Auerbach's *Dichter und Kaufmann:* Enlightenment Thought and Jewish Identity." *Lessing Yearbook* 19 (1987): 267–85.

———. "The 'Frauenfrage' and the Reception of Wilhelm Raabe's Female Characters." In Leo A. Lensing and Hans-Werner Peter, eds. *Wilhelm Raabe: Studien zu seinem Leben und Werk.* Braunschweig: pp-Verlag, 1981.

Dittmann, Ulrich. "*Brigitta* und kein Ende: Kommentierte Randbermerkungen." *Jahrbuch des Adalbert Stifter Institutes* 3 (1996): 24–28.

Doderer, Heimito von. *Grundlagen und Funktion des Romans.* Nuremberg: Glock & Lutz, 1959.

Downing, Eric. *Double Exposure: Repetition and Realism in Nineteenth-Century German Fiction.* Stanford, CA: Stanford UP, 2000.

Eggert, Hartmut. "Der historische Roman des 19. Jahrhunderts." In Helmut Koopmann, ed. *Handbuch des deutschen Romans.* Düsseldorf: Bagel, 1983. 342–55.

Eisele, Ulf. *Realismus und Ideologie: Zur Kritik der literarischen Theorie nach 1848 am Beispiel des "Deutschen Museums."* Stuttgart: Metzler, 1976.

Eke, Norbert Otto. "Eine Gesamtbibliographie des deutschen Romans 1815–1830: Anmerkungen zum Problemfeld von Bibliographie und Historiographie." *Zeitschrift für Germanistik,* n.s. 2 (1993): 295–308.

Elias, Norbert. "On the Sociogenesis of the Difference between *Kultur* and *Zivilisation* in German Usage." In his *The Civilizing Process.* Trans. Edmund Jephcott. Oxford: Blackwell, 1994. 1–28.

Ellis, Havelock. "Sexual Inversion." In his *Studies in the Psychology of Sex.* Vol. 1. New York: Random House, 1905. 1–391.

Elsaghe, Y. A. "'Herr und Frau X. Beliebig'? Zur Funktion des Vornamensinitiale bei Thomas Mann." *German Life and Letters* 52, no. 1 (1999): 58–67.

Engel, Eduard. "Stereographischer Bericht über die Gerichtsverhandlungen im Prozesse: 'Angela.' Roman von Friedrich Spielhagen." *Magazin für die Literatur des In- und Auslandes* 50 (1881): 399–404, 413–17.

Engelhardt, Ulrich. *"Bildungsbürgertum": Begriffs- und Dogmengeschichte eines Etiketts.* Stuttgart: Klett, 1986.

Enzinger, Moriz. "Stifters Erzählung 'Brigitta' und Ungarn." In his *Gesammelte Ausfsätze zu Adalbert Stifter*. Vienna: Österreichische Verlagsanstalt, 1967. 134–53.

Eulenburg, Albert. *Sexuale Neuropathie: Genitale Neurosen und Neuropsychosen der Männer und Frauen*. Leipzig: Vogel, 1895.

Evans, Richard J. *The Feminist Movement in Germany 1894–1933*. SAGE Studies in 20th Century History 6. London: SAGE, 1976.

Fendri, Mounir. "Neues zu Karl Mays Krüger-Bei: Das Manuskript des Muhammad ben Abdallah Nimsi alias Johann Gottlieb Krüger." *Jahrbuch der Karl-May-Gesellschaft* (1992): 277–98.

Festausschuss der Spielhagen-Feier, ed. *Friedrich Spielhagen: Dem Meister des deutschen Romans zu seinem 70. Geburtstag von Freunden und Jüngern gewidmet*. Leipzig: Staackmann, 1899.

Feuerlicht, Ignace. "Thomas Mann and Homoeroticism." *Germanic Review* 57, no. 3 (1982): 89–97.

Finney, Gail. "Poetic Realism: Theodor Storm, Gottfried Keller, Conrad Ferdinand Meyer." In J. Barzun and G. Stade, eds. *European Writers*. Vol. 6: *The Romantic Century*. New York: Scribners, 1985. 913–42.

Fischbacher-Bosshardt, Andrea. *Anfänge der modernen Erzählkunst: Untersuchungen zu Friedrich Spielhagens theoretischem und literarischem Werk*. Bern, Frankfurt am Main, New York & Paris: Peter Lang, 1988.

Fischer, Fritz. *Germany's Aims in the First World War*. New York: Norton, 1967.

Fohrmann, Jürgen, and Wilhelm Vosskamp, eds. *Wissenschaftsgeschichte der Germanistik im 19. Jahrhundert*. Stuttgart: Metzler, 1994.

Fontane, Theodor. *Briefe*. Eds. Walter Keitel and Helmuth Nürnberger. 5 Vols. Munich: Hanser, 1976–94.

———. *Fontanes Werke in Fünf Bänden*. Vol. 4. Berlin & Weimar: Aufbau, 1969.

———. "Gustav Freytag: *Soll und Haben*." *Literatur-Blatt des Deutschen Kunstblattes* 2 (1855): 59–63.

———. "Gustav Freytags Die Ahnen." In his *Sämtliche Werke*. Vol. 21.1. Ed. Kurt Schreinert. Munich: Nymphenburger Verlagshandlung, 1963. 231–48.

Forel, August. *Die sexuelle Frage: Eine naturwissenschaftliche, psychologische, hygienische und soziologische Studie für Gebildete*. Munich: Reinhardt, 1909.

Foucault, Michel. *The History of Sexuality*. Vol. 1: *An Introduction*. Trans. Robert Hurley. New York: Vintage, 1978.

Fox, Thomas C. "Louise von François: A Feminist Reintroduction." In Marianne Burkhard and Jeanette Clausen, eds. *Women in German Yearbook* 3 (1985): 123–38.

———. *Louise von François and Die letzte Reckenburgerin: A Feminist Reading*. New York: Lang, 1989.

———."Louise von François: Between *Frauenzimmer* and *A Room of One's Own*." Diss. Yale U., 1983.

———. "Louise von François Rediscovered." In Gerhard P. Knapp, ed. *Autoren Damals und Heute: Literaturgeschichtliche Beispiele veränderter Wirkungshorizonte*. Atlanta: Rodopi, 1991. 303–19.

———. "Sexist Literary History? The Case of Louise von François." In Ginette Adamson and Eunice Myers, eds. *Continental, Latin-American, and Francophone Women Writers*. Lanham, MD: UP of America, 1987. 129–38.

Francke, Kuno. *Weltbürgertum in der deutschen Literatur von Herder bis Nietzsche*. Berlin: Weidmann, 1928.

François, Louise von. *Frau Erdmuthens Zwillingssöhne*. Zurich: Manesse, [1954].

———. *Frau Erdmuthens Zwillingssöhne: Roman aus dem Zeitalter der Befreiungskriege*. Bayreuther Feldpostausgaben. [Bayreuth]: Gauverlag, 1944.

———. "Fräulein Muthchen und ihr Hausmeier." In her *Gesammelte Werke*. Vol. 1. Leipzig: Lippold, [1930]. 491–519.

———. *Die letzte Reckenburgerin*. Leipzig: Insel, [1918].

———. *Die letzte Reckenburgerin: Geschichte einer deutschen Frau*. Bayreuther Feldpostausgaben. [Bayreuth]: Gauverlag, 1943.

———. "Der Posten der Frau." In her *Gesammelte Werke in fünf Bänden*. Vol. 4. Leipzig: Insel, [1918]. 181–266.

Freiligrath, Ferdinand. *Freiligraths Werke in 6 Teilen*. Ed. Julius Schwering. Berlin: Bong, n.d.

Freud, Sigmund. *Gesammelte Werke Chronologisch geordnet*. Vols. 5 and 8. Ed. Anna Freud et al. London: Imago, 1973; rpt. Frankfurt: Fischer, 1999.

Frevert, Ute. *Women in German History: From Bourgeois Emancipation to Sexual Liberation*. Trans. Stuart McKinnon-Evans et al. Oxford: Berg, 1990.

Frey, John R. "Author-Intrusion in the Narrative: German Theory and Some Modern Examples." *Germanic Review* 23 (1948): 274–89.

Freytag, Gustav. *Die Ahnen: Roman*. 35th ed. 6 vols. Leipzig: S. Hirzel, 1906–1907.

———. *Gesammelte Werke.* 22 vols. Leipzig: S. Hirzel, 1896–98.

———. *Gustav Freytag und Herzog Ernest von Coburg im Briefwechsel 1853 bis 1893.* Ed. Eduard Tempeltey. Leipzig: S. Hirzel, 1904.

———. "Ein Roman von Louise von François." In his *Vermischte Aufsätze.* Leipzig: Hirzel, 1901. 139–47.

———. *Soll und Haben.* In his *Werke,* vol. 1.2. Ed. Heike Menges Karben: Verlag Petra Wald, 1996.

Friedemann, Käte. *Die Rolle des Erzählers in der Epik.* Berlin: Haessel, 1910; rpt. Darmstadt: Wissenschaftliche Buchgesellschaft, 1965.

Friedlaender, Benedikt. *Die Renaissance des Eros Uranios: Die physiologische Freundschaft, ein normaler Grundtrieb des Menschen und eine Frage der männlichen Gesellungsfreiheit.* Berlin: Renaissance, 1904.

Friedrichsmeyer, Sara, Sara Lennox, and Susanne Zantop, eds. *The Imperialist Imagination: German Colonialism and Its Legacy.* Ann Arbor: U of Michigan P, 1998.

Fuchs, Hans. *Richard Wagner und die Homosexualität.* Berlin: Barsdorf, 1903.

Fuld, Werner. Wilhelm Raabe: Eine Biographie. Munich: Hanser, 1993.

Fulda, Daniel. "Telling German History: Forms and Functions of the Historical Narrative against the Background of the National Unifications." In Walter Pape, ed. *1870/71–1989/90: German Unifications and the Change of Literary Discourse.* Berlin: de Gruyter, 1993. 195–230.

Furst, Lilian R. *All Is True: The Claims and Strategies of Realist Fiction.* Durham, NC: Duke UP, 1995.

Geller, Martha. *Friedrich Spielhagens Theorie und Praxis des Romans.* Berlin: Grote, 1917.

Giddens, Anthony. *The Consequences of Modernity.* Stanford, CA: Stanford UP, 1990.

Gilbert, Sandra M., and Susan Gubar. *The Madwoman in the Attic: The Woman Writer and the Nineteenth-Century Literary Imagination.* New Haven: Yale UP, 1979.

Gilman, Sander L. *The Jew's Body.* New York: Routledge, 1991.

———, and Jack Zipes, eds. *Yale Companion to Jewish Writing and Thought in German Culture 1096–1996.* New Haven & London: Yale UP, 1997.

Ginzburg, Carlo. *The Cheese and the Worms: The Cosmos of a Sixteenth-Century Miller.* Trans. John and Addne Tedeschi. Baltimore: Johns Hopkins UP, 1980.

Giseke, Robert. "Soll und Haben." *Novellen-Zeitung* 3 (1855): 311–18.

Glaser, Horst Albert, ed. *Deutsche Literatur: Eine Sozialgeschichte. Vol. 7: Vom Nachmärz zur Gründerzeit: Realismus 1848–1880.* Reinbek: Rowohlt, 1982.

———. *Deutsche Literatur: Eine Sozialgeschichte. Vol. 8: Jahrhundertwende: Vom Naturalismus zum Expressionismus 1880–1918.* Reinbek: Rowohlt, 1982.

Goessl, Alfred F. "Die Darstellung des Adels in Prosaschriften Friedrich Spielhagens." Diss. Tulane U, 1966.

Goethe, Johann Wolfgang von. *Collected Works.* 12 vols. Eds. Victor Lange, Eric A. Blackall, and Cyrus Hamlin. New York: Suhrkamp, 1983–89.

———. *Sämtliche Werke.* Münchner Ausgabe. Ed. Karl Richter. Vol. 19: *Johann Peter Eckermann Gespräche mit Goethe.* Ed. Heinz Schlaffer. Munich: Hanser, 1986.

———. *Werke.* Vol. 12. Ed. Erich Trunz. Hamburg: Wegner, 1953.

Gohrbandt, Elisabeth. "'Selbst bei einem drei Jahre langen Urbarmachen einer Wildnis wird man nur ein Settler, aber kein Westman': Auswanderer und Siedler in Karl Mays Nordamerikaerzählungen." *Jahrbuch der Karl-May-Gesellschaft* (1995): 165–205.

Goldhagen, Daniel Jonah. *Hitler's Willing Executioners: Ordinary Germans and the Holocaust.* New York: Vintage, 1997.

Gooch, G. P. *History and Historians in the Nineteenth Century.* 3rd ed. Boston: Beacon Press, 1959.

Graf, Andreas. "Literarisierung und Kolportageroman: Überlegungen zu Publikum und Kommunikationsstrategie eines Massenmediums im 19. Jahrhundert." *Jahrbuch der Karl-May-Gesellschaft* (1999): 191–203.

Grafton, Anthony. *The Footnote: A Curious History.* Cambridge, MA: Harvard UP, 1997.

Gregor-Dellin, Martin. "Louise von François." In his *Was ist Größe? Sieben Deutsche und ein deutsches Problem.* Munich: Piper, 1985. 175–96.

Greenberg, Valerie D. "The Resistance of *Effi Briest:* An (Un)told Tale." *PMLA* 103 (1988): 770–82.

Grüllich, Schulrath. *Was können wir aus Freytags "Ahnen" lernen. Vortrag, gehalten im Bezirks-Lehrerverein Dresden-Land.* Meißen: H. W. Schlimpert, 1888.

Gurlitt, Ludwig. *Pestalozzi: Eine Auswahl aus seinen Schriften.* Stuttgart: Greiner & Pfeiffer, 1907?

Gutzkow, Karl. "Ein neuer Roman." *Unterhaltungen am häuslichen Herd* 3 (1855): 558–60.

Härle, Gerhard. *Männerweiblichkeit: Zur Homosexualität bei Klaus und Thomas Mann*. Frankfurt am Main: Athenäum, 1988

Hahl, Werner. *Reflexion und Erzählung: Ein Problem der Romantheorie von der Spätaufklärung bis zum programmatischen Realismus*. Stuttgart: Kohlhammer, 1971.

Hajek, Siegfried. "'Meister Autor.' — Sprachschichten und Motive." *Jahrbuch der Raabe-Gesellschaft* (1981): 149–68.

Hammer, Wolfgang. "Karl Mays Novelle 'Leilet' als Beispiel für seine Quellenverwendung." *Jahrbuch der Karl-May-Gesellschaft* (1996): 205–30.

Harder, Hermann. "Ein Rassenroman der Louise v. François." *Die Sonne: Monatsschrift für Rasse, Glauben, und Volkstum. Im Sinne Nordischer Weltanschauung und Lebensgestaltung* 12 (1935): 265–68.

Hardin, James, and Siegfried Mews, eds. *Dictionary of Literary Biography*. Vol. 129: *Nineteenth-Century German Writers, 1841–1900*. Detroit: Gale Research, 1993.

Hart, Heinrich and Julius. *Kritische Waffengänge*. Ed. Mark Boulby. New York & London: Johnson Reprint, 1969.

Hartung, Rudolf. "Mensch und Werk: Zu den Tagebüchern 1933–34 von Thomas Mann." *Neue Rundschau* 89, no. 2 (1978): 285–91.

Hatfield, Henry C. "Realism in the German Novel." *Comparative Literature* 3 (1951): 234–52.

Heermann, Christian. *Der Mann, der Old Shatterhand war: Eine Karl-May-Biographie*. Berlin: Verlag der Nation, 1988.

Heilbut, Anthony. *Thomas Mann: Eros and Literature*. New York: Knopf, 1996.

Heine, Heinrich. *Sämtliche Schriften*. Ed. Klaus Briegleb. Vol. 2. Munich: Hanser, 1976.

Hellmann, Winfried. "Objektivität, Subjektivität und Erzählkunst: Zur Romantheorie Friedrich Spielhagens." In Reinhold Grimm, ed. *Deutsche Romantheorien*. Frankfurt am Main: Athenäum, 1968. 165–217.

Henning, Hans. *Friedrich Spielhagen*. Leipzig: Staackmann, 1910.

Henkel, Gabriele. *Studien zur Privatbibliothek Wilhelm Raabes: Vom "wirklichen Autor," von Zeitgenossen und "ächten Dichtern."* Braunschweig: Stadtbibliothek, 1997.

Hermand, Jost. "Zur Literatur der Gründerzeit." In his *Von Mainz nach Weimar (1793–1919): Studien zur Deutschen Literatur.* Stuttgart: Metzler, 1969. 211–49.

Herminghouse, Patricia. "Schloß oder Fabrik? Zur Problematik der Adelsdarstellung im Roman des Nachmärz." In Peter Uwe Hohendahl and Paul Michael Lützeler, eds. *Legitimationskrisen des deutschen Adels 1200–1900.* Stuttgart: Metzler, 1979. 245–61.

———, and Magda Mueller. *Gender and Germanness: Cultural Productions of Nation.* Providence, RI: Berghahn, 1997.

Hesekiel, George. *Stille vor dem Sturm.* Vol. 2. Berlin: Janke, 1863.

Hettche, Walter. "Nach alter Melodie: Die Gedichte von Julius Rodenberg, Wilhelm Jensen und Paul Heyse zum 70. Geburtstag Wilhelm Raabes." *Jahrbuch der Raabe-Gesellschaft* (1999): 144–56.

Hobohm, Cornelia. "Geliebt; Gehaßt; Erfolgreich: Eugenie Marlitt (1825–1887)." In Karin Tebben, ed. *Beruf: Schriftstellerin: Schreibende Frauen im 18. und 19. Jahrhundert* Göttingen: Vandenhoek & Ruprecht, 1998. 244–75.

———. *Das literarische Arnstadt.* Wandersleben: Gleichen, 1997.

Hohendahl, Peter Uwe. *Building a National Literature: The Case of Germany 1830–1870.* Trans. Renate Baron Franciscono. Ithaca, NY: Cornell UP, 1989.

———, ed. *A History of German Literary Criticism 1730–1980.* Trans. Franz Blaha et al. Lincoln: U of Nebraska P, 1988.

Holbeche, Brian. "Innstetten's 'Geschichte mit Entsagung' and Its Significance in Fontane's *Effi Briest.*" *German Life and Letters* 41 (1987): 21–32.

Holub, Robert C. "Raabe's Impartiality: A Reply to Horst Denkler." *German Quarterly* 60 (1987): 617–22.

———. *Reflections of Realism: Paradox, Norm, and Ideology in Nineteenth-Century German Prose.* Detroit: Wayne State UP, 1991.

Holz, Claus. *Flucht aus der Wirklichkeit. "Die Ahnen" von Gustav Freytag: Untersuchungen zum realistischen historischen Roman der Gründerzeit 1872–1880.* Europäische Hochschulschriften, ser. no. 1, Deutsche Sprache und Literatur 624. Frankfurt am Main: Peter Lang, 1983.

Horch, Hans Otto. "Gustav Freytag and Berthold Auerbach — eine repräsentive deutsch-jüdische Schriftstellerfreundschaft im 19. Jahrhundert." *Jahrbuch der Raabe-Gesellschaft* (1985): 154–74.

———. "Historische Standortbestimmung vor Guinea: Zu Wilhelm Raabes Erzählung 'Sankt Thomas' (1865)." *Jahrbuch der Raabe-Gesellschaft* (1986): 114–28.

Hovanec, Evelyn A. *Henry James and Germany.* Amsterdam: Rodopi, 1979.

Hughes, Arthur H. "Wilhelm von Humboldt's Influence on Spielhagen's Esthetics." *Germanic Review* 5 (1930): 211–24.

Hunter-Lougheed, Rosemarie. "Adalbert Stifter: Brigitta (1844/47)." In Paul Michael Lützeler, ed. *Romane und Erzählungen zwischen Romantik und Realismus: Neue Interpretationen.* Stuttgart: Reclam, 1983. 354–85.

Huyssen, Andreas. *Twilight Memories: Marking Time in a Culture of Amnesia.* New York: Routledge, 1995.

Iggers, Georg G. *The German Conception of History: The National Tradition of Historical Thought from Herder to the Present.* Hanover, NH: Wesleyan UP, 1983.

Jackson, Paul. *Bürgerliche Arbeit und Romanwirklichkeit: Studien zur Berufsproblematik in Romanen des deutschen Realismus.* Frankfurt am Main: Rita G. Fischer, 1981.

Jacobs, Jürgen. *Wilhelm Meister und seine Brüder: Untersuchungen zum deutschen Bildungsroman.* Munich: Fink, 1972.

Jaeger, Friedrich, and Jörn Rüsen. *Geschichte des Historismus.* Munich: Beck, 1992.

Jahrbuch der Interessengemeinschaft Marlitt. Wandersleben: Gleichen Verlag, 1997 and 2000.

James, Henry. "Pandora." In his *The Complete Tales.* Ed. Leon Edel. Vol. 5. Philadelphia & New York: Lippincott, 1963. 357–412.

Jameson, Fredric. *The Political Unconscious: Narrative as Socially Symbolic Act.* Ithaca NY: Cornell UP, 1981.

Jankowsky, Karen, and Carla Love, eds. *Other Germanies: Questioning Identity in Women's Literature and Art.* Albany: State U of New York P, 1997.

Joeres, Ruth-Ellen Boetcher. *Respectability and Deviance: Nineteenth-Century German Women Writers and the Ambiguity of Representation.* Chicago: U of Chicago P, 1998.

Jones, James W. *"We of the Third Sex": Literary Representations of Homosexuality in Wilhelmine Germany.* New York: Lang, 1990.

Kafitz, Dieter. *Figurenkonstellation als Mittel der Wirklichkeitserfassung: Dargestellt an Romanen der zweiten Hälfte des 19. Jahrhunderts (Freytag — Spielhagen — Fontane — Raabe)*. Kronberg: Athenäum, 1978.

Kahn, Lothar, and Donald D. Hook. *Between Two Worlds: A Cultural History of German-Jew Writers*. Ames: Iowa UP, 1993.

Kaiser, Gerhard. *Gottfried Keller: Das gedichtete Leben*. Frankfurt am Main: Insel, 1981.

———. "Um eine Neubegrundung des Realismusbegriffs." *Zeitschrift für deutsche Philologie* 77 (1958): 161–76.

Kaiser, Nancy A. "Berthold Auerbach." In James Hardin and Siegfried Mews, eds. *Dictionary of Literary Biography*. Vol. 133: *Nineteenth-Century German Writers to 1840*. Detroit: Gale Research, 1993. 114–19.

———. "Berthold Auerbach: The Dilemma of the Jewish Humanist from 'Vormärz' to Empire." *German Studies Review* 6:3 (1983): 399–419.

Kandolf, Franz. "Kara Ben Nemsi auf den Spuren Layards: Ein Blick in die Werkstätte eines Schriftstellers." *Karl-May-Jahrbuch* (1922): 197–207.

Kant, Immanuel. "Beantwortung der Frage: Was ist Aufklärung?" In his *Werkausgabe*. Vol. 11. Ed. Wilhelm Weischedel. Frankfurt am Main: Suhrkamp, 1978. 53–61.

Katz, Jacob. "Berthold Auerbach's Anticipation of the Jewish Tragedy." *Hebrew Union College Annual* 53 (1982): 215–40.

Kaufmann, Walter. *Nietzsche: Philosopher, Psychologist, Antichrist*. Cleveland: Meridian, 1956.

Kayserling, M. *Der Dichter Ephraim Kuh*. Berlin: Springer, 1864.

Keindorf, Gudrun. "Formen und Funktion des Reisens bei Karl May: Ein Problemaufriß." *Jahrbuch der Karl-May-Gesellschaft* (1996): 291–314.

Keiter, Heinrich, and Tony Kellen. *Der Roman: Theorie und Technik des Romans und der erzählenden Dichtung, nebst einer geschichtliche Einleitung*. 4th ed. Essen: Fredebeul & Koenen, 1912.

Kienzle, Michael. *Der Erfolgsroman: Zur Kritik seiner poetischen Ökonomie bei Gustav Freytag und Eugenie Marlitt*. Stuttgart: Metzler, 1975.

Klemperer, Victor. *Curriculum vitae: Jugend um 1900*. Berlin: Siedler, 1989.

———. *Die Zeitromane Friedrich Spielhagens und ihre Wurzeln*. Weimar: Duncker, 1913.

Klippenberg, August. *Deutsches Lesebuch für höhere Mädchenschulen*. Edition A, pt. 3, 22nd ed. Hannover: Norddeutsche Verlagsanstalt O. Goedel, 1903.

———. *Deutsches Lesebuch für höhere Lehranstalten: Bearbeitung des Döbelner Lesebuchs für Mittel- und Norddeutschland in engem Anschluß an die neuesten preußischen Lehrpläne von Direktor M. Evers und Professor H. Walz.* Edition A, pt. 5: *Für evangelische Anstaltungen.* Leipzig: Teubner, 1903.

Klotz, Marcia. "White Women and the Dark Continent: Gender and Sexuality in German Colonial Discourse from the Sentimental Novel to the Fascist Film." Diss. Stanford U, 1994.

Klüglein, Norbert. *Coburg Stadt und Land.* 3rd ed. Coburg: Verkehrsverein Coburg e.V., 1995.

Koepke, Wulf. *Die Deutschen: Vergangenheit und Gegenwart,* 5th ed. Fort Worth: Holt, Rinehart & Winston, 2000.

Kohlschmidt, Werner. *Geschichte der deutschen Literatur vom Jungen Deutschland bis zum Naturalismus.* Vol. 4. Stuttgart: Reclam, 1975.

Kokora, Michel Gnéba. "Die Ferne in der Nähe: Zur Funktion Afrikas in Raabes 'Abu Telfan' und 'Stopfkuchen.'" *Jahrbuch der Raabe-Gesellschaft* (1994): 54–69.

Kolbe, Jürgen. *Goethes "Wahlverwandtschaften" und der Roman des 19. Jahrhunderts.* Stuttgart, Berlin, Cologne & Mainz: Kohlhammer, 1968.

Kontje, Todd. *The German Bildungsroman: History of a National Genre.* Columbia, SC: Camden House, 1993.

———. "Passing for German: Politics and Patriarchy in Kleist, Körner, and Fischer," *German Studies Review* 22 (1999): 67–84.

———. *Women, the Novel, and the German Nation 1771–1871: Domestic Fiction in the Fatherland.* Cambridge: Cambridge UP, 1998.

Koopmann, Helmut, ed. *Handbuch des deutschen Romans.* Düsseldorf: Bagel, 1983.

Kord, Susanne, and Friederike Eigler, eds. *The Feminist Encyclopedia of German Literature.* Westport, CT: Greenwood Press, 1997.

Kremer, Detlef, and Nikolaus Wegmann. "Wiederholungslektüre(n): Fontanes *Effi Briest:* Realismus des wirklichen Lebens oder realistischer Text?" *Deutschunterricht* 47, no. 6 (1995): 56–75.

Kuczynski, Jürgen. *Gestalten und Werke: Soziologische Studien zur deutschen Literatur.* Vol. 1. Berlin & Weimar: Aufbau, 1969.

Küppers, Petra. "Karl Mays Indianerbild und die Tradition der Fremdendarstellung: Eine kulturgeschichtliche Analyse." *Jahrbuch der Karl-May-Gesellschaft* (1996): 315–45.

Kurth-Voigt, Lieselotte E., and William H. McClain. "Louise Mühlbach's Historical Novels: The American Reception." *Internationales Archiv für Sozialgeschichte der deutschen Literatur* 6 (1981): 52–77.

Laane, Tiiu V. "Comic Mirrors and Sociological Implications in Louise von François's Narratives." In Ginette Adamson and Eunice Myers, eds. *Continental, Latin-American, and Francophone Women Writers.* Vol. 4. Lanham, MD: UP of America, 1998. 95–107.

———. "The Incest Motif in Louise von François's *Der Katzenjunker:* A Veiled Yet Scathing Indictment of Patriarchal Abuse." *Orbis Litterarum* 47 (1992): 11–30.

———. "Louise von François and the Education of Women." In Ginette Adamson and E. Myers, eds. *Continental, Latin-American, and Francophone Women Writers.* Vol. 3. Lanham, MD: UP of America, 1997. 1–16.

———. "Louise von François's Critical Perspectives of Society." *European Studies Journal* 8, no. 2 (1991): 13–41.

Ladd, Brian. *The Ghosts of Berlin: Confronting German History in the Urban Landscape.* Chicago: U of Chicago P, 1997.

Lämmert, Eberhard, ed. *Romantheorie: Dokumentation ihrer Geschichte in Deutschland.* 2 vols. Berlin: Kiepenheuer & Witsch, 1971. 1975.

Lamers, Henrike. *Held oder Welt? Zum Romanwerk Friedrich Spielhagens.* Bonn: Bouvier, 1991.

Landes, Joan B. *Women and the Public Sphere in the Age of the French Revolution.* Ithaca, NY: Cornell UP, 1988.

Landmann, Karl. "Deutsche Liebe und deutsche Treue in Gustav Freytags 'Ahnen.'" *Zeitschrift für den deutschen Unterricht* 6 (1892): 81–167.

Laqueur, Thomas. *Making Sex: Body and Gender from the Greeks to Freud.* Cambridge, MA: Harvard UP, 1990.

Lehnert, Herbert. Review of Thomas Mann's diaries. *Orbis litterarum* 39 (1984): 79–88.

Lesér, Esther. *Thomas Mann's Short Fiction: An Intellectual Biography.* Ed. Mitzi Brunedale. Rutherford, NJ: Farleigh Dickinson UP, 1989.

Leventhal, Jean. "Fact into Fiction: *Effi Briest* and the Ardenne Case." *Colloquia Germanica* 24 (1991): 181–83.

Lieblang, Helmut. "'Der Inhaber dieses Buiruldu . . .': Alfred Edmund Brehms Orient in Karl Mays Frühwerk." *Jahrbuch der Karl-May-Gesellschaft* (1997): 232–71.

Liebs, Elke. *Kindheit und Tod: Der Rattenfänger-Mythos als Beitrag zu einer Kulturgeschichte der Kindheit.* Munich: Fink, 1986.

Lindemann, C. "Verdrängte Revolutionen? Eichendorffs 'Schloß Dürande' und Karl Mays Klekih-Petra-Episode im *Winnetou*-Roman." *Jahrbuch der Eichendorff-Gesellschaft* 34 (1974): 24–38.

Löwenthal, Leo. *Erzählkunst und Gesellschaft: Die Gesellschaftsproblematik in der deutschen Literatur des 19. Jahrhunderts.* Neuwied & Berlin: Luchterhand, 1971.

Lubbock, Percy. *The Craft of Fiction.* New York: Viking, 1957.

Ludwig, Otto. "Der poetische Realismus." In Gerhard Plumpe, ed. Theorie des bürgerlichen Realismus. Stuttgart: Reclam, 1985. 148–50.

Lukács, Georg. *Essays on Realism.* Ed. Rodney Livingstone. Trans. David Fernbach. Cambridge, MA: MIT Press, 1980.

———. *German Realists in the Nineteenth Century.* Ed. Rodney Livingstone. Trans. Jeremy Gaines and Paul Keast. Cambridge, MA: MIT Press, 1993.

———. *The Historical Novel.* Trans. Hannah and Stanley Mitchell. Lincoln: U of Nebraska P, 1983.

———. *Realism in Our Time: Literature and the Class Struggle.* New York: Harper & Row, 1962.

———. *The Theory of the Novel: A Historico-Philosophical Essay on the Forms of Great Epic Literature.* Trans. Anna Bostock. Cambridge, MA: MIT Press, 1971.

Maimon, Salomon. *Lebensgeschichte.* 2 vols. Ed. K. P. Moritz. Berlin: Vieweg, 1972.

Mandelkow, Karl Robert. *Goethe in Deutschland: Rezeptionsgeschichte eines Klassikers.* Vol. 1: *1773–1918.* Munich: Beck, 1980.

Mann, Thomas. *An die gesittete Welt: Politische Schriften und Reden im Exil.* Eds. Peter de Mendelssohn and Hanno Helbling. Frankfurt am Main: Fischer, 1986.

———. *Betrachtungen eines Unpolitischen.* Frankfurt am Main: Fischer, 1988.

———. *Briefe an Otto Grautoff 1894–1901 und Ida Boy-Ed 1903–1928.* Ed. Peter de Mendelssohn. Frankfurt am Main: Fischer, 1975.

———. *Briefe: 1889–1936.* Ed. Erika Mann. Frankfurt am Main: Fischer, 1962.

———. *Death in Venice: A New Translation, Backgrounds and Contexts, Criticism.* Trans. and ed. Clayton Koelb. New York: Norton, 1994.

———. *Gesammelte Werke in zwölf Bänden*. Vol. 11. Frankfurt am Main: Fischer, 1960.

———. *Schwere Stunde: Erzählungen 1903–1912*. Frankfurt am Main: Fischer, 1991.

———. *Tagebücher 1918–1920*. Ed. Peter de Mendelssohn. Frankfurt am Main: Fischer, 1979.

———. *Tagebücher 1933–1934*. Ed. Peter de Mendelssohn. Frankfurt am Main: Fischer, 1977.

———. *Tagebücher 1949–1950*. Ed. Inge Jens. Frankfurt am Main: Fischer, 1991.

———. *"Von deutscher Republik": Politische Schriften und Reden in Deutschland*. Eds. Peter de Mendelssohn and Hanno Helbling. Frankfurt am Main: Fischer, 1984.

———. *Der Wille zum Glück: Erzählungen 1893–1903*. Frankfurt am Main: Fischer, 1991.

Marbacher Magazin Sonderheft 36 (1985).

Marggraff, Hermann. "Ein Roman, 'der das deutsche Volk bei seiner Arbeit sucht.'" *Blätter für literarische Unterhaltung* 25 (1855): 445–52.

Marlitt, E. *Gesammelte Romane und Novellen*. Vol. 6. Leipzig: Ernst Keil's Nachfolger, n.d. Vol. 10. Leipzig: Ernst Keil's Nachfolger, 1890.

"Ein Marlitt-Blatt." *Gartenlaube* (1875): 68–80.

Martini, Fritz. *Deutsche Literatur im bürgerlichen Realismus 1848–1898*. Stuttgart: Metzler, 1964; 4th rev. ed. Stuttgart: Metzler, 1981.

———. "Realismus." In Paul Merker und Wolfgang Stammler, eds. *Reallexikon der deutschen Literaturegeschichte*. 2nd ed. Eds. Werner Kohlschmidt and Wolfgang Mohr. Vol. 3. Berlin: de Gruyter, 1976. 343–65.

Martino, Alberto. *Die Deutsche Leihbibliothek: Geschichte einer literarischen Institution (1756–1914)*. Wiesbaden: Otto Harrasowitz, 1990.

———. "Publikumsschichten und Leihbibliotheken." In Horst Glaser, ed. *Deutsche Literatur: Eine Sozialgeschichte*. Vol. 7. Reinbek bei Hamburg: Rowohlt, 1982. 59–69.

Marx, Leonie. "Der deutsche Frauenroman im 19. Jahrhundert." In Helmut Koopmann, ed. *Handbuch des deutschen Romans*. Düsseldorf: Bagel, 1983. 439–59.

Mauthner, Fritz. *Nach berühmten Mustern: Parodistische Studien*. Stuttgart: Spemann, [1878].

May, Karl. *Winnetou I*. Zurich: Haffmans, 1996.

———. *Winnetou II*. Zurich: Haffmans, 1996.

———. *Winnetou III*. Zürich: Haffmans, 1996.

Mayer, Hans. *Thomas Mann*. Frankfurt am Main: Suhrkamp, 1980.

———. *Von Lessing bis Thomas Mann: Wandlungen der bürgerlichen Literatur in Deutschland*. Pfullingen: Neske, 1959.

McClain, William H., and Lieselotte E. Kurth-Voigt, eds. "Clara Mundts Briefe an Hermann Costenoble: Zu L. Mühlbach's historischen Romanen." *Archiv für Geschichte des Buchwesens* 22 (1981): 917–52.

McClintock, Anne. *Imperial Leather: Race, Gender and Sexuality in the Colonial Contest*. New York: Routledge, 1995.

McInnes, Edward. "Auerbach's *Schwarzwälder Dorfgeschichten* and the Quest for 'German Realism' in the 1840s." In *Perspectives on German Realist Writing*. Ed. Mark G. Ward. Lewiston, Queenstown & Lampeter: Edwin Mellen Press, 1995. 95–111.

McMurtrie, Douglas. "Die konträre Sexualempfindung des Weibes in den Vereinigten Staaten von Amerika." *Archiv für Kriminal-Anthropologie und Kriminalistik* 55, nos. 1–2 (1913): 141–47.

Medlicott, W. N., and Dorothy K. Coveney, eds. *Bismarck and Europe*. New York: St. Martin's Press, 1972.

Mehring, Franz. *Beiträge zur Literaturgeschichte*. Ed. Walter Heist. Berlin: Weiss, 1948.

Meier, Albert. "Diskretes Erzählen: Über den Zusammenhang von Dichtung, Wissenschaft und Didaktik in Adalbert Stifters Erzählung 'Brigitta.'" *Aurora* 44 (1984): 213–23.

Mensch, Ella. "Erinnerungen an Friedrich Spielhagen." *Westermanns Monatshefte* 110 (1911): 356–60.

Merbach, Günter. *E. Marlitt: Das Leben einer großen Schriftstellerin*. Hamburg: Martin Kelter, 1992.

Meyer, Michael A. *The Origins of the Modern Jew: Jewish Identity and European Culture in Germany, 1749–1824*. Detroit: Wayne State UP, 1967.

Meyer, Richard M. *Die deutsche Literatur des Neunzehnten Jahrhunderts*. Volksausgabe. Berlin: Bondi, 1912.

Mielke, Hellmuth. *Der Deutsche Roman des 19. Jahrhunderts*. 3rd ed. Berlin: Schwetschke, 1898.

Milde, Caroline S. J. *Der deutschen Jungfrau Wesen und Wirken: Winke für das geistige und praktische Leben*. 4th ed. Leipzig: C. F. Amelang, 1878.

Möhrmann, Renate. *Die andere Frau: Emanzipationsansätze deutscher Schriftstellerinnen im Vorfeld der Achtundvierziger-Revolution*. Stuttgart: Metzler, 1977.

Mojem, Hellmuth. "Literaturbetrieb und literarisches Selbstverständnis: Der Briefwechsel Wilhelm Raabes mit Eduard Engel." *Jahrbuch der Raabe-Gesellschaft* (1995): 27–87.

Mommsen, Wolfgang J. *Imperial Germany, 1867–1918: Politics, Culture, and Society in an Authoritarian State*. London: Arnold, 1995.

Mosse, George L. *The Crisis of German Ideology: Intellectual Origins of the Third Reich*. 2nd rev. ed. New York: Schocken, 1981.

———. *German Jews beyond Judaism*. Bloomington: Indiana UP / Cincinnati: Hebrew Union College, 1985.

———. *Nationalism and Sexuality: Middle-Class Morality and Sexual Norms in Modern Europe*. Madison: U of Wisconsin P, 1985.

———. *The Nationalization of the Masses: Political Symbolism and Mass Movements in Germany from the Napoleonic Wars through the Third Reich*. Ithaca NY: Cornell UP, 1975.

———. "Was die Deutschen wirklich lasen: Marlitt, May, Ganghofer." In Reinhold Grimm and Jost Hermand, eds. *Popularität und Trivialität* Frankfurt am Main: Athenäum, 1974. 101–20.

———. "What the Germans Really Read." In his *Masses and Man: Nationalist and Fascist Perceptions of Reality*. New York: Fertig, 1980. 52–68.

Mühlbach, Luise. *Berlin und Sanssouci oder Friedrich der Große und seine Freunde: Historischer Roman*. 4 vols. Berlin: Simion, 1854.

———. *Deutschland in Sturm und Drang: Historischer Roman*. 17 vols. Jena: Costenoble, 1867–68.

———. *Friedrich der Große und seine Geschwister: Historischer Roman*. 3 vols. Berlin: Janke, 1855.

———. *Friedrich der Große und sein Hof: Historischer Roman*. 3 vols. Berlin: Janke, 1853.

Müller, Klaus. *"Aber in meinem Herzen sprach eine Stimme so laut": Homosexuelle Autobiographien und medizinische Pathographien im neunzehnten Jahrhundert*. Berlin: Verlag rosa Winkel, 1991.

Müller, Klaus-Detlef, ed. *Bürgerlicher Realismus: Grundlagen und Interpretationen*. Königstein: Athenäum, 1981.

Müller-Donges, Christa. *Das Novellenwerk Friedrich Spielhagens in seiner Entwicklung zwischen 1851 und 1899*. Marburg: Elwert, 1970.

Näcke, Paul. "Über Kontrast-Träume und speziell sexuelle Kontrast-Träume." *Archiv für Kriminal-Anthropologie und Kriminalistik* 28 (1903): 1–19.

Neubauer, H., Schuldirektor a.D. *Zur Erinnerung an Gustav Freytag: Vortrag, gehalten in der ordentlichen Sitzung der Königlichen Akademie gemeinnütziger Wissenschaften zu Erfurt am 29. Mai 1895.* Sonderdruck aus den Jahrbüchern der Königl. Akademie gemeinnütziger Wissenschaften zu Erfurt, n.s. 22. Erfurt: Carl Villaret, 1896.

Neuhaus, Volker. "Friedrich Spielhagen — Critic of Bismarck's Empire." In *1870/71–1898/90: German Unifications and the Change of Literary Discourse*. Ed. Walter Pape. Berlin & New York: de Gruyter, 1993. 135–43.

———. "Der Unterhaltungsroman im 19. Jahrhundert." In *Handbuch des deutschen Romans*. Ed. Helmut Koopmann. Düsseldorf: Bagel, 1983. 410–11.

Neumann, Bernd. "Friedrich Spielhagen: Sturmflut 1877. Die Gründerjahre als die 'Signatur des Jahrhunderts.'" In *Romane und Erzählungen des Bürgerlichen Realismus: Neue Interpretationen*. Ed. Horst Denkler. Stuttgart: Reclam, 1980. 260–73.

Nietzsche, Friedrich. "Vom Nutzen und Nachteil der Historie für das Leben." In his *Werke*. Vol. 1. Ed. Karl Schlechta. Frankfurt am Main: Ullstein, 1976. 209–85.

Nochlin, Linda. *Realism*. Harmondsworth UK: Penguin, 1971; New York: Penguin, 1971.

Nollendorfs, Valters. "The Field, the Boundaries, and the Cultivators of German-American Studies." *Monatshefte* 86 (1994): 319–30.

Nutz, Maximilian. "Das Beispiel Goethe: Zur Konstituierung eines nationalen Klassikers." In *Wissenschaftsgeschichte der Germanistik im 19. Jahrhundert*. Eds. Jürgen Fohrmann and Wilhelm Vosskamp. Stuttgart: Metzler, 1994. 605–37.

Ohl, Hubert. "Eduards Heimkehr oder Le Vaillant und das Riesenfaultier: Zu Wilhelm Raabes 'Stopfkuchen.'" In *Raabe in neuer Sicht*. Ed. Hermann Helmers. Stuttgart: Kohlhammer, 1968. 247–78.

Osterkamp, Barbara. *Arbeit und Identität: Studien zur Erzählkunst des bürgerlichen Realismus*. Würzburg: Königshausen & Neumann, 1983.

Ott, Ulrich, ed. *Literatur im Industriezeitalter: Eine Austellung des Deutschen Literaturarchivs im Schiller-Nationalmuseum*. Vol. 1. Marbach am Neckar: Deutsche Schillergesellschaft, 1987.

Ozment, Steven. *The Bürgermeister's Daughter: Scandal in a Sixteenth-Century German Town*. New York: St. Martin's Press, 1996.

Pape, Walter, ed. *1870/71 — 1989/90: German Unifications and the Change of Literary Discourse.* Berlin: de Gruyter, 1993.

Paret, Peter. *Art as History: Episodes in the Culture and Politics of Nineteenth-Century Germany.* Princeton: Princeton UP, 1988.

Pascal, Roy. *The German Novel: Studies.* Manchester, UK: Manchester UP, 1956.

Pavel, Thomas G. *Fictional Worlds.* Cambridge, MA: Harvard UP, 1986.

Pazi, Margarita. "Wie gleicht man auch ethisch Soll und Haben aus?" *Zeitschrift für deutsche Philologie* 106, no. 2 (1987): 198–218.

Peterson, Brent O. "E. Marlitt (Eugenie John)." In James Hardin and Siegfried Mews, eds. *Dictionary of Literary Biography.* Vol. 129: *Nineteenth-Century German Writers, 1841–1900.* Detroit: Gale Research, 1993. 223–28.

———. "German Nationalism after Napoleon: Caste and Regional Identities in Historical Fiction, 1815–1830." *German Quarterly* 68, no. 3 (1995): 287–303.

———. "The Fatherland's Kiss of Death: Gender and Germany in Nineteenth-Century Historical Fiction." In Patricia Herminghouse and Magda Mueller, eds. *Gender and Germanness: Cultural Productions of Nation.* Providence, RI: Berghahn, 1997. 82–97.

———. "Luise Mühlbach." In James Hardin and Siegfried Mews, eds. *Dictionary of Literary Biography.* Vol. 133: *Nineteenth-Century German Writers to 1840.* Detroit: Gale Research, 1993. 204–10.

———. *Popular Narratives and Ethnic Identity: Literature and Community in* Die Abendschule. Ithaca, NY: Cornell UP, 1991.

———. "Towards a 'Cultural' German-American Studies." *Monatshefte* 86 (1994): 354–60.

Pinson, Koppel S. *Modern Germany: Its History and Civilization.* 2nd ed. New York: Macmillan, 1966.

Plessen, Marie-Louise von. *"Germania aus dem Fundus," Marianne und Germania 1789–1889: Frankreich und Deutschland: zwei Welten — eine Revue.* Berlin: Argon, 1996.

Plessner, Helmuth. *Die verspätete Nation: Über die Verführbarkeit bürgerlichen Geistes.* In his *Gesammelte Schriften.* Ed. Günter Dux et al. Vol. 6. Frankfurt am Main: Suhrkamp, 1982. 7–223.

Potthast, Bertha. "Eugenie Marlitt: Ein Beitrag zur Geschichte des deutschen Frauenromans." Diss. U of Cologne, 1926.

Preisendanz, Wolfgang. *Humor als dichterische Einbildungskraft*. 2nd ed. Munich: Fink, 1976.

———. *Wege des Realismus: Zur Poetik und Erzählkunst im 19. Jahrhundert*. Munich: Fink, 1977.

Raabe, Wilhelm. *Pfisters Mühle*. Stuttgart: Reclam, 1980.

———. *Sämtliche Werke*. 26 vols. Eds. Karl Hoppe et al. Göttingen: Vandenhoeck & Ruprecht, 1960–94.

———. *Werke: Braunschweiger Ausgabe*. Ed. Hans Oppermann. Göttingen: Vandenhoeck & Ruprecht, 1970.

Radek, Heide. "Zur Geschichte von Roman und Erzählung in der *Gartenlaube* (1853 bis 1914): Heroismus und Idylle als Instrument nationaler Ideologie." Diss. U of Erlangen-Nuremberg, 1967.

Ranke, Leopold von. *Sämmtliche Werke*. 2nd ed. 54 vols. in 43. Leipzig: Duncker & Humblot, 1867–90.

Rebing, Günter. *Der Halbbruder des Dichters: Friedrich Spielhagens Theorie des Romans*. Frankfurt am Main: Athenäum, 1972.

Reed, T. J. *Thomas Mann: The Uses of Tradition*. Oxford: Clarendon Press, 1974.

Reich-Ranicki, Marcel. "Die ungeschminkte Wahrheit" (1978) and "Die Geburt der Kritik aus dem Geiste der Epik" (1986). In his *Thomas Mann und die Seinen*. Stuttgart: Deutsche Verlags-Anstalt, 1987. 29–49, 63–81.

Remak, Henry H. "The German Reception of French Realism." *PMLA* 69 (1954): 410–31.

———. "Politik und Gesellschaft als Kunst: Güldenklees Toast in Fontanes *Effi Briest*." In Jörg Thunecke, ed. *Formen realistischer Erzählkunst: Festschrift for Charlotte Jolles*. Nottingham, UK: Sherwood Press, 1979. 550–62.

Rhöse, Franz. *Konflikt und Versöhnung: Untersuchungen zur Theorie des Romans von Hegel bis zum Naturalismus*. Stuttgart: Metzler, 1978.

Rhotert, Hans. "Ephraim Moses Kuh." Diss. U of Munich, 1927.

Riehl, Wilhelm Heinrich. *Die deutsche Arbeit*. Stuttgart: Cotta, 1861.

Riffaterre, Michael. *Fictional Truth*. Baltimore: Johns Hopkins UP, 1990.

Rindisbacher, Hans J. *The Smell of Books: A Cultural-Historical Study of Olfactory Perception in Literature*. Ann Arbor: U of Michigan P, 1992.

Robertson, Ritchie. *The "Jewish Question" in German Literature 1749–1939: Emancipation and Its Discontents*. London & New York: Oxford UP, 1999.

Roebling, Irmgard. *Wilhelm Raabes doppelte Buchführung: Paradigma einer Spaltung*. Tübingen: Niemeyer, 1988.

Röhse, Franz. *Konflikt und Versöhnung: Untersuchungen zur Theorie des Romans von Hegel bis zum Naturalismus*. Stuttgart: Metzler, 1978.

Roper, Katherine. "Friedrich Spielhagen." In James Hardin and Siegfried Mews, eds. *Dictionary of Literary Biography*. Vol. 129: *Nineteenth Century German Writers, 1841–1900*. Detroit & London: Gale Research, 1993. 348–60.

[Rosegger, Hans Ludwig, ed.] "Briefe von Friedrich Spielhagen an den alten Heimgärtner." *Roseggers Heimgarten* 35 (1911): 608–15.

Rosenstrauch, Hazel E. "Zum Beispiel: *Die Gartenlaube*." In Annamaria Rucktäschel and Hans Dieter Zimmermann, eds. *Trivialliteratur*. Munich: Fink, 1976. 169–89.

Rothe-Buddensieg, Margret. *Spuk im Bürgerhaus: Der Dachboden in der deutschen Prosaliteratur als Negation der gesellschaftlichen Realität*. Kronberg/Ts.: Scriptor, 1974.

Roxin, Claus. "Vernunft und Aufklärung bei Karl May: Zur Deutung der Klekih-Petra Episode im *Winnetou*." *Mitteilungen der Karl-May-Gesellschaft* 28 (1976): 25–30.

Sälter, Rolf. *Entwicklungslinien der deutschen Zola-Rezeption von den Anfängen bis zum Tode des Autors*. Bern, Frankfurt am Main, New York & Paris: Peter Lang, 1989.

Sagarra, Eda. *Tradition and Revolution: German Literature and Society 1830–1890*. London: Weidenfeld & Nicolson, 1971.

Sammons, Jeffrey L. "The Evaluation of Freytag's *Soll und Haben*." *German Life and Letters* 22 (1968–69): 315–24.

———. *Ideology, Mimesis, Fantasy: Charles Sealsfield, Friedrich Gerstäcker, Karl May, and Other German Novelists of America*. Chapel Hill & London: U of North Carolina P, 1998.

———. "The Mystery of the Missing Bildungsroman, or: What Happened to Wilhelm Meister's Legacy?" *Genre* 14 (1981): 229–46.

———. *Wilhelm Raabe: The Fiction of the Alternative Community*. Princeton: Princeton UP, 1987.

Sassen, Saski. *Migranten, Siedler, Flüchtlinge: Von der Massenauswanderung zur Festung Europa*. Frankfurt am Main: Fischer, 1996.

Schama, Simon. *Dead Certainties (Unwarranted Speculations)*. New York: Knopf, 1991.

Scheidemann, Uta. *Louise von François: Leben und Werk einer deutschen Erzählerin des neunzehnten Jahrhunderts*. Bern: Lang, 1988.

Schenda, Rudolf. *Volk ohne Buch: Studien zur Sozialgeschichte der populären Lesestoffe 1770–1910*. Frankfurt am Main: Klostermann, 1970.

Scherer, Wilhelm. *Geschichte der deutschen Litteratur*. Berlin: Weidmann, 1883.

———. *Poetik*. Berlin: Weidmann, 1888.

Schieder, Theodor. "Friedrich der Große — eine Integrationsfigur des deutschen Nationalbewußtseins im 18. Jahrhundert?" In Otto Dahn, ed. *Nationalismus in vorindustrieller Zeit*. Munich: Oldenbourg, 1986. 115–128.

Schieding, Hermann. *Untersuchungen über die Romantechnik Friedrich Spielhagens*. Borna-Leipzig: Noske, 1914.

Schiller, Friedrich. *Sämtliche Werke*. Vol. 1. Eds. Gerhard Fricke and Herbert G. Göpfert. Munich: Hanser, 1980.

———. *Werke: Nationalausgabe*. Vol. 20. Eds. Benno von Wiese and Helmut Koopmann. Weimar: Hermann Böhlau, 1962.

———. *Werke: Nationalausgabe*. Vol. 29. Eds. N. Oellers and F. Stock. Weimar: Böhlau, 1977.

Schivelbusch, Wolfgang. *Disenchanted Night: The Industrialization of Light in the Nineteenth Century*. Trans. Angela Davies. Berkeley: U of California P, 1995.

Schlechta, Karl. *Goethes Wilhelm Meister*. Frankfurt am Main: Klostermann, 1953.

Schmidt, Julian. "Friedrich Spielhagen." *Westermann's Jahrbuch der Illustrirten Deutschen Monatshefte* 29 (1870–71): 442–49.

Schmiedt, Helmut. "Karl May gibt es gar nicht: Beobachtungen und Überlegungen aus neuerer literaturwissenschaftlicher Sicht." *Jahrbuch der Karl-May-Gesellschaft* (1998): 152–63.

———, ed. *Karl May*. Frankfurt am Main: Suhrkamp, 1983.

Schoeps, Julian H. *Leiden an Deutschland: Vom antisemitischen Wahn und der Last der Erinnerung*. Munich: Piper, 1990.

Schorsch, Ismar. *From Text to Context: The Turn to History in Modern Judaism*. Hanover, NH & London: Brandeis UP, published by UP of New England, 1994.

Schrader, Hans-Jürgen. "Gedichtete Dichtungstheorie im Werk Raabes. Exemplifiziert an 'Alte Nester.'" *Jahrbuch der Raabe-Gesellschaft* (1989): 23–27.

Schuch, Uta. *"Die im Schatten stand." Studien zum Werk einer vergessenen Schriftstellerin: Louise von François*. Stockholm: Almqvist & Wiksell International, 1994.

Schulte-Sasse, Jochen. *Literarische Wertung*. 2nd ed. Stuttgart: Metzler, 1976.

———, and Renate Werner. "E. Marlitts 'Im Hause des Kommerzienrates': Analyse eines Trivialromans in paradigmatischer Absicht." In E. Marlitt, *Im Hause des Kommerzienrates*. Munich: Fink, 1977. 389–434.

Schwerte, Hans. *Faust und das Faustische: Ein Kapitel deutscher Ideologie*. Stuttgart: Klett, 1962.

Sedgwick, Eve Kosofsky. *Epistemology of the Closet*. Berkeley: U of California P, 1990. 82–86.

Seferens, Gregor. "'Immer . . . wenn ich an den Indianer denke': Eine Studie zur Entwicklung des Indianerbildes bei Karl May." *Jahrbuch der Karl-May-Gesellschaft* (1994): 86–103.

Seidenspinner, Wolfgang. "Oralisierte Schriftlichkeit als Stil: Das Literarische Genre Dorfgeschichte und die Kategorie Mündlichkeit." *Internationales Archiv für Sozialgeschichte der deutschen Literatur* 22:2 (1997 [1998]): 36–51.

Seiffert, Hans Werner, and Christel Laufer. "Zeugnisse und Materialien zu Fontanes 'Effi Briest' und Spielhagens 'Zum Zeitvertrieb.'" In Seiffert, ed. *Studien zur neueren deutschen Literatur*. Berlin: Akademie, 1964. 255–300.

Seiler, Friedrich. *Gustav Freytag, mit 28 Abbildungen*. Leipzig: Voigtländer, 1898.

Sent, Eleonore, ed. *Louise von François: Zum 100. Todestag am 25.9.1993*. Weissenfels: Druckhaus Naumburg, 1993.

Sheehan, James J. *German History 1770–1866*. Oxford: Clarendon Press, 1989.

———. *German Liberalism in the Nineteenth Century*. Chicago: U of Chicago P, 1978.

Showalter, Elaine, ed. *The New Feminist Criticism: Essays on Women, Literature, and Theory*. New York: Pantheon, 1985.

Silber, Kate. *Pestalozzi: The Man and His Work*. London: Routledge & Kegan Paul, 1960.

Silz, Walter. *Realism and Reality: Studies in the German Novelle of Poetic Realism.* Chapel Hill: U of North Carolina P, 1954.

Simmel, Georg. "Das Abenteuer." In his *Philosophische Kultur: Über das Abenteuer, die Geschlechter und die Krise der Moderne. Gesammelte Essais.* Berlin: Wagenbach, 1986. 25–38.

Skolnik, Jonathan. "Writing Jewish History Between Gutzkow and Goethe: Auerbach's *Spinoza* and the Birth of Modern Jewish Historical Fiction." *Prooftexts* 19 (1999): 101–25.

Solms, Wilhelm. "Effi und Innstetten: 'ein Musterpaar'? Zum poetischen Realismus Fontanes." *Germanisch-Romanische Monatsschrift* 35 (1985): 189–208.

Sorkin, David. "The Jewish Community: Emancipation, Secular Culture, and Jewish Identity in the Writings of Berthold Auerbach." In Jehuda Reinharz and Walter Schatzberg, eds. *The Jewish Response to German Culture.* Hanover, NH & London: UP of New England, 1985. 100–109.

———. "Jews, the Enlightenment and Religious Toleration — Some Reflections." *Yearbook for the Leo Baeck Institute* 37 (1992): 3–16.

Spielhagen, Friedrich. *Am Wege: Vermischte Schriften.* Leipzig: Staackmann, 1903.

———. *Ausgewählte Romane.* Leipzig: Staackmann, 1889–93.

———. *Beiträge zur Theorie und Technik des Dramas.* Leipzig: Staackmann, 1883.

———. *Finder und Erfinder: Erinnerungen aus meinem Leben.* Leipzig: Staackmann, 1890.

———. *Neue Beiträge zur Theorie und Technik der Epik und Dramatik.* Leipzig: Staackmann, 1898.

Spiero, Heinrich. *Geschichte des deutschen Romans.* Berlin: de Gruyter, 1950.

Spivak, Gayatri Chakravorty. "Can the Subaltern Speak?" In Cary Nelson and Lawrence Grossberg, eds. *Marxism and the Interpretation of Culture.* Urbana: U of Illinois P, 1988. 271–313.

Sprengel, Peter. "Der Liberalismus auf dem Weg ins 'neue Reich': Gustav Freytag und die Seinen 1866–1871." In Klaus Amann and Karl Wagner, eds. *Literatur und Nation: Die Gründung des deutschen Reiches.* Vienna: Böhlau, 1996. 153–82.

Stahr, Adolf. *Aus Adolf Stahrs Nachlaß: Briefe von Stahr nebst Briefe an ihn.* Ed. Ludwig Geiger. Oldenburg: Schulze, 1903.

Steakley, James. *The Homosexual Emancipation Movement in Germany (1862–1945).* New York: Arno, 1975.

Steinecke, Hartmut. "Gustav Freytag: *Soll und Haben* (1855): Weltbild und Wirkung eines deutschen Bestsellers." In Horst Denkler, ed. *Romane und Erzählungen des bürgerlichen Realismus: Neue Interpretationen*. Stuttgart: Reclam, 1980. 138–52.

———. *Romantheorie und Romankritik in Deutschland*. 2 vols. Stuttgart: Metzler, 1975, 1976.

———. "*Wilhelm Meister* und die Folgen: Goethes Roman und die Entwicklung der Gattung im 19. Jahrhundert." In Wolfgang Wittkowski, ed. *Goethe im Kontext*. Tübingen: Niemeyer, 1984. 89–118.

Steinmetz, Hans-Dieter. "'Es werden hier deutsche Werke massenhaft nachgedruckt': Zeitgenössische finnische, tschechische und slowenische Karl-May-Übersetzungen in Einwanderer-Verlagen der USA." *Jahrbuch der Karl-May-Gesellschaft* (1994): 312–37.

Stern, J. P. *Idylls and Reality: Studies in Nineteenth-Century German Literature*. New York: Ungar, 1971.

———. *Re-Interpretations: Seven Studies in Nineteenth-Century German Literature*. New York: Basic Books, 1964.

Stifter, Adalbert. *Brigitta: Urfassung/Studienfassung*. Ed. Max Stefl. Augsburg: Adam Kraft Verlag, 1957.

———. *Indian Summer*. Trans. Wendell Frye. New York: Lang, 1985.

———. *Der Nachsommer*. Frankfurt am Main: Insel, 1982.

———. *Werke*. Eds. Kamill Eben and Franz Hüller. Vols. 6–8. Prague: Verlag der Gesellschaft zur Föderung deutscher Wissenschaft, Kunst und Literatur in Böhmen, 1916–21.

———. *Werke und Briefe: Historisch-Kritische Ausgabe*. Vol. 1, part 5. Eds. Alfred Doppler and Wolfgang Frühwald. Stuttgart: Kohlhammer, 1982.

Storck, Jochim W. "Eros bei Stifter." In Hartmut Laufhütte and Karl Möseneder, eds. *Adalbert Stifter: Dichter und Maler, Denkmalpfleger und Schulmann: Neue Zugänge zu seinem Werk*. Tübingen: Niemeyer, 1996. 135–56.

Strecker, Gabriele. *Frauenträume — Frauentränen: Über den deutschen Frauenroman*. Weilheim/Oberbayern: Otto Wilhelm Barth, 1969.

Strodtmann, Adolf. *Dichterprofile: Literaturbilder aus dem neunzehnten Jahrhundert*. Stuttgart: Abenheim, 1879.

Struck, Wolfgang. "See- und Mordgeschichten: Zur Konstruktion exotischer Räume in realistischen Erzähltexten." *Jahrbuch der Raabe-Gesellschaft* (1999): 60–70.

Struik, Dirk J., ed. *Birth of the Communist Manifesto: With Full Text of the Manifesto, All Prefaces by Marx and Engels, Early Drafts by Engels and Other Supplementary Material*. New York: International Publishers, 1971.

Subiotto, Frances M. "The Ghost in Effi Briest." *Forum for Modern Language Studies* 21 (1985): 137–50.

Swales, Martin. *Buddenbrooks: Family Life as the Mirror of Social Change*. Boston: Twayne, 1991.

———. *Epochenbuch Realismus: Romane und Erzählungen*. Munich: Schmidt, 1997.

Tatlock, Lynne. "Regional Histories as National History: Gustav Freytag's Bilder aus der deutschen Vergangenheit (1859–67)." In Nicholas Vazsonyi, ed. *Searching for Common Ground: Diskurse zur deutschen Identität*. Cologne: Böhlau, 2000. 161–78.

Tatum, John Hargrove. *The Reception of German Literature in U.S. German Texts, 1864–1914*. New York, Bern, Frankfurt am Main & Paris: Peter Lang, 1988.

Taubert, Erich. *Classical Road Thuringia*. 2nd ed. Weimar: Weimardruck GmbH, 1994.

Taylor, A. J. P. *Germany's First Bid for Colonies 1884–1885: A Move in Bismarck's European Policy*. 1938; rpt. Hamden, CT: Archon, 1967.

Tebben, Karin, ed. *Beruf: Schriftstellerin: Schreibende Frauen im 18. und 19. Jahrhundert*. Göttingen: Vandenhoek & Ruprecht, 1998.

Tewarson, Heidi Thomann. "Die Aufklärung im jüdischen Denken des 19. Jahrhunderts." *Forum Vormärz Forschung Jahrbuch* (1998): 44–51.

Thomas, Keith, ed. *The Oxford Book of Work*. Oxford: Oxford UP, 1999.

Touaillon, Christine. *Der deutsche Frauenroman des 18. Jahrhunderts*. Vienna: Braumüller, 1919.

Trommler, Frank. "Die Nationalisierung der Arbeit." In Reinhold Grimm and Jost Hermand, eds. *Arbeit als Thema in der deutschen Literatur vom Mittelalter bis zur Gegenwart*. Königstein: Athenäum, 1979. 102–5.

Tuchmann, Barbara. *The Guns of August*. New York: Macmillan, 1962.

Turner, David. "Marginalien und Handschriften zum Thema: Fontane und Spielhagens Theorie der 'Objektivität.'" *Fontane-Blätter* 1 (1968–69): 265–81.

Ueding, Gert, and Reinhard Tschapke, eds. *Karl-May-Handbuch*. Stuttgart: Kröner, 1987.

Ulrichs, Karl Heinrich. *Forschungen über das Räthsel der mannmännlichen Liebe*. Ed. Hubert Kennedy. 4 vols. Berlin: Verlag rosa Winkel, 1984.

Vazsonyi, Nicholas. *Searching for Common Ground: Diskurse zur deutschen Identität*. Cologne: Böhlau, 2000.

Volkov, Shulamit. *Die Juden in Deutschland 1780–1918*. Trans. Simone Gundi. Enzyklopädie deutscher Geschichte 16. Munich: Oldenbourg, 2000.

Weber, Max. *The Protestant Ethic and the Spirit of Capitalism*. Trans. Talcott Parsons. Los Angeles: Roxbury, 1996.

Wehler, Hans-Ulrich. *The German Empire 1871–1918*. Trans. Kim Traynor. Oxford: Berg, 1985.

Weimar, Klaus. *Geschichte der deutschen Literaturwissenschaft bis zum Ende des 19. Jahrhunderts*. Munich: Fink, 1989.

Weiner, Marc. *Richard Wagner and the Anti-Semitic Imagination*. Lincoln: U of Nebraska P, 1995.

Wellek, René. "The Concept of Realism in Literary Scholarship." *Neophilologus* 45 (1961): 1–20.

White, Hayden. *Metahistory: The Historical Imagination in Nineteenth-Century Europe*. Baltimore: Johns Hopkins UP, 1973.

———. *Tropics of Discourse: Essays in Cultural Criticism*. Baltimore: Johns Hopkins UP, 1978.

Whitesell, Lloyd, and Sophie Fuller, eds. *Secret Passages: Music and Modern Transitional Queer Identity, 1880–1940*. Bloomington: U of Indiana P, forthcoming).

Widhammer, Helmuth. *Die Literaturtheorie des deutschen Realismus (1848–1860)*. Stuttgart: Metzler, 1977.

Wiese, Benno von, ed. *Deutsche Dichter des 19. Jahrhunderts: Ihr Leben und Werk*. 2nd. ed. Berlin: Erich Schmidt, 1979.

Wilkending, Gisela. *Kinder und Jugendliteratur: Mädchenliteratur vom 18. Jahrhundert bis zum Zweiten Weltkrieg, Eine Textsammlung*. Reclam: Stuttgart, 1994.

Wisskirchen, Hans. "Republikanischer Eros: Zur Welt Whitmans und Hans Blühers Rolle in der politischen Publizistik Thomas Manns." In Gerhard Härle, ed. *"Heimsuchung und süßes Gift": Erotik und Poetik bei Thomas Mann*. Frankfurt am Main: Fischer, 1992. 17–40.

Wolff, Charlotte. *Magnus Hirschfeld: A Portrait of a Pioneer in Sexology*. London: Quartet, 1986.

Wollschläger, Hans. "Introduction." *Jahrbuch der Karl-May-Gesellschaft* (1998): 7–8.

Worley, Linda Kraus. "Louise von François: A Reinterpretation of Her Life and Her 'Odd-Women' Fiction." Diss. U of Cincinnati, 1985.

———. "Louise von François (1817–1893): Scripting a Life." In Ruth-Ellen Boetcher Joeres and Marianne Burkhard, eds. *Out of Line/Ausgefallen: The Paradox of Marginality in the Writings of Nineteenth-Century German Women*. Atlanta: Rodopi, 1989. 161–86.

———. "The 'Odd' Woman as Heroine in the Fiction of Louise von François." In Marianne Burkhard and Jeanette Clausen, eds. *Women in German Yearbook 4*. Lanham, MD: UP of America, 1988. 155–65.

Worthmann, Joachim. *Probleme des Zeitromans: Studien zur Geschichte des deutschen Romans im 19. Jahrhundert*. Heidelberg: Winter, 1974.

Zantop, Susanne. *Colonial Fantasies: Conquest, Family, and Nation in Precolonial Germany, 1770–1870*. Durham, NC: Duke UP, 1997.

———. "Crossing the Border: The French Revolution in the German Literary Imagination." In James A. W. Heffernan, ed. *Representing the French Revolution: Literature, Historiography, and Art*. Hanover, NH: UP of New England, 1992. 213–33.

Zimmermann, Christina von. "'Brigitta' — seelenkundlich gelesen: Zur Vewendung 'kalobiotischer' Lebensmaximen Feuchterslebens in Stifters Erzählung." In Harmut Laufhütte and Karl Möseneder, eds. *Adalbert Stifter: Dichter und Maler, Denkmalpfleger und Schulmann: Neue Zugänge zu seinem Werk*. Tübingen: Niemeyer, 1996. 410–34.

Zinken, Rosa-Maria. *Der Roman als Zeitdokument: Bürgerlicher Liberalismus in Friedrich Spielhagens "Die von Hohenstein" (1863/64)*. Frankfurt am Main, Bern, New York & Paris: Peter Lang, 1991.

Zwick, M. I. *Berthold Auerbach's sozialpolitischer und ethischer Liberalismus: Nach seinen Schriften dargestellt*. Stuttgart: Kohlhammer, 1933.

Notes on the Contributors

KIRSTEN BELGUM is associate professor in the Department of Germanic Studies at the University of Texas at Austin. She has published in the areas of nineteenth-century German realism, feminist aesthetics, and the cultural history of German nationalism. Her books are *Interior Meaning: Design of the Bourgeois Home in the Realist Novel* and *Popularizing the Nation: Audience, Representation, and the Production of Identity in Die Gartenlaube, 1853–1900*.

NINA BERMAN is associate professor of German Studies at the Ohio State University. She has published *Orientalismus, Kolonialismus und Moderne: Zum Bild des Orients in der deutschsprachigen Literatur um 1900* and articles on Arab-German minority literature, multiculturalism in Germany, colonialism in German literature, Hugo von Hofmannsthal, and Albert Schweitzer. She is currently finishing a manuscript on German agents of development in Africa. Her next project will explore Arab-German artists and intellectuals in contemporary Germany.

RUSSELL A. BERMAN is the Walter A. Haas Professor in the Humanities at Stanford University. His books include *The Rise of the Modern German Novel*, *Modern Culture and Critical Theory*, *Cultural Studies of Modern Germany*, and *Enlightenment or Empire*. His is currently completing a work on German literary history.

IRENE S. DI MAIO is associate professor of German at Louisiana State University and A&M College. Her publications treat the narrative techniques of Wilhelm Raabe, multiculturalism in Friedrich Gerstäcker's North American narratives, and Jewish identity in the works of Fanny Lewald, Berthold Auerbach, Jean Améry, Elias Canetti, and Theodor Herzl. Currently she is preparing a translation with critical introduction of Friedrich Gerstäcker's narratives set in Louisiana.

THOMAS C. FOX is professor of German at the University of Alabama. He has published numerous articles on nineteenth- and twentieth-century German literature and has written or edited books on medieval literature, Louise von François, East German prose, and East German responses to the Holocaust. He is currently editing a volume of essays on Lessing.

ROBERT C. HOLUB is professor of German at the University of California, Berkeley. He has written books on Heinrich Heine, literary theory, German realism, Jürgen Habermas, and Friedrich Nietzsche. He is currently working on a project involving Nietzsche and the discourses of the nineteenth century.

TODD KONTJE is professor of German at the University of California, San Diego. He has written books on Schiller's aesthetics, the German Bildungsroman, and German women writers of the eighteenth and nineteenth centuries. He is currently working on Orientalism in German literature from *Parzival* to the present.

BRENT O. PETERSON is associate professor of German at Ripon College. He has written *Popular Narratives and Ethnic Identity* and recently published an article, "How (and why) to read German-American Literature." In addition to several articles, his work on German history and historical fiction resulted in a book-length manuscript, "History, Fiction, and Germany: Writing the Nineteenth-Century Nation."

JOHN PIZER is professor of German and comparative literature at Louisiana State University. He has written a wide range of articles and books on German literature and thought of the eighteenth, nineteenth, and twentieth centuries. His current research focus is the history of "world literature" as a discursive paradigm from Goethe to the present day.

HANS J. RINDISBACHER is associate professor of German at Pomona College. His special interest is cultural studies, and his publications include a book on the intersection of literature and the cultural history of olfactory perception (*The Smell of Books*) and several articles. He has been involved in Languages Across the Curriculum projects (LAC), with a CD-ROM of related materials forthcoming. Works in progress include a study of the various Soviet memorials in Berlin and one on narrative aspects of Max Frisch's novel *Mein Name sei Gantenbein*.

JEFFREY L. SAMMONS is Leavenworth Professor of German at Yale University. Among the topics of his books are Heinrich Heine, Wilhelm Raabe, and German novels of America. He is currently working on a book about Friedrich Spielhagen.

LYNNE TATLOCK is the Hortense and Tobias Lewin Distinguished Professor in the Humanities at Washington University, St. Louis. She has published widely on German literature and culture from the seventeenth to the twentieth century, edited or coedited five books on early modern literature and culture, and translated novels by Marie von Ebner-Eschenbach and Gabriele Reuter. She is currently investigating ideas of community in realist fiction in Imperial Germany.

ROBERT TOBIN is associate professor of German and associate dean of the faculty at Whitman College in Walla Walla, Washington. He is the author of *Warm Brothers: Queer Theory and the Age of Goethe* and *Doctor's Orders: Enlightenment Medicine and German Literature*. He is currently working on nationality and sexuality in modern Germany.

Index

Abendschule, 13
Age of Goethe, 1, 46, 138, 140, 141, 143, 144
Aldrich, Robert, 335 n
Alexis, Willibald, 87, 122, 265, 281 n
Alexis, Willibald, works by: *Isegrimm,* 86; *Ruhe ist die erste Bürgerpflicht,* 59, 82 n
Alker, Ernst, 152 n, 155 n
Althusser, Louis, 263
Altmann, Alexander, 255 n
Anderson, Alexander Robinson, 152 n, 156 n
Anderson, Benedict, 25 n, 86, 105 n, 110
Andreas-Salomé, Lou, 313
anti-Semitism, 12, 142, 160, 171, 179 n, 224, 227, 235, 236, 251, 312, 315, 322, 325, 329–30. *See also* Jews in Germany
Applegate, Celia, 103–4, 108 n, 221 n
Arens, Hans, 278 n, 279 n, 281 n
Armstrong, Nancy, 28 n, 278 n
Aston, Louise, 6–7, 19
Aston, Louise, works by: *Aus dem Leben einer Frau,* 270
Auerbach, Berthold, 5, 12, 135, 137, 139, 223–52
Auerbach, Berthold, works by: *Auf der Höhe,* 235–41, 245; *Dichter und Kaufmann,* 223, 225, 226–28, 230–34, 235, 238, 249, 252; *Ein neues Leben,* 235, 236, 238; *Gallerie der ausgezeichneten Israeliten,* 234; *Das Judenthum,* 234; *Das Landhaus am Rhein,* 231, 236, 240, 241–51, 281 n; *Schwarzwälder Dorfgeschichten,* 223, 225–26, 279 n; *Spinoza,* 223, 225, 226–30, 238; *Studien,* 230; *Waldfried,* 236, 246, 251
Auerbach, Erich, 2, 22 n, 30, 49 n, 81 n, 84 n, 112
Auerbach, Jakob, 252 n
Augusti, Brigitte, 104 n
Austen, Jane, 276, 282 n

Bade, Klaus, 294, 303 n, 304 n
Bakhtin, Mikhail, 141, 155 n
Balzac, Honoré de, 6, 29, 147
Bamler, Friedrich, 164, 179 n
Barthes, Roland, 22 n
Baumann, Christiane, 49 n
Bazzanella, Astrid, 265, 280 n, 281 n
Belgum, Kirsten, 12, 19, 26 n, 83 n, 278 n, 279 n, 281 n, 282 n
Ben-Ari, Nitsa, 235, 255 n
Bennett, E. K., 24 n
Berghahn, Volker R., 304 n, 305 n
Berman, Harold, 151 n
Berman, Marshall, 190–91, 220 n
Berman, Nina, 13, 303 n, 305 n
Berman, Russell, 5, 14, 16, 24 n, 26 n, 27 n, 159–60, 162, 167, 170, 178, 178 n, 179 n, 180 n, 195, 203, 220 n, 221 n, 278 n
Bernd, Clifford, 6, 23 n, 24 n, 364 n
Bernstein, Aaron, 235
Bertschik, Julia, 164, 170, 179 n, 180 n
Bethe, Emil, 326, 337 n
Bettelheim, Anton, 252 n, 253 n, 256 n, 257 n
Bieber, Hugo, 154 n

Bildungsroman
 (Entwicklungsroman), 7–8,
 110, 134, 149, 184, 189, 241,
 256 n
Bismarck, Otto von, 5, 6, 11, 14,
 58, 137, 138, 144, 148, 161,
 164, 177, 212, 259, 295, 342,
 343, 344, 347, 348, 351, 358,
 361
Blackbourn, David, 23 n
Bleibtreu, Carl, 136, 137, 138,
 153 n, 156 n
Blüher, Hans, 20–21, 322–27,
 329, 337 n
Blumenberg, Hans, 22 n
Böhm, Klaus Werner, 337 n,
 338 n
Bonaventura, works by:
 Nachtwachen, 38
Börne, Ludwig, 227
Boulby, Mark, 153 n, 154 n
Bovenschen, Silvia, 27 n
Brahm, Otto, 101, 108 n
Bramsted, Ernst K., 25 n, 239,
 243, 256 n, 257 n
Brand, Adolf, 322–24
Brauer, Cornelia (Hobohm),
 278 n
Brecht, 1, 136
Brehm, Alfred Edmund, 285
Brenner, Peter J., 180 n
Bretting, Agnes, 303 n
Brewster, Philip J., 175, 180 n,
 181 n
Brinkmann, Richard, 30, 49 n
Brontë, Charlotte, 276
Bruno, Leonard C., 305 n
Büchler-Hauschild, Gabriele, 187,
 220 n
Büchner, Georg, 5
Bülow, Frieda von, 16, 354

Campbell, Joan, 200, 219 n,
 220 n, 221 n
Carter, T. E., 219 n

Catlin, George, 285
Caudwell, Sarah, works by: *The
 Shortest Way to Hades*, 81 n
Cervantes, Miguel de, works by:
 Don Quixote, 137
Cicero, works by: *De senectute*, 48
Collingwood, R. G., 70, 84 n
colonialism and imperialism
 (German), vii, 12–17, 98–99,
 159–78, 184–85, 299–300,
 351–54
Commines, Philipe de, 83 n
Confino, Alon, 92, 106 n, 213–
 14, 221 n
Conrady, Karl Otto, 25 n
Cooper, James Fenimore, 283
Craig, Gordon A., 257 n
Crane, Susan A., 81 n
Curth, Karl, 162

Dahn, Felix, 86, 87, 105 n
Dahn, Felix, works by: *Ein Kampf
 um Rom*, 81 n
Damerau, Burghard, 80 n
Demetz, Peter, 122, 131 n, 146,
 156 n
Denkler, Horst, 167, 179 n,
 180 n, 181 n
Derks, Paul, 336 n
Dickens, Charles, 6, 8, 29, 59,
 82 n, 139, 147, 282 n, 307
Diethe, Carol, 280 n
Dilthey, Wilhelm, 7, 67
Di Maio, Irene (Stocksieker), 12,
 179 n
Dittmann, Ulrich, 51 n
Doderer, Heimito von, 142,
 155 n
Dorfgeschichten (village tales), 8,
 10, 12, 223, 225–26, 279 n
Dostoyevsky, Feodor, 307, 329
Droste-Hülshoff, Annette von, 5,
 110, 262
Dühring, Euren, 325
Dumas, Alexandre, 61, 62

Ebers, Georg, 81 n
Ebner-Eschenbach, Marie von, 110
Eggert, Hartmut, 61, 82 n, 127 n
Eichendorff, Josef Freiherr von, works by: *Das Marmorbild*, 46
Einstein, Albert, 330
Eke, Norbert Otto, 60–61, 82 n
Eley, Geoff, 23 n
Elias, Norbert, 24 n
Eliot, George, 276
Eliot, George, works by: *Middlemarch*, 143–44
Ellis, Havelock, 336 n
Elsaghe, Y. A., 337 n
emigration, vii, 12–13, 286, 287–94, 300–301
Engel, Eduard, 137, 139, 153 n, 154 n, 156 n
Engels, Friedrich, 146, 186. See also Marx, Karl
Entwicklungsroman. See Bildungsroman
Enzinger, Moriz, 50 n
Ernest II, Duke of Saxe-Coburg-Gotha, 89, 90, 95, 104 n
Eulenberg, Albert, 330, 336 n
Evans, Richard J., 28 n

Fendri, Mounir, 302 n
Feuerlicht, Ignace, 338 n
Fielding, Henry, works by: *Tom Jones*, 137
First World War, 4, 6, 14, 294, 329
Fischbacher-Bosshardt, Andrea, 154 n, 155 n, 157 n
Fischer, Fritz, 23 n
Flaubert, Gustave, 2, 7, 8, 29, 112, 142
Flaubert, Gustave, works by: *Madame Bovary*, 346
Fontane, Theodor, vii, 29, 87, 104 n, 111, 142, 155 n, 186, 219 n, 259, 269, 276, 339–64

Fontane, Theodor, works by: *Effi Briest*, 6, 57, 67, 150, 276, 339–64; *Die Poggenpuhls*, 142; *Stechlin*, 340; *Unterm Birnbaum*, 134
Forel, August, 336 n
Forster, Georg, 159, 178 n
Foucault, Michel, 20, 28 n, 309, 334 n
Fox, Thomas C., 11, 20, 128 n, 131 n
Francke, Kuno, 139, 154 n
François, Louise von, vii, 11, 20, 109–31
François, Louise von, works by: "Der Posten der Frau," 109, 112–15, 117; *Die letzte Reckenburgerin*, 109, 110, 111, 117–22, 124, 125, 126; *Frau Erdmuthens Zwillingssöhne*, 109, 110, 122–26; "Fräulein Muthchen und ihr Hausmeier," 109, 110, 115–17, 120; *Stufenjahre eines Glücklichen*, 126
Franco-Prussian War, 102, 117, 122, 147, 149, 348, 351
Frankfurter, Bernhard, 252 n
Franklin, Benjamin, 242–43, 244
Franzos, Karl Emil, 235
Frederick II, King of Prussia ("the Great"), 55, 67, 59, 62–80, 110, 112, 113, 114, 131 n, 144, 224
Frederick William, Crown Prince of Prussia, 90
Freiligrath, Ferdinand, 107 n, 111, 253 n
French Revolution, 9–10, 46, 115, 116, 119–21, 204
Frenssen, Gustav, 176, 181 n
Freud, Sigmund, 323, 337 n, 346
Freud, Sigmund, works by: *Interpretation of Dreams*, 6
Frevert, Ute, 305 n

Frey, John R., 154 n, 155 n
Freytag, Gustav, vii, 29, 81 n, 85–105, 112, 117, 122, 130 n, 131 n, 139, 235–37, 239, 255 n, 259, 278 n
Freytag, Gustav, works by: *Die Ahnen*, 10, 85–104; *Aus einer kleinen Stadt*, 88, 103; *Bilder aus der deutschen Vergangenheit*, 86, 89, 92–93, 95, 98, 99, 107 n, 108 n; *Die Brüder vom deutschen Hause*, 94–101; *Marcus König*, 98, 99; *Soll und Haben*, 8–9, 11, 12, 92–93, 98, 184, 185, 186–99, 202, 205, 206, 208–9, 211, 215–18, 257 n, 276, 277, 281 n
Friedemann, Käte, 141, 142, 154 n, 155 n
Friedlaender, Benedict, 322–27, 329, 337 n
Friedrich, Friedrich, 263, 280 n
Friedrichs, Hermann, 279 n
Friedrichsmeyer, Sara, 26 n, 27 n
Fuchs, Hans, 336 n
Fuld, Werner, 151 n
Fulda, Daniel, 108 n
Furst, Lillian R., 58, 81 n

Gartenlaube, 12–13, 19, 260–64, 267, 278 n, 279 n, 282 n
Gass, William H., 104 n
Geiger, Abraham, 224
Geller, Martha, 153 n, 154 n
George, Stefan, 331, 333
George Wilhelm, Elector of Brandenburg, 344, 354
Gerber, Paul, 176, 177
Gersdorf, Wilhelmine von, works by: *Aurora Gräfin von Königsmark*, 61
Gerstäcker, Friedrich, 257 n
Gervinus, Georg Gottfried, 1
Giddens, Anthony, 294–95, 305 n
Gilbert, Sandra M., 111, 129 n

Gilman, Sander, 310, 335 n, 337 n
Ginzburg, Carlo, 55, 80 n
Giseke, Robert, 187, 220 n
Glaser, 24 n
Goeden, Wilhelm von, Baron, 310
Goessl, Alfred F., 154 n, 156 n
Goethe, Johann Wolfgang von, 1, 2, 35, 89, 133, 136, 141, 143, 144, 145, 147, 166, 224, 250, 310
Goethe, Johann Wolfgang von, works by: *Faust*, 1, 146, 341; *Die Leiden des jungen Werther*, 67, 143; "Literarischer Sansculottismus," 9; "Der neue Amadis," 171; *Die Wahlverwandtschaften*, 138, 143–44; *Wilhelm Meisters Lehrjahre*, 7–8, 138, 145, 24 n, 242; *Xenien*, 9–10
Gogol, Nicolai, 134
Gohrbandt, Elisabeth, 288, 304 n, 305 n
Goldhagen, Daniel Jonah, 26 n
Goncourt, Edmund, 2
Goncourt, Jules, 2
Gooch, G. P., 80 n
Gottschall, Rudolf von, 155 n, 156 n, 262, 279
Gottsched, Luise, 18
Graf, Andreas, 303 n
Grafton, Anthony, 82 n, 83 n
Grautoff, Otto, 328
Greenberg, Valerie D., 363 n, 364 n
Gregor-Dellin, Martin, 128 n
Die Grenzboten, 5, 236
Grimmelshausen, Hans Jakob Christoffel, works by: *Simplicissimus*, 137
Grosz, Georg, 330
Gubar, Susan, 111, 129 n
Gutzkow, Karl, 111, 143, 155 n, 186, 220 n, 235

Hahl, Werner, 240, 256 n
Hahn-Hahn, Ida Gräfin, 6, 19
Hajek, Siegfried, 170, 180 n
Haley, Alex, 108 n
Hammer, Wolfgang, 302 n
Hamsun, Knut, 6
Hardenberg, Karl August von, 10, 121
Harder, Hermann, 131 n
Härle, Gerhard, 335 n, 336 n, 338 n
Hart, Heinrich, 137, 138, 139, 140, 142, 143, 153 n, 154 n
Hart, Julius, 153 n, 154 n
Hartung, Rudolf, 334 n
Hauptmann, Gerhart, 330
Hauptmann, Gerhart, works by: *Die Weber*, 8
Hausrath, Adolf, 81 n
Heermann, Christian, 304 n
Hegel, Friedrich, 204, 346
Heilbut, Anthony, 328, 336 n, 338 n
Heimat, 87, 92, 96, 100, 104, 185, 213–14
Heimatliteratur, 2, 10, 138, 264
Heine, Heinrich, 46, 134, 135, 136, 227, 255 n, 350
Heine, Heinrich, works by: *Ideen: Das Buch Le Grand*, 38; *Die romantische Schule*, 1
Heller, Erich, 338 n
Hellmann, Winfried, 155 n, 156 n
Henkel, Gabriele, 151 n, 152 n, 153 n
Henning, Hans, 151 n, 152 n, 154 n, 155 n
Herder, Johann Gottfried, 224
Hermand, Jost, 22 n
Herminghouse, Patricia, 129 n, 157 n, 256 n
Herwegh, Georg, 111
Hesekiel, George, works by: *Stille vor dem Sturm*, 83 n
Hesse, Hermann, 330

Hettche, Walter, 151 n
Heyse, Paul, 154 n
Hirschfeld, Magnus, 311, 322, 330
historical fiction, 6, 8, 19–20, 53–80, 109–12, 126–27. *See also* national identity; realism
Hitler, Adolf, 3, 12, 15, 329
Hobohm, Cornelia, 278 n, 281 n
Hoffmann, E. T. A., 5
Hohendahl, Peter Uwe, 5, 22 n, 23 n, 25 n, 84 n
Holbeche, Brian, 364 n
Holocaust, 14, 16, 233, 235
Holub, Robert, 11, 22 n, 25 n, 26 n, 49 n, 110, 128 n, 179 n, 257 n
Holz, Claus, 102, 108 n
Homer, 30, 137, 140, 141, 142, 144
Homer, works by: *Odyssey*, 46
homosexuality (homoeroticism), vii, 20–21, 118, 299, 307–333
Hook, Donald D., 252 n
Horch, Hans Otto, 164, 179 n, 180 n, 226, 235, 252 n, 253 n, 254 n, 255 n
Hughes, Arthur H., 154 n
Humbert, Édouard, 106 n
Humboldt, Wilhelm von, 10, 140
Hunter-Lougheed, Rosemarie, 50
Huyssen, Andreas, 27 n

Ibsen, Henrik, 6
Ibsen, Henrik, works by: *A Doll's House*, 139
Iggers, Georg G., 80 n
Immermann, Karl Leberecht, works by: *Die Epigonen*, 1
imperialism. *See* colonialism

Jackson, Paul, 156 n
Jacobs, Jürgen, 24 n
Jaeger, Friedrich, 80 n
James, G. P. R., 61

James, Henry, 151 n
James, Henry, works by: "Pandora," 134
Jameson, Fredric, 21, 28 n
Janke, Otto, 117
Jean Paul (Friedrich Richter), 224
Jews (German), 18, 20, 160, 179 n, 194, 223–52, 310–12, 315, 325, 327, 329, 331, 349–50. *See also* anti-Semitism
Joeres, Ruth-Ellen Boetcher, 18–19, 24 n, 28 n, 84 n, 115, 126, 128 n, 129 n, 280 n, 281 n
Jones, James W., 334 n
John, Alfred, 279 n, 280 n
Junges Deutschland (Young Germany), 61, 111

Kafitz, Dieter, 157 n
Kafka, Franz, 1, 58
Kafka, Franz, works by: "Das Urteil," 362
Kahn, Lothar, 252 n
Kaiser, Nancy A., 240, 241, 253 n, 256 n
Kandolf, Franz, 285, 302 n
Kant, Immanuel, 5, 23 n
Kant, Immanuel, works by: *Critique of Judgment*, 45, 47
Kapp, Friedrich, 243
Karpeles, Gustav, 133, 146, 150 n, 155 n, 156 n
Karsch, Anna, 18
Katz, Jacob, 255 n
Kaufmann, Walter, 26 n
Kayserling, M., 254 n
Keil, Ernst, 19, 261–62, 279 n
Keindorf, Gudrun, 304 n
Keiter, Heinrich, 142, 155 n
Kellen, Tony, 142, 155 n
Keller, Gottfried, 29, 111, 133, 239, 259, 263, 268, 279 n
Keller, Gottfried, works by: *Die Berlocken*, 15; *Der grüne Heinrich*, 8, 11, 149, 276

Kienzle, 263, 280 n
Klemperer, Victor, 133, 150 n, 153 n, 156 n, 157 n
Klippenberg, August, 91, 106 n
Klotz, Marcia, 364 n
Kock, Paul de, 61
Koepke, Wulf, 111, 129 n
Kohlschmidt, Werner, 128 n
Kokora, Michel Gnéba, 180 n
Kolbe, Jürgen, 156 n, 157 n
Kollwitz, Käthe, 330
Kompert, Leopold, 235
König, Heinrich, 255 n
Kontje, Todd, 24 n, 28 n, 109, 128 n, 280 n
Krafft-Ebing, Richard von, 328, 330
Kremer, Detlef, 363 n
Krüger, Johann Gottlieb, 285
Kruger, Oom Paul, 176–77
Kuczynski, Jürgen, 152 n, 156 n
Kugler, Franz, 56, 81 n
Kuh, Ephraim Moses, 232
Kulturkampf, 11, 245, 259, 361
Küppers, Petra, 286, 303 n
Kurth-Voigt, Lieselotte E., 82 n

Laane, Tiiu V., 128 n, 129 n
Ladd, Brian, 27 n
Lamers, Henrike, 152 n, 153 n, 154 n
Landes, Joan B., 28 n
Landmann, Karl, 87, 105 n
Laqueur, Thomas, 28 n
La Roche, Sophie de, 18
Lassalle, Ferdinand, 148
Laufer, Christel, 157 n
Layard, Austen Henry, 285
Lehnert, Herbert, 334 n
Lennox, Sara, 26 n, 27 n
Lesér, Esther, 337 n
Lessing, Gotthold Ephraim, 60, 136, 231, 233, 360
Lessing, Gotthold Ephraim, works by: *Die Juden*, 233, 247;

Nathan der Weise, 233, 240, 349–50
Leventhal, Jean, 363 n
Lewald, Fanny, 6, 19, 237, 251–52, 257 n
Lewald, Fanny, works by: *Familie Darner,* 252; *Jenny,* 252, 270; *Von Geschlecht zu Geschlecht,* 240; *Wandlungen,* 240
Liberalism (German), 5, 23 n, 105 n, 126, 238, 262, 267, 326, 329, 331, 349, 350
Liebland, Helmut, 302 n
Liebs, Elke, 179 n
Lincoln, Abraham, 244, 249
Lindemann, C., 304 n
Louis Philippe, King of France, 227
Löwenthal, Leo, 147, 152 n, 157 n
Lubbock, Percy, 142, 155 n
Lucas, George, 301
Ludwig, Otto, 4, 140, 143, 259, 265, 278 n
Lukács, Georg, 22 n, 26 n, 84 n, 146
Luther, Martin, 4–5, 18, 89, 90, 93, 144

MacKay, John Henry, 337 n
Mandelkow, Karl Robert, 22 n
Mann, Heinrich, 330
Mann, Thomas, vii, 1, 7, 20–21, 24 n, 58, 136, 152 n, 307–33
Mann, Thomas, works by: "Der Bajozzo," 317; *Betrachtungen eines Unpolitischen,* 317–18, 322, 328, 329; *Buddenbrooks,* 6, 192; "Enttäuschung," 317; "Gefallen," 336 n; "Gerächt," 312–14; *Der kleine Herr Friedemann,* 314; "Der kleine Herr Friedemann," 316–17; "Luischen," 318–19, 321; "Tobias Mindernickel," 317; "Der Tod," 317; *Der Tod in Venedig,* 21, 327, 328, 329, 331–33, 356; "Tonio Kröger," 320–21, 322; *Tristan,* 321; "Tristan," 319–20, 321; *Von deutscher Republik,* 328; "Der Wille zum Glück," 314–16, 332
Marggraff, Hermann, 186–88, 190, 194, 205, 220 n
Maria Theresa, 55
Marlitt, E. (Eugenie), vii, 19, 127, 259–82
Marlitt, E. (Eugenie), works by: *Die Frau mit den Karfunkelsteinen,* 265–76, 281 n; *Goldelse,* 260, 262, 271, 281 n; *Das Haideprinzeßchen,* 271; *Im Hause des Kommerzienrates,* 264, 270, 271, 281 n; "Schulmeisters Marie," 279 n; *Die zweite Frau,* 271
Martini, Fritz, 22 n, 23 n, 24 n, 154 n, 156 n
Martino, Alberto, 61, 82 n, 219 n
Marx, Karl, 263
Marx, Karl, and Friedrich Engels, works by: *The Communist Manifesto,* 9, 184, 186, 188–99, 211, 212, 213, 215–18
Marx, Leonie, 131 n
Matt, Peter van, 278 n
Mauthner, Fritz, 153 n
May, Karl, vii, 13, 283–305
May, Karl, works by: *Ardistan,* 299; *Deutsche Helden,* 285; *Krüger Bei,* 285; "Der Krumir," 285; *Old Firehand,* 285, 286, 290; *Der Ölprinz,* 292; *Orientzyklus,* 286; *Satan und Ischariot,* 285; *Der Schatz im Silbersee,* 290; "Weihnacht," 291; *Winnetou,* 285, 286, 288–92, 296–300

Mayer, Hans, 23 n, 152 n, 334 n, 338 n
McClain, William H., 82 n
McClintock, Anne, 17, 27 n
McInnes, Edward, 225, 252 n, 253 n
McMurtrie, Douglas, 336 n
Mehring, Franz, 135, 152 n, 157 n
Meier, Albert, 50 n
Meier Helmbrecht, 95
Mendelssohn, Moses, 12, 232–34, 255 n
Mendelssohn, Peter de, 334 n
Mensch, Ella, 151 n, 154 n
Menzel, Adoph, 81 n
Menzel, Adolph, works by: *Geschichte des Friedrich des Grossen,* 56
Merbach, Günter, 279 n, 280 n
Metternich, Clemens, 227
Meyer, Conrad Ferdinand, 29, 259
Meyer, Michael A., 226, 253 n
Meyer, Richard M., 152 n
Mielke, Hellmuth, 152 n, 157 n
Milde, Caroline S. J., 104 n
Miller, Norbert, 25 n
modernism, 6, 32, 58, 140, 169, 322, 327, 340
Möhrmann, Renate, 27 n, 82 n
Mojem, Hollmuth, 153 n
Moll, Albert, 328, 330
Mommsen, Wolfgang J., 305 n
Monumenta Germaniae Historia, 55
Morris, William, 185
Morsier, Eduard de, 134, 151 n
Mosse, George L., 23 n, 25 n, 26 n, 233, 255, 263, 280 n, 335 n, 338 n
Mühlbach, Luise, vii, 19–20, 53
Mühlbach, Luise, works by: *Der alte Fritz und die neue Zeit,* 69, 78; *Berlin und Sanssouci,* 76;

Erste und letzte Liebe, 61; *Friedrich der Große und seine Geschwister,* 76; *Friedrich der Große und sein Hof,* 61–62, 64–65, 67–80
Müller, Klaus, 335 n
Müller, Klaus-Detlef, 81 n
Müller-Donges, Christa, 157 n
Mundt, Theodor, 61

Näcke, Paul, 330, 336 n
Napoleon, 10, 59, 86, 88, 99, 105 n, 116, 117, 118, 121, 123–24, 130 n
Napoleonic Wars. *See* Wars of Liberation
national identity (German), vii, 9–12, 21, 54, 66, 68, 74, 78–80, 341; and gender/sexual orientation, 99–101, 109–12, 126–27, 332; and regionalism, 7, 10, 85–104, 213–14, 225–26, 346–51. *See also* colonialism; historical fiction; and realism
naturalism, 6, 60, 136, 138, 139, 140, 316
Naubert, Benedikte, 61, 82 n
Neidhardt von Reuenthal, 95
Neuhaus, Volker, 151 n, 156 n, 157 n
Neumann, Bernd, 155 n
Nibelungenlied, 116, 137
Nietzsche, Friedrich, 6, 12, 21, 26 n, 28 n, 34, 322, 323, 325, 327
Nipperdey, Thomas, 88
Njals Saga, 108 n
Nochlin, Linda, 3–4, 22 n, 60, 81 n
Nolde, Emile, 159, 170, 178 n
Nollendorfs, Valters, 26 n
Novalis (Friedrich von Hardenberg), 24 n
Noyes, John K., 181 n
Nutz, Maximilian, 22 n

Ohl, Hubert, 175, 181 n
Orientalism, 20, 117–18, 123, 126, 310, 312
Osterkamp, Barbara, 51 n
Otto, Louise, 19
Ozment, Steven, 55, 80 n

Paret, Peter, 81 n
Parker, Theodore, 242
Pascal, Roy, 22 n, 25 n
Pavel, Thomas, 59, 82 n
Pazi, Margarita, 236, 255 n, 256 n
Pestalozzi, Johann Heinrich, 204, 221 n
Peterson, Brent O., 13, 19, 26 n, 82 n, 109, 110, 127, 128 n, 131 n
Pinson, Koppel S., 23 n
Pizer, John, 11, 15
Plenzdorf, Ulrich, 67
Plessen, Marie-Louise von, 107 n
Plessner, Helmuth, 23 n, 25 n
Potthast, Bertha, 263, 264, 279 n, 280 n, 281 n

Raabe, Wilhelm, vii, 11, 15, 58, 111, 133, 135, 136, 139, 142, 160–78, 235, 259, 269
Raabe, Wilhelm, works by: *Abu Telfan,* 162, 164, 165–68, 171, 175, 176; *Fabian und Sebastian,* 162, 172–73; *Gutmanns Reisen,* 161, 177; "Die Hämelschen Kinder," 179 n; *Hastenbeck,* 161; *Der Hungerpastor,* 8, 171, 179 n; *Im alten Eisen,* 134; *Meister Autor,* 162, 168–71, 172, 173; *Das Odfeld,* 161; *Pfisters Mühle,* 9, 184, 185, 206–14, 215–18; *Prinzessin Fisch,* 169, 171, 172, 173; *Sankt Thomas,* 160, 162–65; *Stopfkuchen,* 162, 173–77, 180–81; *Unruhige Gäste,* 134; *Zum wilden Mann,* 166

Radek, Heide, 280 n
Ranke, Leopold von, 19, 53, 54, 60, 62–68, 70–71, 73–79, 83 n
realism (German), definitions of, 2, 3–9, 29–33, 58–60, 109–10, 177–78, 339–46; in England, 6, 29; and female desire, 259–60, 275–77; and female development, 270–76; in France, 2, 3–4, 6–7, 29, 112, 149; and gender, 17–21; and imperialism, 351–54; and Judaism, 223; and nationalism, 341, 346–54; "poetic" realism, 5, 6, 29, 150, 183, 259; and religion, 359–63; and repression, 42–49, 339–40, 357; reputation of, 1–2, 147, 225–26; in Russia, 6; in Scandinavia, 6; and work, vii, 8–9, 183–218. *See also* colonialism; historical fiction; and national identity
Rebing, Günter, 154 n, 156 n, 157 n
Reed, T. J., 338 n
Reich-Ranicki, Marcel, 334 n
Remak, Henry H., 24 n, 363 n
Revolution of 1848, 1, 5, 11, 19, 46, 142, 144, 204, 216, 238, 288–91, 293, 339
Rhöse, Franz, 153 n, 155 n, 156 n, 157 n, 240, 256 n
Rhotert, Hans, 254 n
Riehl, Wilhelm Heinrich von, 110, 112, 201–2, 220 n
Riffaterre, Michael, 53, 80 n, 84 n
Rilke, Rainer Maria, 330
Rindisbacher, Hans J., 9
Robertson, Ritchie, 232, 254 n
Roebling, Irmgard, 160, 179 n
Röhm, Ernst, 329
Romanticism, 5, 6, 32, 38, 89, 121, 178, 342, 343, 354, 357
Roper, Katherine, 152 n

Rosegger, Peter, 135, 156 n
Rothe-Buddensieg, Margret, 278 n
Roxin, Claus, 304 n
Rüsen, Jörn, 80 n
Ruskin, John, 185

Sagarra, Eda, 153 n
Sälter, Rolf, 154 n, 157 n
Salza, Hermann von, 96, 98, 107 n
Sammons, Jeffrey L., 5, 8, 25 n, 26 n, 164, 171, 177, 178 n, 179 n, 180 n, 181 n, 236, 243, 256 n, 283–84, 302 n
Sand, George, 6, 276
Saphra, B. (Benjamin Segel), 235
Sassen, Saski, 26 n
Schama, Simon, 81 n
Scherer, Wilhelm, 141, 155 n
Scheidemann, Uta, 128 n
Schieder, Theodor, 84 n
Schieding, Hermann, 151 n, 157 n
Schiller, Friedrich, 1, 9–10, 25 n, 89, 136, 140, 141, 144, 145, 224
Schiller, Friedrich, works by: *Aesthetic Education,* 46–48; *Geschichte des Abfalls der vereinigten Niederlande,* 162; *Die Horen* (ed.), 9; *Kabale und Liebe,* 2; "Das Lied von der Glocke," 120
Schivelbusch, Wolfgang, 295, 305 n
Schlechta, Karl, 24 n
Schmidt, Erich, 133, 143, 156 n, 157 n
Schmidt, Julian, 5, 8, 137, 147, 153 n, 186
Schmiedt, Helmut, 303 n, 304 n
Schnitzler, Arthur, 346
Schoeps, Julian H., 337 n, 338 n
Schorsch, Ismar, 228, 254 n

Schrader, Hans-Jürger, 152 n
Schuch, Uta, 111, 112, 126, 128 n, 129 n
Schücking, Levin, 262
Schulte-Sasse, Jochen, 84 n, 264, 280 n, 281 n, 299, 304 n, 305 n
Schumacher, Adolf, 157 n
Schweichel, Robert, 187–88
Schwerte, Hans, 22 n
Scott, Sir Walter, 6, 61, 63, 67, 73, 83 n, 227
Sedgwick, Eve Kosofsky, 308, 322, 334 n, 335 n, 337 n
Seferens, Gregor, 302 n
Seidenspinner, Wolfgang, 253 n
Seiffert, Hans Werner, 157 n
Seiler, Friedrich, 107 n
Seven Years' War, 110, 112, 126, 161
Shakespeare, William, 114
Sheehan, James J., 23 n, 218, 219 n, 220 n, 221 n
Showalter, Elaine, 17, 28 n
Simmel, Georg, 301, 305 n
Silber, Kate, 221 n
Silz, Walter, 24 n
Skolnik, Jonathan, 228, 253 n
Smith, Anthony D., 110
Socrates, 45
Solms, Wilhelm, 363 n
Sophocles, works by: *Antigone,* 252
Sorkin, David, 227–28, 231, 253 n, 254 n
Spielhagen, Friedrich, vii, 5, 112, 122, 133–57, 239, 259
Spielhagen, Friedrich, works by: *Allzeit voran,* 149; *Altershausen,* 133; *Angela,* 137, 139; *Durch Nacht zum Licht,* 134; *Hammer und Amboß,* 147, 148; *In Reih' und Glied,* 148; *Post Festum,* 133; *Problematische Naturen,* 134, 137, 142, 148; *Die schönen*

Amerikanerinnen, 144; *Das Skelet im Hause, Das,* 134–35; *Sturmflut,* 137, 144, 147, 148; *Susi,* 139, 150; *Die von Hohenstein,* 148; *Was will das werden?,* 134, 150; *Zum Zeitvertreib,* 150
Spiero, Heinrich, 155 n
Spinoza, Benedict, 12, 227–30, 232, 240
Spivak, Gayatri Chakravorty, 169, 180 n
Sprengel, Peter, 105 n
Stahr, Adolf, 156 n
Steakley, James, 334 n
Stein, Karl Freiherr von, 10, 55, 121
Steinecke, Hartmut, 24 n, 25 n, 106 n, 219 n
Steinmetz, Hans-Dieter, 302 n
Stendhal (Henri Beyle), 2, 6, 29, 112
Stifter, Adalbert, vii, 29, 33–49
Stifter, Adalbert, works by: *Brigitta,* 11, 33–49; *Nachsommer,* 8, 9, 33, 34, 44–48, 184, 185, 199–206, 208, 211, 215–18, 276, 277, 281 n; *Studien,* 33
Storck, Jochim W., 51 n
Storm, Theodor, 29, 111, 259, 268
Storm, Theodor, works by: "Ein Doppelgänger," 108 n
Stowe, Harriet Beecher, works by: *Uncle Tom's Cabin,* 243, 245
Strauss, David Friedrich, 224, 256 n
Strecker, Gabriele, 264, 279 n, 280 n
Strodtmann, Adolf, 135, 146, 151 n, 156 n
Struck, Wolfgang, 180 n
Subiotto, Frances M., 364 n
Sue, Eugène, 61

Swales, Martin, 24 n, 58, 81 n, 147, 153 n, 157 n
Sweet, Dennis, 61, 82 n

Tacitus, 130
Tatlock, Lynne, 10, 105 n, 106 n, 107 n
Tatum, John Hargrove, 151 n
Taubert, Erich, 105 n
Taylor, A. J. P., 181 n
Teutonic Knights, 94, 96–99
Tewarson, Heidi Thomann, 255 n
Thackeray, William, 6, 29, 139
Thucydides, works by: *History of the Peloponnesian Wars,* 70–71
Thüna, Ulrich von, 302 n
Tobin, Robert, 20–21, 338 n
Tolstoy, Leo, 236
Tolstoy, Leo, works by: *Anna Karenina,* 346; *War and Peace,* 59
Touaillon, Christine, 27 n
Trommler, Frank, 220 n
Tschapke, Reinhard, 302 n, 303 n
Tuchmann, Barbara, 23 n
Turgenev, Ivan, 6
Turner, David, 155 n

Uhland, Ludwig, 224
Ulrichs, Karl Heinrich, 20–21, 308–12, 315, 324, 326, 334 n, 335 n, 336 n
Utz, Peter, 352

Victoria, Crown Princess of Prussia, 90
Victoria, Queen of England, 55
Vinçon, Hartmut, 25 n
Vischer, Friedrich Theodor, 8, 25 n, 241, 256 n
Vogelsberg, Karl Robert, 279 n
Volkov, Shulamit, 335 n
Voltaire (François-Marie Arouet), 76

Vormärz (pre-March), 1, 5, 6, 19, 33, 111, 224, 243

Wagner, Richard, 12, 26 n, 357
Wagner, Richard, works by: *Lohengrin*, 317; *Ring* cycle, 108 n; *Tannhäuser*, 90, 105 n; *Tristan*, 313, 320
Wars of Liberation (Napoleonic Wars), 10, 110, 126, 130 n, 227, 251
Weber, Carl Maria, 327, 333
Weber, Max, 361, 364 n
Wedekind, Frank, 330, 346
Wegmann, Nikolaus, 363 n
Wehler, Hans-Ulrich, 11, 23 n, 26 n
Wehnert, Jürgen, 302 n
Weimar, Klaus, 25 n
Weiner, Marc A., 26 n
Wellek, René, 29–30, 49 n
Werner, Renate, 264, 280 n, 281 n
White, Hayden, 58, 81 n, 84 n
Whitman, Walt, 313
Wiedenroth, Hermann, 284
Wilkending, Gisela, 104 n
William II, Emperor of Germany, 88, 177
Winckelmann, Johann Joachim, 310
Wisskirchen, Hans, 337 n, 338 n
Wolff, Charlotte, 330, 338 n
Wollschläger, Hans, 284, 303 n
Woolf, Virginia, 30
Worley, Linda Kraus, 114, 115, 129 n
Worthmann, Joachim, 154 n, 155 n, 157 n
Wundt, Wilhelm, 50 n

Zantop, Susanne, 15–16, 26 n, 27 n, 99, 107 n, 120, 124, 130 n, 159–60, 162, 167, 170, 174, 177, 178, 178 n, 180 n, 181 n
Zimmermann, Christina von, 50 n
Zimmermann, Peter, 25 n
Zinken, Rosa-Maria, 151 n, 157 n
Zola, Émile, 2, 7, 137, 138, 139, 149–50
Zweig, Stefan, 330
Zwick, M. I., 235, 253 n, 255

This volume of new essays by leading scholars treats a representative sampling of German realist prose from the period 1848 to 1900, the period of its dominance of the German literary landscape. It includes essays on familiar, canonical authors — Stifter, Freytag, Raabe, Fontane, Thomas Mann — and canonical texts, but also considers writers frequently omitted from traditional literary histories, such as Luise Mühlbach, Friedrich Spielhagen, Louise von François, Karl May, and Eugenie Marlitt.

The introduction situates German realism in the context of both German literary history and of developments in other European literatures, and surveys the most prominent critical studies of nineteenth-century realism. The essays treat the following topics: Stifter's *Brigitta* and the lesson of realism; Mühlbach, Ranke, and the truth of historical fiction; regional histories as national history in Freytag's *Die Ahnen;* gender and nation in Louise von François's historical fiction; theory and reputation and the career of Friedrich Spielhagen; Wilhelm Raabe and the German colonial experience; the poetics of work in Freytag, Stifter, and Raabe; Jewish identity in Berthold Auerbach's novels; Eugenie Marlitt's narratives of virtuous desire; the appeal of Karl May in the Wilhelmine Empire; Thomas Mann's portrayal of male-male desire in his early short fiction; and Fontane's *Effi Briest* and the end of realism.

TODD KONTJE is professor of German and Comparative Literature at the University of California, San Diego. He is author of *The German Bildungsroman: History of a National Genre* (Camden House, 1993).

This outstanding collection of essays on the writing of this period provides an excellent overview of this great age of fiction. The contributors are among the very best of German literary critics. . . .
CHOICE

Major figures of realism are treated — Stifter, Freytag, Raabe and Fontane — but also lesser-known names such as Mühlbach, Louise von Francois, Spielhagen, Auerbach, and even Karl May, author of *Winnetou,* in connection with German emigration to the United States. . . .
ETUDES GERMANIQUES

. . . notable for its welcome focus on national identity and on marginalized voices . . .
GERMAN QUARTERLY

The volume's contribution in documenting current scholarly trends in a field that, according to Kontje, suffers from a "bad reputation," is great: it opens new windows onto neglected areas of consideration.
GERMAN STUDIES REVIEW

These essays are all excellent studies that should stimulate renewed interest in 19th-century German realism.
MONATSHEFTE

www.ingramcontent.com/pod-product-compliance
Lightning Source LLC
Chambersburg PA
CBHW021814300426
44114CB00009BA/171